The Pergamon Dictionary of Perfect Spelling

CHRISTINE MAXWELL

E J Arnold

E. J. Arnold & Son Ltd.
Parkside Lane
Dewsbury Road
LEEDS LS11 5TD

First edition 1977
Second edition 1978
Reprinted 1979, 1983, 1984, 1985, 1987, 1988

ISBN 0-08-022863-1 non net
ISBN 0-08-022865-8 net

Printed in Great Britain by A. Wheaton & Co. Ltd., Exeter

Contents

Preface

This dictionary, the first of its kind in Great Britain (as far as the compiler knows), and its accompanying booklet, *Practise Your Spelling*, aim at being of service to children and adults of all ages who are weak at spelling and who therefore fail to locate quickly and easily the words they seek in standard dictionaries.

Compilers and publishers of English-language dictionaries overseas have long recognised this problem, and have successfully provided phonetically-arranged dictionaries to help pupils overcome these serious difficulties which so impede their progress.

Recent experience gained as a teacher in an Oxford middle school (age-group 9–13) and with students learning English as a foreign language has brought the compiler face to face with the problem. This has made her aware of the inordinate amount of time that has to be spent by teachers helping students with spelling difficulties which they could so easily have overcome for themselves had they had access to a phonetically-arranged dictionary.

The compiler gratefully acknowledges the co-operation of teachers and students in Oxfordshire schools for their help in testing the dictionary and its accompanying booklet, *Practise Your Spelling*, in a classroom environment. These successful tests, which were also carried out in several establishments that teach English as a foreign language, have revealed the following:

I. Students who assisted with the tests quickly understood that words printed in RED were incorrectly spelt and that only words printed in BLACK were correctly spelt. In tests which involved several hundred students, not one copied down incorrect spellings. Some teachers' initial concern over the possible negative effect of showing students incorrect spellings has proved unfounded.

II. Teachers (besides saving themselves time) found that regular use of the dictionary and the exercise booklet improved their pupils' ability to locate words easily and quickly and spell them correctly.

The mis-spellings (mainly phonetic) are printed in RED (RED is wrong), with the correct spellings given alongside in BLACK (BLACK is right). Even when users are unsure of the first two letters in a word, they may still find its correct spelling with the help of this dictionary. For instance, the word 'pheasant' will be found under the phonetic groups fes and fez as well as in its correct alphabetical place under phe:

fesant	pheasant
fezant	pheasant

pheasant

Some of the commonest spelling errors are made in adding suffixes and in forming derivatives from root words which in themselves may be quite easy to spell. In a conventional dictionary a student may be able to find the spellings of infinitives like 'picnic', 'abandon' and 'span', but may encounter difficulties spelling their present and past participles. How is one to know that the words 'spanning' and 'spanned' are not spelt 'spaning' and 'spaned'? There may be no indication that one must insert 'k' after 'picnic' in order to spell 'picnicking' and 'picnicked' correctly. This dictionary leaves no room for error in this respect, as difficult and irregular word derivatives are included.

It is hoped that this dictionary (and its accompanying booklet) will prove to be of practical, daily help, solving spelling problems and helping to increase the spelling skills of both children and adults—in the classroom, at home and at work.

Oxford, July 1977   CHRISTINE MAXWELL

On Choice of Words, Spelling and Arrangement of Entries

The words in this dictionary have been chosen because they are difficult to spell. Accordingly, many common words are omitted. Obsolete and highly technical words have also been left out, though special attention has been given to the selection of scientific and technical words. Very few proper names are given and foreign words are included only if they have passed into common use.

Where alternative spellings exist these have mostly been omitted. In the case of words ending in -ise, -isation, the -ize and -ization versions have not been given (nor have they been given as mis-spelt versions since they cannot be counted as such). In a very few instances two spellings have been given; where only one spelling is given the reader can assume that it is widely accepted as being correct. To help the user decide upon the correct spelling, brief word definitions are given in the case of words that are (1) pronounced alike but differ in meaning and spelling, (2) often mispronounced to give the same or almost the same sound but are entirely different in meaning and spelling, e.g.:

(1) sail (of boat)   (2) poplar (tree)
  sale (of goods)   popular (well known)

The spellings and mis-spellings in the dictionary are arranged in alphabetical order.

Endings of words: It has not been possible to put in every derivation and many comparative endings have been excluded. In many cases there has been insufficient space for all the derivatives to be placed in one entry. They have therefore been split up in what the author considers to be the most obvious and practical way, e.g.:

abnormal /ly
abnormalit*y* /ies

Abbreviations Used in the Dictionary

adj(s).	adjective(s)
fem.	feminine
n.	noun
pl(s).	plural(s)
sing.	singular
v.	verb

How to Use the Dictionary

1. Think hard about the word you wish to spell and try to decide with which two letters it starts.
2. Find the two letters in the dictionary and look down the <u>left-hand column</u> under these two letters until you find the word you want. If you find the word printed in BLACK, then you have found the correct spelling. However, if the word is printed in RED, then you are not spelling the word correctly, but if you look across the same line you will find the correct spelling printed in BLACK, e.g.:

palis   palace

3. (a) It may be necessary to add the word endings which are individually separated by oblique strokes (/) in order to build up the complete word you want. In the example below you can see how this works:

neat /er/est/ly/ness

By adding <u>er</u> to <u>neat</u> you spell <u>neater</u>.
By adding <u>est</u> to <u>neat</u> you spell <u>neatest</u>.
By adding <u>ly</u> to <u>neat</u> you spell <u>neatly</u>.
By adding <u>ness</u> to <u>neat</u> you spell <u>neatness</u>.

(b) Where the last letter or letters of a word are in *italics* these <u>must</u> be left off before adding the endings, e.g.:

nast*y* /ier/iest/ily/iness

Here, the *y* must be left off before making:

nastier, nastiest, nastily, nastiness

(c) The plurals of most nouns may be formed by simply adding the letter **s**. Only where this does not apply, or where the spelling of a plural often gives trouble, is the plural spelling noted, e.g.:

dais*y* /ies	(daisies)	cello /s	(cellos)
cargo /es	(cargoes)	minutia /e	(minutiae)
circus /es	(circuses)		

4. NOTE
If the correct spelling given alongside a mis-spelling has a ⁺ sign after it, then this means that all other given derivations of the word may only be found by looking up the correct spelling again, but in its PROPER ALPHABETICAL PLACE, e.g.:

hapen	happen [1]
hapier	happier +
hapless	
happen [1]	
happi*er* /est/ly/ness	

Where the word <u>happier</u> occurs in its correct alphabetical place other forms of the word are given:

happiest, happily, happiness

If you thought that the word <u>elastic</u> began with an **i** you would find that you are spelling the word wrongly <u>and</u>, as the following example shows, the correct spelling of <u>elastic</u> has a ⁺ sign after it:

ilastic   elastic +

Now if you look up <u>elastic</u> under **e** instead of **i** you will find that other forms of the word are given:

elastic /ally/ity

5. All the words with the number ¹ or ² or ³ or ⁴ after them are verbs (doing words) or may be used as verbs. If you require the word to end in either <u>ed</u> or <u>ing</u>, then you must remember the following:

(a) If you see ¹ after a word you may add <u>ed</u> or <u>ing</u> to the word without changing it, thus:

add¹   add <u>ed</u>   add <u>ing</u>

(b) If you see ² after a word ending in **e**, the **e** must be dropped before adding <u>ed</u> or <u>ing</u>, thus:

name²   nam <u>ed</u>   nam <u>ing</u>

(c) If you see ³ after a word you must double the final consonant (the last letter) before adding <u>ed</u> or <u>ing</u>, thus:

pat³   patt <u>ed</u>   patt <u>ing</u>

(d) If you see ⁴ after a word (all words with a ⁴ after them end in **y**) you MUST change the **y** to an **i** before adding <u>ed</u>, but you may add <u>ing</u> to the word without changing it, thus:

carry⁴   carr**i** <u>ed</u>   carry <u>ing</u>

cry⁴   cr**i** <u>ed</u>   cry <u>ing</u>

BEWARE

A word having an asterisk (*) after it has the same sound, or almost the same sound, as another word, but it has a different meaning and spelling.

Explanations in brackets (not exact definitions) are only included where the words occur in their correct alphabetical place in the book, e.g.:

berr *y* * (fruit) /ies

berry   bury⁴*

bury⁴* (cover)

If you want to check the meaning of the word <u>bury</u>⁴*, you must look it up in its correct alphabetical place under <u>bu</u> and not under <u>be</u>.

NOTES. (1) Where a dagger (†) appears after the *, the word definition is given on the next line, e.g.:

farth *er* *† /est

†(distant)

(2) The **hyphen** (-) is a sign used to join words and must not be left out, e.g.:

far /-fetched/-flung (far-fetched, far-flung)

fire-engine

KEY TO DICTIONARY SYMBOLS

A list of meanings of the various symbols used appears on the inside back cover of the dictionary.

Dictionary Exercises

Although the instructions on the use of the dictionary are set out clearly enough for a pupil to follow and understand, it would be helpful for the teacher to read through the rules with the pupils and make them do the exercises set out below. There is an exercise to help reinforce each rule, and the final exercise (V) gives the pupil practice in the use of all the rules.

Most pupils will quickly learn how to use the dictionary and the teacher can check whether they are using it accurately simply by giving a verbal test requiring written answers. For those who may need further practice, the teacher may use the exercises set out in *Practise Your Spelling* (O. B. Gregory/C. Maxwell, Wheaton, 1977), which exploit further the special features of the dictionary—and are designed to aid spelling, word study and development of vocabulary.

EXERCISE I

Look up the following words and write out in full all the other words that you can make up from the information you find. (The first question has been done for you.)

1. bite *(biting, bitten)*
2. abundant
3. bleak
4. bush
5. door
6. feeble
7. wealth
8. luck
9. sharp
10. tooth

EXERCISE II

Remember: When the last letter or letters of a word are in *italics*, these must be LEFT OFF before adding the other endings, e.g.:

nast*y* /ier/iest/ily/iness

The *y* in <u>nasty</u> must be left off before making the words

nastier, nastiest, nastily, nastiness

Look up the following words and write out in full all the other words that you can make up from the information you find. (The first question has been done for you.)

1. difficulty *(difficulties)*
2. rowdy
3. geography
4. giddy
5. mightier
6. lady
7. someone
8. greedier
9. busier
10. army

EXERCISE III **Using the numbers 1, 2, 3, and 4**

Use the following example as a guide,

Verb	*Past participle*	*Present participle*
peck	pecked	pecking

and write out the corresponding parts of the verbs listed in the following sections A–D. (The first items of sections A–D, respectively, have been done for you.)

A. Using the number **1**
1. tick *(ticked, ticking)*
2. bang
3. dismay
4. help
5. thump
6. link
7. lisp
8. hurl
9. shatter
10. drill

10

B. Using the number **2**
1. cripple *(crippled, crippling)*

2. mime	5. slope	8. fuse
3. rinse	6. tremble	9. chuckle
4. blaze	7. wrestle	10. ache

C. Using the number **3**
1. dab *(dabbed, dabbing)*

2. skid	5. jar	8. zigzag
3. beg	6. chip	9. prod
4. whiz	7. hum	10. expel

D. Using the number **4**
1. dignify *(dignified, dignifying)*

2. satisfy	5. busy	8. try
3. disqualify	6. marry	9. fry
4. pity	7. terrify	10. crucify

EXERCISE IV

Combination of numbers and other word endings: e.g. dance² /r
In the above entry the ² tells us that we can write <u>dancing</u> and <u>danced</u>.
If we add the **r** to the main word <u>dance</u>, we get <u>dancer</u>.

See if you can do this exercise. Write out in full as many forms of the words as you can from the information given. (The first question has been done for you.)

1. attract *(attracting, attracted, attraction)*

2. coach	5. guide	8. thin
3. narrow	6. hedge	9. mouth
4. dissatisfy	7. learn	10. travel

EXERCISE V

You are now ready to tackle an exercise containing a mixture of all the rules.

Look up the following words and write out as many words as you can from the information given. (The first question has been done for you.)

1. close *(closed, closing, closure)*

2. further	5. young	8. wide
3. playful	6. clever	9. knife
4. run	7. police	10. water

Your teacher will now ask you to spell a number of words, and if you use the dictionary correctly, you will get every word right.

You may also work with another member of your group or class, taking turns to ask each other how to spell words that you are presently using, until you are quite confident that you can use the dictionary successfully.

Remember, on the inside back cover there is a key to the symbols used in this dictionary.

A

à la carte
aback
abac *us* /i (pl.)
abait   abate [2+]
abanden   abandon [1+]
abandon [1] /ment
abash /ed
abate [2] /ment
abawd   aboard
abawshun   abortion [+]
abawt   abort [1+]
abawtion   abortion [+]
abayans   abeyance [+]
abbey /s
abb *ot* /ess (fem.)
abbreviat *e* [2] /ion
abdicat *e* [2] /ion
abdomen
abdomin *al* /ally/ous
abduct [1] /ion/or
abet [3] /tor
abetor   abettor
abeyan *ce* /t
abeyans   abeyance [+]
abhaw   abhor [3+]
abhor [3] /rence
abhorence   abhorrence
abhorens   abhorrence
abhorent   abhorrent [+]
abhorrent /ly
abidans   abidance
abid *e* [2] /ance
abilit *y* /ies
abismal   abysmal [+]
abiss   abyss
abject /ion/ly/ness
ablative
ablbodid   able-bodied

able /-bodied/r/st
ablie   ably
ably
abnawmal   abnormal [+]
abnawmalitey abnormality [+]
abnormal /ly
abnormalit *y* /ies
aboard
abode
aboli *sh* [1] /tion
abolishun   abolition
A-bomb
abominabl *e* /y
abominabul abominable [+]
abominashun abomination
abominat *e* [2] /ion
abord   aboard
aborigin *al* /es
aborshun   abortion [+]
abort [1] /ive
abortion /ist
abound [1]
about
above /-board
abownd   abound [1]
abowt   about
abracadabra
abrashun   abrasion [+]
abras *ion* /ive
abrawd   abroad
abreast
abrecadabra abracadabra
abrest   abreast
abreviashun abbreviation
abreviate   abbreviate [2+]
abreviation abbreviation
abridge [2] /ment
abrige   abridge [2+]

abroad		abyewse	abuse [2]+
abrord	abroad	abysmal /ly	
abrupt /ly/ness		abyss	
absaloot	absolute +	abyusiv	abusive
absawb	absorb [1]+	abzawb	absorb [1]+
absawbency	absorbency +	abzawbent	absorbent
absawbensey	absorbency +	abzolv	absolve [2]+
absawbent	absorbent	acacia	
absawpshun	absorption +	academic /al/ally	
abscess /es		academician	
abscond [1] /er		academishun	academician
absent [1] /ee/eeism		academ*y* /ies	
abserd	absurd +	acapuncture	acupuncture
abserditey	absurdity	accede [2] /nce	
absess	abscess +	accelerat*e* [2] /ion/or	
absolushun	absolution	accent [1] /ual	
absolut*e* /ely/ism		accentuat*e* [2] /ion	
absolution		accept [1] /ability	
absolv*e* [2] /able		acceptabl*e* /y	
absorb [1] /able		acceptabul	acceptable +
absorben*cy* /t		acceshun	accession +
absorbensey	absorbency +	access /ibility/ible	
absorpshun	absorption +	accessar*y* ★ (legal) /ies	
absorpt*ion* /ive		accession /al	
abstain [1] /er		accessor*y* ★† /ies	
abstayn	abstain [1]+	† (accompaniment)	
abstemious /ness		accident /al/ally	
abstemius	abstemious +	acclaim [1] /er	
abstenshun	abstention	acclamashun	acclamation +
abstention		acclamat*ion* /ory	
abstinen*ce* /t		acclaym	acclaim [1]+
abstinens	abstinence +	acclimatis*e* [2] /ation	
abstract [1] /ion/or		accolade	
abstroos	abstruse +	accommodat*e* [2] /ion	
abstruse /ness		accompani*st* /ment	
absurd /ity/ities		accompany [4]	
abul	able +	accomplice	
abundanc*e* /y		accomplish [1] /ment	
abundans	abundance +	accompliss	accomplice
abundant /ly		accord [1] /ance/ingly	
abundent	abundant +	accordion /ist	
abunduns	abundance +	accordyun	accordion+
abus*e* [2] /ive/iveness		accost [1]	
abut [3] /ment		account [1] /ancy/ant	
abuv	above +	accountab*le* /ility	

accountabul	accountable +	acootrements	accoutrements
accoutrements		acord	accord 1+
accredit 1 /ation		acorn	
accru e 2 /al		acost	accost 1
accumpany	accompany 4	acount	account 1+
accumulat e 2 /ion/or		acoustic /s	
accumulative		acownt	account 1+
accuracy		acquaint 1 /ance	
accurasey	accuracy	acquiesce 2 /nce/nt	
accurate /ly/ness		acquire 2 /ment	
accursed /ly/ness		acquisit ion /ive	
accusative		acquit 3 /tal	
accus e 2 /ation/er		acre /age	
accustom 1		acrid /ity/ness	
ace		acrimonious /ly	
acer	acre +	acrimonius	acrimonious +
acerige	acreage	acrimony	
acetate		acrobat /ic/ically	
acetic		acromatic	achromatic
acetone		acronim	acronym
acetylen e /ic		acronym	
ache 2		acropolis	
achevabul	achievable	across	
acheve	achieve 2+	acseed	accede 2+
achievable		acselerate	accelerate 2+
achieve 2 /ment/r		acselerater	accelerator
achromatic		acsent	accent 1+
acid /ic/ity		acsentuate	accentuate 2+
acidul ate 2 /ous		acsept	accept 1+
acknoledge	acknowledge 2+	acseptable	acceptable +
acknolidge	acknowledge 2+	acsesary	accessary *+
acknowledge 2 /ment		acsesary	accessory *+
aclaim	acclaim 1+	acseshun	accession +
aclamashun	acclamation +	acsess	access +
aclamation	acclamation +	acsessorey	accessory *+
aclaym	acclaim 1+	acshun	action +
acme		acsident	accident +
acne		act 1 /able	
acolight	acolyte	actini c /um	
acolyte		action /able	
acommodate	accommodate 2+	activat e 2 /ion/or	
acomodate	accommodate 2+	active /ly/ness	
acompaniment	accompaniment	activis m /t	
acompany	accompany 4	activit y /ies	
acompliss	accomplice	act or /ress (fem.)	

actual /ly		adhearence	adherence
actualit y /ies		adhere² /nce/nt	
actuar y /ies		adheshun	adhesion⁺
actuat e² /ion/or		adhes ion /ive	
acumen		adicshun	addiction
acumpany	accompany⁴	adiction	addiction
acumpliss	accomplice	adidge	adage
acumulate	accumulate²⁺	adieu	
acupuncture		adige	adage
acupunkcher	acupuncture	adikwacy	adequacy
acuracy	accuracy	adikwat	adequate⁺
acurate	accurate⁺	adiquacy	adequacy
acustic	acoustic⁺	adiquate	adequate⁺
acustum	accustom¹	adishun	addition⁺
acute /ly/ness		adition	addition⁺
ad	add¹	adjacent /ly	
ad hoc		adjectiv e /al	
ad infinitum		adjoin¹	
ad-lib³		adjourn¹ /ment	
adage		adjudge²	
adagio /s		adjudicat e² /ion/or	
adamant /ine		adjunct /ion/ive	
adament	adamant⁺	adjust¹ /able/ment	
adapt¹ /ation/ive		adjutan cy /t	
adaptab le /ility		adle	addle²
adaptabul	adaptable⁺	administ er¹ /rable	
adapter ★ (person)		administrat e² /ion/or	
adaptor ★ (electric)		administrater	administrator
add¹		administrative	
addend um /a (pl.)		admirabl e /y	
addenoids	adenoids	admirabul	admirable⁺
adder		admiral /ty	
addict¹ /ion/ive		admirashun	admiration
addition /al/ally		admir e² /ation/er	
addle²		admirul	admiral⁺
address¹ /ee/er		admishun	admission⁺
ade	aid¹⁺	admisibul	admissible⁺
adement	adamant⁺	admissib le /ility	
adendum	addendum⁺	admiss ion /ive	
adenoids		admit³ /tedly	
adept /ly/ness		admitance	admittance
adequacy		admitans	admittance
adequasey	adequacy	admittance	
adequate /ly/ness		admonish¹ /er/ment	
adhear	adhere²⁺	ado	

adobe		advis *edly* /er/ory	
adobi	adobe	advocacy	
adolescen *ce* /t		advocasey	advocacy
adolesence	adolescence +	advocat *e²* /or	
adolesens	adolescence +	advurse	adverse +
adolesent	adolescent	advurtisment	advertisement
adoor	adore ²+	aegis	
adopshun	adoption	aerat *e²* /ion/or	
adopt ¹ /er/ion/ive		aerial /ly	
adorabl *e* /y		aerobatics	
adorabul	adorable +	aerodrome	
ador *e²* /ation		aerodynamics	
adorn ¹ /ment		aerofoil	
adrenal /in		aeronaut /ical/ics	
adrift		aeroplane	
adroit /ly/ness		aerosol	
adsorpshun	adsorption +	aesthet *e* /ic/icism	
adsorpt *ion* /ive		afable	affable +
adue	adieu	afabul	affable +
adul	addle ²	afair	affair
adulashun	adulation	afare	affair
adulat *e²* /ion/or		afecshun	affection
adult /hood		afecshunate	affectionate +
adulterat *e²* /ion		afect	affect ¹+
adulterus	adulterous	afectation	affectation
adulter *y* /er/ous		afection	affection
advance ² /ment		afectionate	affectionate +
advans	advance ²+	afective	affective
advencher	adventure ²+	afeild	afield
advencherous	adventurous +	afeld	afield
advencherus	adventurous +	aferm	affirm ¹+
advent		afermativ	affirmative +
adventishus	adventitious +	affab *le* /ility/ly	
adventitious /ly/ness		affair	
adventure ² /some		affect ¹ /ion/ive	
adventurous /ly/ness		affectation	
adverb /ial		affectionate /ly/ness	
adversar *y* /ies		affidavit	
adverse /ly/ness		affiks	affix ¹+
adversit *y* /ies		affiliat *e²* /ion	
advertise ² /ment		affinit *y* /ies	
advice ★ (suggestion)		affirm ¹ /ation	
advisabl *e* /y		affirmative /ly	
advisabul	advisable +	affix ¹ /er	
advise ² ★ (suggest)		afflict ¹ /ion	

affluen *ce* /t		after	
affluens	affluence +	afterbirth	
afford [1] /able		afterburth	afterbirth
afforest [1] /ation		aftermath	
affray /s		afternoon	
affront [1]		afterthort	afterthought
afid	aphid +	afterthought	
afidavit	affidavit	afterwards	
afield		afterwerds	afterwards
afiks	affix [1]+	afurm	affirm [1]+
afiliashun	affiliation	afurmashun	affirmation
afiliate	affiliate [2]+	afurmation	affirmation
afiliation	affiliation	afurmativ	affirmative +
afinitey	affinity +	again	
afire		against	
afirm	affirm [1]+	agast	aghast
afirmativ	affirmative +	agate	
afix	affix [1]+	agayn	again
aflaim	aflame	age [2] /less	
aflame		agen	again
aflicshun	affliction	agenc *y* /ies	
aflict	afflict [1]+	agenda	
afliction	affliction	agensey	agency +
afloat		agenst	against
aflote	afloat	agent /ial	
afluence	affluence +	agglomerat *e* [2] /ion	
afluens	affluence +	aggrandise [2] /ment	
afluent	affluent	aggravat *e* [2] /ion	
aford	afford [1]+	aggregat *e* [2] /ely/ion	
aforesaid		aggreshun	aggression +
aforest	afforest [1]+	aggress *ion* /or	
aforestashun	afforestation	aggressive /ly/ness	
aforestation	afforestation	aggrieved	
aforism	aphorism +	aghast	
aforistic	aphoristic	agil *e* /ity	
aforsed	aforesaid	agitat *e* [2] /ion/or	
afrade	afraid	aglomerashun	agglomeration
afraid		aglomerate	agglomerate [2]+
afray	affray +	aglomeration	agglomeration
afrayd	afraid	aglow	
African		agnostic /ism	
Afrikaans		agonie	agony +
Afrikans	Afrikaans	agonis *e* [2] /ingly	
afrodisiac	aphrodisiac	agon *y* /ies	
afront	affront [1]	agorafobia	agoraphobia

agoraphobia		air hostess /es	
agrafobia	agoraphobia	airial	aerial +
agrandise	aggrandise ²⁺	airily	
agrarian		airline /r	
agravate	aggravate ²⁺	air-lock	
agree /d/ing/ment		airmail ¹	
agreeabl e /y		airmale	airmail ¹
agregate	aggregate ²⁺	airobatics	aerobatics
agrement	agreement	airodinamics	aerodynamics
agreshun	aggression +	airodrome	aerodrome
agresion	aggression +	airofoil	aerofoil
agresiv	aggressive +	airofoyl	aerofoil
agression	aggression +	aironort	aeronaut +
agreved	aggrieved	aironortics	aeronautics
agriculcher	agriculture +	airoplane	aeroplane
agricultur e /al/ally		airosol	aerosol
agrieved	aggrieved	air-pocket	
aground		airport	
agrownd	aground	air raid	
agu e /ish		airworth y /iness	
ahead		airy /-fairy	
ahed	ahead	aisle ★ (passage)	
ahoi	ahoy	aisle	isle ★
ahoy		ajar	
aid ¹ /er		ajasent	adjacent +
ail ¹★ (trouble)		ajectiv	adjective +
ail	ale ★	ajency	agency +
ailment		ajenda	agenda
aim ¹ /less/lessly		ajensey	agency +
air ¹★ (gases)		ajent	agent +
air	ere ★	ajile	agile +
air	heir ★	ajilitey	agility
airate	aerate ²⁺	ajitashun	agitation
airborne		ajitate	agitate ²⁺
air-brake		ajoyn	adjoin ¹
aircondishner	air-conditioner	ajudicate	adjudicate ²⁺
air-conditioner		ajunct	adjunct +
air-cooled		ajurn	adjourn ¹⁺
aircraft		ajusment	adjustment
aires	Aries	ajust	adjust ¹⁺
airey	airy +	ajustable	adjustable
airfeild	airfield	ajutancy	adjutancy +
airfield		akimbo	
air force		akin	
air-gun		aksiomatic	axiomatic +

19

aksis	axis +	alegation	allegation
aksium	axiom	alege	allege ²+
akwaintance	acquaintance	alegiance	allegiance
akwalung	aqualung	alegians	allegiance
akwamarine	aquamarine	alegorey	allegory +
akwaplane	aquaplane	alegorical	allegorical +
akwarium	aquarium +	alelooya	alleluia
akwarius	Aquarius	aleluia	alleluia
akwatic	aquatic	alergey	allergy +
akwatint	aquatint	alergic	allergic
akwiduct	aqueduct	alert ¹ /ly/ness	
akwiesence	acquiescence	aleviate	alleviate ²+
akwiesent	acquiescent	alfa	alpha
akwiline	aquiline	alfabet	alphabet +
akwire	acquire ²+	alfabetical	alphabetical
akwisition	acquisition +	alfresco	
akwisitiv	acquisitive	alga /e (pl.)	
akwit	acquit ³+	algebra	
akwital	acquittal	algibra	algebra
alabaster		ali	ally ⁴+
alack		aliance	alliance
alacrit y /ous		alians	alliance
alagro	allegro	alias /es	
alah	Allah	alibi /s	
alarm ¹ /ist		aliby	alibi +
alas		alien /able	
alay	allay ¹+	alienat e ² /ion/or	
albatross		aligater	alligator
albeit		alight ¹	
albeno	albino +	align ¹ /ment	
albino /s		alike /ness	
album		alimenta ry /tion	
albumen *†		alimentrey	alimentary +
† (white of egg)		alimony	
albumin *†		aline	align ¹+
† (soluble protein)		alite	alight ¹
alchem y /ist		aliterashun	alliteration
alcohol /ic/ism		aliterate	alliterate ²+
alcove		aliteration	alliteration
alder		alive	
alderman /cy		alkali /s	
ale * (drink)		alkalin e /ity	
ale	ail ¹*	alkemey	alchemy +
alegashun	allegation	alkemist	alchemist
alegater	alligator	all * (everyone)	

all	awl ★	almon *er* /ry	
all right		almost	
Allah		alms ★ (charity)	
allay [1] /er		alms	arms ★
allegashun	allegation	alms-house	
allegation		alocate	allocate [2+]
allege [2] /dly		aloft	
allegiance		aloi	alloy [1]
allegorical /ly		alone	
allegor *y* /ies		along /side	
allegro		alood	allude [2★]
alleluia		aloof /ness	
allergic		alot	allot [3+]
allerg *y* /ies		alotment	allotment
alleviat *e* [2] /ion		aloud	
alley /s/way		alow	allow [1+]
all-fours		alowable	allowable
alli	ally [4+]	alowabul	allowable
alliance		alowance	allowance
alligator		alowans	allowance
alliterat *e* [2] /ion/ive		alowd	aloud
allmost	almost	aloy	alloy [1]
allocat *e* [2] /ion		alp	
allot [3] /ment		alpaca	
allotropes		alpaka	alpaca
allow [1] /able/ance		alpha	
alloy [1]		alphabet /ical/ically	
all-round		alpine	
allrite	all right	already	
allso	also	alredy	already
allude [2★] (refer to)		alright	all right
allude	elude [2★]	alrite	all right
allure [2] /ment		alsashun	Alsatian
allushun	allusion ★	Alsatian	
allusion★ (reference to)		also	
allusion	illusion ★	altar ★ (church)	
allusive ★† /ly/ness		altarpiece	
† (suggestive)		alter [1★] (change)	
allusive	elusive ★+	altera *ble* /tion	
allusive	illusive ★	alterabul	alterable +
alluvi *al* /um		alterashun	alteration
all *y* [4] /ies		altercat *e* [2] /ion	
ally	alley +	alternashun	alternation
almanac		alternat *e* [2] /ion/or	
almighty			

21

alternative /ly		ambishun	ambition
alterpeace	altarpiece	ambishus	ambitious +
alterpiece	altarpiece	ambit	
altho	although	ambition	
although		ambitious /ly/ness	
altimeter		ambivalen ce /t	
altitude		amble² /r	
alto /s		amboosh	ambush ¹+
altogether		ambrosia /l	
altrooism	altruism	ambul	amble ²+
altrooist	altruist +	ambulance	
altrooistic	altruistic	ambulans	ambulance
altruism		ambulat e² /ory	
altruist /ic/ically		ambush¹ /er	
alude	allude ²★	ame	aim ¹+
alum		ameba	amoeba
aluminium		amelierashun	amelioration
aluminum	aluminium	amelierate	ameliorate ²+
alure	allure ²+	ameliorat e² /ion	
alurt	alert ¹+	amen	
alushun	allusion ★	amenabl e /y	
alusion	allusion ★	amenabul	amenable +
alusiv	allusive ★+	amend¹ /ment	
always		amenit y /ies	
amaise	amaze ²+	American	
amalgam		ameter	ammeter
amalgamashun	amalgamation	amethyst /ine	
amalgamat e² /ion		amfibian	amphibian
amass¹ /able/ment		amfibious	amphibious +
amater	amateur +	amfibius	amphibious +
amateur /ish/ism		amfitheater	amphitheatre
amaze² /ment		amiab le /ility/ly	
Amazon /ian		amiabul	amiable +
ambasader	ambassador +	amicab le /ility/ly	
ambassador /ial		amicabul	amicable +
amber		amid /st	
ambiant	ambient	amiss	
ambidekstrus	ambidextrous	amiter	ammeter
ambidextrous		amitey	amity
ambidextrus	ambidextrous	amithist	amethyst +
ambien ce /t		amity	
ambiens	ambience +	ammeter	
ambiguit y /ies		ammonia /c/cal	
ambiguous /ly/ness		ammonya	ammonia +
ambiguus	ambiguous +	ammunishun	ammunition

22

ammunition		anakey	anarchy +	
amnest *y* /ies		anakronism	anachronism	
amoeba		anal		
amoner	almoner +	analgesi *a* /c		
among /st		analise	analyse 2+	
amonia	ammonia +	analisis	analysis +	
amonya	ammonia +	analist	analyst	
amoral /ity/ly		analitic	analytic +	
amorfus	amorphous +	analog	analogue	
amorous /ly		analogey	analogy +	
amorphous /ly/ness		analogous /ly		
amortise 2		analogue		
amorus	amorous +	analogus	analogous +	
amount 1		analog *y* /ies		
amownt	amount 1	anals	annals	
ampar	ampere +	analyse 2 /r		
amper *e* /age		analys *is* /es (pl.)		
amperige	amperage	analyst		
amphibian		analytic /al/ally		
amphibious /ly/ness		anarchi *c* /sm/st		
amphitheatre		anarch *y* /ical		
ampl *e* /y		anarkey	anarchy +	
amplie	amply	anarkick	anarchic +	
amplifi	amplify 4+	anarkism	anarchism	
amplif *y* 4 /ier		anarkist	anarchist	
amplitude		anathema		
ampool	ampoule	anatomic *al* /ally		
ampoule		anatomise 2		
ampul	ample +	anatom *y* /ist		
amputashun	amputation	ancest *or* /ress (fem.)		
amputat *e* 2 /ion		ancestr *y* /al		
amulet		anchor 1 /age		
amung	among +	anchov *y* /ies		
amunishun	ammunition	ancient /ly/ness		
amunition	ammunition	ancillar *y* /ies		
amuse 2 /ment/r		andante		
anachronism		androginus	androgynous +	
anachronistic /ally		androgyn *ous* /y		
anaconda		anecdot *e* /al/ic		
anacronism	anachronism	aneks	annex 1★+	
anacronistic	anachronistic +	aneks	annexe ★	
anaemi *a* /c		anelise	analyse 2+	
anaesthe *sia* /tic/tist		aneksation	annexation	
anaesthetis *e* 2 /ation		anemia	anaemia +	
anagram /matic		anemic	anaemic	

23

anemomet *er* /ry	
anemone	
anemya	anaemia [+]
aneroid	
anesthesia	anaesthesia [+]
anesthetic	anaesthetic
anesthetise	anaesthetise [2+]
anesthetist	anaesthetist
anew	
angel ★ (heavenly)	
angel	angle [2]★
angelic /al/ally	
angena	angina
anger	
angina	
angle [2]★ (fish, geometry)	
angler	
Anglican /ism	
anglicise [2]	
anglisise	anglicise [2]
anglosaksen	Anglo-Saxon
Anglo-Saxon	
angora	
angrie	angry [+]
angr *y* /ier/iest/ily	
angsietey	anxiety [+]
anguish [1]	
angular /ity	
anguler	angular [+]
angwish	anguish [1]
anhidrus	anhydrous
anhydrous	
anihilate	annihilate [2+]
aniilate	annihilate [2+]
anilen	aniline
aniline	
animal /ism/istic	
animashun	animation
animat *e* [2] /ion	
animatedly	
animosit *y* /ies	
animul	animal [+]
aniseed	
aniversarey	anniversary [+]
anjelic	angelic [+]

anjelical	angelical
anker	anchor [1+]
ankerage	anchorage
ankerige	anchorage
ankle /bone/t	
ankshous	anxious [+]
ankshus	anxious [+]
ankul	ankle [+]
annals	
anneal [1]	
annex [1]★† /ation	
†(take possession of)	
annexe ★ (of house)	
annihilat *e* [2] /ion	
anniversar *y* /ies	
Anno Domini	
annon	anon
annotat *e* [2] /ion/or	
announce [2] /ment/r	
announs	announce [2+]
annoy [1] /ance/ingly	
annoyans	annoyance
annual /ly	
annuit *y* /ies	
annul [3] /ment	
annular /ity	
annunciat *e* [2] /ion	
Ano domini	Anno Domini
anod *e* /al	
anodine	anodyne
anodyne	
anoi	annoy [1+]
anoiance	annoyance
anoians	annoyance
anoint [1] /er/ment	
anomaley	anomaly [+]
anomalous /ly	
anomalus	anomalous [+]
anomal *y* /ies	
anon	
anonimitey	anonymity
anonimous	anonymous [+]
anonimus	anonymous [+]
anonymity	
anonymous /ly/ness	

anorak		anthology /ies/ist	
anotashun	annotation	anthracit e /ic	
anotate	annotate [2+]	anthraks	anthrax
anotation	annotation	anthrasite	anthracite [+]
another		anthrax	
anounce	announce [2+]	anthropoid /al	
anouns	announce [2+]	anthropologey	anthropology [+]
anounser	announcer	anthropologist	
anownce	announce [2+]	anthropolog y /ical	
anowns	announce [2+]	anthropoyd	anthropoid [+]
anoy	annoy [1+]	anti-aircraft	
anoyance	annoyance	antibiotic	
anoyans	annoyance	antibod y /ies	
anoynt	anoint [1+]	antic	
anser	answer [1+]	antichamber	antechamber
anserable	answerable	antichrist	
anserabul	answerable	anticiclone	anticyclone [+]
ansester	ancestor [+]	anticipat e [2] /ion/ory	
ansestrul	ancestral	anticlimaks	anticlimax [+]
ansestry	ancestry [+]	anticlima x /ctic	
anshent	ancient [+]	anticyclon e /ic	
ansilarey	ancillary [+]	antidate	antedate [2]
answer [1] /able/er		antidiloovian	antediluvian
ant /-eater/-hill		antidot e /al/ally	
ant	aunt [+]	anti-freeze	
antacid		antihistamine	
antagonis e [2] /m		antikwarian	antiquarian
antagonist /ic/ically		antikwate	antiquate [2]
Antarctic		antikwerey	antiquary [+]
antasid	antacid	antikwitey	antiquity [+]
anteceden ce /t		antilope	antelope
antecedens	antecedence [+]	antimon y /ial	
antechamber		antinatul	antenatal
antedate [2]		antipathey	antipathy [+]
antediluvian		antipath y /etic	
anteek	antique [+]	antipodes	
antelope		antiquar y /ies/ian	
antena	antenna [+]	antiquate [2]	
antenatal		antique /ness	
antenna /e (pl.)		antiquit y /ies	
anterier	anterior	antiroom	anteroom
anterior		antisedens	antecedence [+]
anteroom		anti-semiti c /sm	
anthem		antiseptic /ally	
anther		antisiclone	anticyclone [+]

antisipashun	anticipation	aparishun	apparition
antisipate	anticipate ²⁺	aparition	apparition
antisipation	anticipation	apart	
antisocial /ly		apartat	apartheid
antisoshal	antisocial ⁺	apartheid	
antithes *is* /es (pl.)		apartied	apartheid
antithisis	antithesis ⁺	apartment	
antitoksic	antitoxic ⁺	apase	apace
antitoksin	antitoxin	apathetic /al/ally	
antitoxi *c* /n		apathy	
antler /ed		ape ²	
anu	anew	apeace	apiece
anual	annual ⁺	apeal	appeal ¹⁺
anuitey	annuity ⁺	apear	appear ¹⁺
anul	anal	apearance	appearance
anul	annul ³⁺	apearans	appearance
anular	annular ⁺	apease	apiece
anulment	annulment	apeel	appeal ¹⁺
anunciashun	annunciation	apeer	appear ¹⁺
anunciate	annunciate ²⁺	apeice	apiece
anunciation	annunciation	apeks	apex ⁺
anunsiashun	annunciation	apellant	appellant ⁺
anunsiate	annunciate ²⁺	apellashun	appellation
anunsiation	annunciation	apellation	appellation
anus		apend	append ¹⁺
anuther	another	apendage	appendage
anvil		apendicitis	appendicitis
anxiet *y* /ies		apendige	appendage
anxious /ly/ness		apendiks	appendix ⁺
any		apendisitis	appendicitis
anybody		apendix	appendix ⁺
anyhow		aperance	appearance
anyone		aperans	appearance
anything		apercher	aperture
anyual	annual ⁺	apergey	apogee ⁺
anyway		aperitif	
anywere	anywhere	apertain	appertain ¹
anywhere		aperture	
aorta		apetiser	appetiser
apace		apetising	appetising ⁺
Apache		apetite	appetite
apal	appal ³⁺	ap *ex* /e**x**es/ices (pls.)	
aparatus	apparatus ⁺	aphid /ian	
aparel	apparel ⁺	aphoris *m* /tic	
aparent	apparent ⁺	aphrodisiac	

apiar *y* /ies
apiece
apissul — epistle [+]
apitite — appetite
aplaud — applaud [1]
aplause — applause
aplawd — applaud [1]
aplawse — applause
aple — apple [+]
apli — apply [4]
apliance — appliance
aplians — appliance
aplicable — applicable [+]
aplicabul — applicable [+]
aplicant — applicant
aplicashun — application
aplication — application
aplom — aplomb
aplomb
apocalips — apocalypse [+]
apocalyp *se* /tic
apocrifal — apocryphal
apocryphal
apoge *e* /an
apoint — appoint [1+]
apologetic /ally
apologey — apology [+]
apologise [2]
apolog *y* /ies/ist
apoplectic /ally
apopleksey — apoplexy
apoplexy
aporshun — apportion [1+]
aportion — apportion [1+]
aposishun — apposition
aposit — apposite
aposition — apposition
aposle — apostle [+]
apost *le* /olate/olic
apostrofey — apostrophe
apostrophe
aposul — apostle [+]
apothecar *y* /ies
apoynt — appoint [1+]
appal [3] /lingly

apparatus /es
apparel /led
apparent /ly
apparishun — apparition
appart — apart
apparition
appeal [1] /ingly
appear [1] /ance
appease [2] /ment/r
appella *nt* /tion
append [1] /age
appendicitis
appendiks — appendix [+]
appendi *x* /xes/ces (pls.)
appertain [1]
apperture — aperture
appetiser
appetising /ly
appetite
applaud [1]
applause
applawd — applaud [1]
applaws — applause
apple /-cart/-pie
appli — apply [4]
appliance
applians — appliance
applicab *le* /ility
applicant
applicashun — application
application
apply [4]
appoint [1] /ment
apporshun — apportion [1+]
apportion [1] /ment
apposishun — apposition
apposite
apposition
appreciabl *e* /y
appreciabul — appreciable [+]
appreciat *e* [2] /ion/ive
apprehend [1]
apprehenshun — apprehension
apprehension
apprehensive /ly/ness

apprentice² /ship		aproximation	approximation
apprentis	apprentice²⁺	apt /ly/ness	
apprise²		aptitude	
approach¹ /able		aptley	aptly
approbation		apul	apple⁺
approch	approach¹⁺	aqualung	
appropriate² /ly/ness		aquamarine	
appropriat*ion* /or		aquaplane	
approval		aquarelle	
approve²		aquari*um* /a/ums (pls.)	
approximashun	approximation	Aquarius	
approximate² /ly		aquatic	
approximation		aquatint	
aprehend	apprehend¹	aqueduct	
aprehenshun	apprehension	aqueous	
aprehensiv	apprehensive⁺	aquiline	
apren	apron¹	aquius	aqueous
aprentis	apprentice²⁺	ar	are⁺
apreshabul	appreciable⁺	arabel	arable
apreshiable	appreciable⁺	arabesk	arabesque
apreshiativ	appreciative	arabesque	
apresiashun	appreciation	Arabi*an* /c	
apricot		arable	
April		arabul	arable
aprise	apprise²	araign	arraign¹⁺
aprize	apprise²	arain	arraign¹⁺
aproach	approach¹⁺	Aramaic	
aprobashun	approbation	arange	arrange²⁺
aprobation	approbation	arant	arrant⁺
aproch	approach¹⁺	aray	array¹⁺
aprochabul	approachable	arayn	arraign¹⁺
aproksimashun	approximation	arber	arbour
aproksimat	approximate²⁺	arbiter	
aproksimation	approximation	arbitrar*y* /ily/iness	
apron¹		arbitrashun	arbitration
aproov	approve²	arbitrat*e*² /ion/or	
aprooval	approval	arbour	
apropo	apropos	arc ★ (curved line)	
apropos		arc	ark ★
apropriashun	appropriation⁺	arcade	
apropriate	appropriate²⁺	arch /es/ly/ness	
apropriation	appropriation⁺	archaeolog*y* /ical/ist	
aproval	approval	archai*c* /sm	
aprove	approve²	archangel	
aproximate	approximate²⁺	archaologey	archaeology⁺

archbishop	
archdeacon	
archduke	
archeologey	archaeology +
archer /y	
archetype	
archfeind	archfiend
archfiend	
archipelago /s	
architect /ure	
architectural /ly	
archiv es /ist	
archley	archly
archway	
arcipeligo	archipelago +
arcitect	architect +
arcitectural	architectural +
arcives	archives +
arc -lamp /-light	
Arctic	
ardent /ly	
arder	ardour
ardewus	arduous +
ardour	
arduous /ly/ness	
arduus	arduous +
are /n't	
area * (surface)	
area	aria *
arears	arrears
arees	Aries
arena	
arent	aren't
arest	arrest 1+
argew	argue 2+
argu	argue 2+
arguabul	arguable
argu e 2 /able/ably	
argument /ative	
ari	awry
aria * (song)	
aria	area *
arial	aerial +
arid /ity	
Aries	

aright	
ariley	airily
arina	arena
arise /n	
aristocracy	
aristocrasey	aristocracy
aristocrat /ic	
arite	aright
arithmetic /ian	
arithmetical /ly	
arival	arrival
arive	arrive 2+
arizen	arisen
ark * (floating vessel)	
ark	arc *
arkade	arcade
arkaic	archaic +
arkangel	archangel
arkiologey	archaeology +
arkiologist	archaeologist
arkipeligo	archipelago +
arkitect	architect +
arkitectural	architectural +
arkives	archives +
arktic	Arctic
arktipe	archetype
arm 1 /ful/let	
armada	
armadillo /es	
armament	
armchair	
armer	armour +
armey	army +
armistice	
armistis	armistice
armoner	almoner +
armour /ed	
arms * (limbs)	
arms	alms *
arm y /ies	
arnt	aren't
arogance	arrogance +
arogans	arrogance +
arogant	arrogant
arogate	arrogate 2+

29

aroma /s/tic		artiller *y* /ies	
arora	aurora	artisan	
aroroot	arrowroot	artist ★ (painter)	
arose		artiste ★ (performer)	
around		artistic /ally	
arouse²		artistry	
arow	arrow⁺	artizan	artisan
arownd	around	artless /ly/ness	
arowroot	arrowroot	asail	assail¹⁺
arowse	arouse²	asailant	assailant
arpeggio /s		asalant	assailant
arpejo	arpeggio⁺	asale	assail¹⁺
arraign¹ /ment		asalt	assault¹⁺
arrange² /ment		asassin	assassin
arrant /ly		asassinashun	assassination
array¹ /s		asassinate	assassinate²⁺
arrears		asassination	assassination
arrest¹ /er		asault	assault¹⁺
arrival		asay	assay¹⁺
arrive² /r		asayl	assail¹⁺
arrogan *ce* /t/tly		asbestos /is	
arrogans	arrogance⁺	ascend¹ /ancy/ant	
arrogat *e*² /ion		ascenshun	ascension
arrow /-head		ascension	
arrowroot		ascent ★ (rise)	
arsenal		ascent	assent¹★
arsenic /al		ascertain¹ /able	
arsnic	arsenic⁺	ascetic /ally/ism	
arson /ist		ascrib *e*² /able	
artefact		ase	ace
arter *y* /ies		asemblage	assemblage
arteshun	artesian	asemble	assemble²⁺
artesian		asembley	assembly⁺
artful /ly/ness		asemblige	assemblage
arthriti *c* /s		asembul	assemble²⁺
arthropod		asend	ascend¹⁺
artichoke		asendancy	ascendancy
article²		asendansey	ascendancy
articul	article²	asendant	ascendant
articular		asenshun	ascension
articulat *e*² /ion		asension	ascension
artifice /r		asent	ascent★
artificial /ity/ly		asent	assent¹★
artifis	artifice⁺	asep *sis* /tic	
artifishal	artificial⁺	asershun	assertion

asert	assert [1+]	asistance	assistance
asertain	ascertain [1+]	asistans	assistance
asertane	ascertain [1+]	asistant	assistant
asertayn	ascertain [1+]	asitic	acetic
asertion	assertion	ask [1]	
asertive	assertive	askance	
asess	assess [1+]	askans	askance
asesser	assessor	askew	
asessment	assessment	asku	askew
aset	asset	asleep	
asetic	ascetic [+]	asma	asthma [+]
aseticism	asceticism	asmatic	asthmatic
asfalt	asphalt	asociate	associate [2+]
asfixia	asphyxia	asociation	association
asfixiate	asphyxiate [2+]	asonance	assonance [+]
ash /es/en/-tray/y		asonans	assonance [+]
ashamed		asonant	assonant
ashfalt	asphalt	asort	assort [1+]
ashor	assure [2★]	asoshiashun	association
ashorance	assurance	asoshiate	associate [2+]
ashorans	assurance	aspadistra	aspidistra
ashore ★ (on beach)		asparagus	
ashore	assure [2★]	aspect	
aside		aspen	
asiditey	acidity	asperit y /ies	
asidulate	acidulate [2+]	aspershun	aspersion
asiduous	assiduous [+]	aspersion	
asiduus	assiduous [+]	asphalt	
asign	assign [1+]	asphyxia	
asignashun	assignation	asphyxiat e [2] /ion	
asignation	assignation	aspic	
asignment	assignment	aspidistra	
asilum	asylum	aspirashun	aspiration
asimetrical	asymmetrical	aspir e [2] /ation	
asimilashun	assimilation	aspirin	
asimilate	assimilate [2+]	asprin	aspirin
asimilater	assimilator	ass /es	
asimilation	assimilation	assail [1] /able/ant	
asimitrey	asymmetry [+]	assassin	
asinable	assignable	assassinat e [2] /ion	
asinabul	assignable	assault [1] /er	
asine	assign [1+]	assay [1] /er	
asinement	assignment	assembl e [2] /age	
asinin e /ity		assembl y /ies	
asist	assist [1+]	assembul	assemble [2+]

31

assend	ascend [1+]
assendancy	ascendancy
assendant	ascendant
assenshun	ascension
assension	ascension
assent [1]★ (agree)	
assent	ascent ★
assert [1] /ion/ive	
assess [1] /ment/or	
asset	
assiduous /ly	
assign [1] /able/ation/ment	
assignee	
assimilat*e* [2] /ion/or	
assine	assign [1+]
assist [1] /ance/ant	
associat*e* [2] /ion	
assonan*ce* /t	
assonans	assonance [+]
assort [1] /ment	
assoshiate	associate [2+]
assuage [2] /ment	
assum*e* [2] /able/ably	
assumption	
assumshun	assumption
assurance	
assurans	assurance
assure [2]★ (make certain)	
aster ★ (flower)	
aster	astir ★
asterisk	
astern	
asteroid	
asthma /tic	
astigmati*c* /sm	
astir ★ (motion)	
astonish [1] /ment	
astound [1] /ingly	
astownd	astound [1+]
astral /ly	
astray	
astrel	astral [+]
astride	
astringen*cy* /t	
astrolog*y* /er/ical	

astronaut /ic/ical	
astronomy	
astronort	astronaut [+]
astronortic	astronautic
astrul	astral [+]
astur	astir ★
asturn	astern
astute /ly/ness	
asume	assume [2+]
asumpshun	assumption
asumption	assumption
asunder	
aswage	assuage [2+]
asylum	
asymetrey	asymmetry [+]
asymmetr*y* /ical	
atach	attach [1+]
atachable	attachable
atachabul	attachable
atachay case	attaché case
atack	attack [1+]
atain	attain [1+]
atane	attain [1+]
ate ★ (did eat)	
ate	eight ★
ateen	eighteen [+]
atempt	attempt [1+]
atend	attend [1+]
atendance	attendance
atendans	attendance
atendant	attendant
atenshun	attention [+]
atention	attention [+]
atentiv	attentive
atenuashun	attenuation
atenuate	attenuate [2+]
atenuation	attenuation
aterney	attorney [+]
atest	attest [1+]
atestashun	attestation
atestation	attestation
atey	eighty [+]
atheis*m* /t/tic	
athiism	atheism [+]
athiist	atheist

athleet	athlete
athlete	
athletic /ism/s	
atic	attic
atipical	atypical +
atire	attire ²
atitude	attitude
Atlantic	
atlas /es	
atmosfere	atmosphere +
atmosferic	atmospheric
atmospher e /ic	
atom /ic/ically	
atomise ² /r	
atone ² /ment	
atract	attract ¹+
atraction	attraction
atractiv	attractive +
atribushun	attribution
atributable	attributable
atributabul	attributable
atribute	attribute ²+
atribution	attribution
atrishun	attrition
atrition	attrition
atrium	
atrocious /ly/ness	
atrocit y /ies	
atrofey	atrophy ⁴+
atroph y ⁴ /ic	
atroshus	atrocious +
atrositey	atrocity +
attach ¹ /able	
attachabul	attachable
attaché case	
attachment	
attack ¹ /er	
attain ¹ /able/ment	
attempt ¹ /able	
attend ¹ /ance	
attendant	
attenshun	attention +
attent ion /ive	
attenuat e ² /ion	
atterney	attorney +

attest ¹ /ation	
attic	
attire ²	
attitude	
attorney /s	
attract ¹ /ion	
attractive /ly/ness	
attributable	
attribut e ² /ion/ive	
attrishun	attrition
attrition	
attune ²	
atune	attune ²
aturney	attorney +
atypical /ly	
au pair	
aubergine	
auburn	
aucshun	auction ¹+
auction ¹ /eer	
audacious /ly	
audacity	
audashus	audacious +
audasitey	audacity
audib le /ility/ly	
audibul	audible +
audience	
audiens	audience
audiomet er /ric/ry	
audio-typist	
audio-visual	
audishun	audition ¹
audit ¹	
audition ¹	
auditor	
auditorium	
auditory	
auditrey	auditory
auger ★ (tool)	
aught ★ (anything)	
aught	ought ★
augment ¹ /ation	
augur ¹★ (predict)	
augur y /ies	
August	

P.D.P.S.—C

33

aunt /ie/y	
aura	
aural ★ (of the ear) /ly	
auric *le* /ular	
aurora	
auspic *es* /ious	
auspishus	auspicious
austere /ly/ness	
austerit *y* /ies	
Australian	
authentic /ally/ity	
authenticat *e* ² /ion	
author /ess (fem.)	
authoris *e* ² /ation	
authoritarian /ism	
authoritative /ly	
authorit *y* /ies	
autis *m* /tic	
autobiografey	autobiography +
autobiografical	autobiographi-cal +
autobiographical /ly	
autobiograph *y* /ies	
autocrac *y* /ies	
autocrasey	autocracy +
autocrat	
autocratic /ally	
autograf	autograph ¹+
autograph ¹ /ic	
automat *e* ² /ion	
automatic /ally	
automatism	
automaton	
automobile	
autonomous /ly	
autonomus	autonomous +
autonomy	
autopilot	
autops *y* /ies	
autum	autumn +
autumn /al	
auxiliar *y* /ies	
avaidable	available +
avaide	evade ²+
avail ¹	

availab *le* /ility	
avalable	available +
avalabul	available +
avalanche	
avale	avail ¹
avarey	aviary +
avaric *e* /ious	
avenew	avenue
avenge ² /r	
avenue	
aver ³ /ment	
average ² /ly	
averige	average ²+
averishus	avaricious
averiss	avarice +
averse /ly/ness	
avershun	aversion
aversion	
avert ¹ /edly	
aviar *y* /ies	
aviashun	aviation +
aviater	aviator
aviat *ion* /or	
avid /ity/ly	
avlanch	avalanche
avocado	
avocashun	avocation
avocation	
avoid ¹ /able/ably	
avow ¹ /al/edly	
avoyd	avoid ¹+
avoydable	avoidable
avoydabul	avoidable
avrige	average ²+
avur	aver ³+
avurs	averse +
avurshun	aversion
avursion	aversion
avurt	avert ¹+
await ¹	
awake ²	
awaken ¹	
award ¹ /able/er	
aware /ness	
awate	await ¹

away			**B**
awb	orb [1]		
awe [2]*(fear)/some/struck		babble [2]	
awear	aware [+]	babie	baby [+]
awful /ly/ness		babmingten	badminton
awgsiliarey	auxiliary [+]	babminten	badminton
Awgust	August	baboon	
awgy	orgy [+]	babul	babble [2]
awhile		bab y /ies	
awile	awhile	baby-sitter	
awiyul	awhile	baccarat	
awkward /ly/ness		bach	batch
awl * (tool)		bacheler	bachelor [+]
awning		bachelor /hood	
awoard	award [1+]	bacill us /i (pl.)	
awoke		back [1] /ache/bone/er	
awry		backara	baccarat
axe [2]		backbencher	
axial		backbit e /er/ing	
a:cident	accident [+]	backbone	
axiom		backcloth	
axiomatic /ally		backfire [2]	
ax is /es (pl.)		backgammon	
axle		background	
axseed	accede [2+]	backgrownd	background
axsel	axle	backhand /ed/er	
axselerate	accelerate [2+]	backlash	
axsent	accent [1+]	backlog	
axsentuate	accentuate [2+]	backslid e /er/ing	
axsept	accept [1+]	backspace [2]	
axseptable	acceptable [+]	backstage	
axseptabul	acceptable [+]	backstitch [1]	
axsesorey	accessory *[+]	backstroke	
axsess	access [+]	backward /ness/s	
axsessible	accessible	backwater	
axsessibul	accessible	bacon	
ay * (yes) /es *		bacteriological /ly	
ay	eye [2*+]	bacteriolog y /ist	
ay	I *[+]	bacteri um /a (pl.)	
aya	ayah	bad * (no good) /ly	
ayah		bade * (asked)	
aye * (always)		badge	
azalea		badger [1]	
azalia	azalea	badley	badly
azure			

badminton		balistic	ballistic +
baffle² /r		balk¹	
baful	baffle² +	balkoney	balcony +
bag³ /gy/gier/giest		ball ★ (dance) /room	
bagatelle		ball	bawl ★+
baggage		ballad /ry	
baggidge	baggage	ballast	
baggi *ly* /ness		ball-bearing	
bagier	baggier	ballerina	
bagiley	baggily +	ballet	
bagpipe /r		ballistic /s	
baige	beige	balloon¹ /er/ist	
bail ★ (security, sport)		ballot¹	
bail	bale²★	ball-point	
bailee ★ (person)		ballyhoo	
bailey ★ (castle wall)		balm /y ★ (mild)	
bailful	baleful +	balmoral	
bailiff		baloney	
bain	bane +	baloon	balloon¹+
bainful	baneful	balot	ballot¹
bairn		balsa	
baist	baste²	balsam	
bait¹★ (fishing)		baluster	
bait	bate²★	balustrade	
baize		bamboo	
baje	beige	bamboozle² /r	
Balaclava		bamboozul	bamboozle²+
balad	ballad +	ban³	
balalaika		banal /ity/ities	
balalika	balalaika	banalitey	banality
balance² /r		banana	
balans	balance²+	band ★(stripe, group)/s★	
balast	ballast	band	banned ★
balay	ballet	bandage²	
balcon *y* /ies		bandanna	
bald ★ (no hair)		bandey	bandy +
bald	bawled ★	bandie	bandy +
balderdash		bandige	bandage²
bald-headed		bandit /ry	
bald *ing* /ness		bands	banns ★
bale²★ (bundle)		bandstand	
bale	bail ★	bandwagon	
baleful /ly		bandy /-legged	
balerina	ballerina	bane /ful/fully	
balihoo	ballyhoo	baner	banner

bang [1]		barge [2] /-pole	
bangle		bargen	bargain [1+]
bangul	bangle	baricade	barricade [2]
banish [1] /ment		barier	barrier
banister		barige	barrage
banjo /s		baring * (exposing)	
bank [1] /er/note		baring	barring *
bankrupt [1] /cy		baring	bearing *
bankwet	banquet [1]	barister	barrister
banned * (barred)		baritone	
banner		barium	
banns * (marriage)		bark [1] /er	
banquet [1]		barley /-sugar	
bans	banns *	barly	barley +
bantam /-weight		barm	balm +
banter [1] /ingly		barmade	barmaid
Bantu		barmaid	
baonet	bayonet [3]	barmy * (crazy)	
baptis *e* [2] /m		barmy	balmy *
bar /red * (stop) /ring *		barn /yard	
barack	barrack [1]	barn	bairn
barb		barnacle /d	
barbarian		barnicul	barnacle +
barbar *ic* /ism/ous		barograf	barograph
barbarit *y* /ies		barograph	
barbarus	barbarous	barok	baroque
barbecue		baromet *er* /ric	
barbed wire		baron * (noble) /et/y	
barber		baroness (fem.)	
barbican		baroque	
barbique	barbecue	barow	barrow
barbiturate		barrack [1]	
bard * (poet)		barrage	
bard	barred *	barrel [3] /ful	
bare [2]* (naked) /foot		barren * (empty) /ness	
bare	bear *	barricade [2]	
bareback		barrier	
barefaced		barrister	
bareheaded		barrow	
barel	barrel [3+]	barter [1] /er	
barelegged		barul	barrel [3+]
baren	baron *+	basalt	
baren	barren *+	base * (station,	
bareskin	bearskin	foundation)	
bargain [1] /er		base	bass *

baseball	
base *less* /ly/ness	
basement	
baset	basset
bashful /ly/ness	
basic /ally	
basillus	bacillus +
basin /ful	
bas *is* ★ (groundwork)/es	
basit	basset
bask [1]	
basket /ball/ful/ry	
baskit	basket +
basoon	bassoon
bas-relief	
bass ★ (deep tone)	
bass clef	
bass drum	
basset	
bassoon	
bastard /ly	
bastardis *e* [2] /ation	
baste [2]	
basterd	bastard +
bastion	
bastyun	bastion
bat [3] /sman	
batalion	battalion
batalyun	battalion
batch	
bate [2]★ (lessen)	
bate	bait [1]★
baten	baton ★
baten	batten [1]★
bater	batter [1]
baterey	battery +
batering ram	battering-ram
bathe [2] /r	
bathroom	
batie	batty +
batik	
batle	battle [2]+
baton ★ (staff of office)	
battalion	
batten [1]★ (wood, grow fat)	

batter [1]	
battering-ram	
batter *y* /ies	
battle [2] /dress/ship	
battle-axe	
batt *y* /ier/iest	
batul	battle [2]+
baty	batty +
bauble	
baubul	bauble
bauxite	
bawble	bauble
bawdie	bawdy +
bawdi *ly* /ness	
bawd *y* /ier/iest	
bawk	balk [1]
bawksite	bauxite
bawl ★ (cry)/ed ★ /ing	
bawl	ball ★+
bawl-baring	ball-bearing
bawldedash	balderdash
bawldheded	bald-headed
bawldness	baldness
bawlpoint	ball-point
bawlroom	ballroom
baylif	bailiff
bayonet [3]	
bayth	bathe [2]+
bazaar	
bazar	bazaar
bazooka	
be ★ (is-[verb]) /ing	
be	bee ★+
beach [1]★ (shore) /es	
beach	beech ★+
beachcomber	
beachhead	
beacon	
bead /y	
beadle	
beadul	beadle
beaf	beef +
beafeter	beefeater
beafstake	beefsteak
beagl *e* /ing	

beagul	beagle +	bed ³ /ridden/rock	
beak /er		bedaub ¹	
beam ¹		bedawb	bedaub ¹
bean * (vegetable)		beday	bidet
bean	been *	bedevil ³	
beanstalk		bedlam	
bear * (carry, animal)		bedouin	
bear	bare ²*+	bedowin	bedouin
bearback	bareback	bedraggle ²	
beard¹		bedragul	bedraggle ²
bearfased	barefaced	bedriden	bedridden
bearfoot	barefoot	bedroom	
bearheded	bareheaded	bed-sitter	
bearing * (carrying)		bedspread	
bearing	baring *	bedstead	
bearleggid	barelegged	bedtime	
bearskin		bee * (insect) /hive	
beast /ly		beech * (tree) /es	
beastli er /est/ness		beech	beach ¹*+
beat * (strike) /en		beechcomer	beachcomber
beat	beet *	beechhed	beachhead
beatif y ⁴ /ic/ication		beecon	beacon
beatitude		beed	bead +
beatle	beetle	beedle	beadle
beatroot	beetroot	beef /y	
beatul	beetle	beefeater	
beau * (dandy)		beefi er /est/ly/ness	
Beaufort scale		beefsteak	
beauteous		beegle	beagle +
beautician		beek	beak +
beautie	beauty +	beekun	beacon
beautiful /ly		beeline	
beautify ⁴		Beelzebub	
beautishun	beautician	beem	beam ¹
beaut y /ies		been * (past of be)	
beaver		been	bean *
becalmed		beenstork	beanstalk
became		beer * (drink)	
becarmed	becalmed	beer	bier *
because		beerd	beard ¹
beck		beest	beast +
beckon ¹ /ingly		beestlier	beastlier +
becom e /ing		beeswaks	beeswax
becon	beacon	beeswax	
becos	because	beet * (vegetable)	

beet	beat ★+	bel	bell ★
beetle		bel	belle ★
beetroot		belaber	belabour [1]
beetul	beetle	belabour [1]	
beever	beaver	belated /ly	
befall /en		belay [1]	
befell		belch [1]	
befier	beefier +	beleaf	belief
befit [3]		beleager	beleaguer [1]
before /hand		beleaguer [1]	
befrend	befriend [1]	beleavabul	believable +
befriend [1]		beleave	believe [2+]
befuddle [2]		belfrey	belfry +
befudul	befuddle [2]	belfr y /ies	
beg [3]		Belgian	
began		beli	belie ★+
beger	beggar [1+]	belicose	bellicose +
beggar [1] /liness/ly		belie ★ (untruth) /d	
begile	beguile [2+]	belief	
begin /ner/ning		believabl e /y	
begone		believe [2] /r	
begot /ten		beliful	bellyful
begrudge [2]		beligerence	belligerence +
beguile [2] /ment/r		beligerency	belligerency
begun		beligerent	belligerent
behalf		beline	beeline
beharf	behalf	belittle [2] /r	
behave [2]		belittul	belittle [2+]
behavier	behaviour +	beliying	belying
behaviour /ism		bell ★ (rings)	
behead [1]		belle ★ (beauty)	
behed	behead [1]	bellicos e /ity	
beheld		belligerenc e /y	
behest		belligerent	
behind		bellow [1] /er	
behive	beehive	bellows	
behold /en/er/ing		bell y ★ (stomach) /ies/ied	
behove		bellyful	
beige		belong [1] /ings	
being		belose	bellows
bekoz	because	beloved	
bekweath	bequeath [1+]	below ★ (beneath)	
bekwest	bequest	below	bellow [1+]
bel ★†		below	billow [1★+]
†(unit = 10 decibels)		belows	bellows

40

bely	belly★+	beril	beryl +
belying		berilium	beryllium
bemoan [1]		berkelium	
bemuse [2]		berlap	burlap
bench /er/es		berli	burly +
bend /ing		bern	burn [1]+
beneath		bernish	burnish [1]+
benefaction		berr *y* ★ (fruit) /ies	
benefact *or* /ress (fem.)		berry	bury [4]★
beneficen *ce* /t		berserk	
beneficial		bersurk	berserk
beneficiar *y* /ies		berth [1]★ (moor, bunk)	
benefisens	beneficence +	berth	birth ★+
benefisent	beneficent	bery	berry ★+
benefisharey	beneficiary +	bery	bury [4]★
benefishul	beneficial	beryl /line	
benefit [1]		beryllium	
benevolen *ce* /t/tly		beseech /er	
benevolens	benevolence +	beseige	besiege [2]+
benifacshun	benefaction	beset /ting	
benifacter	benefactor +.	beside /s	
benifactress	benefactress	besiege [2] /ment	
benifit	benefit [1]	besort	besought
benign /ant/ly		besot [3]	
benine	benign +	besought	
bent		bespatter [1]	
benum	benumb [1]+	best /-seller	
benumb [1] /ment		bester	bestir [3]
benzene ★†		bestial /ism/ly	
†(from coal-tar)		bestialit *y* /ies	
benzine ★ (from		bestir [3]	
mineral oils)		bestow [1] /al/er	
bequeath [1] /ment		bestrew [1] /n	
bequest		bet /ting	
berate [2]		beta particles	
beray	beret	betle	beetle
bereave [2] /ment		betoken [1]	
bereft		betray [1] /al/er	
beret		betroth [1] /al	
bereve	bereave [2]+	better [1] /ment	
bergler	burglar	betul	beetle
berial	burial	between	
beriberi		betwixt	
berie	berry ★+	beverage	
berie	bury [4]★	beveridge	beverage

41

beverige	beverage
bevie	bevy [+]
bev*y* /ies	
bewail[1] /er	
beware	
bewayl	bewail[1+]
bewich	bewitch[1+]
bewilder[1] /ment	
bewitch[1] /er	
beyond	
bezurk	berserk
bi election	by-election
biannual *† /ly	
†(twice a year)	
biannual	biennial [*+]
bias[1] /es	
biatifi	beatify[4+]
biatitude	beatitude
Bibl*e* /ical	
bibliografey	bibliography [+]
bibliografic	bibliographic [+]
bibliographic /al	
bibliograph*y* /ies/er	
bibul	Bible [+]
bicame	became
bicarbonate	
bicarmed	becalmed
bicentenar*y* /ies	
bicentennial	
bicentenyul	bicentennial
biceps	
bich	bitch [+]
bicicle	bicycle[2+]
biciclist	bicyclist
bicker[1] /er	
bicycl*e*[2] /ist	
bide[2]	
bidet	
bidevil	bedevil[3]
biennial *† /ly	
†(every two years)	
biennial	biannual [*+]
bier * (for coffin)	
bier	beer *
bier	byre *

bifell	befell
bifocal	
bifurcat*e*[2] /ion	
big /ger/gest/gish	
bigam*ist* /ous	
bigamus	bigamous
bigam*y* /ies	
bigan	began
bighead	
bigile	beguile[2+]
bigin	begin [+]
biginer	beginner
bigining	beginning
bigon	begone
bigone	bygone [+]
bigot /ed/ry	
bigrudge	begrudge[2]
bigun	begun
biharf	behalf
bihave	behave[2]
bihavier	behaviour [+]
bihed	behead[1]
bihest	behest
bihove	behove
bike	
bikweath	bequeath[1+]
bikwest	bequest
bil	bill[1]
bilaber	belabour[1]
bilated	belated [+]
bilateral /ism/ly	
bilaw	by-law
bilay	belay[1]
bilberie	bilberry [+]
bilberr*y* /ies	
bild	build [+]
bilding	building
bile	
bileager	beleaguer[1]
bileavable	believable [+]
bileavabul	believable [+]
bileave	believe[2+]
bileger	beleaguer[1]
bileif	belief
bilet	billet[1]

bilge		biografical	biographical +
bilief	belief	biographical /ly	
bilingual /ism/ly		biography /ies/er	
bilingwal	bilingual +	biokemist	biochemist +
bilious		biologey	biology +
bilittle	belittle 2+	biological /ly	
bilitul	belittle 2+	biology /ist	
bilius	bilious	biopsey	biopsy +
bilk 1 /er		biopsy /ies	
bill 1		biparti te /san	
billabong		bipartizan	bipartisan
billet 1		bipass	by-pass 1
billiards		biped	
billion /aire		biplane	
billit	billet 1	biplay	byplay
billow 1* (wave) /y		bipolar /ity	
bilong	belong 1+	biproduct	by-product
bilow	below *	birate	berate 2
bilow	billow 1*+	birch /es	
biluvd	beloved	bird	
bilyards	billiards	birdie	
bilyon	billion +	bird's-eye	
bilyus	bilious	bireft	bereft
bimetalli c /sm		bireve	bereave 2+
bimoan	bemoan 1	birode	byroad
bimonthly		birth * (born) /day	
bimuse	bemuse 2	birth	berth 1*
bin * (box)		biscuit	
bin	been *	bisecshun	bisection
binacle	binnacle	bisect 1 /ion/or	
binacul	binnacle	biseech	beseech +
binary		biseege	besiege 2+
bind /er/ery/ing		biseksual	bisexual +
bineath	beneath	bisentenary	bicentenary +
bineeth	beneath	bisentenial	bicentennial
binge		bisentenyal	bicentennial
bingo		biseps	biceps
binine	benign +	biset	beset +
binnacle		bisexual /ly	
binocular /s		bishop /ric	
binomial		bisicle	bicycle 2+
binum	benumb 1+	bisiclist	bicyclist
biochemist /ry		biside	beside +
biografer	biographer	bisier	busier +
biografey	biography +	bisiley	busily

biskit	biscuit	blaber	blabber
bismuth		black [1] /out	
bisness	business +	black-beetle	
bison		blackberie	blackberry +
bisort	besought	blackberr y /ies	
bisot	besot [3]	blackbird	
bispatter	bespatter [1]	blackboard	
bistander	bystander	blacken [1]	
bistow	bestow [1+]	blackguard	
bistowal	bestowal	blackleg [3]	
bistru	bestrew [1+]	blacklist [1]	
bistur	bestir [3]	blackmail [1] /er	
bisun	bison	blacksmith	
bisy	busy [4]	bladder	
bitch /es		blade	
bit e /ing/ten		blader	bladder
biter	bitter +	blagard	blackguard
bitoken	betoken [1]	blaid	blade
bitray	betray [1+]	blaim	blame [2+]
bitrayal	betrayal	blaimless	blameless +
bitroth	betroth [1+]	blair	blare [2]
bitter /est/ly/ness		blaise	blaze [2]
bitum en /inous		blaizer	blazer
bitween	between	blam e [2] /able	
bitwixt	betwixt	blameless /ly	
bivalve		blameworthy	
bivouac /ked/king		blamonge	blancmange
bivuac	bivouac +	blanch [1]	
biwail	bewail [1+]	blancmange	
biware	beware	bland /ly/ness	
biwàyul	bewail [1+]	blank /ly	
biwear	beware	blanket [1]	
biwhich	bewitch [1+]	blare [2]	
biwich	bewitch [1+]	blarney	
biwilder	bewilder [1+]	blasfeim	blaspheme [2+]
biword	byword	blasfemey	blasphemy +
biyond	beyond	blasfemus	blasphemous
bizar	bizarre +	blasphem e [2] /ous	
bizarre /ly/ness		blasphem y /ies	
bizier	busier +	blast [1] /-off	
biziley	busily	blast-furnace	
bizmuth	bismuth	blatancy	
bizness	business +	blatansey	blatancy
bizy	busy [4]	blatant /ly	
blab [3] /ber		blaze [2]	

blazer		blo	blow +
blazon [1] /er		bloat [1] /edness	
bleach [1] /er		bloater	
blead	bleed +	blob [3]	
bleak /er/est/ly/ness		bloc ★ (group)	
blear [1] /y		blochie	blotchy
bleari er /est/ly		block [1]★† /age	
bleat [1] /er		†(solid piece, stop)	
bled		block	bloc ★
bleech	bleach [1]+	blockade [2] /r	
bleed /er/ing		blockhead /ed	
bleek	bleak +	blond /ish/ness	
bleer	blear [1]+	blone	blown
bleerey	bleary	blood [1] /y	
bleerier	blearier +	blood pressure	
bleet	bleat [1]+	blood vessel	
blemish [1] /er		bloodhound	
blench [1] /er		blood ied /ier/iest	
blend [1] /er		bloodi ly /ness	
bless [1]		blood shed /shot	
blest		bloodthirst y /iness	
blew ★ (wind)		bloom [1] /ers	
blew	blue ★+	blossom [1] /y	
blewbell	bluebell	blosum	blossom [1]+
blewberie	blueberry +	blot [3] /ter	
blewbery	blueberry +	blot	bloat [1]+
blew-chip	blue-chip	blotch [1] /y	
blewish	bluish	bloter	bloater
blewprint	blue-print	bloter	blotter
·blight [1] /er		blouse	
blind [1] /est/ly/ness		blow /er/ing/n/y	
blinder /s		blowse	blouse
blind-man's-buff		blowter	bloater
blink [1]		blowze	blouse
bliss /ful/fully		blowzey	blowzy +
blister [1]		blowz y /ier/iest	
blite	blight [1]+	blu	blue ★+
bliter	blighter	blubber [1] /y	
blith	blithe +	blubell	bluebell
blithe /ly/ness		bluberie	blueberry +
blithering		blubery	blueberry +
blits	blitz [1]	blud	blood [1]+
blitz [1]		blud presher	blood pressure
blizard	blizzard	blud vesel	blood vessel
blizzard		bludey	bloody

bludgen	bludgeon [1]	bob-sled	
bludgeon [1]		bob-sleigh	
bludhound	bloodhound	boby	bobby [+]
bludhownd	bloodhound	boch	botch [1+]
bludid	bloodied [+]	bode [2]	
bludie	bloody	bodice	
bludily	bloodily [+]	bodie	body [+]
bludshed	bloodshed [+]	bodi ed /ly	
bludshot	bloodshot	bodigard	bodyguard
bludthurstey	bloodthirsty [+]	bodiley	bodily
blue * (colour) /bell		bodiss	bodice
blue	blew *	bodkin	
blueberr y /ies		bod y /ies	
bluebottle		bodyguard	
blue-chip		bogey * (golf)	
blue-print		bogey	bogy *[+]
bluf	bluff [1+]	boggle [2]	
bluff [1] /er		bogul	boggle [2]
bluish		bogus	
blummers	bloomers	bog y * (devil) /ies	
blunder [1] /er		bohemian	
blunderbuss		boi	boy *
blunt [1] /er/est/ly/ness		boi	buoy [1]*
blur [3] /riness/ry		boiansey	buoyancy [+]
blurb		boiant	buoyant
blurie	blurry	boicot	boycott [1+]
blurt [1]		boil [1] /er	
blush [1] /es/ingly		boisterous /ly	
bluster [1] /y		boisterus	boisterous [+]
boa-constrictor		boks	box [1+]
boar * (swine)		Boksing Day	Boxing Day
boar	boor *	bolard	bollard
boar	bore [2]*[+]	bolaro	bolero
board [1] /er * (lodger)		bold	
boarding /-house/-school		bolder * (braver)	
boast [1] /er		bolder	boulder *
boastful /ly/ness		bold ly /ness	
boat [1] /-house/-race		bole * (tree trunk)	
boater		bole	bowl [1]*
boatswain		bolero	
bobbin		bollard	
bobb y /ies		boloney	
bobie	bobby [+]	Bolshevi k /sm/st	
bobin	bobbin	bolster [1] /er	
bobslay	bob-sleigh	bolt [1]	

bom	bomb ¹+	boraks	borax
bomb ¹ /er		borasic	boracic
bombard ¹ /ment		borax	
bombardier		bord	board ¹+
bombast /ic/ically		border ¹* (edge) /line	
bomberdeer	bombardier	border	boarder *
bomer	bomber	bording	boarding +
bona fide		bordum	boredom
bonanza		bordy	bawdy +
bond ¹ /age		bore ²*† /dom	
bondige	bondage	† (drill, dull)	
bon e ² /y		bore	boar *
bonet	bonnet	bore	boor *
bonfire		born * (birth)	
bonie	bonny	borne * (carried)	
bonier	bonnier +	boron	
bonit	bonnet	borough * (town)	
bonnet		borow	borrow ¹+
bonni er /est/ly/ness		borrow ¹ /er	
bonny		borstal	
bonus /es		bort	bought
bony	bonny	bos	boss ¹+
boo ¹ /er		bosie	bossy
boobie	booby +	bosier	bossier +
boob y /ies		bosily	bossily
boodwar	boudoir	bosn	boatswain
book /able/ish/let		bosn	bosun
bookay	bouquet	bosom	
bookie		boss ¹ /es/y	
boolvar	boulevard	bossi er /est/ly/ness	
boomerang		bost	boast ¹+
boor * (bad-mannered)		bostful	boastful +
boor	boar *	bosun	
boorgwa	bourgeois	bosy	bossy
boost ¹ /er		bot	boat ¹+
boot /ee * (shoe) /less		botaney	botany +
booteek	boutique	botanical /ly	
booth		botan y /ist	
bootie	booty *	botch ¹ /y	
bootik	boutique	boter	boater
bootleg ³ /ger		both	
booty * (spoils)		bother ¹ /ation/some	
booty	bootee *	botherashun	botheration
booze ² /r		bothersum	bothersome
boracic		botom	bottom +

bottle²		boy	buoy¹*
bottom /less/most		boyancy	buoyancy+
botul	bottle²	boyansey	buoyancy+
boudoir		boyant	buoyant
bough * (tree)		boycott¹ /er	
bough	bow¹*	boykot	boycott¹+
bought		boyl	boil¹+
boukay	bouquet	boysterus	boisterous +
boulder * (big rock)		brace²* (strap up)	
boulder	bolder *	bracelet	
boulevard		bracken	
bounc e² /y		bracket¹	
bound¹ /er		brackish	
boundar y /ies		brackit	bracket¹
boundless		brade	braid¹
bounteous		brag³ /gart	
bountius	bounteous	braget	braggart
bount y /ies/iful		Brahm a /in	
bouquet		brai	bray¹
bourgeois		braid¹	
bourgwa	bourgeois	brail	Braille
bout		Braille	
bouteek	boutique	brain /wave/y	
boutique		brain-drain	
bovine		braini er /est/ly	
bow¹* (bend, arrow)		brainwash¹	
bow	beau *	braise²* (cook)	
bow	bough *	braise	braze²*+
bowel		braisen	brazen +
bower		brakable	breakable
bowl¹* (cricket, basin)		brakabul	breakable
bowl	bole *	brake²* (stop)	
bownce	bounce²+	brake	break *+
bowncy	bouncy	brakedown	breakdown
bownd	bound¹+	braken	bracken
bowndarey	boundary +	brakeneck	breakneck
bowndless	boundless	brakethrew	breakthrough
bowns	bounce²+	brakethrough	breakthrough
bowntey	bounty +	brakewater	breakwater
bowntiful	bountiful	brakige	breakage +
bowntius	bounteous	braking	breaking
bowt	bout	brakish	brackish
box¹ /er/es/-office		brale	Braille
Boxing Day		brama	Brahma +
boy * (lad)		brambl e /y	

48

brambul	bramble +
bramin	Brahmin
branch [1] /es	
brand [1] /-new	
brandie	brandy +
brandnu	brand-new
brandy /-snap	
brane	brain +
branedrain	brain-drain
branewash	brainwash [1]
branier	brainier +
bras	brass +
brase	brace [2]★
brase	braise [2]★
brase	braze [2]★+
brash /ly	
brasier	brassiere ★
brasier	brazier ★
braslet	bracelet
brass /iest/ily/y	
brassiere ★†	
†(undergarment)	
brasy	brassy
brasyer	brazier ★
brat	
bravado	
brave [2] /ly/ry	
bravo	
bravoora	bravura
bravrey	bravery
bravura	
brawd	broad +
brawl [1] /er	
brawn /ier/iest/y	
bray [1]	
brayd	braid [1]
braze [2]★ (solder) /r	
braze	braise [2]★
brazen /ly/ness	
brazier ★ (fire basket)	
breach [1]★†	
† (gap, violation)	
breach	breech ★
bread ★ (food)	
bread	bred ★

breadth	
break ★ (destroy) /able	
break	brake [2]★
break age /er/ing	
breakdown	
breakfast	
breakneck	
breakthrew	breakthrough
breakthrough	
breakwater	
bream	
breast [1] /bone/plate	
breast stroke	
breath /less/lessly	
breathalyse [2] /r	
breathe [2] /r	
breathtaking	
bred ★ (reared)	
bred	bread ★
bredth	breadth
breech ★ (part of gun)	
breech	breach [1]★
breed /er/ing	
breef	brief [1]+
breef case	brief-case
breem	bream
breez e [2] /ily/iness	
breez y /ier/iest	
breif	brief [1]+
breif case	brief-case
brekfast	breakfast
Bren-gun	
brest	breast [1]+
brestbone	breastbone
brestplait	breastplate
breststroke	breast stroke
breth	breadth
breth	breath +
brethalise	breathalyse [2]+
brethless	breathless
brethren	
brethtaking	breathtaking
brevit y /ies	
brew [1] /er	
brewer y /ies	

breze	breeze ²⁺	brisket	
brezy	breezy ⁺	brisle	bristle ²⁺
briar		bristl e² /y	
bribabul	bribable	brisul	bristle ²⁺
brib e² /able/er		brite	bright ⁺
briber y /ies		briten	brighten¹
bric-à-brac		brittle /ness/r/st	
brick /bat/yard		britul	brittle ⁺
bricklay er /ing		broach¹ ★†	
bridal ★ (of bride)		† (tool, discuss)	
bridal	bridle ²★⁺	broach	brooch ★⁺
bride /groom		broad /ly	
bridel	bridal ★	broadcast	
bridel	bridle ²★⁺	broadcloth	
bridelpath	bridle-path	broaden¹	
bridesmaid		broadside	
bridge ² /able		broad ways /wise	
bridle ²★† /-path		brocade²	
†(for a horse)		broccoli	
bridle	bridal ★	broch	broach ¹★
brief¹ /s/ly		broch	brooch ★⁺
brief-case		brochure	
brigade		brock	
brigadear	brigadier	brocoli	broccoli
brigadier		brog	brogue
brigand /age		brogue	
brige	bridge ²⁺	broil¹ /er	
bright /ly/ness		broke /r	
brighten¹		broken /-hearted	
brillianc e /y		bromide	
brilliant /ly		bromine	
brilliantine		bronchial	
brilyance	brilliance ⁺	bronchitis	
brilyancy	brilliancy	bronco	
brilyans	brilliance ⁺	bronkitis	bronchitis
brilyansey	brilliancy	bronkiul	bronchial
brilyant	brilliant ⁺	bronkyul	bronchial
brilyantine	brilliantine	bronze²	
brim³ /ful		brooam	brougham
brimstone		brooch ★ (clasp) /es	
brindled		brood¹ /iness/y	
brin e /y		brook¹ /let	
bring /ing		broom /stick	
brink		broonet	brunette
brisk /ly/ness		broose	bruise ²⁺

broot	brute +	buccaneer /ing	
brootal	brutal +	buck [1]	
brootalitey	brutality +	buckaneer	buccaneer +
brorn	brawn +	bucket /ful	
brornie	brawny	buckle [2] /r	
brorny	brawny	buckshot	
brort	brought	buckskin	
brosher	brochure	buckwheat	
broth		bucolic	
brothel		Buddhis *m* /t	
brother /hood		budge [2]	
brother(s)-in-law		budgerigar	
brotherl *y* /iness		budget [1] /ary	
brougham		budgigar	budgerigar
brought		Budism	Buddhism +
brow /s ★ (eyebrows)		budist	Buddhist
browbeat /en/ing		buf	buff
brown [1] /er/est		bufalo	buffalo +
browney	brownie	bufer	buffer [1]
Brownian motion		bufet	buffet [1]
brownie		buff	
browse [2]★ (read) /r		buffalo /es	
broyl	broil [1]+	buffer [1]	
brud	brood [1]+	buffet [1]	
brudy	broody	buffoon [1]	
bruer	brewer	buffooner *y* /ies	
bruerey	brewery +	bufit	buffet [1]
bruise [2] /r		bufoonerey	buffoonery +
brunet	brunette	bufune	buffoon [1]
brunette		bufunerey	buffoonery +
brunt		bug [3] /bear	
bruse	bruise [2]+	bugbare	bugbear
brush [1] /wood		bugerigar	budgerigar
brusk	brusque +	buget	budget [1]+
brusque /ly/ness		bugg *y* /ies	
Brussels sprouts		bugie	buggy +
brutal /ly		bugl *e* [2] /er	
brutalis *e* [2] /ation		bugul	bugle [2]+
brutalit *y* /ies		bugy	buggy +
brut *e* /ish		build /er/ing	
bubbl *e* [2] /y		built	
bublie	bubbly	buksom	buxom +
bubly	bubbly	buksomness	buxomness
bubonic plague		bulb /ous	
bubul	bubble [2]+	bulbus	bulbous

buldoze	bulldoze [2]+
bulet	bullet +
buletin	bulletin
bulfinch	bullfinch +
bulfite	bullfight
bulg e [2] /y	
bulie	bully [4]+
bulit	bullet +
bulit proof	bullet-proof
bulk /ier/iest/iness/y	
bulkey	bulky
bulkhead	
bull /fight	
bulldoze [2] /r	
bullet /-proof	
bulletin	
bullfinch /es	
bullion	
bullock	
bullring	
bull's-eye	
bull y [4] /ies	
bulock	bullock
bulring	bullring
bulrush	
bulseye	bull's-eye
bulwark	
buly	bully [4]+
bulyon	bullion
bumbelbe	bumble-bee
bumble-bee	
bump [1] /er/ily/iness	
bumpey	bumpy +
bumpkin	
bumpshus	bumptious +
bumptious /ly/ness	
bump y /ier/iest	
bumshus	bumptious +
bunch [1] /es/y	
bundle [2]	
bundul	bundle [2]
bung [1] /-hole	
bungalow	
bungkum	bunkum
bungle [2] /r	

bungul	bungle [2]+
bunie	bunny +
bunion	
bunk [1]	
bunker [1]	
bunkum	
bunn y /ies	
Bunsen burner	
buny	bunny +
bunyon	bunion
buoy [1]★ (float)	
buoyan cy /t	
buoyansey	buoyancy +
bur	
bura	borough ★
burble [2] /r	
burbul	burble [2]+
burch	birch +
burd	bird
burden [1] /some	
burdey	birdie
burdie	birdie
burds eye	bird's-eye
bureau /x (pl.)	
bureaucrac y /ies	
bureaucrat /ic	
burgandey	Burgundy
burger	burgher
burgher	
burglar	
burglar y /ies	
burgle [2]	
burgler	burglar
burgul	burgle [2]
Burgundy	
burial	
burlap	
burlesk	burlesque [2]+
burlesque [2] /r	
burlie	burly +
burl y /ier/iest/iness	
burn [1] /able/er/t	
burnish [1] /er	
buro	bureau +
burocracy	bureaucracy +

burocrasey	bureaucracy +	butress	buttress [1]+
burocrat	bureaucrat +	butrey	buttery +
burow	burrow [1]★+	butt [1] ★ (end)	
burra	borough ★	butter [1] /-fingered	
burro	bureau +	buttercup	
burrow [1]★ (hole, dig) /er		butterey	buttery +
burrow	borough ★	butterfly	
bursar /y		buttermilk	
burser	bursar +	butterscotch	
burst /ing		butter y /ies	
burth	birth ★+	buttock	
burthday	birthday	button [1] /hole	
bur y [4]★ (cover)		buttress [1] /es	
bus [3] /es		buxom /ness	
busbie	busby +	buy ★† /ing/er ★	
busb y /ies		†(purchase)	
bush /ily/iness		buy	by ★
bushel		buy	bye ★
bushie	bushy +	buzz [1] /es	
bush y /ier/iest		buzzard	
busi er /est/ly		by ★ (near)	
business /-like		by	buy ★+
bust		by	bye ★
bustle [2] /r		by-and-by	
busul	bustle [2]+	bycicle	bicycle [2]+
busy [4]		byciclist	bicyclist
but ★ (however)		bye ★ (sport)	
but	butt [1]★	by-election	
butcher [1] /y		byer	buyer ★
buten	button [1]+	byfocal	bifocal
buter	butter [1]+	bygone /s	
buter fingerd	butter-fingered	bying	buying
butercup	buttercup	byke	bike
buterfly	butterfly	by-law	
butermilk	buttermilk	byle	bile
buterscotch	butterscotch	bylore	by-law
butey	beauty +	bymetalic	bimetallic +
butician	beautician	bymonthly	bimonthly
butify	beautify [4]	bynomial	binomial
butique	boutique	byopsey	biopsy +
butishun	beautician	bypartisan	bipartisan
butler		bypartite	bipartite +
butn	button [1]+	bypass [1]	
butock	buttock	byped	biped
buton	button [1]+	byplane	biplane

byplay	
bypolar	bipolar +
by-product	
byre * (barn)	
byroad	
byrode	byroad
bysecshun	bisection
bysect	bisect ¹+
bysection	bisection
byseksual	bisexual +
bysexual	bisexual +
bystander	
byvalv	bivalve
byword	

C

cab /man	
cabal ³	
cabaray	cabaret
cabaret	
cabbage	
cabbidge	cabbage
cabb y /ies	
cabie	cabby +
cabin /-boy	
cabinet	
cable ² /gram/way	
cabul	cable ²+
cacao	
cach	catch +
cachay	cachet
cache ²* (hidden store)	
cache	cash ¹*
cachet	
cachou	cashew
cachwerd	catchword
cackle ²	
cacofony	cacophony +
cacophon y /ous	
cact us /i (pl.)	
cacul	cackle ²
cad /dish	
cadaver /ous	

caddey	caddie *
caddie * (golf)	
caddis /-worm	
cadd y ⁴* (for tea) /ies	
cadence	
cadens	cadence
cadentsa	cadenza
cadenza	
cadet corps	
cadge ²	
cadis	caddis +
cadmium	
Caesar	
Caesarean	
caesium	
café /s	
cafene	caffeine
cafeteria	
caffeine	
cafiene	caffeine
cafiteria	cafeteria
cage ² /y	
cagi er /est/ly/ness	
cain	cane ²+
cairn	
cairngorm	
caison	caisson
caisson	
cajole ² /ry	
cake ²	
calabash	
calamine	
calamit y /ies/ous	
calcareous	
calcarius	calcareous
calcif y ⁴ /ication	
calcin e /ation	
calcium	
calculable	
calculabul	calculable
calculashun	calculation
calculat e ² /ion/or	
calculus	
cale	kale
Caledonian	

calendar ★ (time)		Calvary	
calender ¹★ (machine)		calve ²★ (produce a calf)	
cal f /ves (pl.)		calve	carve ²★
caliber	calibre	Calvinis m /t/tic	
calibrashun	calibration	calypso	
calibrat e ² /ion/or		calyx /es	
calibre		cam /shaft	
calicks	calyx ⁺	camaflage	camouflage ²
calico /es		camaraderie	
calif	caliph ⁺	camber ¹	
californium		Cambrian	
caligrafey	calligraphy ⁺	cambric	
caligraphy	calligraphy ⁺	came	
calipers	callipers	camellia	
caliph /ate		camelya	camellia
calipso	calypso	Camembert	
calix	calyx ⁺	cameo /s	
calk ¹★ (horseshoe)		camera /man	
calk	caulk ¹★	camerarderey	camaraderie
call ¹★ (cry out)		camfor	camphor ⁺
call	caul ★	camforated	camphorated
calligraph y /er/ist		camio	cameo ⁺
callipers		camisole	
callisthenics		camombare	Camembert
callosity		camomile	
callous ★ (unfeeling)		camouflage ²	
callous ly /ness		camp ¹ /-follower	
callow		campaign ¹	
callus ★ (hard skin)		campain	campaign ¹
calm ¹ /ly/ness		campanile	
calomel		campanology	
calorie /s		camphor /ated	
calorific		campus /es	
calorif y ⁴ /ier		can ³ /not/'t ★	
calorimet er /ric/ry		canabis	cannabis
calory	calorie ⁺	Canadian	
calositey	callosity	canal	
calow	callow	canalis e ² /ation	
calsify	calcify ⁴⁺	canar y /ies	
calsine	calcine ⁺	cancan	
calsium	calcium	cancel ³ /lation	
calumniat e ² /ion/or		cancer /ous	
calumn y /ies/ious		cancerus	cancerous
calus	callous ★	candela	
calus	callus ★	candelabrum	

55

cander	candour	cantankerous /ly/ness	
candey	candy +	cantata /s	
candid * (frank)		canteen	
candid	candied *	canter [1]	
candidac y /ies		cantilever /ed	
candidat e /ure		cantle	
candie	candy +	canton [1] /al/ment	
candied * (sugared)		cantul	cantle
candle /light/stick		canvas * (cloth) /es	
candour		canvass [1]* (solicit)	
candul	candle +	cany	canny
cand y /ies		canyon	
cane [2] /-sugar		caolin	kaolin
canery	cannery +	caos	chaos +
cangaroo	kangaroo	caotic	chaotic
canibal	cannibal +	cap [3]	
canibalise·	cannibalise [2]+	capabilit y /ies	
canie	canny	capabl e /y	
canine		capabul	capable +
canister		capacious /ly/ness	
canker [1]		capacit ance /ive/or	
cannabis		capacitans	capacitance +
canner y /ies		capacitate [2]	
cannibal /ism/istic		capacit y /ies	
cannibalis e [2] /ation		capashus	capacious +
cannon [1]* (gun)		capasitey	capacity +
cannonade		capasitor	capacitor
canny		cape	
canoe [2] /s		caper [1]	
canoeist		capilarey	capillary +
canon * (law) /ical		capillar y /ies	
canon	cannon [1]*	capital /ism/ly	
canonaid	cannonade	capitalis e [2] /ation	
canonis e [2] /ation		capitalist /ic	
canonry		capitashun	capitation
canooist	canoeist	capitation	
canop y [4] /ies		capitulat e [2] /ion	
cansel	cancel [3]+	capon	
canselashun	cancellation	capric e /ious	
canselation	cancellation	Capricorn	
canser	cancer +	caprishus	capricious
canserus	cancerous	capshun	caption [1]
cant * (hypocrisy)		capshus	captious
cant	can't *	capsiz e [2] /able	
cantaloup		capstan	

capsul *e* ² /ar	
captain ¹ /cy	
capter	captor
captin	captain ¹+
caption ¹	
captious	
captivashun	captivation
captivat *e* ² /ion	
captiv *e* /ity	
captor	
capture ² /r	
car /park	
caracter	character
caracteristic	characteristic +
carafe	
caramel	
carat ★ (unit of gems)	
carat	caret ★
carate	karate
caravan ³	
caraway	
carbine	
carbohydrate	
carbolic	
carbon /aceous/ate	
carbon dioxide	
carbon monoxide	
carbonis *e* ² /ation	
carbuncle	
carbuncul	carbuncle
carbureter	carburettor
carburettor	
carcass	
carcino *ma* /genic	
card /board	
cardiac	
cardigan	
cardinal	
cardiograf	cardiograph +
cardiogram	
cardiograph /y	
care ² /worn	
careen ¹	
career ¹ /ism/ist	
carefree	

careful /ly	
careless /ly/ness	
caress ¹	
caret ★ (mark)	
caret	carat ★
caretak *er* /ing	
cargo /es	
cariage	carriage +
caribou	
caricacher	caricature ²+
caricatur *e* ² /ist	
caricter	character
caricteristic	characteristic +
caridge	carriage +
carie	carry ⁴+
carier	carrier
carion	carrion
carisma	charisma
carkey	khaki
carki	khaki
carm	calm ¹+
carmine	
carnage	
carnal /ity/ly	
carnashun	carnation
carnation	
carngorm	cairngorm
carnidge	carnage
carnival	
carnivor *e* /ous	
carol ³ /ler	
carot	carrot +
carous *e* ² /al	
carowsal	carousal
carowse	carouse ²+
carp ¹ /er	
carpent *er* ¹ /ry	
carpet ¹	
carpus	
carriage /way	
carrier	
carrion	
carrot /y	
carr *y* ⁴ /ier	
carryon	carrion

carsinoma	carcinoma +	casserole ²	
cart ¹ /-horse		casset	cassette
cartel		cassette	
cartilage		cassock	
cartilidge	cartilage	cast ★ (throw) /ing	
cartografer	cartographer	cast iron	
cartografey	cartography +	castanet	
cartograph y /er/ic		castaway	
carton		caste ★† /less	
cartoon ¹ /ist		† (social class)	
cartridge		castigat e ² /ion/or	
cartrite	cart-wright	castle ²	
cart-wheel		cast-off	
cart-wright		castor	
carve ²★ (cut)		castor-oil	
carve	calve ²★	castrashun	castration
cary	carry ⁴+	castrat e ² /ion	
cascade ²		casual /ly/ness	
cascara		casualt y /ies	
case ²		casuist /ic/ry	
casein		cat /tish/ty/walk	
casement		catabolism	
caserole	casserole ²	cataclysm /ic	
casette	cassette	catacomb	
cash ¹★ (money)		catacoom	catacomb
cash	cache ²★	catalep sy /tic	
cashay	cachet	catalise	catalyse ²+
casheer	cashier ¹	catalisis	catalysis +
cashew		catalist	catalyst
cashier ¹		catalitic	catalytic
cashmere		catalog	catalogue ²+
cashoo	cashew	catalogue ² /r	
cashual	casual +	catalys e ² /ation	
cashuist	casuist +	cataly sis /tic	
cashultey	casualty +	catalyst	
casing		catamaran	
casino /s		catapiler	caterpillar
cask ★ (wine)		catapult ¹	
cask	casque ★	catar	catarrh +
caskaid	cascade ²	cataract	
casket		catarrh /al	
caskit	casket	catastrofey	catastrophe
casock	cassock	catastrofic	catastrophic +
casque ★ (helmet)		catastrophe	
cassel	castle ²	catastrophic /ally	

catcall [1]
catcawl — catcall [1]
catch /ing/ment
catchword
catechis e [2] /m
categoric /al/ally
categorise [2]
categor y /ies
cater [1] /er
caterpillar
caterwaul [1]
catgut
cathar *sis* /tic
cathedral
Catherine-wheel
cathod e /ic
catholic /ism
caticise — catechise [2+]
catigorey — category [+]
catigoric — categoric [+]
catigorise — categorise [2]
catikism — catechism
catish — cattish
catkin
catle — cattle
catnap [3]
cat-o'-nine-tails
cat's-eye
cattle
catul — cattle
caucashun — Caucasian
Caucasian
caucus /es
caught ★ (did catch)
caught — court [1]★
cauk — caulk [1]★
caul ★ (membrane)
caul — call [1]★
cauldron
cauliflower
caulk [1]★ (seal)
caulk — calk [1]★
causal
causat *ion* /ive
cause [2] /less

causeway
caustic /ally
cauteris e [2] /ation
caution [1] /ary
cautious /ly/ness
cavalcade
cavalier
cavalr y /ies
cave [2] /man
cavern /ous
caveson
caviare
cavil [3]
cavisun — caveson
cavit y /ies
cavort [1]
caw [1]★ (cry of a crow)
caw — core ★
caw — corps ★
cawcashun — Caucasian
cawcasian — Caucasian
cayenne
cazm — chasm
cease [2] /-fire/less
cedar
cede [2]★ (give up)
cede — seed [1]★
ceder — cedar
cedilla
ceeling — ceiling ★
ceese — cease [2+]
cefalic — cephalic [+]
ceiling ★ (roof)
ceiling — sealing ★
celandine
celebrant
celebrashun — celebration
celebrat e [2] /ion
celebrit y /ies
celerey — celery
celerity
celery
celestial /ly
celiba *cy* /te
celibasey — celibacy [+]

59

celibrant	celebrant	centileter	centilitre
celibrate	celebrate [2+]	centilitre	
cell ★ (prison, unit)		centime	
cell	sell ★+	centimeter	centimetre
cellar ★ (cave)		centimetre	
celler	seller ★	centipede	
cellist		centor	centaur
cello /s		central /ity/ly	
cellophane		centralis e [2] /ation	
cellular		centre [2] /board	
cellule		centre-forward	
celluler	cellular	centrifugal /ly	
celluloid		centrifuge	
cellulose		centripetal	
celofane	cellophane	centuple	
Celsius		centupul	centuple
Celt /ic		centurion	
cement [1] /ation		centur y /ies	
cemeter y /ies		cephali c /tis	
cemetrey	cemetery +	ceramic /s	
cemical	chemical +	cerculer	circular
cemist	chemist +	cercumcise	circumcise [2+]
cemistrey	chemistry	cercumference	circumference
cenotaf	cenotaph	cercumferens	circumference
cenotaph		cercumflex	circumflex
censer ★ (for incense)		cercumnavigate	circumnavi-gate [2+]
censer	censor [1]★+		
censership	censorship	cercumscribe	circumscribe [2]
censher	censure [2+]	cercumscripshun	circumscription
censor [1]★† /ious/ship †(moral overseer)		cercumscription	circumscription
		cercumsise	circumcise [2+]
censur e [2] /able		cercumspect	circumspect +
census /es		cercumstance	circumstance
cent ★ (money)		cercumstans	circumstance
cent	scent [1]★	cercumstanshul	circumstantial +
cent	sent ★	cercumstantial	circumstantial +
centaur		cercumvent	circumvent [1+]
centeem	centime	cercus	circus +
centenarian		cereal ★ (grain)	
centenar y /ies		cereal	serial ★+
centennial /ly		cerebellum	
center	centre [2+]	cerebra l /tion	
center forwud	centre-forward	cerebrum	
centigrade		ceremonial /ly	
centigram		ceremonious /ly	

ceremonius	ceremonious +	chalenge	challenge 2+
ceremon y /ies		chalet	
cerial	cereal ★	chalice	
cerial	serial ★+	chalinge	challenge 2+
ceribelum	cerebellum	chalis	chalice
ceribrum	cerebrum	chalk 1 /y	
cerise		challenge 2 /r	
cerkit	circuit 1+	chamber /-music	
cert		chamberlain	
certain /ly		chamberlin	chamberlain
certaint y /ies		chambermade	chambermaid
certen	certain +	chambermaid	
certifiabl e /y		chameleon	
certifiabul	certifiable +	chamie	chamois
certificat e 2 /ion		chamois	
certif y 4 /ier		champ 1	
certinty	certainty +	champagne	
certitude		champain	champagne
cervical		champion 1 /ship	
cervicul	cervical	champyun	champion 1+
cerviks	cervix +	chamwa	chamois
cervix /es		chanc e 2 /y	
cesashun	cessation	chancel	
cesation	cessation	chanceller y /ies	
ceshun	cession ★	chancellor	
ceshun	session ★	chancelor	chancellor
cespit	cesspit	chancelrey	chancellery +
cespool	cesspool	chancer y /ies	
cessation		chandelier	
cession ★ (yielding)		chandler	
cession	session ★	chane	chain 1+
cesspit		chane reacshun	chain-reaction
cesspool		chanel	channel 3
chacoal	charcoal	change 2 /able/-over	
chafe 2★ (rub)		changeling	
chaff ★ (grain husks)		channel 3	
chaffer 1		chans	chance 2+
chaffinch /es		chansel	chancel
chagrin /ed		chanseler	chancellor
chain 1 /-gang		chanselrey	chancellery +
chain-armour		chanserey	chancery +
chain-mail		chansey	chancy
chain-reaction		chansie	chancy
chain-store		chant 1	
chair 1 /man		chao s /tic	

chap [3]		chat [3] /ty	
chapel		chateau /x (pl.)	
chaperon [1] /age		chater	chatter [1+]
chaplain /cy		chaterbox	chatterbox
chaplet		chattel	
chaplin	chaplain +	chatter [1] /er	
chapter /-house		chatterbox	
char [3] /woman/women		chaty	chatty
character		chauffeur	
characteris *e* [2] /ation		chauvinis *m* /t/tic	
characteristic /ally		cheap ★ (inexpensive)	
charade		cheap	cheep [1★]
charcoal		cheap *ish* /ly/ness	
chare	chair [1+]	chear	cheer [1+]
charey	chary +	chearful	cheerful +
charge [2] /able		chease	cheese +
chargé-d'affaires		cheat [1] /er	
charger		check [1★] (stop) /er [1]	
charie	chary +	check	cheque ★+
chariot /eer		Check	Czech ★
charisma		checkmate [2]	
charitabl *e* /y		check-up	
charitabul	charitable +	Cheddar	
charit *y* /ies		cheder	Cheddar
charlatan		cheef	chief +
charlot	charlotte	cheek *y* /ier/iest/ily/iness	
charlotte		cheep [1★] (bird sound)	
charm [1] /er		cheep	cheap ★
charman	chairman	cheer [1] /less	
chart [1]		cheerey	cheery +
charter [1] /er		cheerful /ly/ness	
chartis *m* /t		cheerie	cheery +
char *y* /ily/iness		cheerio	
chas *ed* ★ (pursued) /ing		cheer *y* /ier/iest/ily/iness	
chased	chaste ★	chees *e* /y	
chasen	chasten [1]	cheesecake	
chasis	chassis	cheese-cloth	
chasm		cheet	cheat [1+]
chassie	chassis	cheeta	cheetah +
chassis		cheetah /s	
chaste ★ (pure)		cheeter	cheetah +
chaste	chased ★+	chef	
chasten [1]		chef-d'oeuvre	
chastise [2] /ment		cheif	chief +
chastity		cheiften	chieftain +

chelist	cellist	chilli *er* /est/ly/ness	
chelo	cello +	chime ²	
chemical /ly		chimeric /al	
chemise		chimney /-piece	
chemist /ry		chimnie	chimney +
chemistrey	chemistry	chimpanzee	
cheque *† /-book		chin	
†(money)		china /-clay	
cherie	cherry +	Chinese	
cherio	cheerio	chink ¹	
cherish ¹		chintz /es	
cheroot		chip ³	
cherp	chirp ¹+	chipendale	Chippendale
cherr*y* /ies		chipmunk	
cherub /ic		chipolata	
chery	cherry +	Chippendale	
ches	chess +	chiropod*y* /ist	
chesbord	chessboard	chirp ¹ /y	
chess /board		chirrup ¹	
chest		chisel ³ /ler	
Chesterfield		chit /-chat	
chestnut		chivalrus	chivalrous
chevalier		chivalr*y* /ous	
chevron		chive	
chew ¹ /ing-gum		chlorate	
chic * (stylish)		chloride	
chicanery		chlorinat *e* ² /ion	
chick *† /en/weed		chlorine	
†(baby bird)		chlorofill	chlorophyll
chicory		chloroform ¹	
chide ²		chlorophyll	
chief /s		chloroplast	
chieftain /cy		chock /-a-block	
chiffon		chock-full	
chil	chill ¹+	choclut	chocolate
chilblain		chocolate	
child /ren (pl.)		choice /st	
childbaring	childbearing	choir * (singers)	
childbearing		choir	quire *
child *birth* /hood		chois	choice +
child *ish* /less/like		choke ² /r	
chili * (food) /es		choler * (rage) /ic	
chilie	chilly *	choler	collar ¹*+
chilier	chillier +	cholera	
chill ¹ /y * (cold)		cholester *in* /ol	

choo	chew [1]+	chub /by	
choos e /ing/y		chubbi er /est/ly/ness	
chop [3] /per		chubier	chubbier +
chopp y /ier/iest		chuck [1]	
chopsooey	chop-suey	chuckle [2]	
chopstick		chucul	chuckle [2]
chop-suey		chug [3]	
chopy	choppy +	chukker	
choral ★ (singing) /ly		chum [3] /my	
chorale ★ (metric hymn)		chump	
chord ★ (music)		chunk /y	
chord	cord ★+	church /es/warden	
chore		churl /ish	
choreograph y /er		churn [1]	
chorister		churp	chirp [1]+
chork	chalk [1]+	chute ★ (drop)	
chortle [2]		chute	shoot ★+
chortul	chortle [2]	chutney	
chorus [1] /es		chyle	
chose /n		chyme	
chow		cianide	cyanide
chrisalis	chrysalis +	cibernetics	cybernetics
chrisanthemum	chrysanthemum	cicada	
Christ		cicatrice	
christen [1]		cicatriss	cicatrice
Christendom		ciclamate	cyclamate
Christian /ity		ciclamen	cyclamen
Christmas /sy		cicle	cycle [2]
chromate		ciclic	cyclic +
chromatic /ally		ciclist	cyclist +
chromatin		ciclometer	cyclometer
chromatograf	chromatograph +	ciclone	cyclone +
chromatogram		ciclops	Cyclops
chromatograph /y		ciclostile	cyclostyle
chrom e /ic/ium		ciclotron	cyclotron
chromosome		cicul	cycle [2]
chronic /ally		cider	
chronicle [2] /r		cifer	cipher [1]
chronicul	chronicle [2]+	cigar /ette	
chronograph /ic		cigaret	cigarette
chronological /ly		cignet	cygnet ★
chronolog y /ies		cignet	signet ★
chronometer		cilestial	celestial +
chrysalis /es		cilinder	cylinder
chrysanthemum		cilindrical	cylindrical +

cilium	
cimbal	cymbal ★+
cimbal	symbol ★+
ciment	cement [1]+
cinamon	cinnamon
cinch /es	
cinder	
Cinderella	
cine camera	
cinema /tic	
cinematograph /er/y	
cinerama	
cinic	cynic +
cinical	cynical +
cinicul	cynical +
cinima	cinema +
cinimatograf	cinematograph +
cinimatograph	cinematograph +
cinnamon	
cinosure	cynosure
cipher [1]	
cipress	cypress
circa	
circit	circuit [1]+
circle [2]	
circuit [1] /ous/ry	
circul	circle [2]
circular	
circularis e^2 /ation	
circulat e^2 /ion	
circulator /y	
circumcis e^2 /ion	
circumference	
circumferens	circumference
circumflex	
circumfrence	circumference
circumnavigat e^2 /or	
circumscribe [2]	
circumscription	
circumspect /ion	
circumstance	
circumstans	circumstance
circumstanshul	circumstantial +
circumstantial /ly	
circumvent [1] /ion	

circus /es	
cirosis	cirrhosis
cirrhosis	
cirro-cumulus	
cirro-stratus	
cist	cyst +
cistern	
cistitis	cystitis
citadel	
cit e^2★ (quote) /ation	
cite	sight [1]★+
cite	site [2]★
citie	city +
citizen /ship	
citologey	cytology
citric acid	
citr on /ate	
citrus	
cit y /ies	
civet	
civic /ism/s	
civil /ian/ly	
civilis e^2 /ation	
civilit y /ies	
civit	civet
clad /ding	
claim [1] /able/ant	
clairvoyan ce /t	
clam	
clamant	
clamber [1]	
clame	claim [1]+
clamer	clamour +
clamerous	clamorous
clamerus	clamorous
clamm y /ily/iness	
clamo ur /rous	
clamp [1]	
clamy	clammy +
clan /nish	
clandestine /ly	
clang [1] /our	
clank [1]	
clansman	
clap [3] /per	

claptrap
claret
clarif*y*[4] /ication/ier
clarinet /tist
clarion
clarity
clark — clerk[+]
claryun — clarion
clash[1]
clasify — classify[4+]
clasroom — classroom
class[1] /less/y
classic /al/ally/s
classicis*m* /t
classif*y*[4] /ication/ier
classroom
clatter[1]
clause
claustrofobia — claustrophobia
claustrophobia
clavichord
clavic*le* /ular
clavicord — clavichord
clavicul — clavicle[+]
claw[1]
clay /more
claym — claim[1+]
clean[1] /able/liness/ly
cleanse[2]
clear[1] /ance/ly/ness
cleav*e*[2] /age
cleavidge — cleavage
cleek — clique[+]
clef
cleft
clematis
clemen*cy* /t
clemensey — clemency[+]
clench[1]
clenliness — cleanliness
clense — cleanse[2]
clergy /man
cleric /al/alism
clerk /ship
clever /er/est/ly

clew[1★] (thread)
clew — clue[★+]
clichay — cliché
cliché
click[1]
client /ele
cliff /s
climactic /ally
climaks — climax[1+]
climat*e* /ology
climatic /ally
climax[1] /es
climb[1★] (go up) /er
clime[★] (climate)
clinch[1]
cling /ing
clinic /al/ally
clink[1]
clinker /-built
cliontell — clientele
clip[3] /per
cliqu*e* /ish/y
clitoris
cloak /room
clobber[1]
cloche
clock[1] /wise/work
clod /-hopper
clog[3]
cloister[1]
clorate — chlorate
clore — claw[1]
cloride — chloride
clorinate — chlorinate[2+]
clorine — chlorine
clorofill — chlorophyll
cloroform — chloroform[1]
clorophil — chlorophyll
cloroplast — chloroplast
clos*e*[2] /ure
closet[1]
closher — closure
clot[3]
cloth
cloth*e*[2] /ier

cloud [1] /ier/less/y
clout [1]
clove /n
clover /-leaf
clowd   cloud [1]+
clown [1] /ish
club [3] /bable
cluch   clutch [1]
cluck [1]
clue ★ (guide) /less
clue   clew [1]★
clump [1]
clumsi *ly* /ness
clums *y* /ier/iest
clung
cluster [1]
clutch [1]
clutter [1]
coach [1] /ful/man
coagulant
coagulat *e* [2] /ion/or
coaks   coax [1]
coal /field/-mine
coala   koala
coalesans   coalescence
coalesce [2] /nce/nt
coalesent   coalescent
coaless   coalesce [2]+
coalishun   coalition +
coalition /ist
coal-scuttle
coarse ★ (rough) /ly/ness
coarse   course ★+
coarsen [1]
coast [1] /al
coast *guard* /line
coat [1] /ee
coax [1]
cob
cobalt
cobble [2] /r
cobra
cobul   cobble [2]+
cobweb /bed
coca

cocaine
cocane   cocaine
coccyx /es
coch   coach [1]+
cochineal
cock [1] /crow/erel
cockato   cockatoo
cockatoo
cockchafer
cocker
cocket   coquette +
cocketrey   coquetry
cock-eyed
cockle
cockney /ish/ism/s
cockpit
cockroach
cockscomb
cockshore   cocksure
cocksis   coccyx +
cocksure
cocktail
cockul   cockle
cock *y* /ier/iest/ily
coco ★ (palm tree)
coco   cocoa ★
cocoa ★ (cacao powder)
coconut
cocoon
cocotte
cod [3] /ling
codak   Kodak
coddle [2]
code [2]
codecks   codex +
codeine
cod *ex* /ices (pl.)
codger
codicil
codif *y* [4] /ication/ier
codisil   codicil
codle   coddle [2]
co-educate [2]
co-education /al
coefficient

coefishent	coefficient
coegsist	coexist [1]⁺
coequal /ity/ly	
coerce [2] /ible	
coercion /ive	
coerse	coerce [2]⁺
coershun	coercion ⁺
coersive	coercive
coexist [1] /ence/ent	
cofee	coffee
cofer	coffer
cofey	coffee
coff	cough [1]⁺
coffee	
coffer	
coffin	
cog [3] /-wheel	
cogen cy /t	
coger	codger
cogitat e [2] /ion	
cognac	
cognate	
cognisabl e /y	
cognisan ce /t	
cognishun	cognition ⁺
cognition /al	
cognitive	
cognomen	
cohabit [1] /ation	
cohear	cohere [2]⁺
cohearent	coherent ⁺
cohere [2] /nce	
coherent /ly	
coheshun	cohesion ⁺
cohes ion /ive	
cohort	
coifer	coiffeur ★⁺
coiffeu r ★† /se (fem.) †(hairdresser)	
coiffure ★ (hair style)	
coifur	coiffure ★
coil [1]	
coin [1] /age/er	
coincide [2]	
coinciden ce /t	

coinidge	coinage
coinside	coincide [2]
coinsidence	coincidence ⁺
coinsidens	coincidence ⁺
coinsident	coincident
coir ★ (coconut fibre)	
coir	choir ★
coit us /ion	
coke [2]	
coket	coquette ⁺
cokoon	cocoon
col	
cola	koala
colaborate	collaborate [2]⁺
colage	collage
colander	
colaps	collapse [2]⁺
colate	collate [2]⁺
cold /er/est/ly/ness	
cold-blooded	
cold-shoulder [1]	
cole	coal ⁺
colean	colleen
colecshun	collection
colect	collect [1]⁺
colectabul	collectable ⁺
colection	collection
colectiv	collective ⁺
coleeg	colleague
colege	college ⁺
colegian	collegian
colegiate	collegiate
coler	choler ★⁺
coler	collar [1]★⁺
colera	cholera
coleric	choleric
colesterin	cholesterin ⁺
colesterol	cholesterol
colic /ky	
colide	collide [2]
colier	collier
colinder	colander
colinear	collinear
colishun	collision
colision	collision

colitis
collaborat *e* ² /ion/or
collage
collaps *e* ² /ible
collar ¹★† /-bone
  †(seize, neckband)
collar   choler ★+
collat *e* ² /ion/or
collateral
colleague
collect ¹ /ion/or
collect *able* /edly
collectiv *e* /ism/ist
colleen
colleg *e* /ian/iate
coller   choler ★+
coller   collar ¹★+
collide ²
collie
collier
collinear
collision
collocate ²
colloid /al
colloquial /ism/ly
colloqu *y* /ies
collude ²
collus *ion* /ive
colly   collie
colokwey   colloquy +
colokwial   colloquial +
colon
colonade   colonnade
colonel ★ (officer)
colonial /ism
colonis *e* ² /ation/er
colonnade
colon *y* /ies/ist
coloqual   colloquial +
coloquy   colloquy +
color   colour ¹+
coloration
colorful   colourful +
colossal /ly
colossus /es

colour ¹ /less
colourful /ly
coloyd   colloid +
colt /ish
colude   collude ²
colum   column +
columbine
column /ar/ist
colushun   collusion +
colusion   collusion +
coma ★ (deep sleep)
coma   comma ★
comand   command ¹+
comandment   commandment
comando   commando +
comb ¹
combat ¹ /ant/ive
combinashun   combination
combin *e* ² /ation
combuschun   combustion
combustib *le* /ility
combustibul   combustible +
combustion
com *e* /ing
come   comb ¹
comedi *an* /enne (fem.)
comed *y* /ies
comel *y* /ier/iest
comemorashun   commemoration
comemorate   commemorate ²+
comence   commence ²+
comend   commend ¹+
comendabul   commendable +
comendashun   commendation
comendation   commendation
comens   commence ²+
comenshurate   commensurate
coment   comment ¹+
comentater   commentator
comentrey   commentary +
comerce   commerce
comercial   commercial +
comercialise   commercialise ²+
comercialism   commercialism
comerse   commerce

comershal	commercial [+]
comershalise	commercialise [2+]
comershalism	commercialism
comestibles	
comet	
comfert	comfort [1+]
comfort [1] /er/less	
comfortabl e /y	
comic /al/ally	
comicalit y /ies	
comiserate	commiserate [2+]
comiserey	commissary [+]
comishun	commission [1+]
comission	commission [1+]
comit	comet
comit	commit [3+]
comital	committal
comitey	comity ★
comitment	commitment
comittal	committal
comittey	committee ★
comity ★ (courtesy)	
comma ★(punctuation)	
comma	coma ★
command [1] /ant/er	
commandeer [1]	
commandment	
commando /s	
commemorat e [2] /ion	
commence [2] /ment	
commend [1] /ation	
commendabl e /y	
commensurate	
comment [1] /ator	
commentar y /ies	
commentrey	commentary [+]
commerce	
commercial /ism/ly	
commercialis e [2]/ation	
commershal	commercial [+]
commershalise	commercialise [2+]
commiserat e [2] /ion	
commissar /iat	
commissar y /ies	
commission [1] /aire/er	

commit [3] /ment/tal	
committee ★ (body)	
commity	comity ★
commod e /ious	
commodit y /ies	
commodore	
common /er/est/ly	
Common Market	
commonplace	
Commons	
Commonwealth	
commoshun	commotion
commotion	
communal /ly	
communalise [2]	
commune [2]	
communicable	
communicat e [2] /ion	
communicat ive /or	
communikay	communiqué
communi on /cant	
communiqué	
communis m /t/tic	
communit y /ies	
commute [2] /r	
comode	commode [+]
comodious	commodious
comodity	commodity [+]
comodius	commodious
comodoor	commodore
comon	common [+]
Comon Market	Common Market
Comonwelth	Commonwealth
comoshun	commotion
comotion	commotion
compact	
compair	compère [2★]
companion /ship	
compan y /ies	
companyun	companion [+]
comparabl e /y	
comparabul	comparable [+]
comparative /ly	
compare [2★] (liken to)	
compare	compère [2★]

70

comparison		composition	
compartment		compositor	
compashonate	compassionate	compost	
compashun	compassion +	composure	
compass [1] /es		compot	compote
compassion /ate/ately		compote	
compatib le /ility		compound [1] /able	
compatibul	compatible +	comprehen d [1] /sible	
compatriot		comprehens ion /ive	
compel [3]		compress [1] /ion/or	
compendium		compressib le /ility	
compensat e [2] /ion		compris e [2] /able	
compensator /y		compromise [2]	
compère [2]★ (presenter)		compulshun	compulsion +
competant	competent	compuls ion /ive	
compet e [2] /ition		compulsor y /ily	
competen ce /t		compulsrey	compulsory +
competit ive /or		compuncshun	compunction
compil e [2] /ation		compunction	
complacenc e /y		comput e [2] /ation/er	
complacens	complacence +	computeris e [2] /ation	
complacent /ly		comrad	comrade +
complain [1] /ant/t		comrade /ly/ship	
complane	complain [1]+	comunal	communal +
complasense	complacence +	comunalise	communalise [2]
complasent	complacent +	comune	commune [2]
complement [1]★† /ary		comunicable	communicable
†(complete)		comunicant	communicant
complete [2] /ly		comunicashun	communication
completion		comunicate	communicate [2]+
complex		comunication	communication
complexion /ed		comunikay	communiqué
complexit y /ies		comunion	communion+
complian ce /t		comunism	communism +
complicat e [2] /ion		comunist	communist
complicity		comunitey	community +
compliment [1]★† /ary		comunyun	communion+
† (praise)		comute	commute [2]+
compl y [4] /iable		con [3]	
component		concave	
comport [1] /ment		concavit y /ies	
compose [2]		conceal [1] /ment	
composher	composure	concede [2]	
composishun	composition	conceit /ed	
composite /ly		conceivabul	conceivable

conceiv e^2 /able/ably
concentrat e^2 /ion
concentric /ity
concept /ual/ually
conception
concern [1]
concert /ina
concerto /s
concession /ary
conch
concherto   concerto [+]
conciet   conceit [+]
concievabul   conceivable
concieve   conceive [2+]
conciliat e^2 /ion
conciliator /y
concise /ly/ness
conclave
conclude [2]
conclus *ion* /ive
concoct [1] /ion
concomitant
concord /ance/ant
concorse   concourse
concourse
concrete /ly/ness
concubine
concur [3]
concurren *ce* /t/tly
concuss [1] /ion
condemn [1] /ation
condens e^2 /ation/er
condescen d^1 /sion
condiment
condisend   condescend [1+]
condisenshun   condescension
condisension   condescension
condishun   condition [1+]
condit   conduit
condition [1] /al/ally
condole [2] /nce
condon e^2 /ation/er
conduc e^2 /ive
conduct [1] /ion
conductiv *e* /ity

conduct *or* /ress (fem.)
conduit
cone
conect   connect [1+]
conerbashun   conurbation
conerbation   conurbation
confabulat e^2 /ion
confection /er/ery
confederac *y* /ies
confederasey   confederacy [+]
confederat e^2 /ion
confer [3] /ment
conference
confeser   confessor
confess [1] /or
confession /al
confetti
confidant **†* /e (fem.)
 †(trusted friend)
confide [2] /nce
confidenshal   confidential [+]
confident **†* /ly
 †(self-assured)
confidential /ity/ly
configerashun   configuration
configuration
confine [2] /ment
confirm [1] /ation
confirmat *ive* /ory
confiscat e^2 /ion
conflagration
conflict [1]
conform [1] /able/ation
conform *ist* /ity
confound [1]
confownd   confound [1]
confurm   confirm [1+]
confus e^2 /ion
confut e^2 /ation
congeal [1]
congenial /ity/ly
congenital /ly
conger /-eel
congest [1] /ion/ive
conglomerat e^2 /ion

congratulat *e*² /ion/ory
congregat *e*² /ion
congregational /ist
congress /ional
conic /al/ally
conifer /ous
conjectcher   conjecture ²⁺
conjectur *e*² /al
conjoin¹ /t
conjucive   conducive
conjugal
conjugat *e*² /ion
conjuice   conduce ²⁺
conjuncshun   conjunction
conjunction
conjunctiv *e* /itis
conjur *e*² /ation/er
conker*(horse chestnut)
conker   conquer ¹*⁺
conkwest   conquest
connect¹ /ion/ive
conneser   connoisseur
conning-tower
conniv *e*² /ance/er
connoisseur
connot *e*² /ation
connubial /ly
conosseur   connoisseur
conote   connote ²⁺
conquer ¹*(defeat) /or
conquest
consanguin *eous* /ity
conscience
conscienshus   conscientious ⁺
conscientious /ly
conscious /ly/ness
conscript¹ /ion
conseal   conceal ¹⁺
conseat   conceit ⁺
consecrat *e*² /ion
consecutive
consekwence   consequence ⁺
consensus
consent¹
consequen *ce* /t

consequential /ly
conservancy
conservansey   conservancy
conservashun   conservation
conservation
conservat *ive* /ism
conservatoire
conservator *y* /ies
conservatrey   conservatory ⁺
conserv *e*²
consider¹ /able/ably
considerat *e* /ion
considrabul   considerable
consign¹ /ment
consiliate   conciliate ²⁺
consine   consign ¹⁺
consise   concise ⁺
consist¹ /ence
consistenc *y* /ies
consistensey   consistency ⁺
consolabul   consolable
consolashun   consolation
consol *e*² /able/ation
consolidat *e*² /ion
consommé
consonan *ce* /t
consonans   consonance ⁺
consort¹ /ium
conspicuous /ly/ness
conspirac *y* /ies
conspirasey   conspiracy ⁺
conspirater   conspirator ⁺
conspirator /y
conspire²
constable
constabul   constable
constabular *y* /ies
constan *cy* /t
constansey   constancy ⁺
constelashun   constellation
constellation
consternat *e*² /ion
constipat *e*² /ion
constituenc *y* /ies
constituensey   constituency ⁺

constituent
constitute [2]
constitution /al/ally
constrain [1] /t
constrict [1] /ion
construct [1] /ion
constructive /ly
constru *e* [2] /able
consul /ar/ate
consult [1] /ant
consultat *ion* /ive
consumashun consummation
consum *e* [2] /able/er
consummate [2] /ly
consummation
consumpt *ion* /ive
consumshun consumption [+]
consumtion consumption [+]
contact [1] /or
contag *ion* /ious
contagus contagious
contain [1] /er/ment
contaminat *e* [2] /ion
contemplat *e* [2] /ion
contemplative /ly
contemporaneous
contemporar *y* /ies
contempt /ible/uous
contend [1]
content [1] /ment
content *ion* /ious
contest [1] /able/ant
context
contigu *ous* /ity
continence
continens continence
continent /al
contingenc *y* /ies
contingensey contingency [+]
contingent
continual /ly
continua *nce* /tion
continu *e* [2] /ity
continuous /ly
contorshun contortion [+]

contort [1]
contortion /ist
contour
contraband
contracept *ion* /ive
contract [1] /ion/or
contractual /ly
contradict [1] /ion/ory
contralto /s
contrapshun contraption
contraption
contrar *y* /ily/iness
contrast [1]
contraven *e* [2] /er/tion
contribut *e* [2] /ion
contributor /y
contrit *e* /ion
contriv *e* [2] /ance
control [3] /lable/ler
controvershal controversial [+]
controversial /ly
controvers *y* /ies
contus *e* [2] /ion
conurbation
convalesce [2] /nce/nt
convaless convalesce [2+]
convalessence convalescence
convect *ion* /ive/or
convene [2] /r
convenien *ce* /t
conveniens convenience [+]
convenshun convention
convenshunal conventional [+]
convent
convention
conventional /ism/ly
converge [2] /nce/nt
conversant
conversation /al/alist
converse [2] /ly
conversion
convert [1] /er/ible
convex /ity
convey [1]
conveyanc *e* /ing

conveyor belt		coral ★ (sea life)	
convict [1] /ion		coral	choral ★+
convinc e [2] /ingly		coral	corral [3]★
conviscate	confiscate [2]+	corcus	caucus +
convivial /ity/ly		cord ★ (rope) /age	
convocashun	convocation	cord	chord ★
convocation		cordial /ity/ly	
convoke [2]		cordite	
convolut e [2] /ion		cordon [1]	
convoy [1]		cordon bleu	
convuls e [2] /ion		corduroy	
convulsive /ly		core ★ (centre)	
con y /ies		core	caw [1]★
conyac	cognac	core	corps ★
coo [1]		corecshun	correction
cooger	cougar	corect	correct [1]+
cook [1] /able		corection	correction
cooker /y		corectiv	corrective
cool [1] /ant/est/ness		corespond	correspond [1]+
coolie ★ (labourer)		corespondence	correspondence
coolly ★ (calmly)		corespondens	correspondence
coop [1]		co-respondent	
co-op		coridoor	corridor
cooper /age		coriografey	choreography +
co-operat e [2] /ion/or		corispondence	correspondence
co-operative /ly/ness		corispondens	correspondence
co-opt [1] /ion		corister	chorister
co-ordinat e [2] /ion		cork /age/screw	
co-partner /ship		corm	
cope [2]		cormorant	
copeck		corn /flour	
Copernican system		cornea /l	
co-pilot		corner [1] /-stone	
copious /ly		cornet	
copiss	coppice	cornia	cornea +
copper /plate		cornice	
coppice		cornucopia	
copra		corny	
copse		coroborate	corroborate [2]+
copulat e [2] /ion		coroborativ	corroborative +
cop y [4] /ies/ier		corode	corrode [2]+
copyright		corollary	
copyrite	copyright	corona	
coquetry		coronary	
coquett e /ish		coronashun	coronation

coronation	
coroner	
coronet	
coroshun	corrosion +
corosion	corrosion +
corosiv	corrosive
corporal	
corporat e /ion	
corporeal	
corps ★ (army)	
corpse ★ (body)	
corpulen ce /t	
corpus	
corpusc le /ular	
corpussel	corpuscle +
corral [3] ★ (animal pen)	
corral	coral ★
correct [1] /ion/ive/or	
correlat e [2] /ion	
correlative /ly	
correspond [1] /ence/ent	
corridor	
corrigend um /a (pl.)	
corrigible	
corroborat e [2] /ion	
corroborative /ly	
corrod e [2] /ible	
corros ion /ive	
corrugat e [2] /ion	
corrupt [1] /ive/ness	
corruptib le /ility	
corsashun	causation +
corsation	causation +
corse	coarse ★+
corse	course ★+
corsen	coarsen [1]
corset /ed	
corshun	caution [1]+
corshus	cautious +
corslet	
corstic	caustic +
cort	caught ★
cort	court [1]★
cort marshal	court-martial [3]+
cortège	
corterise	cauterise [2]+
cort ex /ices (pl.)	
cortion	caution [1]+
cortious	cautious +
cortisan	courtesan
cortisone	
cortship	courtship
cortyard	courtyard
corugate	corrugate [2]+
corupt	corrupt [1]+
coruptible	corruptible +
coruptibul	corruptible +
corus	chorus [1]+
corvet	corvette
corvette	
cosecant	
coset	cosset [1]
cosh [1]	
cosi er /est/ly/ness	
co-signator y /ies	
cosine	
cosmetic /ian	
cosmic /ally	
cosmografey	cosmography +
cosmograph y /ic	
cosmolog y /ical	
cosmonaut	
cosmonort	cosmonaut
cosmopolitan /ism	
cosmos	
cosmotron	
co-sponsor	
Cossack	
cosset [1]	
cost /ly	
cost	coast [1]+
costgard	coastguard +
costive	
costli er /est/ness	
costum e /ier	
cosy	
cot	
cotage	cottage +
cotangent	
cote	coat [1]+

coterie
cotidge — cottage +
coton — cotton +
cottage /r
cotton /wool
cou dayta — coup d'état
couch¹ /es
cougar
cough¹ /er
could /n't
coulomb
council * (assembly)
councillor * (member of assembly)
counsel³* (advice)
counsellor * (adviser)
count¹ /ess (fem.) /less
countenance
counter¹ /foil
counteract¹ /ion
counter-attack¹
counterbalance²
counter-charge²
counter-claim¹
counter-clockwise
counterfeit¹ /er
countermand¹
countermine²
counterpane
counterpart
counterpoint
counterpoise²
countersign¹
countersine — countersign¹
counterway — counter-weigh¹
counter-weigh¹
countie — county +
countr y /ies
countryside
count y /ies
coup d'état
couple² /t
coupon
courage /ous/ously
courier

cours e *† /ing
  †(conduct, passage)
course — coarse *+
coursen — coarsen¹
court¹* (law)
court — caught*
courtesan
courtes y /ies
courtier
courtley — courtly +
courtl y /iness
court-martial³ /s
courtship
courtyard
cousin
covalent bond
cove
coven
covenant
Coventry
cover¹ /age/let
covert
covet¹ /er/ous
covey /s
cow
coward *(runaway)/ice
cowardl y /iness
cowboy
cowch — couch¹+
cower /ed * (cringed)
cowerd — coward *+
cowl /ing
cownt — count¹+
cowntenance — countenance
cowntenans — countenance
cownter — counter¹+
cownteract — counteract¹+
cowpox
cowslip
cox¹ /swain
coxcomb
coy /ly/ness
coyn — coin¹+
coyote
crab³ /-apple

crack¹ /er	
crackle²	
cracknel	
crackul	crackle²
cradel	cradle²
cradle²	
cradul	cradle²
craft /y	
crafti er /est/ly/ness	
craftsman /ship	
crag /gy	
crain	crane²⁺
cram³ /mer	
cramp¹ /on	
cranberie	cranberry⁺
cranberr y /ies	
crane² /-fly	
crani um /al	
crank¹ /case/shaft/y	
crann y /ies	
crape²	
crash¹	
crash-land¹	
crass	
crate²	
crater	
cravat	
crave² /n	
crawl¹ /er	
crayfish	
crayon	
craz e² /y	
crazi er /est/ly/ness	
creacher	creature
creak¹* (noise) /y	
creak	creek*
cream¹ /y	
creamer y /ies	
creami er /est/ness	
crease²	
creat e² /ion/or	
creativ e /ity	
creature	
crèche	
crecher	creature

credence	
credens	credence
credential	
credib le /ility/ly	
credibul	credible⁺
credit¹ /or	
creditabl e /y	
creditabul	creditable⁺
crediter	creditor
credul ity /ous	
creed	
creek* (stream)	
creek	creak¹*⁺
creem	cream¹⁺
creep /er/ing/s/y	
creepi er /est/ly/ness	
cremat e² /ion	
crematorium	
Cremlin	Kremlin
crenellated	
creole	
crep	crêpe
crêpe	
crept	
crepuscular	
crescendo /s	
crescent	
cresent	crescent
cresh	crèche
creshendo	crescendo⁺
cresit	cresset
cresset	
crest /fallen	
cretin /ism/ous	
cretonne	
creture	creature
crevasse	
crevice	
crevis	crevice
crew¹ /s* (sailors)	
crews	cruise²*⁺
crewsifix	crucifix⁺
crib³ /ber	
cribbage	
cribidge	cribbage

crick ¹
cricket /er
crime
criminal /ity/ly
criminolog *ist* /y
crimson
crincul   crinkle ²⁺
cringe ²
crinkl *e* ² /y
crinoline
cripple ²
cript   crypt ⁺
criptograf   cryptograph ⁺
criptogram   cryptogram
criptograph   cryptograph ⁺
cripul   cripple ²
crisalis   chrysalis ⁺
crisanthemum   chrysanthemum
crisen   christen ¹
Crisendum   Christendom
Crishna   Krishna
cris *is* /es
Crismas   Christmas ⁺
crisp /iness/ly/y
criss-cross ¹
Crist   Christ
cristal   crystal ⁺
cristaline   crystalline
cristalise   crystallise ²⁺
cristalografer   crystallographer ⁺
Cristian   Christian ⁺
Cristianity   Christianity
criteri *on* /a (pl.)
critic /al/ally
criticis *e* ² /able
criticism
critisize   criticise ²⁺
criy   cry ⁴⁺
croak ¹
croch   crotch
crochet ¹
crock /ery
crocodile
crocus /es
croft /er

croissant
crokay   croquet
cromatic   chromatic ⁺
cromatin   chromatin
cromatograf   chromatograph ⁺
cromatogram   chromatogram
crome   chrome ⁺
cromic   chromic
cromium   chromium
crone ★ (hag)
crone   krone ★⁺
cronic   chronic ⁺
cronicul   chronicle ²⁺
cronie   crony ⁺
cronograf   chronograph ⁺
cronograph   chronograph ⁺
cronologey   chronology ⁺
cronological   chronological ⁺
cronometer   chronometer
cron *y* /ies
crood   crude ⁺
crook
crooked /ly/ness
croon ¹
croop   croup
croopier   croupier
crop ³ /per
croquet
cross ¹ /ly/ness
cross -*breed* /-bred
cross-country
cross-cut /ting
cross-examin *e* ² /ation
cross-fertilis *e* ² /ation
cross-fire
cross-legged
crosspatch
cross-purpose
cross-question ¹
cross-reference ²
cross-road
crosswise
crossword
crotch
crotchet /y

crouch [1]
croup
croupier
crow [1]
crowbar
crowd [1]
crown [1]
crucial /ly
crucible
crucibul   crucible
crucifix /ion
crucify [4]
crude /ly/ness/st
cruditey   crudity +
crudit y /ies
cruel /ler/lest/ly
cruelt y /ies
cruet
cruise [2]* (voyage) /r
crum   crumb +
crumb /iness/y
crumbl e [2]*(break up)/y
crumbul   crumble [2]*+
crumpet
crumple [2]* (crease)
crumpul   crumple [2]*
crumy   crumby
crunch [1] /iness/y
cruper   crupper
crupper
crusade [2] /r
crush [1]
crushal   crucial +
crusible   crucible
crusibul   crucible
crust /y
crustace a /an/ous
crustasha   crustacea +
crutch
crux /es
cruze   cruise [2]*+
cr y [4] /ies/ier
crypt /ic/ically
cryptogram
cryptograph /ic

crysalis   chrysalis +
crystal /line
crystallis e [2] /ation
crystallograph er /y
cub
cubby-hole
cub e /age
cubical * (cube-shaped)
cubicle * (small room)
cubihole   cubby-hole
cubis m /t
cuboard   cupboard
cuckold [1]
cuckoo
cucumber
cuddle [2]
cudgel [3]
cudul   cuddle [2]
cue [2]* (billiards)
cue   queue [2]*
cuff [1]
cuisine
culcher   culture [2]+
cul-de-sac
culer   colour [1]+
culerashun   coloration
culinary
culinder   colander
culinrey   culinary
cull [1]
culminat e [2] /ion
culpab le /ility
culpabul   culpable +
culprit
cult
cultivat e [2] /ion/or
cultur e [2] /al/ist
culvert
cumbersome /ly/ness
cumbersum   cumbersome +
Cumbrian
cumfert   comfort [1]+
cumpas   compass [1]+
cumulative
cumulus

cuneiform	
cuniform	cuneiform
cunning	
cuntreyside	countryside
cup [3] /ful	
cupboard	
cupidity	
cupola	
cupro-nickel	
cur /rish	
curab *le* /ility	
curabul	curable +
curac *y* /ies	
curant	currant ★
curasey	curacy +
curate	
curater	curator +
curator /ship	
curb [1]★ (chain in bit)	
curb	kerb [1]★
curd	
curdle [2]	
curdul	curdle [2]
cur *e* [2] /ative	
curent	current ★+
curfew	
curiculum	curriculum +
curie	
curio /s	
curiosit *y* /ies	
curious /ly/ness	
curium	
curius	curious +
curl [1] /er/iness/y	
curlew	
curnel	colonel ★
currage	courage +
curragus	courageous
currant ★ (fruit)	
currenc *y* /ies	
currensey	currency +
current ★ (flow) /ly	
curricul *um* /a (pl.)	
curry [4] /comb	
curse [2]	

cursive /ly	
cursory	
curt /ly/ness	
curtail [1] /ment	
curtain [1]	
curtale	curtail [1]+
curts *y* [4] /ies	
curv *e* [2] /ature	
curvilinear	
cushion [1]	
cushon	cushion [1]
cusp	
cuss [1] /edness	
custard	
custod *y* /ial/ian	
custom /er	
customar *y* /ily	
cut /ter/ting	
cute /ly/ness/r/st	
cuticle	
cuticul	cuticle
cutlass /es	
cutlery	
cutlet	
cuttle-fish	
cuvenant	covenant
cuver	cover [1]+
cuvet	covet [1]+
cuvey	covey +
cyanide	
cybernetics	
cyclamate	
cyclamen	
cycle [2]	
cyclic /al/ally	
cycl *ist* /ometer	
cyclon *e* /ic	
Cyclops	
cyclostyle	
cyclotron	
cygnet ★ (swan)	
cygnet	signet ★
cyle	chyle
cylinder	
cylindrical /ly	

cymbal *† /ist
  †(musical instrument)
cymbal   symbol *+
cynic /ism
cynical /ly
cynosure
cypress
cyst /itis
cytology
czar   tsar
Czech * (nationality)
Czechoslovakian

D

dab ³ /ber
dabble ² /r
dable   dabble ²+
dabul   dabble ²+
dabutant   débutant +
dace
dachshund
dactill   dactyl
dactyl
daddy /-long-legs
daffodil
daft /er/est
dagger
dahlia
dail   dale
dailie   daily +
dail y /ies
daintie   dainty +
daint y /ier/iest/ily/iness
dairie   dairy +
dairimade   dairymaid
dair y /ies
dairymaid
daisie   daisy +
dais y /ies
daitee   deity +
dakshound   dachshund
dale
dalia   dahlia

dalie   dally ⁴+
dall y ⁴ /ier
dam ³* (water)
dam   damn ¹*+
damage ² /able
damask
dame
damidge   damage ²+
damn ¹* (curse) /ation
damnabl e /y
damnabul   damnable +
damp /er/est/ness
dampen ¹
damsel
damson
dance ² /r
dandelion
dandie   dandy +
dandifi   dandify ⁴
dandify ⁴
dandilion   dandelion
dandruff
dand y /ies
Dane * (from Denmark)
dane   deign ¹*
danger /ous/ously
dangerus   dangerous
dangle ² /r
dangul   dangle ²+
danjer   danger+
danjerus   dangerous
dank /ness
danse   dance ²+
daper   dapper +
daple   dapple ²
dapper /ness
dapple ²
dapul   dapple ²
dare ² /-devil
dark /er/est/ly/ness
darken ¹
darling
darn ¹ /er
darnel
dart ¹

dase	dace
dash[1] /board	
dastard /ly	
data	
dat e[2] /able	
dater	data
dative	
daub[1] /er/y	
daufin	dauphin
daughter /(s)-in-law	
daunt[1] /less	
dauphin	
dauter	daughter[+]
davenport	
Davielamp	Davy lamp
davit	
Davy lamp	
dawb	daub[1+]
dawdle[2] /r	
dawdul	dawdle[2+]
dawn[1]	
dawnt	daunt[1+]
dawter	daughter[+]
day /-break/s * (dates)	
daybu	début
day-dream /t/ing	
dayify	deify[4+]
dayism	deism[+]
dayist	deist
dayity	deity[+]
daylight	
daylite	daylight
day-nurser y /ies	
daytant	détente
daze[2]* (stun)	
dazle	dazzle[2+]
dazul	dazzle[2+]
dazzl e[2] /er/ingly	
de luxe	
deacon /ess (fem.)	
deactivat e[2] /ion	
dead /-beat/-line	
deaden[1] /er	
dead-heat[1]	
deadlock	

deadl y /ier/iest/iness	
dead-nettle	
deaf /-mute/ness	
deafen[1] /ingly	
deal /er/ing/t	
deam	deem[1]
dean /ery	
deap	deep[+]
dear * (loved)	
dear	deer *
dear er /est/ly	
dearth	
death /-mask/-rate	
death ly /less/like	
death -trap /-watch	
débâcle	
debacul	débâcle
debar[3] /ment	
debark[1] /ation	
debase[2] /ment	
debat e[2] /able/ably	
debauch[1] /ery	
debilitat e[2] /ion	
debility	
debit[1] /able	
debonair /ness	
deborch	debauch[1+]
debree	debris
debrief[1]	
debris	
debt /or * (owe money)	
debunk[1] /er	
début	
débutant /e (fem.)	
decade	
decaden ce /t	
decagon /al	
deca gram /litre/metre	
decamp[1] /ment	
decant[1] /er	
decapitat e[2] /ion	
decapod	
decarbonis e[2] /ation	
decathlon	
decay[1]	

decease ²	
deceit /ful/fully/fulness	
deceive ² /r	
decelerat *e* ² /ion	
December	
decenc *y* /ies	
decensey	decency +
decent ★ (good) /ly	
decent	descent ★
decentralise ²	
decepshun	deception
deception	
deceptive /ly/ness	
decerus	decorous +
decibel	
decide ² /dly	
deciduous	
decifer	decipher ¹+
deci *gram* /litre/metre	
decimal /ism	
decimalis *e* ² /ation	
decimat *e* ² /ion	
decipher ¹ /able	
decision	
decisive /ly/ness	
deck ¹ /-chair/-hand	
declaim ¹ /er	
declamashun	declamation +
declamat *ion* /ory	
declarat *ion* /ory	
declare ²	
declassif *y* ⁴ /ication	
declension	
declin *e* ² /able/ation	
declivit *y* /ies	
declutch ¹	
decockshun	decoction
decoction	
decode ² /r	
decoi	decoy ¹
décollet *é* /age	
decompos *e* ² /able/ition	
decompress ¹ /ion	
decompress *ive* /or	
decon	deacon +

decongestant	
decontaminat *e* ² /ion	
decontrol ³	
décor	
decorashun	decoration
decorat *e* ² /ion/ive/or	
decorous /ly/ness	
decorum	
decorus	decorous +
decoy ¹	
decreas *e* ² /ingly	
decree /d/ing	
decrepit /ude	
decrese	decrease ²+
decri	decry ⁴+
decr *y* ⁴ /ier	
ded	dead +
deden	deaden ¹+
dedheat	dead-heat ¹
dedicat *e* ² /ion	
dedlie	deadly +
dedlier	deadlier
dedlock	deadlock
dedly	deadly +
dednetle	dead-nettle
dednetul	dead-nettle
deduc *e* ² /ible	
deduct ¹ /ible/ion	
deed /-poll	
deel	deal +
deem ¹	
deen	dean +
deep /er	
deepen ¹	
deep-freez *e* /er/ing	
deep-frozen	
deep-fry ⁴	
deer ★ (animal)	
deer	dear ★
de-escalat *e* ² /ion	
def	deaf +
deface ² /ment	
defamatory	
defamatrey	defamatory
defam *e* ² /ation	

default¹ /er	
defeat¹ /ism/ist	
defecat e² /ion	
defect¹ /ion/ive/or	
defeet	defeat¹⁺
defen	deafen¹⁺
defence /less	
defend¹ /able/ant	
defens	defence⁺
defensib le /ility	
defensibul	defensible⁺
defensive /ly/ness	
defensless	defenceless
defer³★ (postpone)	
deferen ce /tial	
deferens	deference⁺
deferenshal	deferential
defesit	deficit
defi	defy⁴
defian ce /t/tly	
defians	defiance⁺
deficienc y /ies	
deficient /ly	
deficit	
defile² /ment/r	
defin e² /able/ition	
definishun	definition
definit	definite⁺
definite /ly	
definitive /ly	
defishency	deficiency⁺
defishent	deficient⁺
defisit	deficit
deflashun	deflation
deflat e² /ion/ionary	
deflecshun	deflection
deflect¹ /ion/ive/or	
deflour	deflower¹
deflower¹	
defmute	deaf-mute
deforest¹ /ation	
deform¹ /ation	
deformashun	deformation
deformit y /ies	
defraud¹ /er	

defray¹ /able/al	
defreez e /ing	
defrord	defraud¹⁺
defrost¹ /er	
defrozen	
deft /ly/ness	
defunct /ive/ness	
defy⁴	
degeneracy	
degenerat e² /ion	
degrad e² /ation	
degree	
dehidrate	dehydrate²⁺
dehydrat e² /ion	
de-ice² /r	
deifi	deify⁴⁺
deif y⁴ /ier	
deign¹★ (condescend)	
de-ise	de-ice²⁺
deis m /t	
deitee	deity⁺
deit y /ies	
deject¹ /ion	
dejeneracy	degeneracy
dejenerate	degenerate²⁺
dejeneration	degeneration
dekstrose	dextrose
dekstrus	dextrous
delay¹ /er	
delectabl e /y	
delectabul	delectable⁺
delegac y /ies	
delegasey	delegacy⁺
delegat e² /ion	
delet e² /ion	
deleterious /ly	
deliberat e² /ely/ion	
delibratley	deliberately
delicac y /ies	
delicate /ly/ness	
delicatessen	
delicious /ly/ness	
deligacy	delegacy⁺
deligashun	delegation
deligate	delegate²⁺

85

delight [1] /ful/fully		demobilis *e* [2] /ation	
delineat *e* [2] /ion		democrac *y* /ies	
deliniashun	delineation	democrasey	democracy [+]
deliniate	delineate [2+]	democratic /ally	
delinkwasey	delinquency [+]	democratis *e* [2] /ation	
delinkwens	delinquence [+]	demolish [1] /able	
delinquen *ce* /t		demolishun	demolition [+]
delinquenc *y* /ies		demolition /ist	
delirious /ly/ness		demon /ic	
delirium		demonstra *ble* /tive	
delirius	delirious [+]	demonstrashun	demonstration
delishus	delicious [+]	demonstrat *e* [2] /ion/or	
delite	delight [1+]	demoralise [2]	
deliteful	delightful	demot *e* [2] /ion	
deliterius	deleterious [+]	demur [3]★ (object)	
deliver [1] /ance/er		demure ★(quiet, coy)/ly	
deliver *y* /ies		denationalise [2]	
delivrey	delivery [+]	dencher	denture
dell		dendrology	
delouse [2]		deni	deny [4]
delt	dealt	denial	
delta		denier	
delude [2]		denigrat *e* [2] /ion/or	
deluge [2]		denim	
deluks	de luxe	denizen	
delushun	delusion [+]	denominat *e* [2] /or	
delusion /al		denomination /al	
delus *ive* /ory		denot *e* [2] /able/ation/ive	
delve [2] /r		denounce [2] /ment	
demagog	demagogue [+]	denownse	denounce [2+]
demagog *ue* /y		dense /ly/r	
demand [1] /able/er		densitey	density [+]
demarcat *e* [2] /ion		densitie	density [+]
demarch	démarche	densit *y* /ies	
démarche		dent [1]	
demean [1] /our		dental	
demeaner	demeanour	dentifrice	
demented		dentifriss	dentifrice
demerara		denti *ne* /tion	
demerit		dentishun	dentition
demesne		dentist /ry	
demigod		denture	
demilitarise [2]		denud *e* [2] /ation	
demis *e* [2] /able		denunciat *e* [2] /ion	
demist [1] /er		deny [4]	

deoderant	deodorant	deput e^2 /ation	
deoderise	deodorise $^{2+}$	deputey	deputy $^+$
deodorant		deputise ^{2}	
deodorise ^{2} /r		deput y /ies	
deparcher	departure	derail ^{1} /ment	
depart ^{1} /ure		derale	derail $^{1+}$
department /al/ally		derange ^{2} /ment	
departmentalise ^{2}		derelicshun	dereliction
depen	deepen ^{1}	derelict /ion	
depend ^{1} /able/ence		derick	derrick
dependant $\star$ (n.)		deride ^{2} /r	
dependenc y /ies		derishun	derision
dependensey	dependency $^+$	derision	
dependent $\star$ (adj.)		deris ive /ory	
depict ^{1} /ion		derivashun	derivation $^+$
depilat e^2 /ion/or		derivat ion /ive	
depilatory		derivativ	derivative
deplet e^2 /ion		deriv e^2 /able/er	
deploi	deploy $^{1+}$	dermatitis	
deplor e^2 /able/ably		dermatolog y /ist	
deploy ^{1} /ment		derogat e^2 /ive/ory	
depo	depot	derrick	
depopulat e^2 /ion		dert	dirt $^+$
deport ^{1} /ment		derth	dearth
deportashun	deportation	derty	dirty $^{4+}$
deportation		dervish	
depos e^2 /able		desalinat e^2 /ion	
deposishun	deposition	descant ^{1} /er	
deposit ^{1} /ion/or		descend ^{1} /er	
depositor y /ies		descendant $\star$ (n.)	
depositrey	depository $^+$	descendent $\star$ (adj.)	
depot		descent $\star$ (go down)	
deprav e^2 /ity		describ e^2 /able	
deprecat e^2 /ion/ory		descript ion /ive	
depreciat e^2 /ion		descry ^{4}	
depredat e^2 /ion		deseat	deceit $^+$
depresherise	depressurise ^{2}	deseave	deceive $^{2+}$
depreshurise	depressurise ^{2}	desecrat e^2 /ion	
depresiv	depressive	desegregat e^2 /ion	
depress ^{1} /ion/ive		desel	diesel
depressant		deselerashun	deceleration
depressurise ^{2}		deselerate	decelerate $^{2+}$
depricate	deprecate $^{2+}$	Desember	December
depriv e^2 /ation		desency	decency $^+$
depth		desend	descend $^{1+}$

desensitise²	
desent	decent ★+
desent	descent ★
desentralise	decentralise²
desershun	desertion
desert¹★ (abandon, dry land)	
desert	dessert ★
desert er /ion	
deserve² /dly	
desese	disease +
desibel	decibel
desiccat e² /ion	
desiduous	deciduous
design¹ /er	
designat e² /ion/or	
desimal	decimal +
desimalise	decimalise²+
desimate	decimate²+
desimation	decimation
desine	design¹+
desirab le /ility	
desirabul	desirable +
desir e² /ous	
desist¹	
desk	
deskant	descant¹+
desolat e² /ion	
despair¹	
desperado /es	
desperashun	desperation
desperate /ly/ness	
desperation	
despicabl e /y	
despise² /r	
despite	
despoil¹ /ment	
despoliation	
despond¹ /ent	
despondenc e /y	
despondens	despondence +
despot /ism	
despotic /ally	
dessert ★ (food)	
dessert	desert¹★

destinashun	destination
destination	
destine²	
destin y /ies	
destitut e /ion	
destroy¹ /er	
destructib le /ility	
destructibul	destructible +
destruct ion /ive	
desultor y /ily	
det	debt +
detach¹ /ment	
detail¹	
detain¹ /ment	
detale	detail¹
detane	detain¹+
detecshun	detection
detect¹ /ion/or	
detective	
détente	
detention	
deter³★ (hinder)	
deter	debtor ★
deterent	deterrent
detergent	
deteriorat e² /ion	
determinant	
determinashun	determination
determination	
determin e² /able	
deterrent	
detest¹ /able/ation	
deth	death +
dethrone² /ment	
detiriarate	deteriorate²+
detonat e² /ion/or	
detoor	detour
detour	
detract¹ /ion/or	
detriment /al	
detrishun	detrition
detrition	
deuce	
deuterium	
deuteron	

devalu *e*² /ation
devastat *e*² /ion/or
develop¹ /er/ment
devian *ce* /t
deviat *e*² /ion
device ★ (scheme, means)
devil /ry
devilish /ly
devious /ly
devis *e*²★ (invent) /able
devitalis *e*² /ation
devius — devious⁺
devoid
devolushun — devolution
devolution
devolve²
devot *e*² /ee/ion
devour¹
devout /ly/ness
dew ★ (moisture)
dew — due ★
dew *y* /-drop
dext *erity* /rous
dextrose
dextrus — dextrous
dhoti
dhow
diabetes
diabetic
diabolic /al/ally
diadem
diafanous — diaphanous⁺
diafanus — diaphanous⁺
diafram — diaphragm⁺
diagnose²
diagnos *is* /es (pl.)
diagnostic /ian
diagnostishun — diagnostician
diagonal /ly
diagram
diagrammatic /ally
dial³ /er
dialect /al/ally
dialectic /al/ally
dialisis — dialysis⁺

dialog — dialogue
dialogue
dialy *sis* /tic
diamet *er* /ral
diametric /al/ally
diamond
diapason
diaper
diaphanous /ly
diaphragm /atic
diarea — diarrhoea
diarey — diary⁺
diarrhoea
diar *y* /ies/ist
diatonic
diatribe

If you cannot find your word under **di** *look under* **de**

dibase — debase²⁺
dibate — debate²⁺
dibble² /r
dice² (pl. of die)
dichotom *y* /ies
diciple — disciple
dicipul — disciple
dicotomey — dichotomy⁺
dicotyledon
dicshun — diction
dicshunrey — dictionary⁺
dictafone — dictaphone
dictaphone
dictat *e*² /ion
dictator /ial
diction
dictionar *y* /ies
dictum
didactic /ally/ism
diddle² /r
didget — digit⁺
didgitalis — digitalis
didn't (did not)
didnt — didn't
die ★ (sing. of dice)
die ★ (death) /d ★

die-hard		dignity	
dieing	dyeing ★	digress [1] /ion/ive	
dieing	dying ★	dike [2]	
diernal	diurnal [+]	dil	dill
diesel		dilapidat e [2] /ion	
diet [1] /ary		dilatashun	dilatation
dietetic /s		dilat e [2] /ation/or/ory	
dietician		dilemma	
dietishun	dietician	diletant	dilettante [+]
difer	differ [1]★	dilettant e /i (pl.)	
diference	difference [+]	dilidalie	dilly-dally [4]
diferens	difference [+]	diligen ce /t	
diferenshal	differential [+]	diligens	diligence [+]
diferenshiate	differentiate [2+]	dill	
diferent	different	dilly-dally [4]	
diferential	differential [+]	dilut e [2] /ion/or	
diferentiate	differentiate [2+]	diluvial	
differ [1]★ (disagree)		dim [3] /ly/ness	
differ	defer [3]★	dime	
differen ce /t		dimenshun	dimension [+]
differential /ly		dimension /al	
differentiat e [2] /ion		dimer	dimmer [+]
difficult		diminish [1] /able	
difficult y /ies		diminuendo	
diffiden ce /t		diminut ive /ion	
diffract /ion		dimm er /est	
diffus e [2] /ion/ive		dimpl e [2] /y	
dificult	difficult	dimpul	dimple [2+]
dificultey	difficulty [+]	dinamic	dynamic [+]
difidence	diffidence [+]	dinamite	dynamite [2]
difident	diffident	dinamo	dynamo [+]
difract	diffract [+]	dinastey	dynasty [+]
diftheria	diphtheria	dinastic	dynastic [+]
difthong	diphthong	dine [2]★ (eat) /r	
difuse	diffuse [2+]	dine	dyne ★
difushun	diffusion	diner	dinner
difusion	diffusion	dingh y /ies	
dig [3] /ger		dingie	dinghy [+]
digest [1] /ion/ive		ding y /ily/iness	
digestib le /ility		dinner	
digit /al/ally		dinosaur	
digitalis		dinosore	dinosaur
dignify [4]		dioces e /an	
dignitar y /ies		diode	
dignitrey	dignitary [+]	diokside	dioxide

diosees	diocese +	disarange	disarrange ²+
dioxide		disaray	disarray
dip ³ /per		disarm ¹ /ament	
diper	diaper	disarrange ² /ment	
diphtheria		disarray	
diphthong		disasoshiate	disassociate ²+
diploma /s		disassociat e ² /ion	
diplomac y /ies		disast er /rous/rously	
diplomasey	diplomacy +	disastrus	disastrous
diplomat /ist		disatisfi	dissatisfy ⁴+
diplomatic /ally		disavow ¹ /al	
dipsomania /c		disband ¹ /ment	
dire /ful/ly/r/st		disbar ³ /ment	
direcshun	direction	disbeleif	disbelief
direct ¹ /ion/ive		disbeleive	disbelieve ²+
director /ate		disbelief	
director y /ies		disbelieve ² /r	
directrey	directory +	disberden	disburden ¹+
dirge /ful		disberse	disburse ²+
dirigib le /ility		disbileaf	disbelief
dirigibul	dirigible +	disbileve	disbelieve ²+
dirt /iness		disburden ¹ /ment	
dirt y ⁴ /ier/iest/ily		disburse ² /ment	
disabilit y /ies		disc /-brake/-jockey	
disable ² /ment		discard ¹	
disabul	disable ²+	discern ¹ /ible/ment	
disabuse ²		discernibul	discernible
disadvantage /ous		discharge ²	
disadvantidge	disadvantage +	disciple	
disafecshun	disaffection	disciplinar y /ian	
disaffected		discipline ²	
disaffection		discipul	disciple
disagreabul	disagreeable +	disclaim ¹	
disagree /d/ing/ment		disclaym	disclaim ¹
disagreeabl e /y		disclos e ² /ure	
disagrement	disagreement	discolor	discolour ¹+
disallow ¹		discolo ur ¹ /ration	
disapear	disappear ¹+	discomfert	discomfort ¹
disapearance	disappearance	discomfort ¹	
disapoint	disappoint ¹+	discompos e ² /ure	
disapoynt	disappoint ¹+	disconcert ¹	
disappear ¹ /ance		disconect	disconnect ¹+
disappoint ¹ /ment		disconnect ¹ /ion	
disapprov e ² /al		disconsert	disconcert ¹
disaproval	disapproval	disconsolate /ly	

discontent[1]
discontinu*e*[2] /ance
discontinu*ity* /ous
discord /ance/ant
discorse   discourse[2]
discotek   discotheque
discotheque
discount[1] /able/er
discountenance[2]
discourage[2] /ment
discourse[2]
discourteous /ly/ness
discourtes*y* /ies
discourtius   discourteous +
discover[1] /er
discover*y* /ies
discownt   discount[1]+
discowntenans   discountenance[2]
discredit[1] /able
discreet /ly/ness
discrepanc*y* /ies
discrepant
discrepensey   discrepancy +
discreshun   discretion +
discretion /ary
discribable   describable
discribe   describe[2]+
discriminat*e*[2] /ion
discripshun   description +
discriptiv   descriptive
disculer   discolour[1]+
discuridge   discourage[2]+
discurs*ion* /ive
discurtesey   discourtesy +
discurtius   discourteous +
discus *† /es
    †(heavy disc)
discushun   discussion
discuss[1]* (debate)
discussion
disdain[1] /ful/fully
dise   dice[2]
disease /d
diseave   deceive[2]+
disecshun   dissection

disect   dissect[1]+
disembark[1] /ation
disembarrass[1] /ment
disemble   dissemble[2]+
disembodie   disembody[4]+
disembod*y*[4] /iment
disembowel[3] /ment
disembroil[1]
disembul   dissemble[2]+
diseminashun   dissemination
diseminate   disseminate[2]+
disenchant[1] /ment
disengage[2] /ment
disenshent   dissentient
disenshun   dissension
disentangle[2] /ment
disentient   dissentient
disentrey   dysentery
disern   discern[1]+
disernible   discernible
disernibul   discernible
disertashun   dissertation
disertation   dissertation
diserviss   disservice
disfaver   disfavour[1]
disfavour[1]
disfiger   disfigure[2]+
disfigure[2] /ment
disfranchise[2] /ment
disgise   disguise[2]+
disgorge[2] /ment
disgrace[2] /ful/fully
disgruntled
disguise[2] /r
disgust[1]
dish /-cloth/ful
dishabille
disharmoney   disharmony +
disharmon*y* /ious
disharten   dishearten[1]
dishearten[1]
dishevel[3]
dishonest /ly/y
dishonour[1] /able/ably
dishonrabul   dishonourable

92

disidence	dissidence +	disobey [1]	
disidens	dissidence +	disoblige [2]	
disident	dissident	disoloot	dissolute +
disillusion [1] /ment		disoluble	dissoluble
disilushun	disillusion [1]+	disolute	dissolute +
disimilar	dissimilar +	disolution	dissolution
disimulashun	dissimulation	disolve	dissolve [2]+
disincentive		disonance	dissonance +
disinclinashun	disinclination	disonans	dissonance +
disinclin e [2] /ation		disonant	dissonant
disinfect [1] /ant/ion		disone	disown [1]
disinherit [1] /ance		disoner	dishonour [1]+
disinsentiv	disincentive	disonerabul	dishonourable
disintegrat e [2] /ion		disonest	dishonest +
disinter [3] /ment		disonist	dishonest +
disinterest [1]		disonrabul	dishonourable
disintigrate	disintegrate [2]+	disorder [1] /ly	
disipate	dissipate [2]+	disorganis e [2] /ation	
disiple	disciple	disorientate [2]	
disiplin	discipline [2]	disoshiate	dissociate [2]+
disiplinarey	disciplinary +	disown [1]	
disipul	disciple	disparage [2] /ment	
disjoint [1]		disparate /ly/ness	
diskwiet	disquiet [1]+	disparidge	disparage [2]+
diskwolification	disqualification	disparige	disparage [2]+
diskwolify	disqualify [4]+	disparitey	disparity +
dislik e [2] /able		disparit y /ies	
dislocat e [2] /ion		dispashonate	dispassionate +
dislodge [2] /ment		dispassionate /ly	
disloge	dislodge [2]+	dispatch [1] /er	
disloial	disloyal +	dispel [3] /ler	
disloialtey	disloyalty	dispensar y /ies	
disloyal /ly/ty		dispens e [2] /ation/er	
dismal /ly		dispepsia	dyspepsia +
dismantle [2]		dispeptic	dyspeptic
dismantul	dismantle [2]	dispers e [2] /al	
dismast [1]		dispershun	dispersion
dismay [1]		dispersion	
dismember [1] /ment		dispirit [1]	
dismisal	dismissal	displace [2] /ment	
dismiss [1] /al		displase	displace [2]+
dismount [1]		display [1]	
dismownt	dismount [1]	displeas e [2] /ure	
disobay	disobey [1]	displese	displease [2]+
disobedien ce /t		displesher	displeasure

disport[1]		dissidens	dissidence +
dispos e[2] /able/al		dissimilar /ity/ities	
disposeshun	dispossession	dissimulat e[2] /ion	
disposess	dispossess[1]+	dissipat e[2] /ion	
disposishun	disposition	dissociat e[2] /ion	
disposition		dissoluble	
dispossess[1] /ion		dissolute /ly/ness	
disproof		dissolution	
disproov	disprove[2]	dissolve[2] /nt	
disproporshun	disproportion +	dissonan ce /t	
disproportion /ate		dissuade[2]	
disprosium	dysprosium	dissuas ion /ive	
disprove[2]		distaff	
dispursal	dispersal	distance	
dispurse	disperse[2]+	distans	distance
dispurshun	dispersion	distant /ly	
disputashun	disputation +	distaste /ful/fully	
disputat ion /ious		distemper[1]	
disput e[2] /able		distend[1]	
disqualif y[4] /ication		distenshun	distension
disquiet[1] /ude		distens ible /ion	
disregard[1] /ful		distensibul	distensible +
disrepair		disterb	disturb[1]+
disreputabl e /y		disterbance	disturbance
disrepute		distil[3] /lation/ler	
disrespect /ful/fully		distiller y /ies	
disrigard	disregard[1]+	distinct /ive/ly	
disripair	disrepair	distinction	
disrispect	disrespect +	distinguish[1] /able	
disrobe[2] /ment		distingwish	distinguish[1]+
disrupt[1] /ion/ive		distorshun	distortion
dissapear	disappear[1]+	distort[1] /ion	
dissapoint	disappoint[1]+	distracshun	distraction
dissaproov	disapprove[2]+	distract[1] /ion	
dissatisf y[4] /action		distrain[1] /t	
dissect[1] /ion/or		distrane	distrain[1]+
dissemble[2] /r		distraught	
disseminat e[2] /ion/or		distrawt	distraught
dissension		distress[1] /ful	
dissent[1]★ (disagreement)		distribut e[2] /ion	
dissentient		distribut ive /or	
dissentious		district /nurse	
dissertation		distrort	distraught
disservice		distrust[1] /ful	
dissiden ce /t		disturb[1] /ance	

disunion
disunit e² /y
disurn — discern ¹⁺
disurnible — discernible
disuse²
diswade — dissuade²
diswashun — dissuasion⁺
diswasion — dissuasion⁺
diswasiv — dissuasive
ditch¹ /er
dither¹ /y
ditie — ditty⁺
dito — ditto
ditto
ditt y /ies
dity — ditty⁺
diurnal /ly
divan
dive² /r
diverge² /nce/nt
divergens — divergence
divers — diverse⁺
diverse /ly
divershun — diversion
diversifi — diversify⁴⁺
diversif y⁴ /ication
diversion
diversitey — diversity⁺
diversity /ies
divert¹ /er
divest¹
divide² /r
dividend
divin e² /ation/ely/er
divinitey — divinity⁺
divinit y /ies
diviser — divisor
divishun — division⁺
divis ible /ive/ively
divisibul — divisible⁺
division /al
divisiv — divisive
divisor
divorce² /é/ée (fem.)
divorse — divorce²⁺

divulge² /nce/r
dizier — dizzier⁺
dizmal — dismal⁺
dizolve — dissolve²⁺
dizy — dizzy
dizzi er /est/ly/ness
dizzy
do ★ (perform) /er/ing
do ★ (music) /s ★ (pl.)
do — doe ★⁺
docile /ly
docility
dock¹ /er/yard
docket¹
dockit — docket¹
docter — doctor¹⁺
doctor¹ /ate/ial
doctrin — doctrine⁺
doctrinair — doctrinaire
doctrin e /aire/al
document¹ /ation
documentar y /ies
documentrey — documentary⁺
dodder¹ /er/y
dodecagon
doder — dodder¹⁺
dodg e² /er/y
dodgi er /est/ness
doe ★ (deer) /s ★ (pl.)
doe — do ★⁺
doe — dough ★⁺
does ★ (do-[verb])
doesn't (does not)
doff¹
dofin — dauphin
dog³ /fight/fish
dog-eared
dogeared — dog-eared
dogeral — doggerel
dogfite — dogfight
doggerel
dogma /tic/tically
dogmatis e² /m
doilie — doily⁺
doil y /ies

doldrum	
dole²	
doleful /ly	
doler	dollar
dolerus	dolorous⁺
dolfin	dolphin
doll¹ /y	
dollar	
doller	dollar
dollop	
dolman	
dolomite	
dolorous /ly/ness	
dolorus	dolorous⁺
dolphin	
domain	
domane	domain
dome	
Domesday Book	
domestic /ally	
domesticate²	
domesticity	
domestisitey	domesticity
domicil e /iary	
dominan ce /t	
dominans	dominance⁺
dominat e² /ion/or	
dominear	domineer¹
domineer¹	
dominion	
domino /es	
dominyon	dominion
domisile	domicile⁺
don³*† /nish	
†(put on, tutor)	
donat e² /ion/or	
done * (finished)	
doner	donor
donkey /s	
donky	donkey⁺
donor	
donut	doughnut
dooch	douche²
doodle² /r	
doodul	doodle²⁺

doom¹	
doomsday book	Domesday Book
door /step/way	
door	dour
doordle	dawdle²⁺
doormouse	dormouse
doosh	douche²
dope² /y	
dophin	dauphin
dore	door⁺
dorman cy /t	
dormansey	dormancy⁺
dormice	
dormise	dormice
dormitor y /ies	
dormitrey	dormitory⁺
dormouse	
dorn	dawn¹
dorsal /ly	
dorter	daughter⁺
dos e² /age	
dosidge	dosage
dosile	docile⁺
dosilitey	docility
dossier	
dot³	
dot age /ard	
dote² /r	
doti	dhoti
dotidge	dotage⁺
dotti er /est/ly/ness	
dotty	
double² /-barrelled	
double-bass	
double-cross¹	
doublet	
doubloon	
doubly	
doubt¹ /er/less	
doubtful /ly/ness	
douche²	
dough * (bread) /nut/y	
dought y /ily	
dour	
douse²* (shower) /r	

douse	dowse ²★	draftiness	draughtiness
dout	doubt ¹⁺	drafts	draughts ★
doutey	doughty ⁺	draftsman ★ (drafter	
doutful	doubtful ⁺	of documents)	
doutless	doubtless	draftsman	draughtsman ★
dove /-cot		drafty	draughty ⁺
dovetail ¹		drag ³ /ger	
dow	dhow	dragon	
dow	doe ★⁺	dragonfl y /ies	
dow	dough ★⁺	dragoon ¹	
dowager		drain ¹ /age/er	
dowdie	dowdy ⁺	drainidge	drainage
dowd y /ily/iness		drake	
dowey	doughy	dram	
down ¹ /cast/hill		drama /s/tist	
downey	downy	dramatic /ally	
downfall /en		dramatis e ² /ation	
downgrade ²		drank	
downharted	downhearted	drape ² /r	
downhearted		draper y /ies	
downie	downy	drastic /ally	
downpoor	downpour	draught ★† /s ★	
downpour		†(air current, game)	
downright		draughtiness	
downrite	downright	draughtsman ★†	
downstairs		†(drawer of plans)	
downtrodden		draught y /ier/iest	
downward		draw /ing/n	
downwerd	downward	drawback	
downy		drawbridge	
dowrie	dowry ⁺	drawer	
dowr y /ies		drawing-room	
dowse ²★ (divine with rod)		drawl ¹ /er	
dowse	douse ²★⁺	dray ★ (low cart)	
dowt	doubt ¹⁺	dray	drey ★
dowtey	doughty ⁺	dread ¹ /ful/fully	
dowtful	doubtful ⁺	dreadnort	dreadnought
doz e ²★ (sleep) /y		dreadnought	
doze	does ★	dream ¹ /ily/less/t/y	
dozen		drearey	dreary
dozi ly /ness		drearie	dreary
drab		dreari er /est/ly/ness	
draft ¹★ (bank, military)		dreary	
draft	draught ★⁺	dred	dread ¹⁺
draftey	draughty ⁺	dredful	dreadful

dredge² /r		dropper	
drednort	dreadnought	dropsey	dropsy +
dreem	dream ¹+	dropsie	dropsy +
drege	dredge ²+	drops y /ical/ied	
dregs		dross /iness	
dremt	dreamt	drought	
drench¹ /er		drout	drought
drerey	dreary	drove /r	
drerie	dreary	drown¹	
drerier	drearier +	drows e² /y	
dresage	dressage	drowsey	drowsy
dresie	dressy	drowsie	drowsy
dresmaker	dressmaker +	drowsi er /ly/ness	
dress¹ /er/es/iness/y		drowt	drought
dressage		dru	drew
dressmak er /ing		drub³ /ber	
dresy	dressy	drudge² /ry	
drew		drug³	
Drewid	Druid	druge	drudge ²+
drey ★ (squirrel's nest)		drugery	drudgery
dri	dry ⁴+	drugget	
dribble² /r		druggist	
driblet		Druid	
dribul	dribble² +	drum³ /mer/stick	
driclean	dry-clean¹	drumedarey	dromedary +
drift¹ /er/wood		drum-major	
dril	drill¹	drunk /ard/en/enness	
drill¹		dr y⁴ /ier/iest	
drily		dry-clean¹	
drink /able/er		dryer	drier
drip³ /-dry		dual ★ (two) /ism/ity	
driv e /en/er/ing		dual	duel ³★
drivel³ /ler		dub³	
drizul	drizzle ²+	dubbin	
drizzl e² /y		dubious /ly	
droll /ness		dubius	dubious +
droller y /ies		duble	double ²+
dromedar y /ies		dublebareld	double-barrelled
drone²		dublet	doublet
Drooid	Druid	dublie	doubly
drool¹		dubloon	doubloon
droop¹ /y		dubly	doubly
drop³ /let		ducal	
droper	dropper	ducat	
drop-out		duce	deuce

duchess /es	
duchey	duchy +
duchie	duchy +
duch y /ies	
duck [1] /ling	
ducket	ducat
ducktile	ductile +
duct /ing/less	
ductil e /ity	
du e* (owing, expected)	
due	dew *
duedrop	dew-drop
duel [3]* (fight)	
duel	joule *
dueler	dueller +
duelist	duellist
duell er /ist	
duet /tist	
duey	dewy +
dufel	duffel
duffel	
duffer	
dug /-out	
dul	dull +
dulcet	
dulcimer	
duler	duller +
dulie	duly
dull /ard/y	
dull er /est/ish	
dulset	dulcet
dulsimer	dulcimer
duly	
dum	dumb +
dumb /ly/ness	
dumb-bell	
dumbell	dumb-bell
dumbfound [1]	
dumfound	dumbfound [1]
dumfownd	dumbfound [1]
dumm y /ies	
dumness	dumbness
dump [1] /er/y	
dumpling	
dumy	dummy +

dun * (colour)	
dun	done *
dunce	
dune	
dung /hill	
dungaree /s	
dungen	dungeon
dungeon	
dunjon	dungeon
duns	dunce
dunse	dunce
duolog	duologue
duologue	
dup e [2] /able	
dupleks	duplex +
duplex /ity	
duplicat e [2] /ion/or	
duplicity	
duplisitey	duplicity
durab le /ility/ly	
durabul	durable +
durashun	duration
duration	
duress	
durge	dirge +
during	
durt	dirt +
durtie	dirty [4]+
durtier	dirtier
durty	dirty [4]+
dusbin	dustbin +
duse	deuce
dusk /y	
dust [1] /er/y	
dust bin /man/pan	
dusti er /est/ness	
Dutch /man/woman	
dutie	duty +
dutifree	duty-free
dutiful /ly	
dut y /ies	
duty-free	
duv	dove +
duvtail	dovetail [1]
duvtale	dovetail [1]

99

duz   does *
duzn   dozen
duznt   doesn't
dwarf¹ /ish
dwell /er/ing
dwelt
dwindle²
dwindul   dwindle²
dworf   dwarf¹⁺
dye *† /d *† /ing *†
   †(change colour)
dye   die *⁺
dyed   died *
dyehard   die-hard
dying * (death)
dying   dyeing *
dynamic /ally
dynamics
dynamite²
dynamo /s
dynast
dynastey   dynasty⁺
dynastic /ally
dynast y /ies
dyne * (unit of force)
dysentery
dysentrey   dysentery
dyspep sia /tic
dysprosium

E

each
eager /ly/ness
eagle /-eyed/t
eal   eel
ear /-ache/-drum
earie   eerie *
earie   eyrie *
earl /dom
earli er /est
early /ish
earmark¹
earn ¹* (gain) /ings

earnest /ly/ness
ear-ring
earshot
earth¹ /iness
earthen /ware
earthl y /iness
earthquake
earth work /worm
earwig
ease²
easel
east /erly/ward/wards
easten   eastern⁺
Easter
eastern /er
eas y /ier/ily/iness
easy-going
eat /able/en/er/ing
eau-de-Cologne
eaves
eavesdrop³ /per
ebb¹
ebonie   ebony⁺
ebon y /ite
ebulience   ebullience⁺
ebuliens   ebullience⁺
ebulient   ebullient
ebullien ce /t
eccentric /ally/ity
ecclesiastic /al/ally
ecentric   eccentric⁺
ech   each
echelon
echo¹ /es
eclair
eclare   eclair
eclectic
eclesiastic   ecclesiastic⁺
eclipse²
ecliptic
ecolog   ecologue
ecologey   ecology⁺
ecological /ly
ecologue
ecolog y /ist

economic /al/ally/s	
economise²	
economist	
econom y /ies	
ecsema	eczema
ecsentric	eccentric +
ecstas y /ies	
ecstatic /ally	
ectoplasm	
ecumenical	
eczema	
edd y⁴ /ies	
edge² /ways/wise	
edgey	edgy +
edgie	edgy +
edg y /ily/iness	
edib le /ility	
edibul	edible +
edict	
edie	eddy ⁴⁺
edifice	
edifiss	edifice
edif y⁴ /ication	
edishun	edition
edit¹ /ion	
editer	editor +
editor /ial/ially	
educab le /ility	
educashun	education +
educat e² /ive/or	
education /al/ally/ist	
edy	eddy ⁴⁺
eeger	eager +
eegle	eagle +
eel	
eer	ear +
eerie * (strange)	
eerie	eyrie *
eeri er /est/ly/ness	
eermark	earmark ¹
eface	efface ²⁺
efect	effect ¹
efectiv	effective +
efectual	effectual
efeet	effete

efemeral	ephemeral +
efeminacy	effeminacy
efeminasey	effeminacy
efeminate	effeminate +
efert	effort +
efervesence	effervescence
efervesent	effervescent
efervess	effervesce ²⁺
efface² /ment	
effect¹	
effective /ly	
effectual	
effeminacy	
effeminate /ly	
effervesce² /nce/nt	
effervess	effervesce ²⁺
effete	
efficacious /ly/ness	
efficacy	
efficashus	efficacious +
efficienc y /ies	
efficient /ly	
effigey	effigy +
effig y /ies	
efflorescen ce /t	
effluen ce /t	
effluvium	
effort /less/lessly	
effronter y /ies	
effulgen ce /t	
effulgens	effulgence +
effus e² /ion/ive	
eficacious	efficacious +
eficacy	efficacy
eficasey	efficacy
eficashus	efficacious +
eficiency	efficiency +
eficient	efficient +
efigey	effigy +
efishency	efficiency +
efishensey	efficiency +
efishent	efficient +
efloresence	efflorescence +
efluence	effluence +
efluens	effluence +

101

efluent — effluent
efluvium — effluvium
efort — effort [+]
efronterey — effrontery [+]
efulgence — effulgence [+]
efuse — effuse [2+]
efusiv — effusive
eg — egg [1+]
egalitarian /ism
ege — edge [2+]
egg [1] /-cup/-shell
Egipshun — Egyptian
Egiptian — Egyptian
egis — aegis
ego /ism/tism
egocentric /ity
egoist /ic/ically
egosentric — egocentric [+]
egotist /ical/ically
egress [1]

If you cannot find your word under **egs** look under **ex**

egsact — exact [1+]
egsamine — examine [2+]
egsample — example
egsaust — exhaust [1+]
egsecutive — executive
egsempt — exempt [1+]
egsert — exert [1+]
Egyptian
eiderdown
Eiffel (Tower)
eight ★ (number)
eighteen /th
eighth /ly
eight y /ies
einsteinium
either
ejaculat e [2] /ion/ory
eject [1] /ion/or
ejis — aegis
eke [2]
eko — echo [1+]

If you cannot find your word under **eks** look under **ex**

ekscavate — excavate [2+]
ekschange — exchange [2+]
eksclaim — exclaim [1]
eksite — excite [2+]
ekumenical — ecumenical
ekwable — equable [+]
ekwabul — equable [+]
ekwal — equal [3+]
ekwalise — equalise [2+]
ekwalitey — equality [+]
ekwanimitey — equanimity
ekwashun — equation
ekwate — equate [2]
ekwater — equator [+]
ekwation — equation
ekwerey — equerry [+]
ekwestrian — equestrian
ekwianguler — equiangular
ekwidistant — equidistant
ekwilateral — equilateral
ekwilibrium — equilibrium
ekwine — equine
ekwinox — equinox
ekwip — equip [3+]
ekwitable — equitable [+]
ekwitabul — equitable [+]
ekwity — equity [+]
ekwivalence — equivalence [+]
ekwivocate — equivocate [2+]
elaborat e [2] /ely/ion
elapse [2]
elastic /ally/ity
elat e [2] /ion
elbow [1] /-room
elder /ly
elderberie — elderberry [+]
elderberr y /ies
eldest
elect [1] /ive/or/orate
election /eering
electoral /ly
electric /al/ally
electrician

102

electricity
electrif *y* [4] /ication
electrocut *e* [2] /ion
electrode
electrolight   electrolyte [+]
electrolite   electrolyte [+]
electrolysis
electrolyt *e* /ic
electromagnet /ic/ism
electromotive
electron /s
electronic /ally/s
electroplate [2]
electroscope
electrovalency
elefant   elephant [+]
elegan *ce* /t
elegans   elegance [+]
elegey   elegy [+]
eleg *y* /ies/iac
element /al/ary
elephant /ine
elevat *e* [2] /ion/or
eleven /th
elf /in/ish
elfs   elves
elicit [1*] (draw out)
elicit   illicit [*+]
elide [2]
elifant   elephant [+]
eligans   elegance [+]
eligant   elegant
eligib *le* /ility
eligibul   eligible [+]
elikser   elixir
eliment   element [+]
elimental   elemental
elimentarey   elementary
elimentrey   elementary
eliminat *e* [2] /ion/or
elips   ellipse
elipsis   ellipsis
eliptic   elliptic [+]
elision
élit *e* /ism/ist

elivashun   elevation
elivate   elevate [2+]
elivater   elevator
elivation   elevation
elixir
Elizabethan
elk
ellipse
ellipsis
elliptic /al/ally
elocution /ary/ist
elokwence   eloquence [+]
elokwens   eloquence [+]
elokwent   eloquent
elongat *e* [2] /ion
elope [2] /ment/r
eloquen *ce* /t
eloquens   eloquence [+]
else /where
elswere   elsewhere
elucidat *e* [2] /ion/or
elude [2*] (avoid)
elude   allude [2*]
elushun   elusion [*]
elusidate   elucidate [2+]
elusion [*] (escape)
elusive [*] (evasive) /ness
elusive   illusive [*]
elver
elves (pl. of elf)
emaciat *e* [2] /ion
emanat *e* [2] /ion/ive
emancipat *e* [2] /ion/or
emansipate   emancipate [2+]
emasculat *e* [2] /ion
emasiate   emaciate [2+]
embalm [1] /er/ment
embankment
embarass   embarrass [1+]
embargo [1] /es
embark [1] /ation
embarm   embalm [1+]
embarrass [1] /ment
embass *y* /ies
embattle [2]

embatul	embattle [2]	eminens	eminence [+]
embed [3]		eminent	imminent ★[+]
embellish [1] /ment		emisarey	emissary [+]
ember		emishun	emission
embezul	embezzle [2+]	emissar y /ies	
embezzle [2] /ment/r		emission	
embitter [1] /ment		emit [3] /ter	
emblazon [1]		emollient	
emblem		emolument	
emblematic /ally		emoshun	emotion [+]
embodie	embody [4+]	emotion /al/ally	
embod y [4] /iment		emotive	
embolism		empanel [3]	
emboss [1]		emperer	emperor [+]
embrace [2]		emp eror /ress (fem.)	
embrase	embrace [2]	emphas is /es (pl.)	
embrio	embryo [+]	emphasise [2]	
embriologist	embryologist [+]	emphatic /ally	
embrocashun	embrocation	empire ★ (dominion)	
embrocation		empire	umpire [2★]
embroider [1] /y/ies		empiric /ism/ist	
embroil [1] /ment		empirical /ly	
embryo /s/nic		empirisist	empiricist
embryolog ist /y		emplacement	
emend	amend [1+]	emploi	employ [1+]
emerald		employ [1] /able/ee/er	
emerey	emery	emporium /s	
emerge [2] /nce		empower [1]	
emergenc y /ies		empress	impress [1+]
emergensey	emergency [+]	emptie	empty [4]
emergent		empti er /est/ness	
emerie	emery	empty [4]	
emershun	emersion	emulashun	emulation
emersion		emulat e [2] /ion/ive/or	
emery		emulshun	emulsion
emetic		emulsif y [4] /ication	
emfasis	emphasis [+]	emulsion	
emfasise	emphasise [2]	en route	
emfatic	emphatic [+]	enable [2] /ment	
emigrant		enabul	enable [2+]
emigrat e [2] /ion		enact [1] /able/ment	
emigray	émigré [+]	enamel [3] /ler	
émigré /e (fem.)		enamer	enamour [1]
eminen ce /t ★†		enamour [1]	
†(distinguished)		encamp [1] /ment	

encapsulat *e* ² /ion
encase ² /ment
encefalic   encephalic
encephalic
enchant ¹ /ment
enchant *er* /ress (fem.)
enciclical   encyclical
enciclopedia   encyclopedia +
encircle ² /ment
enclave
enclos *e* ² /ure
encompass ¹
encore ²
encounter ¹
encourage ² /ment
encownter   encounter ¹
encroach ¹ /er/ment
encrust ¹
encumb *er* ¹ /rance
encuridge   encourage ²+
encurige   encourage ²+
encyclical
encyclopedi *a* /c
end ¹ /less/lessly
endanger ¹
endear ¹ /ment
endeavour ¹
endeer   endear ¹+
endever   endeavour ¹
endive
endocrine
endorse ² /ment/r
endow ¹ /ment
end-product
endur *e* ² /able/ance
enema /s
enem *y* /ies
energetic /ally
energey   energy +
energise ² /r
energ *y* /ies
enervat *e* ² /ion
enfebul   enfeeble ²+
enfeeble ² /ment
enfold ¹

enforce ² /ment
enforceab *le* /ility
enfors   enforce ²+
enforsible   enforceable +
enforsibul   enforceable +
enfranchise ² /ment
engage ² /ment
engender ¹
engine /-driver
enginear   engineer ¹
engineer ¹
English /man/woman
engraft ¹ /ment
engrain ¹
engrave ² /r
engrayn   engrain ¹
engross ¹
engulf ¹
enhance ² /ment
enhans   enhance ²+
eni   any
enibodie   anybody
enigma /tic/tically
enihow   anyhow
enima   enema +
enithing   anything
eniware   anywhere
eniway   anyway
eniwhere   anywhere
eniwun   anyone
enjender   engender ¹
enjin   engine +
enjineer   engineer ¹
enjoi   enjoy ¹+
enjoiable   enjoyable +
enjoiabul   enjoyable +
enjoiment   enjoyment
enjoin ¹
enjoy ¹ /ment
enjoyabl *e* /y
enlace ²
enlarge ² /able/ment/r
enlase   enlace ²
enlighten ¹ /ment
enlist ¹

enliten	enlighten ¹⁺	enterpris *e* /ing	
enliven ¹		entertain ¹ /er/ment	
enmit *y* /ies		entertane	entertain ¹⁺
ennoble ² /ment		enthral ³ /ment	
ennui		enthrone ² /ment	
enobul	ennoble ²⁺	enthuse ²	
enormit *y* /ies		enthusias *m* /t	
enormous /ly/ness		enthusiastic /ally	
enormus	enormous ⁺	entice ² /ment/r	
enough		entire /ly/ty	
enquire ² /r		entise	entice ²⁺
enquir *y* /ies		entitey	entity ⁺
enrage ²		entitle ² /ment	
enrap	enwrap ³	entitul	entitle ²⁺
enrapcher	enrapture ²	entit *y* /ies	
enrapture ²		entomb ¹ /ment	
enrich ¹ /ment		entomolog *y* /ical/ist	
enrol ³ /ment		entoom	entomb ¹⁺
enroot	en route	entrails	
ensconce ²		entrain ¹	
enscons	ensconce ²	entrales	entrails
ensefalic	encephalic	entrance ² /ment	
ensemble		entrans	entrance ²⁺
ensembul	ensemble	entrant	
ensercal	encircle ²⁺	entrap ³	
enshore	ensure ²★	entreat ¹ /ingly	
enshore	insure ²★⁺	entreat *y* /ies	
enshrine ²		entrée	
enshure	ensure ²★	entreet	entreat ¹⁺
ensiclical	encyclical	entrench ¹ /ment	
ensiclopedia	encyclopedia ⁺	entreprener	entrepreneur ⁺
ensign		entrepreneur /ial	
ensine	ensign	entrey	entry ⁺
enslave ² /ment		entrust ¹	
ensnare ²		entr *y* /ies	
ensue ²		entwine ²	
ensure ²★ (make certain)		enuf	enough
ensure	insure ²★⁺	enumerat *e* ² /ion/or	
entail ¹		enunciat *e* ² /ion/or	
entale	entail ¹	enunsiate	enunciate ²⁺
entangle ² /ment		envelop ¹★† /ment	
entangul	entangle ²⁺	†(to surround)	
enteprise	enterprise ⁺	envelope ★ (stationery)	
enter ¹		envenom ¹	
enteritis		envie	envy ⁴⁺

envious /ly/ness	
environ [1] /s	
environment /al/ally	
envisage [2]	
envisidge	envisage [2]
envisige	envisage [2]
envius	envious +
envoi	envoy
envoy	
env y [4] /iable/ier	
enwrap [3]	
enzime	enzyme
enzyme	
epaulet	
epawlet	epaulet
ephemeral /ly	
epic /ally	
epicenter	epicentre
epicentre	
epicure /an/anism	
epidemic	
epiderm is /al	
epidiascope	
Epifaney	Epiphany
epiglottis	
epigraf	epigraph +
epigram	
epigrammatic /ally	
epigraph /ic	
epilep sy /tic	
epilog	epilogue
epilogue	
Epiphany	
episcopacy	
episcopal /ian	
episcopasey	episcopacy
episod e /ic/ical .	
epist le /olary	
episul	epistle+
epitaf	epitaph
epitaph	
epithet	
epitome	
epitomise [2]	
epoch /al	

epok	epoch +
eporlet	epaulet
equab le /ility/ly	
equal [3] /ly	
equalis e [2] /ation/er	
equalitey	equality +
equalit y /ies	
equanimity	
equashun	equation
equate [2]	
equater	equator +
equation	
equator /ial	
equerr y /ies	
equestrian	
equiangular	
equidistant	
equilateral	
equilibrium	
equine	
equinoks	equinox
equinox	
equip [3] /ment	
equitabl e /y	
equitabul	equitable +
equit y /ies	
equivalen ce /t	
equivalens	equivalence +
equivocal /ly	
equivocat e [2] /ion/or	
equmenical	ecumenical
er	err [1]
era /s	
eradicat e [2] /ion/or	
erand	errand
erant	errant
eras e [2] /er/ure	
erasher	erasure
erata	errata
eratic	erratic +
eratum	erratum +
erban	urban
erbane	urbane +
erbanise	urbanise [2]+
erbanitey	urbanity

107

erchin	urchin	erudit *e* /ely/ion	
ere ★ (before)		erupt [1] /ion/ive	
erecshun	erection	erwig	earwig
erect [1] /ile/or		esay	essay [1+]
erection		escalat *e* [2] /ion/or	
erer	error	escallop [1]	
erge	urge [2+]	escapade	
ergency	urgency	escape [2] /ment	
ergensey	urgency	escapis *m* /t	
ergent	urgent	escarpment	
erie	eerie ★	eschew [1]	
erie	eyrie ★	eschu	eschew [1]
ering	ear-ring	escort [1]	
erk	irk [1+]	esel	easel
erksome	irksome	esence	essence
erksum	irksome	esens	essence
erl	earl [+]	esenshal	essential [+]
erlier	earlier [+]	esential	essential [+]
erly	early [+]	eshelon	echelon
ermine		eshoo	eschew [1]
ern	earn [1★+]	Eskimo /s (pl.)	
ern	urn ★	eskwire	esquire
ernest	earnest [+]	esofagus	esophagus
erode [2]		esophagus	
eroneous	erroneous [+]	esoteric /ally/ism	
eronius	erroneous [+]	especial /ly	
eror	error	espeshal	especial [+]
eroshun	erosion	espi	espy [4]
erosion		espionage	
erotic /a/ally/ism		esplanade	
err [1]		esplanaid	esplanade
errand		espous *e* [2] /al	
errant		espowse	espouse [2+]
erratic /ally		espresso	
errat *um* /a (pl.)		espy [4]	
erroneous /ly		esquire	
erronius	erroneous [+]	essay [1] /s/ist	
error		essence	
erstwhile		essens	essence
erstwile	erstwhile	essenshal	essential [+]
erth	earth [1+]	essential /ly	
erthen	earthen [+]	est	east [+]
erthley	earthly [+]	establish [1] /able/ment	
erthquake	earthquake	estate	
erudishun	erudition	esteam	esteem [1]

esteem [1]

Ester   Easter

estern   eastern [+]

esthet   aesthete [+]

esthetic   aesthetic

estimable

estimabul   estimable

estimat *e* [2] /ion/or

estrange [2] /ment

estuar *y* /ies

et cetera

etch [1] /er

ete   eat [+]

eternal /ly

eternit *y* /ies

ether /eal

ether   either

ethic /al/ally/s

ethnic /ally

ethnolog *y* /ical

etholog *y* /ical

ethos

etiket   etiquette

etimology   etymology [+]

etiquet   etiquette

etiquette

etsetera   et cetera

etymolog *y* /ical/ist

eucalyptus /es

Eucharist

Euclid

eufemism   euphemism

eufoney   euphony [+]

eufonious   euphonious

eufonius   euphonious

eufony   euphony [+]

euforia   euphoria [+]

euforic   euphoric

eugenic /ally/s

Eukarist   Eucharist

Euklid   Euclid

eulogey   eulogy [+]

eulogis *e* [2] /m

eulogistic /ally

eulog *y* /ies

eunuch

euphemism

euphemistic /ally

euphon *y* /ious

euphori *a* /c

Eurashun   Eurasian

Eurasian

eurhythmics

eurithmics   eurhythmics

European

euthanasia

evacuashun   evacuation

evacuat *e* [2] /ion

evacuee

evad *e* [2] /able

evaluat *e* [2] /ion

evangelic /al/ally

evangelis *e* [2] /m/t

evanjelic   evangelic [+]

evaperate   evaporate [2+]

evaporat *e* [2] /ion/or

evaquee   evacuee

evashun   evasion

evasion

evasive /ly/ness

eve

even [1] /ly/ness

even *song* /tide

event /ful

eventual /ly

eventualit *y* /ies

ever /green/lasting

evermore

every /body/day/one

every *thing* /where

eves   eaves

evesdrop   eavesdrop [3+]

evict [1] /ion

eviden *ce* [2] /tial

evidens   evidence [2+]

evident /ly

evil /ly

evince [2]

evins   evince [2]

evocat *ion* /ive

evoke ²	
evolushun	evolution +
evolushunist	evolutionist
evolution /ary/ist	
evolve ²	
evrie	every +
evry	every +
ewe ★ (sheep)	
ewe	yew ★
ewe	you ★
exacerbat e ² /ion	
exacrabul	execrable
exact ¹ /itude/ly/ness	
exaggerat e ² /ion/or	
exalt ¹ /ation	
examination	
examine ² /r	
example	
exampul	example
exaserbate	exacerbate ²+
exasperat e ² /ion	
excavat e ² /ion/or	
exceed ¹ /ingly	
excel ³	
excellen ce /t	
excellenc y /ies	
excellens	excellence +
excellensey	excellency +
excepshun	exception +
except ¹	
exception /able/al/ally	
excerpt ¹	
excess /ive/ively	
exchange ² /able/r	
exchequer	
excis e ² /able/ion	
excitab le /ility	
excitabul	excitable +
excite ² /dly/ment	
exclaim ¹	
exclamashun	exclamation +
exclamat ion /ory	
exclu de ² /sion	
exclusiv e /ely/ity	
excommunicat e ² /ion	

excoriat e ² /ion	
excrement	
excrescence	
excresens	excrescence
excreta	
excret e ² /ion	
excruciating /ly	
excrushiating	excruciating +
excursion /ist	
excus e ² /able/ably	
exebition	exhibition +
execrable	
execrabul	execrable
execrat e ² /ion	
execut e ² /ant/or/rix (fem.)	
execution /er	
executive	
exemplary	
exemplif y ⁴ /ication	
exempt ¹ /ion	
exentric	eccentric +
exentricitey	eccentricity
exercise ²	
exert ¹ /ion	
exhal e ² /ation	
exhaust ¹ /ion	
exhaust ible /ive	
exhibit ¹ /or	
exhibition /er	
exhibitionis m /t	
exhilara te ² /nt/tion	
exhort ¹ /ation	
exhum e ² /ation	
exibition	exhibition +
exigence	
exigenc y /ies	
exigens	exigence
exigensey	exigency +
exigu ous /ity	
exile ²	
exist ¹ /ence/ent	
existens	existence
exit ¹	
exkwisit	exquisite +
exonerat e ² /ion	

110

exorbitan *ce* /t
exorcise [2] /r
exorcis *m* /t
exorsism — exorcism [+]
exorst — exhaust [1+]
exorstibul — exhaustible [+]
exort — exhort [1+]
exortashun — exhortation
exoteric
exotic /ness
expand [1]
expans *e* /ion
expanshun — expansion
expansive /ly/ness
expatriat *e* [2] /ion
expect [1] /ation
expectanc *e* /y
expectans — expectance [+]
expectant /ly
expedien *ce* /t
expedienc *y* /ies
expediens — expedience [+]
expedishun — expedition
expedishus — expeditious [+]
expedite [2] /r
expedition
expeditious /ly/ness
expel [3]
expend [1] /iture
expendab *le* /ility
expendabul — expendable [+]
expendicher — expenditure
expens *e* /ive
experience [2]
experiens — experience [2]
experiment [1] /ation
experimental /ly
expert /ise/ly
expiat *e* [2] /ion
expir *e* [2] /ation/y
explain [1] /able
explanashun — explanation [+]
explanat *ion* /ory
explane — explain [1+]
explanetrey — explanatory

expletive
explicabl *e* /y
explicabul — explicable [+]
explicit /ly
explisit — explicit [+]
explode [2]
exploit [1] /ation/er
explorashun — exploration [+]
explorat *ion* /ory
explore [2] /r
exploshun — explosion [+]
explos *ion* /ive
exponent
export [1] /ation/er
expos *e* [2] /ure
exposher — exposure
expostulat *e* [2] /ion
expound [1]
expreshun — expression [+]
expresibul — expressible [+]
expresive — expressive [+]
express [1]
expressibl *e* /y
expression /less
expressive /ly
expresso — espresso
expropriat *e* [2] /ion/or
expulsion
expunge [2]
expurgate [2]
expurgat *ion* /ory
expurt — expert [+]
exquisite /ly/ness
exseed — exceed [1+]
exsel — excel [3]
exselence — excellence [+]
exselens — excellence [+]
ex-service
exstravagans — extravagance [+]
exsurpt — excerpt [1]
extant
extasey — ecstasy [+]
extatic — ecstatic [+]
extempor *e* /aneous
extemporis *e* [2] /ation

111

extend [1] /ible	
extenshun	extension
extension	
extensive /ly	
extent	
extenuat e [2] /ion	
exterier	exterior
exterior	
exterminat e [2] /ion/or	
external /ly	
exterpate	extirpate [2]+
extinct /ion	
extinguish [1] /er	
extingwish	extinguish [1]+
extirpat e [2] /ion	
extol [3]	
extorshun	extortion +
extort [1]	
extortion /ate/er/ist	
extra	
extract [1] /able/ion/or	
extradishun	extradition
extradit e [2] /able/ion	
extramural	
extraneous /ly/ness	
extranius	extraneous +
extraordinar y /ily	
extra-sensory	
extravagan ce /t/tly	
extravaganza	
extrawdinrey	extraordinary +
extream	extreme +
extreme /ly	
extremist	
extremit y /ies	
extricable	
extricabul	extricable
extricat e [2] /ion	
extrordinary	extraordinary +
extrover t /sion	
exuberan ce /t	
exuberans	exuberance +
exud e [2] /ation	
exult [1] /ant/ation	
exume	exhume [2]+

eye [2]*† /ball/brow/s *† †(sight)	
eyeglass /es	
eyelash /es	
eyelet * (hole for lace)	
eyelet	islet *
eye lid /sight	
eye-opener	
eye-witness	
eyrie * (bird's nest)	
eyrie	eerie *
eze	ease [2]
ezel	easel
ezier	easier
ezy	easy +

F

fable /d	
fabric	
fabricat e [2] /ion/or	
fabul	fable +
fabulous /ly	
fabulus	fabulous +
façade	
face [2] /less	
faceshus	facetious +
facet /ed	
facetious /ly	
facia * (shop-front)	
facia	fascia *
facial /ly	
facile	
facilitat e [2] /ion	
facilit y /ies	
facshun	faction +
facshus	factious
facsimile /s	
fact /ual/ually	
factio n /us	
factishus	factitious
factitious	
factor	
factor y /ies	

facultative		fall /en/er/ing/-out	
facult y /ies		fallacious	
fad /dish/dy		fallac y /ies	
fade [2]		fallasey	fallacy +
faec es /al		fallib le /ility	
faeton	phaeton	fallibul	fallible +
fag [3] /-end		fallow [1]	
faggot /-stitch		fallus	phallus
fagot	faggot +	falout	fall-out
Fahrenheit		falow	fallow [1]
fail [1] /ure		fals	false +
failier	failure	false /hood/ly/r/st	
faim	fame [2]	falsetto /s	
faimus	famous +	falsif y [4] /ication/ier	
fain ★ (glad)		falsit y /ies	
fain	feign [1]★	falt	fault [1]+
faint [1]★ (unconscious)		falter [1]	
faint	feint [1]★	falure	failure
faint-hearted		falus	phallus
fair [1]★ (beauty, just)		fame [2]	
fair	fare [2]★	familey	family +
fair er /est/way		familiar /ity	
fairie	fairy +	familiaris e [2] /ation	
fairwell	farewell	familiaritey	familiarity
fair y /ies		familier	familiar +
fairy land /-tale		famil y /ies	
fait	fate [2]★	famine	
faitful	fateful +	famish [1]	
faith /ful/fully		famous /ly/ness	
faithless /ly		famus	famous +
fake [2] /r ★ (deceiver)		fan [3] /-belt	
fakir ★ (holy man)		fanatic /al/ally/ism	
fal	fall +	fanatisism	fanaticism
falacious	fallacious	fanci er /est/ly/ness	
falacy	fallacy +	fanciful /ly	
falanks	phalanx +	fanc y [4] /ies	
falanx	phalanx +	fane	feign [1]★
falasey	fallacy +	fanfair	fanfare
falashus	fallacious	fanfare	
falcon /er/ry		fansie	fancy [4]+
fale	fail [1]+	fansier	fancier +
falibility	fallibility	fansiful	fanciful +
falible	fallible +	fansy	fancy [4]+
falibul	fallible +	fant	faint [1]★
falic	phallic +	fantasey	fantasy +

fantasia		fascia ★ (architecture)	
fantasm	phantasm	fascia	facia ★
fantasmagoria	phantasmagoria +	fascinat e ² /ion	
fantastic /ally		fascis m /t	
fantas y /ies		fase	face ²+
fantharted	faint-hearted	fase	phase ²
fantom	phantom	fasees	fasces
far /-fetched/-flung		fasen	fasten ¹+
farad /ay		fasener	fastener
farc e ² /ical/ically		faseshus	facetious +
fare ²★ (get along)		faset	facet +
fare	fair ¹★	fasetious	facetious +
Farenheight	Fahrenheit	fasha	facia ★
Farenhite	Fahrenheit	fasha	fascia ★
farer	fairer +	fashal	facial +
farewell		fashion ¹ /able/ably	
fariland	fairyland +	fashism	fascism +
faringeal	pharyngeal +	fashist	fascist
faringitis	pharyngitis	fashon	fashion ¹+
farinks	pharynx	fashonable	fashionable
farinx	pharynx	fashonabul	fashionable
farisee	Pharisee +	fasile	facile
faritale	fairy-tale	fasilitate	facilitate ²+
farm ¹ /er/house		fasilitey	facility +
farmacist	pharmacist	fasinashun	fascination
farmacologey	pharmacology +	fasinate	fascinate ²+
farmacopea	pharmacopoeia	fasination	fascination
farmacy	pharmacy +	fast ¹	
farmasey	pharmacy +	fasten ¹ /er	
farmasist	pharmacist	fastidious /ly/ness	
farmasutic	pharmaceutic +	fastidius	fastidious +
farm stead /yard		fat ³ /ness/ter/test/ty	
faro	Pharaoh	fatal /ism/ly	
farse	farce ²+	fatalist /ic/ically	
farshal	farcical	fatalit y /ies	
far-sighted		fate ²★ (destiny)	
farth er ★† /est		fate	fête ²★
†(distant)		fateeg	fatigue ²
farther	father ¹★	fateful /ly	
farthing /gale		faten	fatten ¹
faryngeal	pharyngeal +	fath	faith +
faryngitis	pharyngitis	father ¹★ (parent)	
farynx	pharynx	father	farther ★+
fasade	façade	father hood /land	
fasces		father(s)-in-law	

father *less* /ly	
fathom [1] /able	
fatig	fatigue [2]
fatigue [2]	
faton	phaeton
fatten [1]	
fatuous /ly	
fatuus	fatuous +
faty	fatty
faucet	
fault [1] /ily/less/y	
faun ★ (Roman god)	
faun	fawn [1]★
fauna	
faux pas	
faver	favour [1]+
faverable	favourable
faverabul	favourable
faverit	favourite +
faveritism	favouritism
favour [1] /able/ably	
favourit *e* /ism	
favrable	favourable
fawn [1]★ (young deer)	
fawn	faun ★
fawna	fauna
fay ★ (fairy)	
fay	fey ★
fayton	phaeton
fea	fee
feacher	feature [2]+
fealty	
fear [1] /less/some	
fearful /ly	
feasable	feasible +
feasib *le* /ility/ly	
feasibul	feasible +
feast [1]	
feat ★ (act)	
feat	feet ★
feather [1] /weight/y	
featherbed /ding	
feature [2] /less	
February	
Febuary	February

febus	Phoebus
feces	faeces +
fech	fetch [1]
feckless	
fecund /ity	
fed /-up	
federal /ism/ist/ly	
federalis *e* [2] /ation	
federat *e* [2] /ion	
fee	
feeble /r/st	
feebul	feeble +
feed /back/er/ing	
feef	fief
feel /er/ing	
feeld	field [1]+
feend	fiend +
feest	feast [1]
feet ★ (pl. of foot)	
feet	feat ★
feetle	foetal
feetus	foetus +
feif	fief
feign [1]★ (invent)	
feign	fain ★
feild	field [1]+
feildmarshal	field-marshal
feind	fiend +
feint [1]★ (pretend)	
feint	faint [1]★
fekless	feckless
fekund	fecund +
fekunditey	fecundity
fel	fell
fela	fellah
felial	filial +
felicitat *e* [2] /ion	
felicit *y* /ous	
feline	
felisitate	felicitate [2]+
felisitey	felicity +
felisitus	felicitous
fell	
fellah	
fellow /ship	

115

felon /ious		fertil e /ity	
felon y /ies		fertilis e [2] /ation/er	
felow	fellow [+]	fertiv	furtive [+]
felt		ferule	ferrule
femail	female	ferus	ferrous
female		ferven cy /t	
femer	femur	ferver	fervour
feminin e /ity		fervour	
feminis m /t		fery	ferry [4+]
femur		fes	fez
fence [2] /r		fesant	pheasant
fenel	fennel	fesees	faeces [+]
feniks	phoenix	fesible	feasible[+]
fenix	phoenix	fesibul	feasible [+]
fennel		fester [1]	
fenobarbitone	phenobarbitone	festiv e /al	
fenol	phenol	festivit y /ies	
fenomenon	phenomenon [+]	festoon [1]	
fenomina	phenomena	fetch [1]	
fenominal	phenomenal [+]	fête [2★] (festival)	
fense	fence [2+]	fête	fate [2★]
fer	fir ★	feter	fetter [1]
fer	fur ★	fether	feather [1+]
feret	ferret [1]	fetherbed	featherbed [+]
feric	ferric [+]	fetherwait	featherweight
ferie	ferry [4+]	fetid	
feris wheel	Ferris-wheel	fetish /ism/ist	
ferite	ferrite	fetlock	
ferl	furl [1]	fetter [1]	
ferlong	furlong	fettle [2]	
ferment [1] /ation		fetul	fettle [2]
fermium		feud [1]	
fern /ery		feudal /ism	
fernis	furnace	fever /ed/ish	
feroci ous /ty		few	
feroshus	ferocious [+]	fewdal	feudal [+]
ferositey	ferocity	fewdalism	feudalism
ferous	ferrous	fey ★ (fated to die)	
ferret [1]		fey	fay ★
ferr ic /ous		fez	
Ferris-wheel		fezant	pheasant
ferrite		fial	file [2★+]
ferrule		fial	phial ★
ferr y [4] /ies		fiancé /e (fem.)	
ferthest	furthest	fiansay	fiancé [+]

fiasco /s
fib³ /ber
fiber   fibre +
fibr e /ous
fibreglass
fibrus   fibrous
fibula
fickle /ness
ficshun   fiction +
fiction /al
fictishus   fictitious +
fictitious /ly/ness
ficul   fickle +
fiddl e² /er/y
fiddlesticks
fidelity
fidget¹ /iness/y
fidle   fiddle²+
fidul   fiddle²+
fie
fief
field¹ /-day/er
field-marshal
fiend /ish
fierce /ly/ness/r/st
fierey   fiery +
fierse   fierce +
fier y /ier/iest/ily
fife
fifteen /th
fiftey   fifty +
fifth
fift y /ies/ieth
figer   figure²+
figerativ   figurative +
figerhead   figurehead
figerhed   figurehead
figet   fidget¹+
fight /er/ing
figment
figurative /ly
figure² /head
fiks   fix¹+
fiksashun   fixation +
fiksation   fixation +

fiksativ   fixative
fikscher   fixture
filament
filander   philander¹+
filanthropey   philanthropy +
filanthropic   philanthropic
filanthropist   philanthropist
filantropy   philanthropy +
filarmonic   philharmonic
filateley   philately +
filatelist   philatelist
filch¹
file²★ (tool, folder) /r
file   phial ★
filet   fillet¹
filharmonic   philharmonic
filial /ly
filibuster¹
filie   filly +
filigree
filip   fillip¹
filistine   Philistine
fill¹ /er
fillet¹
fillip¹
fill y /ies
film¹ /y
film-star
film-strip
filologey   philology +
filosofer   philosopher +
filosofey   philosophy
filosofical   philosophical +
filosofise   philosophise²
filosopher   philosopher +
filosophical   philosophical +
filosophise   philosophise²
filosophy   philosophy
filter¹★ (pass, strainer)
filter   philtre ★
filth /ier/iest/ily/iness/y
filtrat e² /ion
filum   phylum
fily   filly +
fin /ned/ny

final ★ (at last)
finale ★ (the end)
finalis *e* ² /t
finalit *y* /ies
finally
financ *e* ² /ier
financial /ly
finans   finance ²⁺
finanshul   financial ⁺
finansier   financier
finch /es
find /er/ing
fine ² /r/ry/st
finerey   finery
finess   finesse
finesse
finger ¹ /print/tips
finicky
finikey   finicky
finish ¹ /er
finite
fiord
fir ★ (tree)
fir   fur ★
fire ² /arm
fire-brigade
fire-engine
fire-escape
fire-extinguisher
firefl *y* /ies
fire *place* /work
firm ¹ /er/est/ness
firmament
first /-aid/-class/-rate
firth
firy   fiery ⁺
fiscal /ism/ly
fiseek   physique ★
fish ¹ /ier/iest/iness/y
fisher   fissure
fisherm *an* /en (pl.)
fisher *y* /ies
fish- *hook* /monger
fishmunger   fishmonger
fishun   fission ⁺

fisic   physic ★
fisic   physique ★
fisical   physical ⁺
fisician   physician
fisicist   physicist
fisics   physics
fisile   fissile
fisiologey   physiology ⁺
fision   fission ⁺
fisionomey   physiognomy
fisiotherapey   physiotherapy
fisiotherapist   physiotherapist ⁺
fisique   physique ★
fisishun   physician
fisisist   physicist
fissile
fission /able
fissure
fit ³ /ment/ness/ter/test
fite   fight ⁺
fitful /ly
five /pence/r
fix ¹ /edly
fixat *ion* /ive
fixcher   fixture
fixture
fiy   fie
fizle   fizzle ²
fizul   fizzle ²
fizz ¹ /y
fizzle ²
fjord
flabbergast ¹
flabb *y* /ier/iest/iness
flabergast   flabbergast ¹
flabie   flabby ⁺
flaby   flabby⁺
flaccid /ity/ness
flag ³ /ship/staff
flagellate ²
flagon
flagrancy
flagransey   flagrancy
flagrant /ly
flail ¹

flair ★ (instinct)		fleat	fleet [1]
flair	flare [2]★	flebitis	phlebitis
flak *e* [2] /iness/y		fled	
flaks	flax [+]	fledgling	
flaksen	flaxen	flee ★ (run) /ing	
flaksid	flaccid [+]	flee	flea ★
flamable	flammable	fleec *e* [2] /y	
flamabul	flammable	flees	fleece [2+]
flamboiant	flamboyant	fleet [1]	
flamboyan *ce* /cy/t		flegling	fledgling
flamboyans	flamboyance [+]	flegm	phlegm [+]
flame [2]		flegmatic	phlegmatic
flamingo /es		fleks	flex [1]
flammable		fleksible	flexible [+]
flammabul	flammable	fleksibul	flexible [+]
flanel	flannel [3+]	flem	phlegm [+]
flange [2]		Flemish	
flank [1]		fler de lis	fleur-de-lis
flanle	flannel [3+]	flert	flirt [1+]
flannel [3] /ette/graph		flesh /iness/y	
flanul	flannel [3+]	fleur-de-lis	
flap [3] /per		flew ★ (flight)	
flare [2]★ (light)		flew	flu ★
flare	flair ★	flew	flue ★
flash [1] /ier/iest/ily/y		flex [1]	
flash *back* /light		flexib *le* /ility/ly	
flask		flexibul	flexible [+]
flat /let/ly/test		fli	fly [+]
flaten	flatten [1]	flick [1]	
flater	flatter [1+]	flicker [1]	
flatten [1]		flier	flyer
flatter [1] /er		flight /iness/y	
flatulen *ce* /t		flimsie	flimsy [+]
flatulens	flatulence [+]	flims *y* /ier/iest/ily/iness	
flaunt [1]		flinch [1]	
flautist		fling	
flaver	flavour [1]	flint /y	
flavour [1]		flipancy	flippancy [+]
flaw [1]★ (blemish) /less		flipansey	flippancy [+]
flaw	floor [1]★	flipant	flippant
flax /en		fliper	flipper
flay [1]		flippan *cy* /t	
flea ★ (insect)		flipper	
flea	flee ★[+]	flirt [1] /ation/atious	
flea-bite		flit [3]	

flite	flight +	flower [1]★ (plant) /y	
flo	floe ★	flower	flour [1]★
flo	flow [1]★+	flownder	flounder [1]
float [1]		flownse	flounce [2]
flock [1] /s ★ (groups)		flowt	flout [1]
flocks	phlox ★	flox	phlox ★
floe ★ (ice)		flu ★ (cold)	
floem	phloem	flu	flew ★
flog [3]		flu	flue ★
flood [1] /-gate/lit		fluctuashun	fluctuation
floodlight /ing		fluctuat e [2] /ion	
flooid	fluid +	flud	flood [1]+
floor [1]★ (in room)		fludlight	floodlight +
floor	flaw [1]★+	fludlite	floodlight +
flooride	fluoride +	flue ★ (pipe)	
floorine	fluorine	flue	flew ★
floot	flute [2]	flue	flu ★
flop [3] /pily/py		fluen cy /t	
flora /l/lly		fluff /iness/y	
Florentine		fluid /ity	
florescen ce ★† /t ★†		fluke [2]	
†(flowering)		fluks	flux
florescence	fluorescence ★+	flummox [1]	
floresent	florescent ★	flumuks	flummox [1]
florid		flumux	flummox [1]
floridate	fluoridate [2]+	flung	
florin		fluorescen ce★(light)/t ★	
florist		fluoridat e [2] /ion	
floss /y		fluori de /ne	
flotashun	flotation	flurie	flurry [4]+
flotation		flurish	flourish [1]
flote	float [1]	flurr y [4] /ies	
flotilla		flurt	flirt [1]+
flotsam		flurtashun	flirtation
flotsum	flotsam	flurtation	flirtation
flounce [2]		flury	flurry [4]+
flounder [1]		flush [1]	
flouns	flounce [2]	fluster [1]	
flour [1]★ (powder)		flute [2]	
flour	flower [1]★+	flutter [1]	
flourey	flowery	fluvial	
flourish [1]		flux	
flout [1]		fl y /ies/yer/ying	
flow [1]★ (to move) /n		flycatcher	
flow	floe ★	flylea f /ves (pl.)	

fly *weight* /wheel		fonograph	phonograph +
fo	foe +	fonographic	phonographic
foal [1]		fonologey	phonology +
foam [1]		font	
fob [3]		fony	phony
fobia	phobia	food /s	
focal		fool [1] /proof	
focus [1] /er		foolhard *y* /iness	
fodder [1]		foolscap	
foder	fodder [1]	foot [1] /fall/hold/note	
foe /s		football /er	
foet *us* /al		foot *path* /print	
fog [3] /horn		foot *sore* /step/stool	
fogg *y* /ier/iest/ily/iness		fop /pish	
foible		for ★ (on behalf of)	
foibul	foible	for	fore ★
foier	foyer	for	four ★+
foil [1]		for ever	
foist [1]		forage [2] /r	
foks	fox +	foram *en* /ina (pl.)	
fold [1] /er		forarm	forearm [1]
fole	foal [1]	forbade	
foliage		forbarance	forbearance
foliat *e* [2] /ion		forbare	forbear +
folie	folly +	forbear /ance/ing	
foliidge	foliage	forbid /den/ding	
folio [1] /s		forbode	forebode [2]+
folk /-dance/-song		forbore	
folklor *e* /ist		forcasel	forecastle
follow [1] /er		forcast	forecast +
foll *y* /ies		forcastle	forecastle
folow	follow [1]+	forc *e* [2] /ible/ibly	
foly	folly +	forceful /ly/ness	
fome	foam [1]	forceps	
foment [1] /ation/er		forclose	foreclose [2]+
fon	phon ★	ford [1] /able	
fond /er/est/ly/ness		fore ★ (golf)	
fondant		fore	four ★+
fondle [2]		forearm [1]	
fondul	fondle [2]	forebode [2] /r	
fone	phone [2]★	forecast /er	
fonetic	phonetic +	forecastle	
fonie	phony	foreclos *e* [2] /ure	
fonograf	phonograph +	fored	forehead
fonografic	phonographic	forefathers	

121

forefinger
forefoot
forefront
forego ★(precede)/ing ★/ne ★
foregh   forgo ★+
foreground
forehand
forehead
foreign /er/ness
foreknowledge
foreland
foreleg
forelock
forem *an* /en (pl.)
foremast
foremost
foren   foreign +
forener   foreigner
forenoledge   foreknowledge
forensic
forerunner
foresail
foresaw
foresee /able/ing/n
foreshadow [1]
foreshorten [1]
foresight
foresite   foresight
foreskin
forest [1] /ation/er/ry
forestall [1]
foretaste [2]
foretell
forethought
foretold
forewarn [1]
foreword ★ (preface)
foreword   forward [1]★
forfathers   forefathers
forfeit [1] /ure
forficher   forfeiture
forfinger   forefinger
forfit   forfeit [1]+
forfiture   forfeiture
forfoot   forefoot

forfront   forefront
forfrunt   forefront
forgather [1]
forgave
forge [2] /r
forger *y* /ies
forget /table/ting
forgetful /ness
forget-me-not
forgiv *e* /able/eness/ing
forgo ★(waive)/ing★/ne★
forgo   forego ★+
forgot /ten
forground   foreground
forhand   forehand
forhead   forehead
forhed   forehead
forige   forage [2]+
forin   foreign +
fork [1]
forland   foreland
forleg   foreleg
forlock   forelock
forlorn
form [1] /al/ation
formalis *e* [2] /ation
formalit *y* /ies
formally ★†
  †(conventionally)
formally   formerly ★
forman   foreman +
format
formative
former /ly ★†
  †(before now)
formerly   formally ★
formic
formidabl *e* /y
formidabul   formidable +
formost   foremost
formula /e/s (pls.)
formulat *e* [2] /ion
forn   faun ★
forn   fawn [1]★
fornicat *e* [2] /ion

fornolidge	foreknowledge	forward	foreword ★
forruner	forerunner	forwarn	forewarn [1]
forsable	forcible	forwent	
forsail	foresail	forword	foreword ★
forsak e /en/ing		fosfate	phosphate
forsaw	foresaw	fosforesce	phosphoresce [2+]
forse	force [2+]	fosforescent	phosphorescent
forsee	foresee [+]	fosforess	phosphoresce [2+]
forseps	forceps	fosforus	phosphorous ★+
forsful	forceful [+]	fosforus	phosphorus ★
forshadow	foreshadow [1]	fosil	fossil
forshorten	foreshorten [1]	fosilise	fossilise [2+]
forsible	forcible	fosphate	phosphate
forsite	foresight	fossil	
forsithia	forsythia	fossilis e [2] /ation	
forskin	foreskin	foster [1] /-father/-mother	
forsook		foto	photo [+]
forstall	forestall [1]	fotocopy	photocopy [+]
forsythia		fotoelectric	photo-electric
fort ★ (military)		fotofinish	photo-finish
fort	fought ★	fotogenic	photogenic
fortaste	foretaste [2]	fotograf	photograph [1+]
forte ★ (strong point)		fotografey	photography
forteen	fourteen [+]	fotograph	photograph [1+]
fortel	foretell	fotometer	photometer [+]
forth ★ (forward)		fotometrey	photometry
forth	fourth ★	foton	photon
forthcoming		fotosinthesis	photosynthesis
forthort	forethought	fotostat	photostat
forth right /with		fototropism	phototropism
fortie	forty [+]	fought ★ (did fight)	
fortif y [4] /ication/ier		foul [1★] (dirty) /ly/ness	
Fortin barometer		foul	fowl [1★+]
fortissimo		found [1] /ation/er/ling	
fortitude		foundr y /ies	
fortnight /ly		fount	
fortnite	fortnight [+]	fountain	
fortold	foretold	four ★ (number) /th ★	
fortress		four fold /some	
fortuitous /ly		fourt	fort ★
fortuitus	fortuitous [+]	fourt	fought ★
fortun e [2] /ate/ately		fourteen /th	
fort y /ies/ieth		fourth	forth ★
forum		fourty	forty [+]
forward [1★] (advance)		fow	foe [+]

123

fowl [1]* (bird) /er		frawd	fraud
fowl	foul [1]*+	frawdulence	fraudulence +
fownd	found [1]+	frawdulens	fraudulence +
fowndashun	foundation	frawdulent	fraudulent
fowndation	foundation	frawt	fraught
fowndrey	foundry +	fray [1] /s * (fights)	
fownt	fount	frayl	frail +
fowntain	fountain	frays	phrase [2]*+
fox-hunt /ing		freak [1] /ish	
fox-terrier		freckle [2]	
foyble	foible	frecul	freckle [2]
foyer		free /d/ing/ly/r/st	
fracshun	fraction +	freedom	
fracshus	fractious	free-hand	
fraction /al/ally		freehold /er	
fractious		freek	freak [1]+
fracture [2]		freelance [2]	
fraeltey	frailty	freelans	freelance [2]
fragile /ly		freemason /ry	
fragility		free-wheel [1]	
fragment [1] /ary/ation		freez e * (cold) /er/ing	
fragran ce /t		freeze	frieze *
fragrans	fragrance +	freight /age/er	
frail /ty/ties		freind	friend +
frait	freight +	frekwency	frequency +
frame [2] /work		frekwensey	frequency +
franc * (money)		frekwent	frequent [1]+
franchise [2]		French /man/woman	
francium		frend	friend +
frank [1]* (blunt) /ly/ness		frendly	friendly +
frankfurter		frendship	friendship
frankincense		frenetic	phrenetic
frankium	francium	frenologey	phrenology +
frantic /ally		frenologist	phrenologist
frase	phrase [2]*+	frenzie	frenzy +
frasologey	phraseology	frenz y /ies/ied	
frate	freight +	frequenc y /ies	
fraternal /ly		frequensey	frequency +
fraternis e [2] /ation		frequent [1] /er/ly	
fraternit y /ies		fresco /es	
fraud		fresh /er/ly/ness	
fraudulen ce /t		freshen [1]	
fraudulens	fraudulence +	fresko	fresco +
fraught		fret [3] /ful/fully	
fraut	fraught	fret -saw /work	

Freudian		frostbit *e* /ten	
fri	fry [4]	froth [1] /iness/y	
friable		frown [1]	
friabul	friable	frowzie	frowzy [+]
friar		frowz *y* /ier/iest	
fricshun	friction [+]	froze /n	
friction /al		frugal /ity/ly	
friend /ship		fruishun	fruition
friendl *y* /ier/iest/iness		fruit [1] /ion	
frier	friar	fruiterer	
frieze ★ (ornament)		fruitful /ly/ness	
frigate		fruitless /ly/ness	
fright		fruit *y* /ier/iest/iness	
frighten [1]		frump /ish	
frightful /ly/ness		frunt	front [1+]
frigid /ity		fruntal	frontal
frill [1]		fruntier	frontier
fringe [2]		fruntispiece	frontispiece
fripper *y* /ies		frustrat *e* [2] /ion	
frisk [1] /ily/iness/y		frut	fruit [1+]
frite	fright	fruterer	fruiterer
friteful	frightful [+]	frutful	fruitful [+]
friten	frighten [1]	frutie	fruity [+]
friter	fritter [1+]	frutier	fruiterer
fritter [1] /er		fry [4]	
frivol [3] /ous		fu	few
frivolit *y* /ies		fucher	future [+]
frivolus	frivolous	fucherist	futurist [+]
frizul	frizzle [2+]	fucheristic	futuristic
frizz [1] /y		fuchsia	
frizzl *e* [2] /y		fudal	feudal [+]
frock [1]		fudalism	feudalism
frog /man/men (pl.)		fuddle [2]	
froidian	Freudian	fude	feud [1]
frolic /some		fudge [2]	
frolick *ed* /ing		fudul	fuddle [2]
front [1] /age/al/ally		fuel [3]	
frontier		fug /gy	
frontispiece		fugitive	
froogal	frugal [+]	ful	full [+]
frooishun	fruition	fulblooded	full-blooded
frooition	fruition	fulbluded	full-blooded
froot	fruit [1+]	fulcrum	
frootful	fruitful [+]	fulfil [3] /ment	
frost [1] /ily/y		full /-blooded/er/-time	

125

fulscap	foolscap	furst	first [+]
fulsome /ly/ness		furstaid	first-aid
fulsum	fulsome [+]	furstrate	first-rate
fumble [2] /r		furth	firth
fumbul	fumble [2+]	further [1] /more/most	
fume [2]		furtherance	
fumigat e [2] /ion/or		furthest	
fun /nily/ny		furtive /ly	
funcshun	function [1+]	fur y /ies	
funcshunrey	functionary	furze	
function [1] /ary		fus	fuss [1+]
functional /ly		fus e [2] /ion	
fund [1]		fuselage	
fundamental /ly		fusha	fuchsia
funel	funnel [3]	fusib le /ility	
funer al /eal		fusibul	fusible [+]
fung us /i (pl.)		fusie	fussy
funicular		fusier	fussier [+]
funiculer	funicular	fusilade	fusillade
funily	funnily	fusilage	fuselage
funk [1]		fusilier	
funnel [3]		fusilige	fuselage
funn y /ier/iest/ily		fusillade	
fur ★ (coat)		fuss [1] /y	
fur	fir ★	fussie	fussy
furie	furry [+]	fussi er /est/ly/ness	
furie	fury [+]	fustie	fusty [+]
furier	furrier	fust y /ier/iest/ily/iness	
furious /ly		fusy	fussy
furius	furious [+]	futil e /ity	
furl [1]		futur e /ism/ity	
furlong		futurist /ic	
furm	firm [1+]	fuzz /ily/iness	
furmament	firmament	fwayay	foyer
furment	ferment [1+]	fyord	fiord
furmentashun	fermentation	fyord	fjord
furmentation	fermentation	fysical	physical [+]
furn	fern [+]	fysically	physically
furnace		fysician	physician
furnicher	furniture	fysicist	physicist
furnis	furnace	fysick	physic ★
furnish [1] /er		fysick	physique ★
furniture		fysicks	physics
furrow [1]		fysicley	physically
furr y /ier/iest/iness		fysiologey	physiology [+]

fysionomey	physiognomy	galery	gallery +
fysiotherapey	physiotherapy	Galic	Gaelic *
fysiotherapist	physiotherapist +	Galic	Gallic *
fysique	physique *	galie	galley
fysishun	physician	galium	gallium
fysisist	physicist	galivant	gallivant 1
		gall 1	
		gallant /ry	
		galler y /ies	
G		galley	
		Gallic *†	
gabardine		†(of Gaul, French)	
gabble 2* (talk) /r		gallic	Gaelic *
gable * (on roof)		gallium	
gabul	gabble 2*+	gallivant 1	
gabul	gable *	gallon	
gad 3 /about		gallop 1 /er	
gadget /ry		gallows	
gadolinium		galon	gallon
gael	gale	galop	gallop 1+
Gaelic * (language)		galore	
gaf	gaffe	galoshes	
gaffe		galows	gallows
gag 3		galvanic	
gaga		galvanis e 2 /ation/m	
gage	gauge 2+	galvanometer	
gagercounter	Geiger counter	galy	galley
gaget	gadget +	gambit	
gaggle 2		gamble 2* (games) /r	
gagit	gadget +	gambol 3* (frolic)	
gagul	gaggle 2	game /-bird/-cock	
gai ety /ly		gamekeeper	
gain 1 /er/ful/fully		gamesmanship	
gait * (walk)		gamie	game +
gait	gate 2*+	gaming	
gaiter /ed		gammon	
gaitey	gaiety +	gamon	gammon
gal	gall 1	gamut	
gala		gamy	game +
galactic		gander 1	
galaksey	galaxy +	ganet	gannet
galant	gallant +	gang 1 /er	
galantrey	gallantry	gangling	
galaw	galore	gang-plank	
galax y /ies		gangreen	gangrene +
gale			

127

gangren *e* /ous
gangrenus — gangrenous
gangster /ism
gangway
gannet
gaol [1]★ (prison) /bird/er
gape [2]
garage [2]

garantee — guarantee ★+
garantor — guarantor +
garb [1]
garbage

garbige — garbage
garble [2]

garbul — garble [2]
gard — guard [1+]
garden [1] /er
gardenia

gardian — guardian +
gardroom — guard-room
gardsman — guardsman
garet — garret
gargantuan
gargle [2]

gargoil — gargoyle
gargoyle

gargul — gargle [2]
garish

garison — garrison [1]
garland [1]
garlic /ky
garment [1]
garner [1]
garnet
garnish [1]

garnit — garnet
garot — garrotte [2]
garret
garrison [1]

garrot — garrotte [2]
garrotte [2]
garrulous /ly
garter /ed

garulus — garrulous +
gas [3] /eous/es/-mask

gash [1]
gasha — geisha
gasket
gaslight
gaslite — gaslight
gasoline
gasometer
gasp [1]

gastley — ghastly +
gastri *c* /tis
gastronom *y* /ic/ical
gate [2]★ (entrance) /way
gate — gait ★
gate-crash [1]
gater — gaiter +
gather [1] /er
gauche
gaudie — gaudy +
gaud *y* /ily/iness
gauge [2] /r
gaunt /let
gauze
gave
gawdie — gaudy +
gawk [1] /iness
gawl — gall [1]
gawnt — gaunt +
gawntlet — gauntlet
gawse — gorse
gay /er/est
gayety — gaiety +
Gaylic — Gaelic ★
gayn — gain [1+]
gaysha — geisha
gaze [2] /r
gazel — gazelle
gazelle
gazer — geyser
gazet — gazette [2]
gazette [2]
ge gaw — gew-gaw
gear [1] /box
gees — geese
geese (pl. of goose)
Geiger counter

geisha		genus		
gel [3]		geny	genie	
gelatin	gelatine +	geocentric		
gelatin e /ous		geofisical	geophysical	
gelatinus	gelatinous	geofisics	geophysics +	
geld [1]		geofysical	geophysical	
gelignite		geofysics	geophysics +	
gem [3] /my		geografey	geography +	
Gemini		geografic	geographic	
gendarme		geografical	geographical +	
gender [1]		geographical /ly		
gene		geograph y /er/ic		
genealog y /ist		geological /ly		
genee	genie	geolog y /ist		
general /ly		geometrey	geometry	
generalis e [2] /ation		geometric /al/ally		
generalit y /ies		geometry		
generat e [2] /ion/or		geophysic s /al/ist		
generative		geosentric	geocentric	
generic /ally		geranium /s		
generosity		gerd	gird [1]+	
generous /ly/ness		gerder	girder	
generus	generous +	gerdle	girdle [2]	
genetic /ally/s		gerdul	girdle [2]	
geney	genie	geriatric /ian/s		
genial /ity/ly		gerilla	gorilla ★	
genie		gerilla	guerrilla ★	
geniologey	genealogy +	gerkin	gherkin	
genital /s		gerl	girl +	
genitive		gerlish	girlish	
geni us /i/uses (pls.)		germ		
genocide		German		
genoside	genocide	germane		
genre		Germanic		
genteel /ism/ly		germanium		
gentile		germicid e /al		
gentility		germinat e [2] /ion		
gentle [2] /ness/r/st		germiside	germicide +	
gentlem an /en (pl.)		gerontology		
gentrey	gentry	gerth	girth	
gentry		gerund /ive		
gentul	gentle [2]+	gescher	gesture [2]	
gentulman	gentleman +	gess	guess +	
genuin	genuine +	gesswerk	guesswork	
genuine /ly/ness		gesswork	guesswork	

gest	guest ★
gesticulat *e* [2] /ion	
gesture [2]	
get /ting	
getto	ghetto +
gew-gaw	
geyser	
ghastl *y* /ier/iest/iness	
gherkin	
ghetto /s	
ghost [1] /ly	
ghoul /ish	
giant /ess (fem.)	
gibber [1] /ish	
gibbet [1]	
gibbon	
gibe [2]★ (taunt)	
gibe	gybe [2]★
giber	gibber [1]+
giberish	gibberish
gibet	gibbet [1]
giblets	
gibon	gibbon
gidance	guidance
gidans	guidance
gidd *y*/ier/iest/ily/iness	
gide	guide [2]+
gidie	giddy +
gidily	giddily
gidy	giddy +
gift /ed	
gig	
gigantic /ally	
giggle [2] /r	
gigolo	
gigul	giggle [2]+
gil	gill [1]
gild [1]★ (gold cover)	
gild	guild ★
gilder	guilder
Gildhall	Guildhall
gile	guile +
gileless	guileless
gill [1]	
giloteen	guillotine [2]

gilotine	guillotine [2]
gilt ★ (gold leaf)	
gilt	guilt ★
gilt-edged	
giltey	guilty +
gilty	guilty +
gim	gym +
gimick	gimmick +
gimkana	gymkhana
gimlet	
gimmick /ry/y	
gimnasium	gymnasium +
gimnastics	gymnastics
gin [3]	
ginecologey	gynaecology +
ginecologist	gynaecologist
gingam	gingham
ginger [1] /bread/ly	
gingham	
ginie	guinea +
ginifowl	guinea-fowl
ginipig	guinea-pig
ginjer	ginger [1]+
ginjerbred	gingerbread
gipsey	gipsy +
gipsie	gipsy +
gipsum	gypsum
gips *y* /ies	
giraf	giraffe
giraffe	
girashun	gyration
girate	gyrate [2]+
giration	gyration
gird [1] /er	
girdle [2]	
girdul	girdle [2]
girl /hood/ish	
giro ★ (banking)	
giro	gyro ★+
girth	
gise	guise
gist	
gitar	guitar +
gitarist	guitarist
give /n/r	

giving		gliserin	glycerine
Giy Forks	Guy Fawkes	glisten [1]	
gizerd	gizzard	glitter [1]	
gizzard		glo	glow [1]
glacia l /tion		gloaming	
glacier		gloat [1]	
glad /der/dest/ly		glob e /al/ally	
gladden [1]		globe-trott er /ing	
glade		globul e /ar	
gladen	gladden [1]	globuler	globular
gladiater	gladiator	gloming	gloaming
gladiator		gloo	glue [2+]
gladiol us /i (pl.)		gloocose	glucose
glamer	glamour	glooie	gluey
glamerus	glamorous +	gloom /y	
glamoris e [2] /ation		gloomi er /est/ly/ness	
glamorous /ly/ness		glooten	gluten ★+
glamour		glorie	glory [4+]
glance [2]		glorif y [4] /ication	
gland /ular		glorius	glorious
glanduler	glandular	glor y [4] /ies/ious	
glans	glance [2]	glos	gloss [1+]
glare [2]		glosarey	glossary +
glas	glass +	gloss [1] /ier/iest/iness/y	
glashal	glacial +	glossar y /ies	
glasiashun	glaciation	glote	gloat [1]
glasiation	glaciation	glotis	glottis +
glasier	glacier	glott is /al	
glass /es/ily		glove [2] /r	
glassware		glow [1]	
glaswear	glassware	glower [1]	
glaz e [2] /ier		glucose	
glea	glee +	glue [2] /y	
gleam [1]		glum /ly/mer/mest	
glean [1] /er		glut [3]	
glee /ful/fully		glut en ★† /inous★†	
gleem	gleam [1]	†(sticky substance)	
gleen	glean [1+]	gluten	glutton ★+
glib /ber/best/ly		glutinus	glutinous ★
glicerine	glycerine	gluton	glutton ★+
glide [2] /r		glutonus	gluttonous ★
glimmer [1]		glutony	gluttony
glimpse [2]		glutton ★† /ous ★† /y	
glint [1]		†(greedy)	
glisen	glisten [1]	glutton	gluten ★+

131

gluv	glove [2+]
glycerine	
gnarl [1]	
gnash [1]	
gnat	
gnaw [1]	
gnom *e* /ish	
gnu ★ (animal)	
go /er/es/ing	
goad [1]	
go -*ahead* /-kart	
goal ★† /ie/keeper/less	
†(aim, sport)	
goal	gaol [1]★+
goat /ee	
goatherd	
gobble [2] /r	
go-between	
goblet	
goblin	
gobul	gobble [2+]
gocart	go-kart
god /child/like	
god -*daughter* /son	
goddess (fem.)	
gode	goad [1]
god*father* /mother	
god*forsaken* /head	
goggle [2]	
gogul	goggle [2]
goiter	goitre
goitre	
gold /en/finch/fish	
goldsmith	
gole	goal ★+
golf [1] /er	
golie	goalie
golliwog	
gon	gone +
gondol *a* /ier	
gone /r	
gong [1]	
gonoria	gonorrhoea
gonorrhoea	
good /ly/ness/will	

good-bye	
good-humered	good-humoured
good-humoured	
goodie	goody +
good-looking	
good *y* /ies	
gool	ghoul +
goolash	goulash
goolish	ghoulish
goord	gourd
goormand	gourmand +
goormay	gourmet
goose /flesh	
gooseberie	gooseberry +
gooseberr *y* /ies	
Gordian	
Gordyan	Gordian
gor *e* [2] /y	
gorge [2] /r	
gorgeous /ly/ness	
Gorgonzola	
gorgus	gorgeous +
gorilla ★ (ape)	
gorilla	guerrilla ★
gorse	
gosamer	gossamer
gosip	gossip [1+]
gosling	
gospel /ler	
gossamer	
gossip [1] /er/y	
gost	ghost [1+]
gostly	ghostly
got /ten	
gote	goat +
goteherd	goatherd
Gothic	
gouge [2] /r	
goulash	
gourd	
gourmand /ism	
gourmet	
gout /y	
govern [1] /able/ance	
governer	governor +

government /al		granite	
govern*or* /ess (fem.)		grann*y* /ies	
govner	governor +	grant [1]	
gowge	gouge [2+]	granulat *e* [2] /ion	
gown		granul *e* /ar/arity	
gowt	gout +	grany	granny +
grab [3] /ber		grape /fruit/-shot	
grace [2] /less		graph [1]	
graceful /ly		graphic /al/ally	
gracious /ly/ness		graphite	
gradashun	gradation	grapholog *y* /ist	
grad *e* [2] /ation/er		graple	grapple [2]
gradient		grapnel	
gradual /ly		grapple [2]	
graduat *e* [2] /ion/or		grapul	grapple [2]
graf	graph [1]	gras	grass [1+]
graffiti		grase	grace [2+]
grafic	graphic +	grashus	gracious +
graficley	graphically	grasp [1]	
grafite	graphite	grass [1] /es/hopper	
grafiti	graffiti	grasshoper	grasshopper
grafologey	graphology +	grate [2★] (fire) /r	
grafologist	graphologist	grate	great ★+
graft [1] /er		grateful /ly/ness	
grail		gratif *y* [4] /ication	
grain [1]		gratis	
graling	grayling	gratitude	
gramar	grammar +	gratuitey	gratuity +
gramatical	grammatical +	gratuitous /ly/ness	
gramefone	gramophone	gratuitus	gratuitous +
gramer	grammar +	gratuit *y* /ies	
grammar /ian		grave /ly/yard	
grammatical /ly		gravel [3] /ly	
gramophone		gravie	gravy
granar *y* /ies		gravitashun	gravitation +
grand /ee/eur/stand		gravitate [2]	
grandchild /ren (pl.)		gravitation /al	
grand -*daughter* /son		gravity	
grand *father* /mother		gravy	
grandiloquen *ce* /t		gray	grey +
grandios *e* /ity		grayhound	greyhound
grane	grain [1]	grayhownd	greyhound
grange		grayl	grail
granie	granny +	grayling	
granit	granite	grayn	grain [1]

graz *e* ² /ier	
greas *e* ² /y	
greasie	greasy
greasi *er* /est/ly/ness	
great ★ (big) /er/est	
great	grate ²★+
greatful	grateful +
grede	greed +
greed /y	
greedi *er* /est/ly/ness	
green /er/ery/ness	
green *gage* /grocer	
green *horn* /house	
Greenwich mean time	
greese	grease ²+
greesie	greasy
greet ¹	
gref	grief
gregarious /ly/ness	
gregarius	gregarious +
greif	grief
greive	grieve ²+
greivus	grievous
gremlin	
grenad *e* /ier	
grene	green +
grenegage	greengage +
grengroser	greengrocer
grenich	Greenwich +
gresier	greasier +
grete	greet ¹
grevance	grievance
grevans	grievance
greve	grieve ²+
grevus	grievous
grew	
grey /er/est/hound	
grid	
griddle ²	
gridiron	
gridul	griddle ²
grief	
grievance	
grievans	grievance
griev *e* ² /ous/ously	

griffin	
gril	grill ¹+
grill ¹ /-room	
grim /ly/mer/mest/ness	
grimace ²	
grimas	grimace ²
grim *e* ² /ier/iest/iness/y	
grin ³	
grind /er/ing	
grip ³★ (hold)	
grip	gripe ²★
gripe ²★ (colic pain)	
grisel	gristle
grisly ★ (ghastly)	
grisly	gristly ★
grist	
gristle	
gristly ★ (full of gristle)	
grisul	gristle
grit ³ /tily/ty	
grizul	grizzle ²
grizzle ²	
gro	grow +
groan ¹★ (moan)	
groan	grown ★+
grocer ★ (shop) /y/ies	
grocer	grosser ★
grogg *ily* /iness/y	
groin	
grone	groan¹★
grone	grown ★+
groo	grew
grooel	gruel ³
groom ¹	
groop	group ¹
groosum	gruesome +
groov *e* ² /y	
grope ²	
gros	gross ¹+
groser	grocer ★+
groser	grosser ★
groserey	grocery
gross ¹ /er ★ (fatter) /ly	
grotesk	grotesque +
grotesque /ly	

groto — grotto +
grotto /es
ground [1] /less
ground -*swell* /work
group [1]
grouse [2] /r
grove
grovel [3] /ler
grow /er/ing
growl [1] /er
grown *† /-up
  †(matured)
grownd — ground [1]+
growndswell — ground-swell +
growse — grouse [2]+
growth
grub [3] /by
grubbi *er* /est/ly/ness
grudge [2]
gruel [3]
gruesome /ly/ness
gruf — gruff +
gruff /er/est
gruge — grudge [2]
grumble [2] /r
grumbul — grumble [2]+
grumpie — grumpy +
grump *y* /ily/iness
grunt [1] /er
grusome — gruesome +
grusum — gruesome +
gruyare — gruyère
gruyère
guano
guarantee ★ (pledge) /d/ing
guarant *or* /y ★ (undertaking)
guard [1] /sman
guardian /ship
guard-room
guava
guerrilla ★ (war)
guerrilla — gorilla ★
guess /ing/work
guessed ★ (estimated)
guest ★ (visitor)

gufaw — guffaw [1]
guffaw [1]
guid *e* [2] /ance
guild ★ (association)
guild — gild [1]★
guilder
Guildhall
guile /ful/less
guillotine [2]
guilt ★ (law-breaking)
guilt *y* /ier/iest/ily
guinea /-fowl/-pig
guise ★ (pretence)
guitar /ist
gul — gull [1]
gulash — goulash
gulet — gullet
gulf [1]
Gulf-stream
gulible — gullible +
gulibul — gullible +
gulie — gully [4]+
gull [1]
gullet
gullib *le* /ility
gull *y* [4] /ies
gulp [1]
guly — gully [4]+
gum [3] /boil/my/-tree
gumption
gumshun — gumption
gun [3] /powder
gunl — gunwale
gunner /y
gunwale
gurgle [2]
gurgul — gurgle [2]
gush [1]
gust [1]
gusto
gut [3]
guter — gutter +
guteral — guttural +
gutersnipe — guttersnipe
gutter /snipe

135

guttural /ly	
guvern	govern [1]+
guvernable	governable
guvernabul	governable
guvernance	governance
guvernans	governance
guverness	governess
guvernment	government +
guvnable	governable
guvner	governor +
guy [1] /s * (effigies)	
Guy Fawkes	
guzul	guzzle [2]+
guzzle [2] /r	
gwano	guano
gwave	guava
gybe [2]* (sailing)	
gybe	gibe [2]*
gym /nast/nastics	
gymkana	gymkhana
gymkhana	
gymnasium /s	
gynaecolog y /ist	
gypsum	
gyrat e [2] /ion/ory	
gyro * /compass	
gyro	giro *
gyroscop e /ic	

H

habeas corpus	
haberdasher /y	
habias corpus	habeas corpus
habichual	habitual +
habichuate	habituate [2]+
habitab le /ility	
habitabul	habitable +
habitashun	habitation
habitat	
habitation	
habitual /ly	
habituat e [2] /ion	
hach	hatch [1]+

hacherey	hatchery +
hachet	hatchet
hack [1] /-saw	
hackle [2]	
hackney [1]	
hackul	hackle [2]
had /n't	
haddock	
Hades	
hadock	haddock
haemofilia	haemophilia +
haemoglobin	
haemophilia /c	
haemoroids	haemorrhoids
haemorrhage	
haemorrhoids	
haf	half +
hafnium	
hafpenie	halfpenny +
hafpeny	halfpenny +
hagard	haggard
hagerd	haggard
haggard	
haggis	
haggle [2] /r	
hagis	haggis
hagul	haggle [2]+
hai	hay *+
haifever	hay fever
hail [1]* (salute, icy rain)	
hail	hale *
hailo	halo *+
hailstone	
hair * (on head) /line/y	
hair	hare *+
hair	heir *
hairbreadth	
hairi er /est/ness	
hair-raising	
hake	
halcion	halcyon
halcyon	
hale * (hearty)	
hale	hail [1]*
haleluya	hallelujah

halestone — hailstone
hal*f* /ves (pl.)
half-*cast*/-hearted/-way
halfpenn*y* /ies
half-wit /ted
halibut
halilooya — hallelujah
hall * (room)
hall — haul [1]*+
hallelujah
hall-mark [1]
hallo * (cry)
hallow [1]* (make holy)
Hallowe'en
hallucinat*e* [2] /ion/ory
hallucinogen
halmark — hall-mark [1]
halo *(disc of light) /es
halo — hallow [1]*
halogens
halow — hallow [1]*
Haloween — Hallowe'en
halsiun — halcyon
halt [1] /er/ingly
halusinate — hallucinate [2]+
halusinogen — hallucinogen
halve [2]
halyard
halyerd — halyard
ham /burger
hamer — hammer [1]+
ham-fisted
hamlet
hammer [1] /er
hammock
hamper [1]
hamster
hamstring
hand [1] /ful/fuls
handbag
handcuff [1]
handicap [3]
handicraft
handie — handy +
handiwork

handkerchief /s
handle [2] /bar/r
hand-made
handriten — handwritten
handriting — handwriting +
handshake
handsome * (looks) /ly
handul — handle [2]+
handwrit*ing* /ten
hand*y* /ier/iest/ily
hang [1] /over
hangar * (shelter)
hanger * (for clothes)
hangkerchif — handkerchief +
hangman
hank
hanker [1]
hankerchief — handkerchief +
hankuf — handcuff [1]
hansom * (cab)
hansom — handsome *+
hansum — handsome *+
hapen — happen [1]
haphazard /ly/ness
hapie — happy +
hapier — happier +
hapless
happen [1]
happi*er* /est/ly/ness
happy /-go-lucky
hapy — happy +
hara-kiri
harang — harangue [2]
harangue [2]
haras — harass [1]+
harass [1] /ment
harber — harbour [1]+
harbour [1] /age
hard /er/est/ly/ship
harden [1]
hard-hearted
hardie — hardy +
hardware
hardwear — hardware
hard*y* /ier/iest/ily

hare ★ (animal) /bell		hash ¹	
hare	hair ★+	hashish	
hare-brained		hasock	hassock
harem		hassock	
harico	haricot	hast *e* /ily/iness/y	
haricot		hasten ¹	
harier	hairier +	hat ³ /ter	
hark ¹		hatch ¹ /es/way	
harlekwin	harlequin +	hatcherey	hatchery +
harlequin /ade		hatcher *y* /ies	
harlot /ry		hatchet	
harm ¹ /ful/fully		hate ² /ful/r	
harmless /ness		hatred	
harmonic /a/ally		hatrid	hatred
harmonious /ly/ness		haught *y* /ier/iest/ily	
harmonis *e* ² /ation		haul ¹★ (pull in) /age	
harmonium		haul	hall ★
harmonius	harmonious +	haulm	
harmon *y* /ies		haunch /es	
harness ¹ /er		haunt ¹	
harow	harrow ¹	hav	have +
harp ¹ /ist		Havana	
harpoon ¹ /er		have /n't	
harpsichord		haven	
harpsicord	harpsichord	havent	haven't
harrier		haversack	
harrow ¹		having	
harsh /ly/ness		havoc	
hart ★ (deer)		hawk ¹ /er/ish	
hart	heart ★+	hawl	haul ¹★+
hartbrake	heartbreak +	hawlidge	haulage
hartbroken	heartbroken	hawlige	haulage
hartburn	heartburn +	hawm	haulm
harten	hearten ¹	hawnch	haunch +
harth	hearth	hawnet	hornet
hartie	hearty +	hawnpipe	hornpipe
hartless	heartless +	hawnt	haunt ¹
harty	hearty +	hawser	
harum-scarum		hawthorn	
harve	halve ²	hawticulcher	horticulture +
harvest ¹ /er		hawticulture	horticulture +
harvist	harvest ¹+	hawtie	haughty +
hary	hairy	hawtier	haughtier
has /-been/n't		hawty	haughty +
hasen	hasten ¹	hay ★ (grass) /cock	

hay	hey ★	heavyweight	
hay fever		Hebrew	
hayday	heyday	hebroo	Hebrew
hazard [1] /ous		heckle [2] /r	
haz e /ier/iest/y		heckul	heckle [2]+
hazel		hectic /ally	
hazerd	hazard [1]+	hecto gram /litre/metre	
hazerdus	hazardous	hed	head [1]+
hazi ly /ness		hedake	headache
he /'ll ★ (he will)		heddress	head-dress +
head [1] /ache/board		heder	header +
head -dress /way		hedge [2] /hog/row	
head er /less/line/y		hedland	headland +
head land /long/strong		hedmaster	headmaster +
head master /mistress		hedmistriss	headmistress
headquarters		hedonis m /t	
heal [1]★ (to cure) /er		hedquarters	headquarters
heal	heel [1]★	heed [1] /ful/less	
health /y		heel [1]★ (of foot)	
healthi er /est/ly/ness		heel	heal [1]★+
heap [1]		heep	heap [1]
hear ★ (sound) /er/ing		heet	heat [1]+
hear	here ★	heeth	heath
hearabouts	hereabouts	hefer	heifer
hearafter	hereafter	heftie	hefty +
heard ★ (sound)		heft y /ier/iest/ily/iness	
heard	herd [1]★+	hege	hedge [2]+
hearken [1]		heifer	
hearsay		height	
hearse		heighten [1]	
heart ★ (body) /broken		heinous /ly/ness	
heartbreak /ing		heinus	heinous +
heartburn /ing		heir ★ (inheritance)	
hearten [1]		heir ess /loom	
hearth		hel	hell +
heartless /ly/ness		held	
heart y /ier/iest/ily		helicks	helix +
heat [1] /edly/er/-wave		helicopter	
heath		heliocentric	
heathen /ish		heliograf	heliograph
heather		heliograph	
heave [2]		heliotrope	
heaven /ly		heliport	
heaviwait	heavyweight	helium	
heav y /ier/iest/ily		heli x /ces (pl.)	

139

hell /ish
hello /s
helm /sman
helmet
helo   hello+
help [1] /er
helpful /ly/ness
helpless /ness
helpmate
helter-skelter
helth   health+
helthier   healthier+
hem [3] /stitch
hemerige   haemorrhage
hemeroids   haemorrhoids
hemisfere   hemisphere+
hemispher e /ical
hemlock
hemofilia   haemophilia+
hemoglobin   haemoglobin
hemorige   haemorrhage
hemp /en
hen /pecked
hena   henna
hence /forth
henceforward
hench man /men (pl.)
henna
henrey   henry+
henry /s
hens   hence+
hensforth   henceforth
hensforwerd   henceforward
henus   heinous+
hepatitis
heptagon /al
her /s/self
herald [1] /ic/ry
heraldrey   heraldry
herb /age
herbaceous
herbal /ist
herbashus   herbaceous
herbicide
herbiside   herbicide

herbivor e /ous
herbivorus   herbivorous
herd [1]★ (animals) /sman
herd   heard ★
here ★ (this place)
here   hear ★+
hereabouts
hereafter
here by /in/of
heredit ary /y
hereditey   heredity
hereditrey   hereditary+
heresay   hearsay
heresie   heresy+
heres y /ies
heretic /al
here to /upon/with
hering   herring
heritage
herita nce /ble
heritans   heritance+
heritige   heritage
herl   hurl [1]
hermafrodite   hermaphrodite
hermaphrodite
hermetic /ally
hermit /age
hernia
hero /es/ic/ically/ism
heroin ★ (drug)
heroine ★ (fem. hero)
heron /ry
herring
herse   hearse
hert   hurt+
hertle   hurtle [2]
hertul   hurtle [2]
hertz
hesian   hessian
hesitan cy /t
hesitansey   hesitancy+
hesitat e [2] /ion
hessian
heterodoks   heterodox+
hetero dox /sexual

heterogeneous

heterogenus	heterogeneous
heteroseksual	heterosexual
hethen	heathen +
hether	heather
heve	heave ²
heven	heaven +
hevenly	heavenly
hevie	heavy +
heviwait	heavyweight
heviweight	heavyweight
hevy	heavy +
hew ¹★ (cut) /er/n	
hew	hue ★
hexagon /al	
hexahedr on /al	
hey ★ (call out)	
hey	hay ★+
heyday	

If you cannot find your word
under **hi** *look under* **hy**

---

hi ★ (call attention)	
hi	high ★+
hiasinth	hyacinth
hiatus /es	
hibernat e ² /ion/or	
hibrid	hybrid
hiccup ¹	
hich	hitch ¹+
hichhike	hitch-hike ²+
hicup	hiccup ¹
hid /den/ing	
hide /bound/-out	
hideous /ly/ness	
hidius	hideous +
hier	higher ★
hier	hire ²★+
hierarch /ical	
hierarch y /ies	
hierark	hierarch +
hierarkey	hierarchy +
hieroglif	hieroglyph +
hieroglyph /ic	
hi-fi	

higgledy-piggledy	
high ★ (tall) /est/ly	
higher ★ (taller)	
higher	hire ²★+
highfaluting	
highland	
highlight ¹	
highness	
highway /man/men (pl.)	
hijack ¹ /er	
hike ² /r	
hil	hill +
hiland	highland
hilari ous /ty	
hilaritey	hilarity
hilarius	hilarious +
hilight	highlight ¹
hilite	highlight ¹
hill /ock	
hill y /ier/iest/iness	
him ★ (he) /self	
him	hymn ★+
hind /sight	
hinder ¹	
hindoo	Hindu +
hindrance	
hindrans	hindrance
hindsite	hindsight
Hindu /ism	
hiness	highness
hinge ²	
hint ¹	
hinterland	
hipie	hippy +
hipodrome	hippodrome
hipopotamus	hippopotamus
hippodrome	
hippopotamus	
hipp y /ies	
hipy	hippy +
hire ²★ (employ) /ling	
hire	higher ★
hiroglif	hieroglyph +
hiss ¹	
histerey	history +

141

histeria	hysteria +	holie	holly *+
histerical	hysterical +	holie	holy *
historian		holi *er* /est/ness	
historic /al/ally		holihock	hollyhock
histor*y* /ies		hollow [1]	
histrey	history +	holly * (tree) /hock	
histrionic /s		holly	holy *
hit /ter/ting		holly	wholly *
hitch [1] /es		holm * (river islet)	
hitch-hike [2] /r		holmium	
hite	height	holocaust	
hither /to		holocorst	holocaust
hive [2]		holow	hollow [1]
hiway	highway +	holster [1]	
ho * (surprise)		holy * (sacred)	
ho	hoe [2]*+	holy	holey *
hoaks	hoax [1]+	holy	holly *+
hoard [1] * (collect) /er		holy	wholly *
hoard	horde [2]*	homage	
hoarse * (voice)		home [2] * /ward/work	
hoarse	horse [2]*	home	holm *
hoarse *ly* /ness/st		home *ly* /less	
hoax [1] /es/er		homesick /ness	
hobble [2]		homicid*e* /al	
hobb*y* /ies		homige	homage
hobie	hobby +	homiley	homily
hobnob [3]		homily	
hobul	hobble [2]	homiopath	homoeopath +
hoby	hobby +	homisidal	homicidal
hochpoch	hotchpotch	homiside	homicide +
hock		homoeopath /ic	
hockey		homogene *ity* /ous	
hockie	hockey	homogenius	homogeneous
hocus-pocus		homonim	homonym +
hoe [2]* (dig) /s *		homonym /ic	
hoes	hose [2]*	homoseksual	homosexual +
hog [3] /gish		homosexual /ity	
hogshead		hone [2]	
hogshed	hogshead	honest /ly/y	
hoist [1]		honey /dew	
hold /-all/er/ing		honeycomb [1]	
hole [2]* (cavity) /y *		honeymoon [1] /er	
hole	whole *	honeysuckle	
holey	wholly *	honie	honey +
holiday /er/ing		honorari *um* /a/ums (pls.)	

honorary	
honorific	
honour [1] /able/ably	
hony	honey +
hood [1]	
hoodwink [1]	
hoo *f* [1] /fs/ves (pls.)	
hook [1] /-up	
hooligan /ism	
hoop [1]★ (circle)	
hoop	whoop [1]★
hooping coff	whooping cough
hoot [1] /er	
hoover [1]	
hop [3] /per/scotch	
hope [2] /ful/fully	
hopeless /ness	
horde [2]★ (swarm)	
horde	hoard [1]★+
hore	whore [2]+
horer	horror
horible	horrible +
horibul	horrible +
horid	horrid +
horific	horrific +
horify	horrify [4]
horizon	
horizontal /ly	
hormone	
horn [1] /beam/y	
hornet	
hornpipe	
horology	
horor	horror
horoscope	
horribl *e* /y	
horribul	horrible +
horrid /ness	
horrific /ally	
horrify [4]	
horror	
hors-d'oeuvre	
horse [2]★ (animal)	
horse	hoarse ★
horse *back* /-chestnut	

horsely	hoarsely +
horse *power* /radish	
horseshoe /s	
horsewhip [3]	
horswip	horsewhip [3]
horthorn	hawthorn
horticulcher	horticulture +
horticultur *e* /al/ist	
hortie	haughty +
horty	haughty +
hose [2]★ (stockings, water down)	
hose	hoes ★
hosier /y	
hospitabl *e* /y	
hospitabul	hospitable +
hospital	
hospitalis *e* [2] /ation	
hospitality	
host [1] /ess (fem.)	
hostage	
hostel	
hostelr *y* /ies	
hostige	hostage
hostile /ly	
hostilit *y* /ies	
hot /ly/-plate/ter/test	
hotchpotch	
hotel /ier	
hoter	hotter
hotest	hottest
hotheaded	
hotheded	hotheaded
hound [1]	
hour ★ (time) /ly	
hour	our ★
house [2] /boat/ful	
household /er	
house *keeper* /master	
housewi *fe* /ves (pl.)	
hovel	
hover [1] /craft	
how /ever	
howl [1] /er	
hownd	hound [1]

howse	house [2+]	humock	hummock
howsekeeper	housekeeper [+]	humorist /ic	
howsewife	housewife [+]	humorous ★ (funny)	
howshold	household [+]	humorous	humerus ★
hu	hew [1★+]	humour [1]	
hu	hue ★	hump [1] /back	
hubbub		humus	
huch	hutch [+]	hunch [1] /back/es	
huddle [2]		hundred /fold/th	
hudul	huddle [2]	hundredwait	hundredweight
hudwink	hoodwink [1]	hundredweight	
hue ★ (tint, pursuit)		huney	honey [+]
hue	hew [1★+]	hung	
huf	huff [1+]	hunger [1]	
huff [1] /ily/iness/y		hungrie	hungry
hug [3]		hungri er /est/ly/ness	
huge /ly/r/st		hungry	
Hugeno	Huguenot	huni	honey [+]
Huguenot		hunk	
hul	hull [1]	hunt [1] /er/ress (fem.)	
hulabaloo	hullabaloo	huntsman	
hulk /ing		hura	hurrah
hull [1]		huray	hurray
hullabaloo		hurd	heard ★
hum [3]		hurd	herd [1★+]
human ★ (person) /ly		hurdigurdie	hurdy-gurdy
humane ★ (kindly) /ly		hurdle [2]	
humanis e [2] /ation		hurdul	hurdle [2]
humanis m /t/tic		hurdy-gurdy	
humanitarian /ism		huricane	hurricane
humanit y /ies		hurie	hurry [4]
humble [2] /ness		hurl [1]	
humbly		hurmit	hermit [+]
humbug [3]		hurnia	hernia
humbul	humble [2+]	hurrah	
humdrum		hurray	
humer	humour [1]	hurricane	
humerist	humorist [+]	hurry [4]	
humerus ★ (bone)		hurse	hearse
humerus	humorous ★	hurt /ful/ing	
humid /ity		hurtle [2]	
humidif y [4] /ier		hurtul	hurtle [2]
humiliat e [2] /ion		hurtz	hertz
humility		hury	hurry [4]
hummock		husband [1] /ry	

husel | hustle [2+] | hyperbola ★ (curve)
hush [1] /-hush | | hyperbole ★ (exaggeration)
husie | hussy [+] | hyperbolical /ly
husk [1] /ily/iness | | hypermarket
huskie | husky [+] | hyphenate [2]
husk y /ies | | hypnosis
huss y /ies | | hypnoti c /sm/st
hustle [2] /r | | hypnotise [2]
husul | hustle [2+] | hypochondria /c
husy | hussy [+] | hypocris y /ies
hutch /es | | hypocrit e /ical
hyacinth | | hypodermic
hybrid | | hypotenuse
hydra | | hypothermia
hydrangea | | hypothes is /es (pl.)
hydranja | hydrangea | hypothetical
hydrant | | hysteri a /cs
hydraulic /ally/s | | hysterical /ly
hydrocarbon
hydrochloric
hydro-electric

I

hydrofobia | hydrophobia
hydrofoil | | I ★ /'ll ★ (I will)
hydrogen | | I | eye [2★+]
hydrografey | hydrography | iambic
hydrography | | ice [2] /-apron/berg
hydrokside | hydroxide | ice -*bucket* /-rink
hydrolysis | | ich | itch [1+]
hydromet er /ry | | icicle
hydropath /ic/y | | iclesiastic | ecclesiastic [+]
hydrophobia | | iclips | eclipse [2]
hydroplane | | icliptic | ecliptic
hydrostat /ic | | icon
hydrotherapy | | iconomey | economy [+]
hydrous | | iconomist | economist
hydroxide | | icy
hydrus | hydrous | idea /s
hyena | | ideal /ism
hygene | hygiene [+] | idealise [2]
hygien e /ic/ically | | identical
hygromet er /ric | | identif y [4] /ication
hygroscopic | | identit y /ies
hym | hymn [★+] | ideological /ly
hymen | | ideolog y /ies
hymn ★ (song) /al | | iderdown | eiderdown

idilic	idyllic	igwana	iguana
idill	idyll +	ijaculashun	ejaculation
idioc y /ies		ijaculate	ejaculate ²+
idiologey	ideology +	ijaculation	ejaculation
idiological	ideological +	ijecshun	ejection
idiom /atic		iject	eject ¹+
idiosincrasy	idiosyncrasy +	ijection	ejection
idiosincratic	idiosyncratic	ikon	icon
idiosyncra sy /tic		ikwip	equip ³+
idiot /ic		ikwivocal	equivocal +
idium	idiom +	ikwivocate	equivocate ²+
idle ²★ (lazy) /ness/r		il	I'll ★
idol ★ (worship)		ilaberate	elaborate ²+
idol	idle ²★+	ilaborashun	elaboration
idolatr y /ous		ilaborate	elaborate ²+
idolise ²		iland	island +
idyl	idyll +	ilapse	elapse ²
idyll /ic		ilash	eyelash +
iface	efface ²+	ilashun	elation
ifect	effect ¹	ilastic	elastic +
ifectiv	effective +	ilasticity	elasticity
ifectual	effectual	ilastisitey	elasticity
Ifel	Eiffel	ilate	elate ²+
ifeminate	effeminate +	ilation	elation
ificiency	efficiency +	ile	aisle ★
ificient	efficient +	Ile	I'll ★
ifishensey	efficiency +	ile	isle ★
ifishent	efficient +	ilect	elect ¹+
ifrunterey	effrontery +	ilection	election +
igalitarian	egalitarian +	ilectoral	electoral +
igloo		ilectorate	electorate
igneous		ilectrocute	electrocute ²+
ignishun	ignition	ilectron	electron +
ignit e ² /ion		ilectronic	electronic +
ignius	igneous	ilectroplate	electroplate ²
ignoble		ilegal	illegal +
ignominious /ly		ilegalitey	illegality
ignominius	ignominious +	ilegible	illegible +
ignominy		ilegibul	illegible +
ignor	ignore ²	ilegitimacy	illegitimacy +
ignoramus		ilegitimasey	illegitimacy +
ignoran ce /t		ilegitimate	illegitimate
ignorans	ignorance +	ilet	islet ★
ignore ²		ileven	eleven +
iguana		ilicit	elicit ¹★

146

ilikser	elixir	imaciate	emaciate [2+]
iliminashun	elimination	imaculate	immaculate
iliminate	eliminate [2+]	image [2]	
ilimination	elimination	imagin	imagine [2+]
ilips	ellipse	imaginashun	imagination
iliptic	elliptic [+]	imagin *e* [2] /ation	
iliptical	elliptical	imancipate	emancipate [2+]
ilisit	elicit [1★]	imansipashun	emancipation
iliteracy	illiteracy [+]	imansipate	emancipate [2+]
iliterasey	illiteracy [+]	imansipation	emancipation
iliterat	illiterate	imasculate	emasculate [2+]
ilixir	elixir	imashiate	emaciate [2+]
ill		imaterial	immaterial
illegal /ity		imature	immature [+]
illegib *le* /ility		imaturitey	immaturity
illegibul	illegible [+]	imbalance	
illegitima *cy* /te		imbalans	imbalance
illicit ★ (illegal) /ly		imbecil *e* /ity	
illicit	elicit [1★]	imbesile	imbecile [+]
illitera *cy* /te		imbibe [2]	
illogical /ity		imbue [2]	
illuminat *e* [2] /ion		imediacy	immediacy
illusion ★ (false idea)		imediasey	immediacy
illusion	allusion ★	imediate	immediate [+]
illusion	elusion ★	imense	immense [+]
illusive ★ (deceptive)		imensitey	immensity
illusive	allusive [★+]	imerge	emerge [2+]
illusive	elusive [★+]	imergence	emergence
illustrat *e* [2] /ion		imergency	emergency [+]
illustrious		imergens	emergence
ilogical	illogical [+]	imergent	emergent
ilope	elope [2+]	imerse	immerse [2+]
ilucidate	elucidate [2+]	imershun	immersion
ilude	elude [2★]	imersion	immersion
iluminashun	illumination	imesurable	immeasurable [+]
iluminate	illuminate [2+]	imesurabul	immeasurable [+]
ilumination	illumination	imetic	emetic
ilusidate	elucidate [2+]	imige	image [2]
ilusion	illusion ★	imigrant	immigrant
ilusive	elusive [★+]	imigrashun	immigration
ilusive	illusive ★	imigrate	immigrate [2+]
ilustrate	illustrate [2+]	imigration	immigration
ilustration	illustration	iminent	imminent [★+]
ilustrius	illustrious	imishun	emission
I'm (I am)		imission	emission

imit	emit[3+]
imitat*e*[2] /ion	
immaculate	
immaterial	
immatur*e* /ity	
immeasurabl*e* /y	
immediacy	
immediasey	immediacy
immediate /ly	
immens*e* /ely/ity	
immers*e*[2] /ion	
immigrant	
immigrat*e*[2] /ion	
imminent *† /ly †(about to happen)	
imminent	eminent *
immobil*e* /ity	
immobilis*e*[2] /ation	
immoderate /ly	
immodest /ly/y	
immoral /ity/ly	
immortal /ity/ly	
immortalis*e*[2] /ation	
immovabl*e* /y	
immun*e* /ity	
immunis*e*[2] /ation	
immunology	
imobile	immobile[+]
imoderate	immoderate[+]
imodest	immodest[+]
imodestey	immodesty
imolient	emollient
imolument	emolument
imoral	immoral[+]
imoralitey	immorality
imortal	immortal[+]
imortalise	immortalise[2+]
imortalitey	immortality
imoshun	emotion[+]
imoshunal	emotional
imotion	emotion[+]
imotional	emotional
imotiv	emotive
imovable	immovable[+]
imovabul	immovable[+]

imp /ish/ishness	
impact[1] /ion	
impair[1] /ment	
impalpabl*e* /y	
imparshal	impartial[+]
imparshialitey	impartiality
impart[1]	
impartial /ity/ly	
impas	impasse
impasabul	impassable
impashence	impatience
impashens	impatience
impashent	impatient[+]
impashund	impassioned
impasioned	impassioned
impasiv	impassive[+]
impassable	
impasse	
impassioned	
impassive /ness	
impassivity	
impatience	
impatient /ly	
impeach[1] /able/ment	
impecabul	impeccable[+]
impeccabl*e* /y	
impecunio*us* /sity	
impecunius	impecunious[+]
impede[2]	
impediment /a	
impeech	impeach[1+]
impel[3] /ler	
impend[1]	
impenetrab*le* /ility	
impeniten*ce* /t	
impenitens	impenitence[+]
imperative /ly/ness	
imperceptibl*e* /y	
imperfect /ion	
imperial /ism/ly	
imperialist /ic	
imperil[3] /ment	
imperious /ly/ness	
imperishable	
imperius	imperious[+]

impermeable		imposter	impostor ★
impermiabul	impermeable	impostor ★ (swindler)	
imperseptible	imperceptible +	imposture ★ (deception)	
imperseptibul	imperceptible +	impoten *ce* /t	
impersonal /ly		impotens	impotence +
impersonat *e* ² /ion/or		impound ¹	
imperterbable	imperturbable +	impoverish ¹ /ment	
impertinen *ce* /t		impownd	impound ¹
impertinens	impertinence +	impracticab *le* /ility	
imperturbab *le* /ility		impracticabul	impracticable +
impervious /ly/ness		imprecat *e* ² /ion	
impervius	impervious +	imprecise /ly	
impetuosity		impregnab *le* /ility	
impetuous /ly/ness		impregnat *e* ² /ion	
impetus /es		impres	impress ¹+
impetuus	impetuous +	impresario /s	
impiety		impreshun	impression +
impinge ² /ment		impreshunism	impressionism +
impious /ly		impresible	impressible
impius	impious +	impresibul	impressible
implacabl *e* /y		impresionism	impressionism +
implacabul	implacable +	impresionist	impressionist
implant ¹ /ation		impresise	imprecise +
implement ¹ /ation		impresiv	impressive +
impli	imply ⁴+	impress ¹ /ible	
implicat *e* ² /ion		impression /able	
implicit /ly/ness		impressionis *m* /t/tic	
implisit	implicit +	impressive /ly/ness	
implore ²		imprint ¹	
impl *y* ⁴ /ication		imprison ¹ /ment	
impolite /ly/ness		improbab *le* /ility/ly	
impolitic		improbabul	improbable +
imponderable /s		impromptu	
impondrabul	imponderable +	impromtoo	impromptu
import ¹ /able/ation		improper /ly	
importan *ce* /t/tly		impropriet *y* /ies	
importans	importance +	improve ² /ment	
importunate /ly		improviden *ce* /t/tly	
importun *e* ² /ity		improvidens	improvidence +
imposcher	imposture ★	improvis *e* ² /ation	
impos *e* ² /able/ition		impruden *ce* /t/tly	
imposible	impossible +	imprudens	imprudence +
imposibul	impossible +	impruve	improve ²+
imposishun	imposition	impuden *ce* /t/tly	
impossib *le* /ility/ly		impudens	impudence +

149

impugn [1]
impuls *e* /ion/ive/ively
impune   impugn [1]
impunity
impure /ly
impurit *y* /ies
imput *e* [2] /able/ation
imulshun   emulsion
imulsion   emulsion
imune   immune +
imunise   immunise [2]+
imunitey   immunity
imunologey   immunology
imurge   emerge [2]+
in * (on inside)
in   inn *+
inability
inaccessib *le* /ility
inaccurac *y* /ies
inaccurate /ly
inacsesible   inaccessible +
inacsesibul   inaccessible +
inacshun   inaction
inaction
inactive /ly
inactivit *y* /ies
inacuracy   inaccuracy +
inacurasey   inaccuracy +
inacurate   inaccurate +
inadekwacy   inadequacy +
inadekwasey   inadequacy +
inadekwat   inadequate +
inadequac *y* /ies
inadequate /ly
inadmisibul   inadmissible +
inadmissib *le* /ility
inadverten *ce* /t
inadvertens   inadvertence +
inalienab *le* /ility
inalienabul   inalienable +
inane /ly
inanimate
inanit *y* /ies
inaplicable   inapplicable +
inapplicabl *e* /y

inapplicabul   inapplicable +
inappropriate /ly
inapropriat   inappropriate +
inaptitude
inarticulate /ly
inasmuch
inate   innate +
inatenshun   inattention +
inatention   inattention +
inatentiv   inattentive
inattent *ion* /ive
inaudib *le* /ility
inaugural
inaugurat *e* [2] /ion/ive
inauspicious /ly
inawmus   enormous +
inawspicious   inauspicious +
inawspishus   inauspicious +
inborn
inbred
inbreeding
incalculab *le* /ility
incandescen *ce* /t
incandesence   incandescence +
incant [1] /ation
incapab *le* /ility/ly
incapabul   incapable +
incapacitat *e* [2] /ion
incapacity
incapasitate   incapacitate [2]+
incapasitey   incapacity
incarcerat *e* [2] /ion
incarnat *e* [2] /ion
incarserate   incarcerate [2]+
incendiar *y* /ies
incense [2]
incentive
incept *ion* /ive
incertitude
incessant /ly
incest /uous
inch [1] /es
incidence * (bearing)
incident /al/ally
incidents * (events)

incinerat *e* ² /ion/or
incipient
incis *e* ² /ion
incisive /ly/ness
incisor
incite ²★ (stir up)
incite   insight ★
incivilit *y* /ies
inclemen *cy* /t
inclemensey   inclemency ⁺
inclin *e* ² /ation
inclose   enclose ²⁺
inclu *de* ² /sion
inclusive /ly
incognito
incoheren *ce* /t
incoherens   incoherence ⁺
incombustible
income   tax
incomensurat   incommensurate
incoming
incommensurate
incommod *e* ² /ious
incommunicado
incomparabl *e* /y
incompatib *le* /ility
incompatibul   incompatible ⁺
incompeten *ce* /t/tly
incompetens   incompetence ⁺
incomplete
incomprehensible
incomunicado   incommunicado
inconceivabl *e* /y
inconclusive /ly
incongru *ent* /ous
incongruit *y* /ies
incongruus   incongruous
inconseavable   inconceivable ⁺
inconsiderable
inconsiderate /ly
inconsistenc *y* /ies
inconsistensey   inconsistency ⁺
inconsistent /ly
inconsolable
inconsolabul   inconsolable

inconspicuous /ly
inconstan *cy* /t
incontestabl *e* /y
incontestabul   incontestable ⁺
incontinen *ce* /t
incontinens   incontinence ⁺
incontrovertibl *e* /y
inconvenien *ce* ² /t
inconveniens   inconvenience ²⁺
incorect   incorrect ⁺
incorigible   incorrigible ⁺
incorigibul   incorrigible ⁺
incorporat *e* ² /ion/or
incorrect /ly
incorrigib *le* /ility
incorruptib *le* /ility
increase ²
incredibl *e* /y
incredibul   incredible ⁺
incredul *ity* /ous
incredulus   incredulous
increment /al
increse   increase ²
incriminat *e* ² /ion
incrust   encrust ¹
incubat *e* ² /ion/or
inculcat *e* ² /ion
inculpat *e* ² /ion
incum   income ⁺
incumbenc *y* /ies
incumbensey   incumbency ⁺
incumbent
incur ³
incurab *le* /ility/ly
incurabul   incurable ⁺
incurshun   incursion ⁺
incurs *ion* /ive
indebted /ness
indecenc *y* /ies
indecensey   indecency ⁺
indecent /ly
indecipherable
indecishun   indecision
indecision
indecisive /ly

151

indecorous /ness	
indecorum	
indecorus	indecorous +
indeed	
indefatigabl e /y	
indefatigabul	indefatigable +
indefensibl e /y	
indefensibul	indefensible +
indefinable	
indefinabul	indefinable
indefinite /ly	
indeks	index [1]+
indelibl e /y	
indelibul	indelible +
indelicac y /ies	
indelicasey	indelicacy +
indelicate /ly	
indemnifi	indemnify [4]+
indemnif y [4] /ication	
indemnit y /ies	
indencher	indenture
indent [1] /ation/ure	
independen ce /t	
independens	independence +
indescribabl e /y	
indescribabul	indescribable +
indesency	indecency +
indesensey	indecency +
indesent	indecent +
indesiferable	indecipherable
indestructib le /ility	
indestructibul	indestructible +
indeted	indebted +
indeterminate /ly	
ind ex [1] /exes/ices (pls.)	
Indian	
indicat e [2] /ion/ive/or	
indict [1]★(accuse)/ment	
indiference	indifference +
indiferens	indifference +
indiferent	indifferent
indifferen ce /t	
indigen ce /t	
indigenous	
indigens	indigence +

indigenus	indigenous
indigeschun	indigestion +
indigestibl e /y	
indigestibul	indigestible +
indigest ion /ive	
indignant /ly	
indignashun	indignation
indignation	
indignit y /ies	
indigo	
indipendence	independence +
indipendens	independence +
indipendent	independent
indirect /ly	
indiscre et /tion	
indiscreshun	indiscretion
indiscriminate	
indisishun	indecision
indisision	indecision
indisisiv	indecisive [+]
indispensabl e /y	
indispensabul	indispensable +
indispos e [2] /ition	
indisputabl e /y	
indisputabul	indisputable +
indistinct	
indistinguishable	
indite [2]★ (compose)	
indite	indict [1]★+
indium	
individual /ity/ly	
individualis m /t	
indivisibl e /y	
indivisibul	indivisible +
indoctrinat e [2] /ion	
indolen ce /t/tly	
indolens	indolence +
indomitabl e /y	
indomitabul	indomitable +
indoor /s	
indubitabl e /y	
indubitabul	indubitable +
induce [2] /ment	
inducshun	induction +
inductance	

inductans	inductance	inequity * (injustice)	
induct *ion* /ive/ively		inequity	iniquity *
indulge ² /nce/nt		iner	inner +
indulgens	indulgence	ineradicabl *e* /y	
induse	induce ²+	ineradicabul	ineradicable +
industrey	industry +	inersha	inertia
industrial /ism/ist/ly		inert /ia/ly/ness	
industrialis *e* ² /ation		inescapabl *e* /y	
industrious /ly		inescapabul	inescapable +
industrius	industrious +	inesenshal	inessential
industr *y* /ies		inesential	inessential
inebriat *e* ² /ion		inessential	
inedib *le* /ility		inestimabl *e* /y	
inedibul	inedible +	inestimabul	inestimable +
inefectiv	ineffective +	inestinium	einsteinium
inefectual	ineffectual +	inevitability	
ineffective /ly/ness		inevitabl *e* /y	
ineffectual /ly		inevitabul	inevitable +
inefficienc *y* /ies		inexact /itude	
inefficient /ly		inexcusabl *e* /y	
ineficiency	inefficiency +	inexhaustibl *e* /y	
ineficient	inefficient +	inexorabl *e* /y	
inefishensey	inefficiency +	inexpedient /ly	
inefishent	inefficient +	inexpensive /ly	
inegsact	inexact +	inexperience /d	
inegsactitude	inexactitude	inexperiens	inexperience +
inegsawstible	inexhaustible +	inexplicabl *e* /y	
inekscusable	inexcusable +	inexpressibl *e* /y	
inekserable	inexorable +	inextinguishable	
inekspedient	inexpedient +	inextingwishabul	inextinguishable
inekspensive	inexpensive +	inextricabl *e* /y	
ineksperience	inexperience +	infalible	infallible +
ineksplicable	inexplicable +	infalibul	infallible +
inekspresible	inexpressible +	infallib *le* /ility/ly	
inekstricable	inextricable +	infamey	infamy
inekwitable	inequitable +	infamous /ly	
inekwity	inequity *	infamus	infamous +
inelegan *ce* /cy/t		infamy	
inelegens	inelegance +	infancy	
ineligib *le* /ility		infansey	infancy
ineligibul	ineligible +	infant /icide/ile	
inept /itude/ly		infantrey	infantry +
inequalit *y* /ies		infantr *y* /ies	
inequitabl *e* /y		infatuat *e* ² /ion	
inequitabul	inequitable +	infecshun	infection

infecshus	infectious +	influx	
infect [1] /ion		inform [1] /ative/er	
infectious /ness		informal /ity/ly	
infer [3] /ence		informant	
inferens	inference	informashun	information
inferier	inferior +	information	
inferior /ity		infracshun	infraction
inferm	infirm	infraction	
infermarey	infirmary +	infra-red	
infermitey	infirmity +	infrastructure	
infernal /ly		infrekwency	infrequency +
inferno /s		infrekwent	infrequent
infertil e /ity		infrequen cy /t/tly	
infest [1] /ant/ation		infringe [2] /ment	
infidel		infuriate [2]	
infidelit y /ies		infus e [2] /er/ion	
infiltrat e [2] /ion/or		ingenious /ly	
infinite /ly		ingenius	ingenious +
infinitesimal /ly		ingenuity	
infinitey	infinity +	ingenuous /ly/ness	
infinitive		ingenuus	ingenuous +
infinit y /ies		ingle-nook	
infirm		Inglish	English +
infirmar y /ies		inglorious /ly	
infirmit y /ies		inglorius	inglorious +
inflamable	inflammable +	ingot	
inflamabul	inflammable +	ingrained	
inflamashun	inflammation	ingrashiate	ingratiate [2]
inflamatrey	inflammatory	ingratiate [2]	
inflame [2]		ingratitude	
inflamma ble /tion		ingredient	
inflammatory		ingrowing	
inflashun	inflation +	ingulnook	ingle-nook
inflat e [2] /able		inhabit [1] /able/ant	
inflation /ary		inhal e [2] /ant/ation	
inflect [1] /ion		inherent /ly	
inflexib le /ility		inherit [1] /ance/or	
inflict [1] /ion		inheritans	inheritance
inflooenza	influenza	inhibishun	inhibition
influence [2]		inhibit [1] /ion/or/ory	
influens	influence [2]	inhospitabl e /y	
influenshal	influential +	inhospitabul	inhospitable +
influential /ly		inhuman /ity/ly	
influenza		inikwalitey	inequality +
influks	influx	inikwitey	iniquity ★

inikwitous	iniquitous
inikwitus	iniquitous
inimical	
inimitabl e /y	
inimitabul	inimitable +
inings	innings
iniquitey	iniquity *
iniquitous	
iniquitus	iniquitous
iniquity * (badness)	
iniquity	inequity *
inishal	initial 3+
inishativ	initiative
inishiashun	initiation
inishiate	initiate 2+
inishiation	initiation
initial 3 /ly	
initiat e 2 /ion/ive	
inject 1 /ion/or	
injer	injure 2+
injunction	
injunkshun	injunction
injur e 2 /ious	
injurey	injury +
injurius	injurious
injur y /ies	
injustice	
injustis	injustice

If you cannot find your word
under **ink** *look under* **inc**

---

ink 1 /-pot/-well	
inkalculable	incalculable +
inkeeper	innkeeper
inkling	
inkrement	increment +
inkwest	inquest
inkwire	enquire 2+
inkwisitiv	inquisitive +
inkwisitor	inquisitor
inlade	inlaid
inland	
in-law	
inla y /id	
inlet	

inmate	
inmost	
inn * (tavern) /keeper	
innate /ly	
inner /most	
innings	
innocen ce /t/tly	
innocuous /ly	
innovat e 2 /ion/ive	
innuendo /es	
innumerabl e /y	
inocence	innocence +
inocens	innocence +
inocent	innocent
inoculat e 2 /ion	
inocuous	innocuous +
inocuus	innocuous +
inofensiv	inoffensive +
inoffensive /ly/ness	
inoperative /ness	
inoportune	inopportune +
inopportune /ly	
inordible	inaudible +
inordinate /ly	
inorganic	
inorgural	inaugural
inorgurate	inaugurate 2+
inormitey	enormity +
inormous	enormous +
inormus	enormous +
inorspicious	inauspicious +
inorspishus	inauspicious +
inosent	innocent
inough	enough
inovashun	innovation
inovate	innovate 2+
inovation	innovation
inovativ	innovative
input	
inquest	
inquisitive /ly/ness	
inquisitor	
inroad	
inrode	inroad
insan e /ely/ity	

155

insanitar *y* /iness	
insanitey	insanity
insanitrey	insanitary [+]
insashable	insatiable [+]
insashabul	insatiable [+]
insatiabl *e* /y	
inscribe [2]	
inscripshun	inscription
inscription	
inscrutab *le* /ility	
insect /icide	
insectiside	insecticide
insecure /ly	
insecurity	
inseminat *e* [2] /ion	
insendiarey	incendiary [+]
insense	incense [2]
insensib *le* /ility/ly	
insensibul	insensible [+]
insensitive /ly	
insensitivity	
insentiv	incentive
inseparabl *e* /y	
inseprabul	inseparable [+]
insepshun	inception [+]
inseption	inception [+]
insermountable	insurmountable [+]
insert [1] /ion	
insertitude	incertitude
insesant	incessant [+]
insest	incest [+]
insestuous	incestuous
insestuus	incestuous
inset [3]	
inshorance	insurance
inshorans	insurance
inshore	ensure [2]★
inshore	insure [2]★[+]
inside /r	
insidence	incidence ★
insidens	incidence ★
insidens	incidents ★
insident	incident [+]
insidental	incidental
insidious /ly/ness	

insidius	insidious [+]
insight ★ (keen understanding)	
insight	incite [2]★
insignia	
insignifican *ce* /t/tly	
insincere /ly	
insincerity	
insinerate	incinerate [2+]
insinerater	incinerator
insinsere	insincere [+]
insinseritey	insincerity
insinuat *e* [2] /ion/or	
insipid /ly/ness	
insipient	incipient
insiser	incisor
insishun	incision
insision	incision
insisiv	incisive [+]
insist [1] /ence/ent/ently	
insite	incite [2]★
insite	insight ★
insivilitey	incivility [+]
insolen *ce* /t/tly	
insolens	insolence [+]
insolub *le* /ility/ly	
insolubul	insoluble [+]
insolven *ce* /cy/t	
insolvens	insolvence [+]
insomnia /c	
insomuch	
inspecshun	inspection
inspect [1] /ion	
inspecter	inspector [+]
inspector /ate	
inspir *e* [2] /ation	
instability	
instal	install [1+]
install [1] /ation	
instalment	
instance [2]	
instans	instance [2]
instant /ly	
instantaneous /ly	
instantanius	instantaneous [+]

instead		intangibl *e* /y	
insted	instead	intangibul	intangible +
instep		integer	
instigat *e* ² /ion/or		integral /ly	
instigater	instigator	integrashun	integration
instill ¹		integrat *e* ² /ion/or	
instinct /ive/ively		integrity	
institushun	institution +	intelect	intellect
institut *e* ² /or		intelectual	intellectual +
institution /al		inteligence	intelligence +
institutionalis *e* ² /m		inteligens	intelligence +
instrement	instrument +	inteligensia	intelligentsia
instruct ¹ /ion/ive/or		inteligent	intelligent +
instrument /ation		inteligible	intelligible +
instrumental /ist		intellect	
insubordinashun	insubordination	intellectual / ly	
insubordinat *e*/ely/ion		intelligen *ce* /tsia	
insufferabl *e* /y		intelligent /ly	
insufficien *cy* /t/tly		intelligibl *e* /y	
insuficiency	insufficiency +	intelligibul	intelligible +
insuficient	insufficient	intemperance	
insufishensey	insufficiency +	intemperans	intemperance
insufishent	insufficient	intemperate /ly	
insufrable	insufferable +	intend ¹	
insular /ity		intense /ly	
insulat *e* ² /ion/or		intenshun	intention +
insulin		intensif *y* ⁴ /ication	
insult ¹		intensit *y* /ies	
insuperabl *e* /y		intensive /ly/ness	
insuprabul	insuperable +	intent	
insurance		intention /al/ally	
insurans	insurance	inter ³ /ment	
insure ²★(insurance)/r		interbred	
insure	ensure ²★	interbreeding	
insurecshun	insurrection	intercede ²	
insurection	insurrection	intercept ¹ /ion/or	
insurgen *ce* /t		interceshun	intercession +
insurgens	insurgence +	intercess *ion* /or	
insurmountabl *e* /y		interchange ² /able	
insurrection		interconnect ¹ /ion	
insurshun	insertion	intercorse	intercourse
insurt	insert ¹+	intercourse	
insurtion	insertion	interelate	interrelate ²
intact		interest ¹	
intake		interfere ² /nce	

interier	interior	intervenshun	intervention
interim		interview [1]	
interior		intervue	interview [1]
interject [1] /ion		interweav e /ing	
interlock [1]		interwoven	
interloper		intestin e /al	
interlude		intiger	integer
intermarie	intermarry [4]	intigral	integral +
intermarry [4]		intigrashun	integration
intermediar y /ies		intigrate	integrate [2]+
intermediate		intigration	integration
interment ★ (burial)		intijer	integer
interment	internment ★	intimacy	
interminable		intimasey	intimacy
interminabul	interminable	intimate /ly	
intermingle [2]		intimidashun	intimidation
intermingul	intermingle [2]	intimidat e [2] /ion	
intermishun	intermission	intoksicant	intoxicant
intermission		intoksicate	intoxicate [2]+
intermittent		intolerabl e /y	
intern [1] /ment ★ (detention)		intoleran ce /t	
internal		intolerans	intolerance +
internashunal	international +	intolrabul	intolerable +
international /ly		intonashun	intonation
internecine		intonation	
internisine	internecine	intoxicant	
interogashun	interrogation	intoxicat e [2] /ion	
interogate	interrogate [2]+	intractable	
interplanetary		intractabul	intractable
Interpol		intramuscular	
interpolat e [2] /ion		intransigen ce /t	
interpret [1] /ation		intransigens	intransigence +
interrelate [2]		intransitive	
interrogat e [2] /ion/or		intreeg	intrigue [2]+
interrupt [1] /ion		intrepid /ly	
intersect [1] /ion		intricac y /ies	
interseed	intercede [2]	intricasey	intricacy +
intersepshun	interception	intricate /ly	
intersept	intercept [1]+	intrigue [2] /r	
intersepter	interceptor	intrinsic /ally	
interseshun	intercession +	introduce [2]	
interupshun	interruption	introducshun	introduction +
interuption	interruption	introduct ion /ory	
interval		introduse	introduce [2]
interven e [2] /tion		introod	intrude [2]+

introoshun	intrusion +	invenshun	invention
introosion	intrusion +	invent [1] /ion/or	
introosiv	intrusive	inventer	inventor
introspect [1] /ion /ive		inventive /ness	
introver t [1] /sion		inventor y /ies	
intrude [2] /r		inventrey	inventory +
intrushun	intrusion +	invers e /ion	
intrus ion /ive		invershun	inversion
intuishun	intuition	invert [1] /er	
intuition		invertebrate	
intuitive /ly		invest [1] /ment	
inturn	intern [1+]	investicher	investiture
inturnal	internal	investigashun	investigation
inuendo	innuendo +	investigat e [2] /ion	
inuf	enough	investiture	
inumerable	innumerable +	inveterate	
inumerashun	enumeration	invidious /ly	
inumerate	enumerate [2+]	invidius	invidious +
inumerater	enumerator	invigilat e [2] /ion/or	
inumeration	enumeration	invigilater	invigilator
inumrabul	innumerable +	invigorat e [2] /ion	
inunciashun	enunciation	invincibl e /y	
inunciate	enunciate [2+]	invinsible	invincible +
inunciation	enunciation	inviolate	
inundat e [2] /ion		invisib le /ility/ly	
inunsiate	enunciate [2+]	invisibul	invisible +
inure [2]		invitashun	invitation
inursha	inertia	invit e [2] /ation	
inurt	inert +	invoice [2]	
invade [2] /r		invois	invoice [2]
invalid /ity		invoke [2]	
invalidate [2]		involuntar y /ily	
invaluable		involuntrey	involuntary +
invaluble	invaluable	involve [2] /ment	
invalubul	invaluable	invulnerab le /ility	
invariabl e /y		invulnerabul	invulnerable +
invariabul	invariable +	invurs	inverse +
invashun	invasion	invurt	invert [1+]
invasion		invurtebrate	invertebrate
invay	inveigh [1]	inward /ly/ness/s	
invaygul	inveigle [2]	inwud	inward +
invective		iodene	iodine
inveigh [1]		iodine	
inveigle [2]		iodise [2]	
inveigul	inveigle [2]	ion /ic	

159

ionis *e* ² /ation		ireverence	irreverence +
ionosfere	ionosphere	ireverens	irreverence +
ionosphere		ireverent	irreverent
iota		ireversible	irreversible +
ira	era +	irevocable	irrevocable +
iradiate	irradiate ²+	irevocabul	irrevocable +
iradicate	eradicate ²+	irideemable	irredeemable +
irascib *le* /ility		irideemabul	irredeemable +
irascibul	irascible +	iridium	
irase	erase ²+	irigashun	irrigation
irasher	erasure	irigate	irrigate ²+
irashonal	irrational +	irigation	irrigation
irasible	irascible +	iris	
irate		Irish	
irational	irrational +	irisistible	irresistible +
ire		irisistibul	irresistible +
ireclaimable	irreclaimable	iritable	irritable +
ireconcilable	irreconcilable +	iritant	irritant
ireconcilabul	irreconcilable +	iritashun	irritation
irecoverable	irrecoverable +	iritate	irritate ²+
irect	erect ¹+	iritation	irritation
irecuvrable	irrecoverable +	iriversible	irreversible +
irefutable	irrefutable +	irk ¹ /some	
iregular	irregular +	irode	erode ²
iregularitey	irregularity +	iron ¹ /monger	
ireguler	irregular +	ironeous	erroneous +
irelegious	irreligious	ironey	irony +
irelevance	irrelevance +	ironic /al/ally	
irelevans	irrelevance +	ironie	irony +
irelevansey	irrelevancy +	ironius	erroneous +
irelevant	irrelevant	iron *y* /ies	
ireligus	irreligious	iroshun	erosion
iremediable	irremediable +	irosion	erosion
iremediabul	irremediable +	irotic	erotic +
iremovable	irremovable +	irradiat *e* ² /ion	
iremovabul	irremovable +	irrational /ly	
ireplacable	irreplaceable	irreclaimable	
ireplasable	irreplaceable	irreclaimabul	irreclaimable
ireprable	irreparable	irreconcilabl *e* /y	
ireprabul	irreparable	irreconcilabul	irreconcilable +
irepressible	irrepressible	irrecoverabl *e* /y	
iresolute	irresolute +	irrecoverabul	irrecoverable +
irespectiv	irrespective +	irredeemabl *e* /y	
iresponsible	irresponsible +	irredeemabul	irredeemable +
iresponsibul	irresponsible +	irrefutabl *e* /y	

160

irrefutabul	irrefutable +	ishuans	issuance
irregular /ly		ishue	issue ²+
irregularit y /ies		isicle	icicle
irrelevan ce /t		isight	eyesight
irrelevanc y /ies		isinglass	
irrelevansey	irrelevancy +	isite	eyesight
irreligious		island /er	
irreligus	irreligious	isle ★ (island)	
irremediabl e /y		isle	aisle ★
irremediabul	irremediable +	islet ★ (small island)	
irremovabl e /y		islet	eyelet ★
irremovabul	irremovable +	isn't (is not)	
irreparable		isnt	isn't
irreplacabul	irreplaceable	isobar	
irreplaceable		isolashun	isolation +
irreprabul	irreparable	isolate ²	
irrepresibul	irrepressible	isolation /ist	
irrepressible		isometric /ally	
irresistibl e /y		isosceles	
irresolute /ly/ness		isosilese	isosceles
irrespective /ly		isotherm	
irresponsibility		isotope	
irresponsibl e /y		Israeli	
irresponsibul	irresponsible +	Isralie	Israeli
irretrievabl e /y		issuans	issuance
irretrievabul	irretrievable +	issu e ² /ance	
irreveren ce /t/tly		isthmus	
irreverens	irreverence +	Italian	
irreversibl e /y		italic /s	
irreversibul	irreversible +	italicise ²	
irrevocabl e /y		italisize	italicise ²
irrevocabul	irrevocable +	Italyun	Italian
irrigat e ² /ion/or		itch ¹ /y	
irrisistable	irresistible +	item	
irritab le /ility/ly		itemise ²	
irritabul	irritable +	iternal	eternal +
irritant		iternally	eternally
irritashun	irritation	iternitey	eternity +
irritat e ² /ion		ither	either
irrupt ¹ /ion/ive		itinerant	
irupshun	irruption	itinerar y /ies	
irupt	irrupt ¹+	itinerey	itinerary +
iruption	irruption	it's ★ (it is)	
ise	ice ²+	its ★ (possessive)	
ishuance	issuance	iun	iron ¹+

iunmunger	ironmonger	jackdaw	
ivacuashun	evacuation	jackdoor	jackdaw
ivacuate	evacuate ²⁺	jacket ¹	
ivacuation	evacuation	jack-kni *fe* ² /ves (pl.)	
ivacuee	evacuee	Jacobean	
ivade	evade ²⁺	Jacobi *n* /te	
ivaluashun	evaluation	jade ²	
ivaluate	evaluate ²⁺	Jaffa	
ivaluation	evaluation	jaffer	Jaffa
ivangelise	evangelise ²⁺	jag ³	
ivangelist	evangelist	jaguar	
ivaperator	evaporator	jail ¹ /bird/er	
ivaporashun	evaporation	jam ³★ (preserve) /my	
ivaporate	evaporate ²⁺	jamb ★ (side post)	
ivaporation	evaporation	jamboree	
ivashun	evasion	jambori	jamboree
ivasion	evasion	jangle ²	
ivasiv	evasive ⁺	jangul	jangle ²
I've (I have)		janiter	janitor
Ive	I've	janitor	
ivent	event ⁺	January	
iventful	eventful	Janurey	January
iventual	eventual ⁺	Japanese	
iventualitey	eventuality ⁺	jar ³	
ivicshun	eviction	jargon	
ivict	evict ¹⁺	jasmin	jasmine
iviction	eviction	jasmine	
ivie	ivy	jasper	
ivocashun	evocation ⁺	jaundice ²	
ivocation	evocation ⁺	jaundis	jaundice ²
ivocativ	evocative	jaunt ¹ /ily/iness/y	
ivoke	evoke ²	jauntie	jaunty
ivolve	evolve ²	javelin	
ivory		jaw /bone	
ivry	ivory	jawndice	jaundice ²
ivy		jawndis	jaundice ²
		jawnt	jaunt ¹⁺
		jawntey	jaunty
		jay /-walker	
		jaz	jazz ¹⁺

J

jab ³
jabber ¹ /er
jabot
jack ¹ /boot/pot
jackal
jackass /es

jazz ¹ /y
jealous /ly/y
jeans
jeep
jeer ¹

Jehovah		jingo /es/ism	
jelie	jelly +	jingul	jingle 2
jell y /ies		jirashun	gyration
jelous	jealous +	jirate	gyrate 2+
jelus	jealous +	jiration	gyration
jely	jelly +	jiro	giro ★
jemie	jemmy +	jiro	gyro ★+
jemm y /ies		jiroscope	gyroscope +
jemy	jemmy +	jist	gist
jenes	jeans	jiter	jitter 1+
jeopard ise 2 /y		jitter 1 /y	
jepadise	jeopardise 2+	jive 2	
jepardy	jeopardy	job 3 /less	
jeribilt	jerry-built	jockey 1 /s	
jerie	jerry +	jockie	jockey 1+
jerk 1 /ily/iness/y		jocky	jockey 1+
jerkin		jocose /ly	
jerry /-building/-built		jocular /ity/ly	
jersey /s		jocund /ity	
jersie	jersey +	jodhpurs	
jersy	jersey +	jodpers	jodhpurs
jery	jerry +	jodpurs	jodhpurs
jest 1 /er		jog 3	
jet 3 /-propelled		joggle 2	
jetie	jetty +	jogul	joggle 2
jetison	jettison 1	joi	joy +
jetsam		joiful	joyful
jettison 1		join 1 /er/ery	
jett y /ies		joint 1 /er/ly	
jety	jetty +	joiride	joy-ride +
Jew /ish/ry ★ (Jews)		joist 1	
jewel 3 ★ (gem)		joius	joyous +
jewel	duel 3 ★	jok e 2 /er/ingly	
jewel	joule ★	joll y 4 /ier/iest/ily/ity	
jeweler	jeweller +	jolt 1 /y	
jeweller /y		joly	jolly 4+
jewelrey	jewellery	jonkwil	jonquil
jib 3		jonquil	
jiffy		Joo	Jew +
jifie	jiffy	Jooish	Jewish
jify	jiffy	jool	joule ★
jig 3 /saw		joon	June
jilt 1		joopiter	Jupiter
jim	gym +	joos	juice +
jingle 2		joosey	juicy

joot	jute	jugle	juggle [2+]
jostle [2]		jugular ★ (vein)	
josul	jostle [2]	juic *e* /ier/iest/ily/y	
jot [3]		Juish	Jewish
joule ★ (unit of energy)		jujoob	jujube
joule	duel [3★]	jujube	
joule	jewel [3★]	juke-box	
journal /ism/ist		jukstapose	juxtapose [2+]
journey [1] /s		jukstaposition	juxtaposition
jovial /ity/ly		Juli	July
jowl		July	
joy /ful/fully		jumble [2]	
joyous /ly		jumbo	
joy-rid *e* /ing		jumbul	jumble [2]
joyus	joyous +	jump [1] /er/iness/y	
ju	Jew +	junkcher	juncture
jubilant /ly		junction	
jubilashun	jubilation	juncture	
jubilation		June	
jubilee		jungle	
jubili	jubilee	jungul	jungle
juce	juice +	junier	junior
jucy	juicy	junior	
Judas		juniper	
judder [1]		junk	
judge [2] /ment		junket [1]	
judicacher	judicature	junta	
judicature		Jupiter	
judicial /ly		jurer	juror
judiciar *y* /ies		juri	jury ★ +
judicious /ly		juridical /ly	
judishal	judicial +	juriman	juryman +
judisharey	judiciary +	jurisdicshun	jurisdiction +
judishus	judicious +	jurisdiction /al	
judo		jurispruden *ce* /t	
juel	duel [3★]	jurisprudens	jurisprudence +
juel	jewel [3★]	jur *ist* /or	
juel	joule ★	jurnal	journal +
jueller	jeweller +	jurnalism	journalism
juelrey	jewellery	jurnalist	journalist
jug [3]		jurnie	journey [1+]
juge	judge [2+]	jurny	journey [1+]
jugernawt	juggernaut	jur *y* ★(legal)/ies	
juggernaut		jury *man* /men (pl.)	
juggle [2] /r ★ (conjurer)		juse	juice +

jusie	juicy	karicteristic	characteristic +
just		karizma	charisma
justice		kayak	
justifiabl *e* /y		kedgeree	
justifiabul	justifiable +	keel ¹ /age	
justificashun	justification	keelige	keelage
justif *y* ⁴ /ication		keen ¹ /ly/ness	
justis	justice	keep /er/ing/sake	
jut ³		keg	
jute		kegeree	kedgeree
juvenil *e* /ity		kejery	kedgeree
juwel	jewel ³★	kelp	
juweller	jeweller +	kelsius	Celsius
juwellrey	jewellery	kelt	Celt +
juxtapos *e* ² /ition		keltic	Celtic
jym	gym +	kemical	chemical +
jymkana	gymkhana	kemist	chemist +
jymnasium	gymnasium +	kemistrey	chemistry
jymnast	gymnast	ken ³	
jymnastics	gymnastics	kenl	kennel
jyroscope	gyroscope +	kennel	
		kept	

K

> *If you cannot find your word under* **k** *look under* **c**

kacao	cacao	kerb ¹★ (stone edging)	
kaen	cayenne	kerb	curb ¹★
Kaiser		kerchief	
kaison	caisson	kernel ★ (seed)	
kakey	khaki	kernel	colonel ★
kakie	khaki	keropodie	chiropody +
kale		keropody	chiropody +
kaleidoscop *e* /ic		keroseen	kerosene
kalidascope	kaleidoscope +	kerosene	
kameliun	chameleon	kestrel	
kangaroo		ketch /es	
kaolin		ketchup	
kaos	chaos +	ketle	kettle +
kaotick	chaotic	kettle /drum	
karate		ketul	kettle +
karicter	character	kew	cue ²★
karicterisashun	characterisation	kew	queue ²★
karicterise	characterise ²+	key ¹★† /hole/stone †(with lock)	
		key	quay ★
		khaki	
		khan	
		khrist	Christ

165

khristianity	Christianity	kiropodey	chiropody +
kiak	kayak	kiropodist	chiropodist
kibbutz		kiropody	chiropody +
kick [1] /er		kiser	Kaiser
kick-off		kiss [1] /er/es	
kid [3]		kit [3]	
kidd *y* /ies		kitchen	
kidie	kiddy +	kite	
kidnap [3] /per		kiten	kitten
kidney		kith	
kidy	kiddy +	kitie	kitty
kile	chyle	kitn	kitten
kill [1] /er		kitten	
kiln		kitty	
kilo		kity	kitty
kilocycle		kiyak	kayak
kilogram		klorate	chlorate
kilohertz		kloride	chloride
kiloliter	kilolitre	klorinashun	chlorination
kilolitre		klorinate	chlorinate [2]+
kilometer	kilometre	klorination	chlorination
kilometre		klorine	chlorine
kilosicle	kilocycle	klorofil	chlorophyll
kilotonne		kloroform	chloroform [1]
kilotun	kilotonne	klorophill	chlorophyll
kilowatt		knack /er	
kilowhat	kilowatt	knapsack	
kilt		knave ★ (rascal) /ry	
kime	chyme	knead [1]★ (press)	
kimono		knee /-cap/d ★†/ing	
kin /dred/ship		† (touch with knee)	
kinaesthesis		kneel [1]	
kind /ly/ness		knell [1]	
kindergarten		knelt	
kindle [2]		knew ★ (did know)	
kindrid	kindred	knew	gnu ★
kindul	kindle [2]	knew	new ★+
kinesthesis	kinaesthesis	knickerbockers	
kinetic		knickers	
king /ly/-pin/-size		knick-knack	
kink /ier/iest/y		kni*fe* [2] /ves (pl.)	
kins *man* /woman/folk		knight ★ (rank)	
kiosk		knit [3]★ (with needles)	
kipper [1]		knob [3]★ (handle) /by	
kirk		knob	nob ★

knock¹ /er/-kneed
knoll¹
knot³★ (what you tie) /ty
know ★† /ing/ingly/s ★†
  †(understand)
knowledge /able
knuckle² /duster
koala
Kodak

kola	koala
koolom	coulomb
kopeck	copeck
koral	choral ★+
koral	coral ★
koral	corral ³★
kord	chord ★
kord	cord ★+

Kremlin

kresh	crèche
krisalis	chrysalis +
krisanthimum	chrysanthemum

Krishna

kroisant	croissant
kromate	chromate
kromatic	chromatic +
kromatin	chromatin
kromatograf	chromatograph +
kromatogram	chromatogram
krome	chrome +
kromic	chromic
kromium	chromium
kromosome	chromosome

krone★(money)/r(pl.)

krone	crone ★
kronicul	chronicle ²+
kronie	crony +
kronik	chronic +
kronologey	chronology +
kuisine	cuisine

Ku-Klux-Klan

kul de sac	cul-de-sac
kurb	curb ¹★
kurb	kerb ¹★
kurchif	kerchief
kurd	curd

kurdle	curdle ²
kurdul	curdle ²
kurk	kirk
kurl	curl ¹+
kurlew	curlew
kurlu	curlew
kurly	curly
kurnel	colonel ★
kurnel	kernel ★

If you cannot find your word under **kw** *look under* **qu**

kwack	quack ¹
kwaff	quaff ¹
kwafur	coiffeur ★+
kwafur	coiffure ★
kwagmire	quagmire
kwail	quail ¹
kwaint	quaint +

L

label³
laber	labour ¹+
labernum	laburnum
labirinth	labyrinth +
labium
labor	labour ¹+
laborator y /ies
laboratrey	laboratory +
laborious /ly
laborius	laborious +
labour¹ /er
Labrador
labrum
laburnum
labyrinth /ine
lac e² /y
lacerat e² /ion
lach	latch ¹+
lachrym al /ose
lack¹ /-lustre
lackadaisical
lackadaysical	lackadaisical
lacker	lacquer ¹

167

lackey /s	
lacky	lackey +
laconic /ally	
lacquer 1	
lacrimal	lachrymal +
lacros	lacrosse
lacrosse	
lactashun	lactation
lactation	
lactic	
lad /die	
ladder 1	
lad e *† /en/ing	
†(load cargo)	
lade	laid *
lader	ladder 1
ladie	lady +
ladilike	ladylike +
ladiship	ladyship
ladle 2	
ladul	ladle 2
lad y /ies	
lady like /ship	
laer	lair *
laer	layer 1*
laerd	laird
laf	laugh 1+
laffing stock	laughing-stock
lafter	laughter
lag 3	
lagard	laggard
lager	
laggard	
lagoon	
laid * (lay)	
laid	lade *+
lain * (did lie on)	
lain	lane *
lair * (den)	
lair	layer 1*
laird	
laitie	laity
laity	
lake	
laker	lacquer 1

lakrimal	lachrymal +
lakross	lacrosse
laks	lax +
laksativ	laxative
lama * (Tibetan monk)	
lama	llama *
lamb /'s-wool	
lame 2 /ly/ness	
lament 1 /ation	
lamentabl e /y	
lamentabul	lamentable +
lamentashun	lamentation
laminate 2	
lamp /light/shade	
lampoon 1 /er/ist	
lampray	lamprey
lamprey	
lance 2 /r/t	
land 1 /lord	
landau	
landaw	landau
landing /-place	
landlad y /ies	
landlocked	
landlubber /ly	
landmark	
landoner	landowner
landowner	
landscape 2	
landsli de /p	
lane * (path)	
lane	lain *
langger	languor +
language	
languid /ly/ness	
languish 1	
languor /ous	
langwid	languid +
langwidge	language
langwige	language
langwish	languish 1
lanjerie	lingerie
lank /iness/y	
lanladie	landlady +
lanlord	landlord

168

lanolin	
lans	lance ²⁺
lanset	lancet
lantern	
lanthanum	
lanyard	
lap ³	
lapel /led	
lapidary	
lapis lazuli	
lapse ²	
larcen y /ies/ous	
larch /es	
larconic	laconic +
lard ¹ /er	
large /ly/r/sse/st	
lariat	
laringitis	laryngitis
larinks	larynx +
larinx	larynx +
lark ¹ /er	
larseny	larceny +
larva *† /e (pl.)/l	
†(of insects)	
larva	lava *
laryn x /gitis	
lascivious /ly/ness	
lase	lace ²⁺
laser	
laserashun	laceration
laserate	lacerate ²⁺
laseration	laceration
lasitude	lassitude
lasivious	lascivious +
lasivius	lascivious +
lasoo	lasso ¹⁺
lassitude	
lasso ¹ /es	
last ¹ /ly	
latch ¹ /key	
late /ly/st	
laten cy /t	
latensey	latency +
later * (afterwards)	
later	latter *⁺

lateral	
lath * (wooden strip)	
lathe * (machine)	
lather ¹	
Latin	
latis	lattice +
latitude	
latrine	
latter * (last) /ly	
lattice /d	
lattis	lattice +
laud ¹* (praise)	
laud	lord ¹*⁺
lauda ble /bly/tory	
laugh ¹ /ter	
laughing-stock	
launch ¹ /er/es	
laund er ¹ /erette/ress	
laundrey	laundry +
laundr y /ies	
laureate	
laurel ³	
lava * (of volcano)	
lava	larva *⁺
lavator y /ies	
lavatrey	lavatory +
lavender	
lavish ¹ /ly/ness	
law * (rule) /-abiding	
law	lore *
law court /suit/yer	
lawd	laud ¹*
lawd	lord ¹*⁺
Lawd Maer	Lord Mayor
lawdable	laudable +
lawdabul	laudable +
lawdatorey	laudatory
lawditrey	laudatory
lawful /ly	
lawless /ness	
lawn	
lawnch	launch ¹⁺
lawnder	launder ¹⁺
lawnderet	launderette
lawndress	laundress

lawndrey	laundry +
lax /ity/ly/ness	
laxative	
lay /by/ing/-out	
laybie	layby
layer ¹★ (thickness)	
layer	lair ★
layman	
laz e ² /y	
lazi er /est/ly/ness	
lea ★ (open ground)	
lea	lee ★+
leach ¹★ (purge)	
leach	leech ★+
lead ★ (guide) /er/ing	
lead ★ (element) /en	
lea f /flet/ves (pl.)	
leaf y /iness	
league	
leak ¹★ (hole) /age/y	
leak	leek ★
lean ¹	
leant ★ (inclined)	
leant	Lent ★
leant	lent ★
leap /ing/t	
leap -frog /-year	
learn ¹ /er/t	
lease ²	
leash ¹	
least /ways/wise	
leather /iness/n/y	
leav e /er ★ (school-)/ing	
leaven ¹	
leaver	lever ★
lebra	libra
lecher /ous/y	
lecherus	lecherous
lectern	
lecture ² /r/ship	
led ★ (did guide)	
led	lead ★+
ledge	
ledger	
ledo	lido

lee ★† /ward/way †(shelter)	
lee	lea ★
leech ★ (worm) /es	
leech	leach ¹★
leed	lead ★+
leef	leaf +
leeflet	leaflet
leeg	league
leege	liege
leek ★ (vegetable)	
leek	leak ¹★+
leen	lean ¹
leep	leap +
leep yeer	leap-year
leer ¹ /y	
leesh	leash ¹
left /ist/ward	
leftenancy	lieutenancy +
leftenansey	lieutenancy +
leftenant	lieutenant
left-hand /ed	
leg ³ /gy	
legac y /ies	
legal /ly	
legalis e ² /ation	
legalit y /ies	
legasey	legacy +
legashun	legation
legation	
legend /ary	
legendrey	legendary
leger	ledger
legib le /ility/ly	
legibul	legible +
legion /ary/aries	
legislacher	legislature
legislashun	legislation
legislat e ² /ion/or	
legislature	
legitima cy /te/tely	
legitimasey	legitimacy +
legitimis e ² /ation	
legonrey	legionary
leisure /ly	

170

lejun	legion +	lest	least +
lejunrey	legionary	lesure	leisure +
leksicografer	lexicographer +	let /table/ting	
leksicographer	lexicographer +	leter	letter [1]
leksicon	lexicon	lethal /ly	
lemon /ade		lethargey	lethargy +
lemur		letharg y /ic	
lend /er/ing		lether	leather +
length /wise/y		letice	lettuce
lengthen [1]		letis	lettuce
lenienc e /y		letre	litre
leniens	lenience +	letter [1]	
lenient /ly		lettuce	
lens /es		letus	lettuce
Lent ★ (40 days)		leucocytes	
lent ★ (did lend)		leukaemia	
lent	leant ★	Levant	
lenth	length +	leve	leave +
lenthen	lengthen [1]	level [3] /ler/ly	
lenticel		level-headed	
lentil		levelheded	level-headed
Leo		leven	leaven [1]
leopard		lever [1] ★ (bar) /age	
leotard		lever	leaver★
lep er /rous		leviathan	
leperd	leopard	levie	levy [4]+
lepidopterous		levitashun	levitation
leprosy		levitat e [2] /ion	
lept	leapt	levity	
lerch	lurch [1]+	levy [4] /ies	
lerk	lurk [1]	lewd /ly/ness	
lern	learn [1]+	lexicografer	lexicographer +
les	less +	lexicograph er /y	
Lesbian		lexicon	
lese	lease [2]	lezbian	Lesbian
lesen	lessen [1]★	li	lie ★
lesher	leisure +	li	lye ★
leshon	lesion	lia	liar ★
lesion		liabilit y /ies	
leson	lessen [1]★	liable	
leson	lesson ★	liabul	liable
less /ee/er ★ (minor)		liaise [2]	
lessen [1]★ (to belittle)		liaison [1]	
lesson ★ (learnt)		liar ★ (tells lies)	
lessor ★ (grants lease)		liar	lyre ★+

171

libel [3] /ler/lous
libelus   libellous
liberal /ity/ly
liberalis *e* [2] /ation
liberashun   liberation
liberat *e* [2] /ion/or
libertey   liberty +
libertine
libert*y* /ies
libid*o* /inal/inous
libra
libralise   liberalise [2]+
librar*y* /ies/ian
lice
licee   lycée
licence ★ (n.)
license [2]★ (v.) /e/r
licenshiate   licentiate
licenshus   licentious +
licentiate
licentious /ness
lichen /ed
lick [1]
licoriss   liquorice
lid /ded
lido
lie ★ (untruth)
lie   lye ★
liege
lieu ★ (place)
lieutenan*cy* /t
li*fe* /ves (pl.)
life *belt* /-blood/less/long
life-size
lift [1] /-off
ligacher   ligature
ligament
ligature
light /er/est/ing
lighten [1]
lighthouse
light *ly* /ness
lightning
light-weight
light-year

lignin
lignite
likeable
likabul   likeable
like [2] /ly/ness
likelihood
liken [1]
liker   liqueur [1]★
liker   liquor [1]★
likewise
likoris   liquorice
likwefi   liquefy [4]+
likwid   liquid +
likwidashun   liquidation
likwidate   liquidate [2]+
likwidation   liquidation
likwiditey   liquidity
lilac
lilak   lilac
lile   lisle
lilie   lily +
Lilipushun   Lilliputian
Lilliputian
lilt [1]
lil*y* /ies
limb [1] /less
limber [1]
limbo /s
lime /-kiln/light
limelite   limelight
limerick
limestone
limf   lymph +
limfatic   lymphatic
limit [1] /ation
limoosene   limousine
limousine
limp [1] /er/ness
limpet
limph   lymph +
limphatic   lymphatic
limpid
linage ★†
    †(number of lines)
linch   lynch [1]

line² /r	
lineage ★ (ancestry)	
lineament ★ (features)	
lineament	liniment ★
linear /ity/ly	
linet	linnet
linger¹	
lingerie	
lingo /es	
lingual	
linguist /ic/ics	
lingwal	lingual
lingwist	linguist +
liniament	lineament ★
linier	linear +
liniige	lineage ★
liniment ★ (salve)	
liniment	lineament ★
link¹ /age	
links ★ (joins)	
links	lynx ★+
linnet	
lino /cut/leum	
linolium	linoleum
linseed	
lint	
lintel /led	
lintul	lintel +
linx	lynx ★+
lio	Leo
lion /ess (fem.)	
lion-hearted	
liotard	leotard
lip³ /stick	
lip-read /er/ing	
liquefy⁴ /action	
liquer	liquor¹★
liqueur¹★†	
†(sweet liquor)	
liquid /ity	
liquidat e² /ion/or	
liquor¹★ (drink)	
liquor	liqueur¹★
liquorice	
liquoris	liquorice

lire	lyre ★+
lirical	lyrical
lisay	lycée
lise	lice
lisen	listen¹+
lisence	licence ★
lisence	license²★+
lisener	listener
lisensee	licensee
lisenshiat	licentiate
lisenshus	licentious +
lisentiate	licentiate
lisentious	licentious +
lisle	
lisp¹	
lissom	
list¹	
listen¹ /er	
listless /ly/ness	
lisum	lissom
lit	
litany /ies	
lite	light +
litehowse	lighthouse
litely	lightly +
liten	lighten¹
liter	litre
liter	litter¹
literacher	literature
literacy /te	
literal /ly	
literary /ily	
literasey	literacy +
literat	literate
literature	
litergic	liturgic +
litergy	liturgy +
litewait	light-weight
lithe /ly/some	
lithium	
lithograf	lithograph +
lithografey	lithography
lithograph /ic/y	
litig ant /ious	
litigashun	litigation

litigat *e* ² /ion		loby	lobby ⁴⁺
litijus	litigious	local ★ (of place)	
litle	little	locale ★ (locality)	
litmus paper		localis *e* ² /ation	
litning	lightning	localit *y* /ies	
litracher	literature	locashun	location
litre		locat *e* ² /ion/or	
litter ¹		loch ★ (lake)	
little		lock ¹★ (door) /er/jaw	
litul	little	locket	
liturgey	liturgy ⁺	locksmith	
liturgic /al		lockwacious	loquacious ⁺
liturg *y* /ies		lockwacity	loquacity
liv	live ²⁺	lockwashus	loquacious ⁺
livable		locomoshun	locomotion ⁺
livabul	livable	locomot *ion* /ive	
live ² /lihood/ly		locum	
liveli *er* /est/ness		locust	
liven ¹		lode ★ (mineral) /stone	
liver /ish		lode	load ¹★⁺
liver *y* /ies		lodge ² /ment/r	
livid		lof	loaf ¹⁺
living-room		loft ¹ /ier/iest/ily/iness	
livlie	lively	log ³ /ger	
livlier	livelier ⁺	loganberie	loganberry ⁺
livrey	livery ⁺	loganberr *y* /ies	
liying	lying	logarithm /ic	
lizard		log-book	
lizerd	lizard	loge	lodge ²⁺
llama ★ (animal)		logerhed	loggerhead
lo	low ¹⁺	loggerhead	
load ¹★† /er		logic /al/ally/ian	
†(heavy weight)		logishun	logician
load	lode ★⁺	logistics	
loa *f* ¹ /ves (pl.)		loial	loyal ⁺
loam /y		loialist	loyalist
loan ¹★ (lending)		loialtey	loyalty ⁺
loan	lone ★⁺	loier	lawyer
loath ★ (reluctant)		loin	
loath *e* ²★ (hate) /some		loiter ¹ /er	
lob ³		lokust	locust
lobby ⁴ /ist		lol	loll ¹
lobe		lolipop	lollipop
lobie	lobby ⁴⁺	loll ¹	
lobster		lollipop	

lom	loam +	lorgnette	
lone ★ (lonely) /r		loriat	laureate
lone	loan ¹★	lorie	lorry +
loneliness		lornch	launch ¹+
lonesome		lornderet	launderette
lonesum	lonesome	lornyet	lorgnette
long ¹ /er/est/wise		lorr y /ies	
longevity		lory	lorry +
longitud e /inal/inally		los	loss
loo ¹★ (card game)		los e ★† /ing/er/t	
loo	lieu ★	†(fail to win)	
loobricant	lubricant	lose	loose ²★+
loobricashun	lubrication	loshun	lotion
loobricate	lubricate ²+	loss	
loocrativ	lucrative	lotery	lottery +
loodicrous	ludicrous +	lothe	loathe ²★+
loodicrus	ludicrous +	lothsum	loathsome
look ¹		lotion	
lookemia	leukaemia	lotter y /ies	
looker	lucre +	lotus	
looking-glass		loud /er/ly/ness	
lookwarm	lukewarm	loud-speaker	
loom ¹		lounge ² /r	
loominus	luminous +	lous e /y	
loona	luna	lout /ish	
loop ¹		lov e ² /able/ely/er	
loose ²★† /ly/ness/r/st		loveli er /est/ness	
†(not tight)		loves	loaves
loose	lose ★+	low ¹ /est/liness/ly	
loosen ¹		lowd	loud +
loosing	losing	lower ¹	
loot ¹★ (booty) /er		lownge	lounge ²+
loot	lute ★	lowse	louse +
lop ³		lowt	lout +
lope ²		loyal /ism/ist/ly	
loquacious /ly/ness		loyalt y /ies	
loquacity		lozenge	
loquashus	loquacious +	lozinge	lozenge
lord ¹★ (noble) /ly/ship		lu	lieu ★
lord	laud ¹★	lu	loo ¹★
lord(s) justice(s)		lubber /ly	
Lord Mayor		luber	lubber +
lore ★ (teaching)		lubricant	
lore	law ★+	lubricat e ² /ion	
lorel	laurel ³	lucer	lucre +

175

lucid /ity/ly/ness		lusid	lucid [+]
luck /ier/iest/ily/y		lust [1] /ful	
lucr e /ative		luster	lustre [+]
lude	lewd [+]	lustie	lusty [+]
ludicrous /ly		lustr e /ous	
luff [1]		lust y /ily/iness	
lug [3] /ger		lute ★ (instrument)	
luggage		lute	loot [1]★[+]
lugige	luggage	lutetium	
lugsuriant	luxuriant	Lutheran	
lugubrious		luv	love [2+]
lukemia	leukaemia	luver	lover
lukewarm		luvley	lovely
luksurey	luxury [+]	luvlier	lovelier [+]
luksuriant	luxuriant	luxurey	luxury [+]
luksuriate	luxuriate [2]	luxurian ce /t/tly	
luksurious	luxurious [+]	luxuriate [2]	
luksurius	luxurious [+]	luxurious /ly	
lul	lull [1]	luxur y /ies	
lulabie	lullaby [+]	lycée	
lull [1]		lye ★ (chemical)	
lullab y /ies		lye	lie ★
lumbago		lying	
lumbar ★ (back)		lymph /atic	
lumber [1]★ (wood)		lynch [1]	
lumberjack		lynx ★ (animal) /es	
luminary		lynx	links ★
lumino us /sity		lyre ★† /-bird	
luminus	luminous [+]	†(instrument)	
lump [1] /iness/y		lyre	liar ★
luna		lyric /al/ism/ist	
luna cy /tic			
lunasey	lunacy [+]		
lunch [1] /eon/es		**M**	
lung			
lunge [2]		ma'am	
lurch [1] /er		mac ★ (macintosh)	
lure [2]		mac	mach ★
lurid /ly		macabre	
lurk [1]		macadam /ise [2]	
lurn	learn [1+]	macaroni	
lurner	learner	macaroon	
lurnt	learnt	mace	
luscious		macerat e [2] /ion	
lushus	luscious	mach ★ (speed ratio)	

mach	match [1]+
machate	machete
machete	
machiage	maquillage
Machiavellian	
machination	
machine [2] /ry	
machinist	
mackerel	
mackintosh /es	
macrocosm	
macroscopic	
mad /der/dest/ly/ness	
madam /e (French)	
madden [1]	
made ★ (built)	
made	maid ★+
Madeira	
mademoiselle	
mademwoisel	mademoiselle
maden	madden [1]
madera	Madeira
madonna	
madrigal	
maelstrom	
maer	mayor +
magazine	
magenta	
maggot /y	
Magi	
magic /al/ally/ian	
magishun	magician
magisterial /ly	
magistracy /ies	
magistrate /ure	
magnanim ity /ous	
magnanimus	magnanimous
magnate ★†	
†(prominent person)	
magnesia /um	
magnet ★† /ic/ism	
†(attracts iron)	
magnetise [2] /ation	
magneto /s	
magnificen ce /t/tly	

magnificens	magnificence +
magnifisence	magnificence +
magnifisent	magnificent
magnif y [4] /ication	
magnitude	
magnolia	
magnum	
magot	maggot +
magpie	
Magyar	
mahara ja /nee (fem.)	
mahem	mayhem
mahjong	
mahogany	
maid ★ (girl) /en/enly	
maid	made ★
mail [1]★ (letters)	
mail	male ★
maim [1]	
main ★† /land/ly	
†(most important)	
main	mane ★
maintain [1]	
maintenance	
maintenans	maintenance
maisonette	
maize ★ (corn)	
maize	maze [2]★
majenta	magenta
majer	major [1]+
majestey	majesty +
majestic /ally	
majest y /ies	
majong	mahjong
major [1] /ette	
majorit y /ies	
mak	mac ★
mak	mach ★
makaber	macabre
makadam	macadam +
makaroon	macaroon
mak e /ing/er/eshift	
Makiavelian	Machiavellian
makination	machination
maksila	maxilla +

maksim	maxim
maksimise	maximise 2
maksimum	maximum +
malachite	
maladey	malady +
maladjust ed /ment	
maladministration	
maladroit /ness	
malad y /ies	
malaise	
malakite	malachite
malaprop ism /os	
malard	mallard
malaria	
malase	malaise
malcontent	
male * (man)	
male	mail 1*
maledicshun	malediction
malediction	
malefactor	
malet	mallet
maleus	malleus
malevolen ce /t	
malevolens	malevolence +
malform 1 /ation	
malformashun	malformation
malfuncshun	malfunction 1
malfunction 1	
maliable	malleable +
malice	
malicious /ly/ness	
malign 1 /er/ity	
malignanc y /ies	
malignansey	malignancy +
malignant	
maline	malign 1+
malinger 1 /er	
malis	malice
malishus	malicious +
mallard	
malleab le /ility	
malleabul	malleable +
mallet	
malleus	

malnutrishun	malnutrition
malnutrition	
malodorous	
Malpighian (layer)	
malstrom	maelstrom
malt 1 /ose	
Maltese	
maltreat 1 /ment	
maltreet	maltreat 1+
mam	ma'am
mamal	mammal +
mamarey	mammary
mame	maim 1
mammal /ian	
mammary	
mammon	
mammoth	
mamon	mammon
mamoth	mammoth
man 3 /fully/ly/-of-war	
mana	manna *
manacle 2	
manacul	manacle 2
manage 2 /able/ment	
manager /ial	
mandarin	
mandat e 2 /ary * (law)	
mandatory *(command)	
mandatrey	mandatory *
mandible	
mandibul	mandible
mandolin	
mane * (hair)	
mane	main *+
maner	manner *+
maner	manor *+
manganese	
mang e /y	
mangel-wurzel	
manger	
mangle 2	
mango /es	
mangrove	
mangul	mangle 2
manhandle 2	

manhandul	manhandle [2]
manhole	
manhood	
mania /c/cal	
manicur *e* [2] /ist	
manidge	manage [2+]
manie	many
manifest [1] /ation	
manifesto /s	
manifold [1]	
manige	manage [2+]
manikin	mannequin
manila	manilla
manilla	
manipulashun	manipulation
manipulat *e* [2] /ion	
manipulat *ive* /or	
manjer	manger
manliness	
manna ★ (food)	
mannequin	
manner ★† /ed/ism/ly	
†(method)	
manoeuvr *e* [2] /able	
manoover	manoeuvre [2+]
manoovrable	manoeuvrable
manoovrabul	manoeuvrable
manor ★ (estate) /ial	
manshun	mansion
mansion	
manslaughter	
manslorter	manslaughter
mantel ★† /piece	
†(shelf at fireplace)	
mantilla	
mantle [2]★ (cloak)	
mantul	mantle [2]★
manual /ly	
manufaccher	manufacture [2+]
manufacture [2] /r	
manure [2]	
manuscript	
many	
maonaise	mayonnaise
map [3]	

maple	
mapul	maple
maquillage	
mar [3]	
marathon	
maraud [1] /er	
marawd	maraud [1+]
marble [2]	
marbul	marble [2]
march [1] /er/es	
marchioness (fem.)	
Marconi	
mare	
mareen	marine +
margarine	
margerit	marguerite
margin /al/ally	
marguerite	
mariage	marriage +
marie	marry [4]
marige	marriage +
marigold	
marijuana	
marina	
marinade	
marinate [2]	
marine /r	
marionet	marionette
marionette	
marital	
maritime	
maritul	marital
mariwana	marijuana
marjoram	
mark [1] /edly/er	
market [1] /ability	
markey	marquee ★
markey	marquis ★
markoni	Marconi
marksism	Marxism +
marksman	
markwis	marquis ★
marline-spike	
marmalade	
marmoreal	

marmorial	marmoreal	maserate	macerate [2]+
marmoset		mash [1]	
marmot		mashene	machine [2]+
maroon [1]		mashenerey	machinery
marow	marrow	mashenist	machinist
marquee ★ (tent)		mashine	machine [2]+
marquis ★ (noble)		mashinerey	machinery
marriage /able		mashinist	machinist
marrow		masiv	massive +
marry [4]		mask [1]★ (cover)	
Mars		mask	masque ★
Marseillaise		maskerade	masquerade [2]
Marselase	Marseillaise	masochis m /t/tic	
marsh /-mallow/y		masocism	masochism +
marshal [3]★†		masocist	masochist
†(arrange in order)		mason /ic/ry	
marshal	martial ★+	masonet	maisonette
marshoness	marchioness	masque ★ (ball)	
marshun	Martian	masque	mask [1]★
marsupial		masquerade [2]	
marten ★ (animal)		mass [1] /es	
marten	martin ★	massacer	massacre [2]
marter	martyr [1]+	massacre [2]	
marterdom	martyrdom	massage [2]	
marterise	martyrise [2]	masseu r /se (fem.)	
martial ★† /ly		massive /ly/ness	
†(relating to war)		massur	masseur +
martial	marshal [3]★	master [1] /ly	
Martian		masterbate	masturbate [2]+
martin ★ (bird)		masterful /ly/ness	
martin	marten ★	masterpeace	masterpiece
martinet		masterpiece	
martyr [1] /dom		masticat e [2] /ion	
martyrise [2]		mastiff /s	
marvel [3] /lous/lously		masturbat e [2] /ion	
Marxis m /t		mat [3]★ (rug)	
mary	marry [4]	mat	matt ★
marzipan		matador	
mas	mass [1]+	match [1] /es/less	
masacer	massacre [2]	mate [2]	
masacre	massacre [2]	mater	matter [1]
masage	massage [2]	material /ism/ist/ly	
mascot		materialis e [2] /ation	
masculin e /ity		maternal /ly	
mase	mace	maternit y /ies	

mathematic s /al/ian
mathematishun   mathematician
maths
matinay   matinée
matinée
mating   matting
matins
matress   mattress +
matriarch /al/y
matriculat e ^{2} /ion
matriks   matrix +
matrikulate   matriculate $^{2+}$
matrimon y /ial
matri x /ces/xes (pls.)
matron /ly
matt * (dull surface)
matter ^{1}
matting
mattress /es
mature ^{2} /ly
maturity
maul ^{1}
mausoleum
mauve
maverick
mawgage   mortgage $^{2+}$
mawkish /ness
mawl   maul ^{1}
mawsoleum   mausoleum
maxilla /e (pl.)
maxim
maximise ^{2}
maxim um /a (pl.)
may /be /-fly
May Day
mayhem
mayonnaise
mayor /al/alty
maypole
maze ^{2}*†
   †(confusing paths)
maze   maize *
mazurka
mead
meadow

meager   meagre +
meagre /ly
meak   meek +
meal /time/y
mean * (nasty) /s
mean   mien *
meander ^{1}
mean er /est/ly/ness
meaning /ful/fully/less
meant
meantime
meanwhile
measl es /y
measuls   measles +
measurable
measure ^{2} /less/ment
meat * (flesh)
meat   meet *+
meat   mete ^{2}*
mecanic   mechanic +
mecanise   mechanise $^{2+}$
mecanism   mechanism
mechanic /al/ally
mechanis e ^{2} /ation/m
medal * (award) /list
medal   meddle ^{2}*+
medallion
medalyon   medallion
medcine   medicine +
meddle ^{2}*† /some/r *
   †(interfere /r)
meddler   medlar *
medeval   medieval
medi an /al/ally
medical /ly
medicament
medicat e ^{2} /ion
medicin e /al
medieval
mediocer   mediocre
mediocre
mediocrit y /ies
medisinal   medicinal
meditat e ^{2} /ion/ive/or
Mediterranean

medi *um* /a/ums (pls.)
medlar * (fruit)

medle   meddle ²*+
medler   meddler *
medler   medlar *

medley

medly   medley
medow   meadow
medsin   medicine +
medul   meddle ²*+

medulla

meed   mead

meek /ly/ness

meel   meal +
meeltime   mealtime
meen   mean *+
meener   meaner +
meening   meaning +
meeningful   meaningful
meens   means
meentime   meantime
meenwile   meanwhile

meerschaum

meershum   meerschaum
meesels   measles +
meesley   measly

meet *(encounter)/ing

meet   meat *
meet   mete ²*

megacycle

megafone   megaphone

megalith /ic
megalomania /c
megaphone

meger   meagre +

megohm

megom   megohm
mekanic   mechanic +
mekanical   mechanical
mekanise   mechanise ²+
mekanism   mechanism

melanchol *y* /ia/ic

melay   mêlée

mêlée

melifluous   mellifluous

melifluus   mellifluous

mellifluous
mellow ¹

melodey   melody +

melodic /ally

melodius   melodious

melodrama /tic
melod *y* /ies/ious
melon

melow   mellow ¹

melt ¹
member /ship

membrain   membrane +

membran *e* /ous
memento /es
memo /s
memoir
memorabl *e* /y
memorand *um*/a/ums(pls.)

memorey   memory +

memorial
memorise ²
memor *y* /ies

memrable   memorable +

men (pl. of man)
menace ²
menagerie

menajerey   menagerie
menas   menace ²

mend ¹
mendacious /ly
mendacity

mendashus   mendacious +
mendasitey   mendacity

mendelevium
mendicity
menial /ly
meningitis

meninjitis   meningitis

menopause

menopaws   menopause
menshun   mention ¹
menstrooal   menstrual
menstrooate   menstruate ²+

menstrual

menstruat *e* ² /ion	
ment	meant
mental /ity/ly	
mentalitey	mentality
menthol	
mention ¹	
mentor	
menu /s	
merang	meringue
mercantil *e* /ism	
mercenar *y* /ies	
mercenrey	mercenary +
merchandise	
merchant	
mercur *y* /ial	
merc *y* /iful/ifully/iless	
mere /ly/st	
meretricious	
meretrishus	meretricious
merge ² /r	
meridian	
meridional	
merie	merry +
meriment	merriment
meringue	
merit ¹	
meritorious	
meritorius	meritorious
mermade	mermaid
mermaid	
merr *y* /ier/ily/iment	
merry-go-round	
merry-making	
mersenrey	mercenary +
mersie	mercy +
mersiful	merciful
mersy	mercy +
mery	merry +
mesenger	messenger
mesh ¹	
Mesia	Messiah +
mesidge	message
mesie	messy
mesige	message
mesmeris *e* ² /m	

mesofill	mesophyll
mesophyll	
mess ¹ /ier/iest/ily/y	
message	
messenger	
Messia *h* /nic	
mesur	monsieur
mesurable	measurable
mesurabul	measurable
mesure	measure ²+
metabol *ic* /ism	
metacarpals	
metafisical	metaphysical +
metafisics	metaphysics
metafor	metaphor
metaforical	metaphorical +
metal ³★ (material)	
metal	mettle ★
metalic	metallic
metalise	metallise ²+
metallic	
metallis *e* ² /ation	
metallurg *y* /ical/ist	
metalurgey	metallurgy +
metamorfose	metamorphose ²+
metamorfosis	metamorphosis
metamorphos *e* ² /is/es (pl.)	
metaphor	
metaphorical /ly	
metaphysical /ly	
metaphysics	
metatarsals	
mete ²★ (measure)	
mete	meat ★
mete	meet ★+
meteor /ic/ite	
meteorolog *y* /ical	
meter ¹★ (machine)	
meter	metre ★+
methane	
methilate	methylate ²
method /ical/ically	
methylate ²	
meticulous /ly	
meticulus	meticulous +

183

metior — meteor [+]
metiorite — meteorite
metiorologey — meteorology [+]
metiorological — meteorological
metr *e* ★ (measure) /ic
metre — meter [1]★
metricashun — metrication
metricat *e* [2] /ion
metronome
metropoli *s* /tan
mettle ★ (spirit)
mettle — metal [3]★
metul — mettle ★
mew [1] /s ★†
  †(cat's cry, stable)
mezanin — mezzanine
mezzanine
mi — my [+]
miander — meander [1]
miaow
mica
mice (pl. of mouse)
Michaelmas
microb *e* /ial
microbiolog *y* /ist
microcosm
microfilm
microfone — microphone [+]
micrometer
micron
micro-organism
microphon *e* /ic
micropyle
microscop *e* /ic/ical/y
microwave
mid-brain
midday
middle /-weight
middling
midge /t
Midlands
midling — middling
midnight
midnite — midnight
midriff

midshipman
midst
midsummer
midul — middle [+]
midwi *fe* /ves (pl.)/fery
mien ★ (bearing)
mige — midge [+]
might ★ (strength, may)
might — mite ★
might *ier* /iest/ily/y
migit — midget
migraine
migrane — migraine
migrant
migrat *e* [2] /ion/or
mika — mica
miklmas — Michaelmas
miks — mix [1+]
miksamatosis — myxomatosis
mikscher — mixture
mikser — mixer
miksture — mixture
mil — mill [1+]
milch-cow
mild /ly/ness
mildew /y
mildu — mildew [+]
mile /age/stone
milenium — millennium [+]
milet — millet
miligram — milligram [+]
milileter — millilitre
milimeter — millimetre
miliner — milliner [+]
milinerey — millinery
milinrey — millinery
milion — million [+]
milionair — millionaire
milipede — millepede
milisha — militia
militan *cy* /t
militansey — militancy [+]
militarey — military [+]
militar *y* /ily/ism/ist
militate [2]

militia	
milivolt	millivolt +
miliwot	milliwatt
milk 1 /er/iness/y	
milkmade	milkmaid +
milk *maid* /sop	
mill 1 /er	
millenni *um* /a (pl.)	
millepede	
millet	
milli *gram* /litre/metre	
milliner /y	
million /aire/th	
milli *volt* /watt	
milyun	million +
milyunair	millionaire
mime 2	
mimeograph 1	
mimic /ry	
mimick *ed* /ing	
mimiograf	mimeograph 1
mimosa	
minaret	
mince 2 /meat/-pie/r	
mind 1 /er/ful/less	
mine 2 /sweeper	
miner *†	
†(works in a mine)	
miner	minor *
mineralog *y* /ical/ist	
minestrone	
minestrony	minestrone
mingle 2	
mingul	mingle 2
mini /skirt	
miniatur *e* /ist	
minicher	miniature +
minim /al/um/a (pl.)	
minimise 2	
minion	
miniscule	minuscule
minister 1	
ministerial /ly	
ministra *tion* /nt	
ministrey	ministry +

ministr *y* /ies	
minit	minute 2+
mink	
minks	minx
minnow	
minor * (lesser)	
minor	miner *
minorit *y* /ies	
minow	minnow
minse	mince 2+
minsmeat	mincemeat
minspie	mince-pie
minster	
minstrel	
mint 1	
minuet	
minus /sign	
minuscule	
minushia	minutia +
minute 2 /ly	
minutia /e (pl.)	
minx	
minyouet	minuet
minyun	minion
miopia	myopia +
miow	miaow
mirac *le* /ulous	
miracul	miracle +
miraculus	miraculous
mirage	
mir *e* /y	
mirer	mirror 1
miriad	myriad
mirror 1	
mirth /ful/fully	
mis	miss 1+
misadvencher	misadventure
misadventure	
misal	missal *
misal	missile *
misaliance	misalliance
misalians	misalliance
misalliance	
misanthrop *e* /ic/ist/y	
misapli	misapply 4+

misappl *y* [4] /ication
misapprehen *d* [1] /sion
misappropriat *e* [2] /ion
misaprehend   misapprehend [1+]
misaprehenshun   misapprehension
misaprehension   misapprehension
misapropriate   misappropriate [2+]
misbehav *e* [2] /iour
misbehavier   misbehaviour
misbihave   misbehave [2+]
miscalculat *e* [2] /ion
miscariage   miscarriage
miscarie   miscarry [4+]
miscarige   miscarriage
miscarr *y* [4] /iage
miscast
miscelanius   miscellaneous
miscellaneous
miscellan *y* /ies
mischance
mischans   mischance
mischie *f* /vous
mischif   mischief [+]
mischivus   mischievous
miscible
misconceive [2]
misconception
misconcieve   misconceive [2]
misconduct [1]
misconsepshun   misconception
misconstru *e* [2] /ction
miscount [1]
miscownt   miscount [1]
miscreant
misdeed
misdemeanour
misdemener   misdemeanour
mise   mice
miselaneous   miscellaneous
miselaney   miscellany [+]
miselanius   miscellaneous
miself   myself
miselium   mycelium
miser /liness/ly
miserabl *e* /y

miserabul   miserable [+]
miser *y* /ies
misfire [2]
misfit
misfortune
misgave
misgidance   misguidance
misgidans   misguidance
misgide   misguide [2+]
misgiv *e* /en/ing
misgovern [1] /ment
misguid *e* [2] /ance
misguven   misgovern [1+]
mishandle [2]
mishandul   mishandle [2]
mishap
mishun   mission [+]
mishunarey   missionary
mishunrey   missionary
misile   missile [*]
misinform [1] /ation
misinterpret [1] /ation
misiv   missive
misjudge [2] /ment
misjuge   misjudge [2+]
miskwotashun   misquotation
miskwotation   misquotation
miskwote   misquote [2+]
mislade   mislaid
mislaid
mislay /ing
misle   missal [*]
misle   missile [*]
mislead /ing
misled
misleed   mislead [+]
misnomer
misogyn *y* /ism/ist
misojinist   misogynist
misojiny   misogyny [+]
mispell   misspell [+]
mispelt   misspelt
mispend   misspend [+]
mispent   misspent
misplace [2] /ment

misplase	misplace 2+	misultoe	mistletoe
misprint 1		misunderstand /ing	
mispronounce 2		misunderstood	
mispronownce	mispronounce 2	misuse 2	
misquot e 2 /ation		mite ★ (very small)	
misrable	miserable +	mite	might ★
misrabul	miserable +	miten	mitten
misread /ing		miter	mitre 2
misred	misread +	mith	myth +
misrepresent 1 /ation		mithical	mythical
misrool	misrule 2	mithologey	mythology
misrule 2		mitie	mighty
miss 1 /es		mitigat e 2 /ion	
missal ★(prayer book)		mitre 2	
missal	missile ★	mitten	
missellaneous	miscellaneous	mix 1 /er/ture	
missellany	miscellany +	mixamatosis	myxomatosis
missel-thrush		mixcher	mixture
misshapen		mnemonic	
missible	miscible	mo	mow +
missile ★ (weapon)		moan ★1 (complain) /er	
mission /ary/aries		moat 1	
missive		mob 3	
misspell /ing		mobil e /ity	
misspelt		mobilis e 2 /ation	
misspend /ing		mobilitey	mobility
misspent		moca	mocha
misstate 2 /ment		moccasin	
mist /ily/iness/y		mocha	
mistak e /able/en/ing		mock 1 /ery	
misterey	mystery +	mod e /ish	
misterious	mysterious +	model 3	
misterius	mysterious +	moderashun	moderation
mistic	mystic ★+	moderat e 2 /ion/or	
mistic	mystique ★	modern /ism/ity	
mistifi	mystify 4+	modernis e 2 /ation	
mistime 2		modest /y	
mistisism	mysticism	modicum /s	
mistletoe		modifi	modify 4+
mistook		modificashun	modification
mistress /es		modif y 4 /ication	
mistrust 1 /ful		modul	model 3
misul	missal ★	modulat e 2 /ion/or	
misul	missile ★	modul us /i (pl.)	
misul thrush	missel-thrush	mohair	

mohare	mohair	monkey /s	
moischer	moisture	monochord	
moisen	moisten [1]	monochrom e /atic/ic	
moist /ness/ure		monocle	
moisten [1]		monocotyledon	
moka	mocha	monocul	monocle
mokasin	moccasin	monogamus	monogamous
molar		monogam y /ist/ous	
molasses		monograf	monograph [1]
mold	mould [1+]	monogram	
molder	moulder [1]	monograph [1]	
moldey	mouldy	monokord	monochord
mole		monokrome	monochrome [+]
molecul e /ar		monokside	monoxide
molest [1] /ation		monolith /ic	
molicodle	mollycoddle [2]	monolog	monologue
molicodul	mollycoddle [2]	monologue	
mollify [4]		monomania /c	
mollusc		monophonic	
mollycoddle [2]		monoplane	
molt	moult [1]	monopoley	monopoly [+]
molten		monopolis e [2] /ation	
molusk	mollusc	monopolist /ic	
molybdenum		monopol y /ies	
moment /arily/ary		monorail	
momentous		monosilabic	monosyllabic
momentum		monosilable	monosyllable [+]
monak	monarch [+]	monosyllab le /ic	
monakey	monarchy [+]	monothaism	monotheism [+]
monarch /al/ical		monotheis m /t/tic	
monarch y /ies		monotipe	Monotype
monaster y /ial/ies		monoton e /ic	
monastic /ism		monoton ous /y	
monastrey	monastery [+]	monotonus	monotonous [+]
Monday		Monotype	
mone	moan [1+]	monoxide	
monetar y /ism/ist		monsieur	
money /s (pl.)/ed		monsoon	
Mongol /ian		monst er /rous	
Mongol ism /oid		monstrosit y /ies	
mongoose /s		monstrus	monstrous
mongrel		month /ly	
moniter	monitor [1]	monument /al/ally	
monitor [1]		moo [1]	
monk /ish		mooch [1]	

188

mood /ily/iness/y
moon [1] /beam/lit/y
moonlight
moor [1]★† /age
   †(waste ground)
moor   more ★+
moose ★ (animal)
moose   mousse ★
moot [1]
moov   move [2]+
moovable   movable
moovabul   movable
mop [3]
mope [2]
moped
moraine
moral /e/ity/ly
moralise [2]
moralitey   morality
morass
moratorium /s
morbid /ity
mordant
more ★† /over
   †(greater quantity)
more   moor [1]★+
morfia   morphia +
morfine   morphine
morg   morgue
morgage   mortgage [2]+
morganatic /ally
morgige   mortgage [2]+
morgue
moribund
morn ★ (morning)
morn   mourn [1]★+
mornful   mournful +
moron /ic
morose /ly
morover   moreover
morow   morrow
morphi a /ne/nism
morrow
Morse
morsel

mortal /ity/ly
mortar [1] /-board
mortary   mortuary +
mortgag e [2] /ee/or
mortifi   mortify [4]+
mortif y [4] /ication
mortise [2]
mortuar y /ies
mos   moss +
mosaic
moshun   motion [1]+
mosk   mosque
moskito   mosquito +
Moslem
mosque
mosquito /es
moss /es/y
most
mote
moteef   motif ★+
motel
moter   motor [1]+
moterboat   motorboat
motercycle   motorcycle
moterise   motorise [2]+
moterist   motorist
moterway   motorway
moth /-eaten
mother [1] /ly/(s)-in-law
mother-tongue
motif ★ (ornament) /s
motion [1] /less
motivat e [2] /ion
motive ★ (movement)
motled   mottled
motley
motlie   motley
motly   motley
moto   motto +
motor [1]/boat/cycle/way
motoris e [2] /t
mottled
motto /es
mould [1] /iness/y
moulder [1]

moult [1]
mound [1]
mount [1]
mountain /eer/ous
mountebank
mountenus   mountainous
mourn [1]★ (grieve) /er
mournful /ly
mous e ★(rodent)/er/y
mouse   moose ★
mousse ★ (pudding)
moustache
mouth [1] /ful/piece
movable
movabul   movable
move [2] /ment
move   mauve
mow /er/n
mownd   mound [1]
mownt   mount [1]
mowntain   mountain +
mowntbank   mountebank
mownten   mountain +
mowntenear   mountaineer
mowntenus   mountainous
mowse   mouse ★+
mowth   mouth [1]+
mowthful   mouthful
mu   mew [1]+
much
muchooal   mutual +
mucilag e /inous
muck [1] /y
mucous ★ (adj.)
mucus ★ (n.)
mud /dy/guard
muddid   muddied +
muddi ed /er/est
muddle [2] /r
mudid   muddied +
mudie   muddy
mudul   muddle [2]+
muff [1]
muffin
muffle [2] /r

mufin   muffin
mufti
muful   muffle [2]+
mug[3] /gy
mukus   mucous ★
mukus   mucus ★
mulatto /s
mulberie   mulberry +
mulberr y /ies
mulch [1]
mulct [1]
mul e /eteer/ish
mulkt   mulct [1]
mullion
multifarious
multifarius   multifarious
multiform
multilateral /ly
multiple
multipleks   multiplex
multiplex
multipli   multiply [4]+
multiplicashun   multiplication
multiplicity
multipl y [4] /ication
multipul   multiple
multiracial
multirashul   multiracial
multitud e /inous
multitudinus   multitudinous
mulyun   mullion
mumble [2]
mumbo-jumbo
mumbul   mumble [2]
mumie   mummy +
mumifi   mummify [4]
mummify [4]
mumm y /ies
mumy   mummy +
munch [1]
mundane
Munday   Monday
munetarey   monetary +
munetrey   monetary +
mungrel   mongrel

municipal /ity/ities	
munie	money +
munificen ce /t	
munifisens	munificence +
munifisent	munificent
munishun	munition 1
munisipal	municipal +
munisipalitey	municipality
munition 1	
munk	monk +
munky	monkey +
munth	month +
muny	money +
mur	myrrh
mural /ly	
murder 1 /er/ess/ous	
murk /ily/iness/y	
murmer	murmur 1
murmur 1	
murth	mirth +
murtle	myrtle
mus	mews ★
mus	muse 2★
muscat /el	
muscle 2★ (in body)	
muscle	mussel ★
muscular /ity	
muse 2★ (think)	
muse	mews ★
musel	muscle 2★
musel	mussel ★
museum /s	
mush /y	
mushroom 1	
music /al/ally/ian	
musilage	mucilage +
musishun	musician
musk	
musket /eer/ry	
muskwash	musquash
musquash	
mussel ★ (shellfish)	
mussel	muscle 2★
must /n't	
mustach	moustache

mustang	
mustard	
muster 1	
mustie	musty +
must y /iness	
mutashun	mutation
mutation	
mute 2 /ly	
muter	mutter 1
mutilat e 2 /ion/or	
mutinear	mutineer +
mutin eer /ous	
mutinus	mutinous
mutin y 4 /ies	
muton	mutton
mutter 1	
mutton	
mutual /ly	
muzie	muzzy +
muzul	muzzle 2
muzzle 2	
muzz y /ily/iness	
my /self	
mycelium	
myopi a /c	
myriad	
myrrh	
myrtle	
mysterious /ly/ness	
mysterius	mysterious +
myster y /ies	
mystic ★† /al/ism	
†(spiritual)	
mystif y 4 /ication	
mystique ★ (mystery)	
myth /ical/ology	
myxomatosis	

N

nab 3	
naber	neighbour +
nabob	
nabour	neighbour +

nacher	nature	nascen *ce* /t	
nacheral	natural +	nasel	nasal +
nacheralise	naturalise [2+]	nash	gnash [1]
nachural	natural +	nashanality	nationality +
nack	knack +	nashnalism	nationalism +
nacker	knacker	nashun	nation +
nader	nadir	nastie	nasty +
nadir		nast *y* /ier/iest/ily/iness	
naftha	naphtha	nat	gnat
nag [3] /ger		natal	
nail [1]		natie	natty
naive /té/ty		nation /al/ally	
naked /ness		nationalis *e* [2] /ation	
nakid	naked +	nationalis *m* /t/tic	
nale	nail [1]	nationalit *y* /ies	
namby-pamby		native	
name [2] /less/ly		Nativity	
nanie	nanny +	natle	natal
nann *y* /ies		natsi	Nazi
nany	nanny +	natty	
nap [3]		natul	natal
napalm		natural /ism/ist/ly	
naparm	napalm	naturalis *e* [2] /ation	
nape		nature	
naphtha		naty	natty
napie	nappy +	naught	
napkin		naughtie *r* /st	
napp *y* /ies		naught *y* /ily/iness	
napsack	knapsack	nause *a* /ous	
narate	narrate [2+]	nauseate [2]	
narativ	narrative	nautical	
narcissis *m* /t/tic		naval * (navy)	
narcissus		nave * (of church)	
narcosis		nave	knave *+
narcotic		navel * (stomach)	
nar-do-well	ne'er-do-well	naverey	knavery
narl	gnarl [1]	navie	navvy *+
narow	narrow [1+]	navie	navy *+
narrat *e* [2] /ion/or		navigab *le* /ility	
narrative		navigabul	navigable +
narrow [1] /er/ly/ness		navigashun	navigation
narsissism	narcissism +	navigat *e* [2] /ion/or	
narsissist	narcissist	navul	naval *
narsisus	narcissus	navv *y* * (labourer) /ies	
nasal /ly		nav *y* * (warships) /ies	

naw	gnaw [1]	négligé	
nay * (no)		negligen ce /t	
nay	neigh [1]*	negligens	negligence +
naybour	neighbour +	negligibl e /y	
nayl	nail [1]	negligibul	negligible +
Nazi		neglijay	négligé
nead	knead [1]*	negoshable	negotiable
nead	need [1]*+	negoshabul	negotiable
neadle	needle [2]	negoshiate	negotiate [2]+
neadless	needless +	negotiable	
Neapolitan		negotiat e [2] /ion/or	
near /-by/ly/ness		negr o /oes/ess (fem.)	
neat /er/est/ly/ness		negroid	
nebul a /ous		neice	niece
nebulus	nebulous	neigh [1]* (horse's cry)	
necesarey	necessary +	neighber	neighbour +
necesitate	necessitate [2]	neighberhood	neighbourhood
necesitey	necessity +	neighbour /ing/ly	
necessar y /ily		neighbourhood	
necessitate [2]		neither	
necessit y /ies/ous		nek	neck +
neck /lace/tie		neklace	necklace
necksus	nexus	necklis	necklace
necrofilia	necrophilia	nekrofilia	necrophilia
necrophilia		nekropolis	necropolis
necropolis		nekst	next +
nectar /y		neksus	nexus
nee	knee +	nell	knell [1]
need [1]* (lack) /ful/y		nelt	knelt
need	knead [1]*	Nemesis	
need	kneed *	nemisis	Nemesis
needle [2]		nemonic	mnemonic
needless /ly		neodimium	neodymium
needul	needle [2]	neodymium	
neel	kneel [1]	neolithic	
neer	near +	neon	
ne'er-do-well		nephew	
neet	neat +	nepotism	
nefarious /ly		Neptune	
nefarius	nefarious +	neptunium	
nefew	nephew	nerv e [2] /y	
negashun	negation	nervous /ly/ness	
negation		nervus	nervous +
negative /ly		nesesarey	necessary +
neglect [1] /ful		nesesitate	necessitate [2]

nesesitey	necessity +	next /-of-kin	
neslin	nestling	nexus	
nest [1] /ling		ni	nigh
net [3] /ball		nibble [2]	
netha	neither	nibul	nibble [2]
nether		nice /ly/ness/r/st	
nettle [2] /rash		nicet y /ies	
netul	nettle [2]+	nich	niche
network		niche	
neumatick	pneumatic	nick [1]	
neural /gia		nickel	
neuritis		nickerbockers	knickerbockers
neurologist		nickers	knickers
neuron		nickle	nickel
neuro sis /tic		nicknack	knick-knack
neuter		nickname [2]	
neuton	newton	nicotine	
neutral /ity		niece	
neutralis e [2] /ation		niether	neither
neutron /s		nifarious	nefarious +
neva	never +	nifarius	nefarious +
never /more/theless		nife	knife [2]+
nevu	nephew	niftie	nifty +
new * (not old) /er/est		nift y /iness	
new	gnu *	nigerd	niggard +
new	knew *	niggard /ly	
newclear	nuclear	niggl e [2] /y	
newcleus	nucleus +	nigh	
new comer /fangled		night *† /dress/gown	
new ly /ness		†(the dark)	
newmatic	pneumatic	night	knight *
newmonia	pneumonia	night fall /jar	
newral	neural +	nightingale	
newritis	neuritis	nightmar e /ish	
newrologist	neurologist	night -shift /-time	
newron	neuron	night-watch /man	
newrosis	neurosis +	nigle	niggle [2]+
newrotic	neurotic	niglect	neglect [1]+
news /-agent/-flash		nigul	niggle [2]+
news paper /print/y		niks	nix
newt		nilon	nylon
newter	neuter	nimble /ness	
newton		nimblie	nimbly
newtralise	neutralise [2]+	nimbly	
newtron	neutron +	nimbul	nimble +

nimbus /es	
nimf	nymph
nimph	nymph
nincompoop	
nin e /th/thly	
nineteen /th	
ninet y /ies/ieth	
ningcumpoop	nincompoop
ninie	ninny +
ninn y /ies	
niobium	
nion	neon
nip 3 /per/py	
nipie	nippy
nipple	
nipul	nipple
nipy	nippy
nise	nice +
nisitey	nicety +
niss	niece
nit * (insect)	
nit	knit 3*
nite	knight *
nite	night *+
niter	nitre
nither	neither
nitrate	
nitre	
nitric	
nitrifi	nitrify 4
nitrify 4	
nitrite	
nitrogen /ous	
nitrogliserine	nitroglycerine
nitroglycerine	
nitrojen	nitrogen +
nitrous /oxide	
nitrus	nitrous +
nitwit	
nives	knives
nix	
no * (negative reply)	
no	know *+
nob * (cribbage)	
nob	knob 3*+

nobie	knobby
nobility	
noble /man/men(pl.)/r/st	
noblie	nobly
nobly	
nobul	noble +
nock	knock 1+
nocker	knocker
nockneed	knock-kneed
nodes	
nodule	
noes * (negative)	
noes	knows *
noes	nose *+
nois e /y	
noledge	knowledge +
nolidge	knowledge +
noll	knoll 1
nome	gnome +
none * (not any)	
none	nun *+
nor	gnaw 1
norsia	nausea +
norsiate	nauseate 2
nort	naught
nortey	naughty +
nortickle	nautical
nortie	naughty +
Norwegian	
nose * (on face) /y	
nose	knows *
nose	noes *
nostril	
not * (no)	
not	knot 3*+
notie	knotty
notty	knotty
nova	
nowing	knowing
nowledge	knowledge +
nu	gnu *
nu	knew *
nu	new *+
nuance	
nuans	nuance

195

nuckle	knuckle [2+]	nuspaper	newspaper [+]
nuclear		nut /cracker/shell	
nucle *us* /i (pl.)		nuta	neuter
nud *e* /ist/ity		nuter	neuter
nudge [2]		nutie	nutty
nuge	nudge [2]	nutmeg	
nugget		nuton	newton
nulifi	nullify [4+]	nutralise	neutralise [2+]
nulitey	nullity	nutrishun	nutrition
null		nutrition	
nullif *y* [4] /ication		nutron	neutron [+]
nullity		nutty	
numatic	pneumatic	nuty	nutty
numb [1] /ness		nuzul	nuzzle [2]
number [1] /-plate		nuzzle [2]	
numer *able* /acy/al		nylon	
numerabul	numerable [+]	nymf	nymph
numerasey	numeracy	nymph	
numerat *e* [2] /ion			
numerical			
numerous /ly/ness			
numerus	numerous [+]		
numismatic /s		O * (addressing)	
numonia	pneumonia	o	oh *
numrable	numerable [+]	o	owe [2*]
numrabul	numerable [+]	oaf /ish	
numskull		oak /en	
nun * (religious) /nery		oakum	
nun	none *	oar * (of a boat)	
nupshal	nuptial	oar	ore *
nuptial		oas *is* /es (pl.)	
nural	neural [+]	oast	
nuralgia	neuralgia	oat /meal	
nurcher	nurture [2]	oath	
nuritis	neuritis	obay	obey [1]
nurologist	neurologist	obduracy	
nuron	neuron	obdurasey	obduracy
nurosis	neurosis [+]	obdurate /ly	
nurotic	neurotic	obedien *ce* /t	
nurse [2]		obediens	obedience [+]
nurser *y* /ies		obelisk	
nursrey	nursery [+]	obes *e* /ity	
nurture [2]		obey [1]	
nurv	nerve [2+]	obituar *y* /ies	
nus	news [+]	objecshun	objection [+]

object [1] /or
objection /able
objectiv e /ely/ity
obligashun — obligation +
obligat ion /ory
obligatrey — obligatory
oblige [2]
oblik — oblique +
oblique /ly/ness
obliterashun — obliteration
obliterat e [2] /ion
obliv ion /ious
oblivius — oblivious
oblivyun — oblivion +
oblokwey — obloquy +
oblong
obloqu y /ies
obnokshus — obnoxious +
obnoxious /ly
obo — oboe +
obo e /ist
obscene /ly
obscure [2] /ly
obscurit y /ies
obseen — obscene +
obsekwies — obsequies
obsekwius — obsequious +
obsequies
obsequious /ly
observable
observabul — observable
observan ce /t
observashun — observation
observator y /ies
observatrey — observatory +
observ e [2] /ation/er
observence — observance +
observens — observance +
obseshun — obsession
obsess [1] /ion/ive
obsolescen ce /t
obsolesens — obsolescence +
obsolesent — obsolescent
obsolete
obstacle

obstacul — obstacle
obstetric /ian/s
obstetrishun — obstetrician
obstinacy
obstinasey — obstinacy
obstinate /ly
obstreperous
obstreperus — obstreperous
obstrucshun — obstruction
obstruct [1] /ion/ive
obtain [1] /able
obtane — obtain [1]+
obtroode — obtrude [2]+
obtrooshun — obtrusion +
obtroosion — obtrusion +
obtroosiv — obtrusive
obtrude [2] /r
obtrus ion /ive
obtuse /ly/ness
obverse
obviate [2]
obvious /ly
obvius — obvious +
ocasion — occasion [1]+
ocasional — occasional
occashun — occasion [1]+
occasion [1] /al/ally
occident /al
occlu de [2] /sion
occlushun — occlusion
occult [1] /ation
occupan cy /t
occupation /al
occupi — occupy [4]+
occup y [4] /ier
occur [3] /rence
occurens — occurrence
ocean
ocell us /i (pl.)
ocelot
ochre
o'clock
oclude — occlude [2]+
oclusion — occlusion
ocsident — occident +

197

octagon /al
octane
octav *e* /o
octet
October
octogenarian
octopus /es
ocul *ar* /ist
ocult — occult [1+]
ocupancy — occupancy [+]
ocupant — occupant
ocupashun — occupation [+]
ocupation — occupation [+]
ocupi — occupy [4+]
ocur — occur [3+]
ocurence — occurrence
ocurens — occurrence
od — odd [+]
odd /er/est/ly/ment
oddit *y* /ies
ode
odecolone — eau-de-Cologne
oder — odour [+]
oderiferus — odoriferous
oderous — odorous
oderus — odorous
odiferus — odoriferous
odious /ly
oditey — oddity [+]
odium
odius — odious [+]
odontology
odoriferous
odorous
odour /less
oesofagus — oesophagus
oesophagus
of ★ (belonging to)
of — oaf [+]
of — off ★[+]
ofal — offal
ofence — offence
ofend — offend [1+]
ofens — offence
ofensiv — offensive [+]

ofer — offer [1]
off ★ (away from) /ing
offal
offence
offend [1] /er
offens — offence
offensive /ly/ness
offer [1]
offhand /ed/edness
office /r
official /ly
officiate [2]
officious /ly/ness
offis — office [+]
offishal — official [+]
offishus — officious [+]
offprint
offset /ting
offshoot
offside
ofhand — offhand [+]
oficial — official [+]
oficiate — officiate [2]
oficious — officious [+]
ofing — offing
ofis — office [+]
ofiser — officer
ofishal — official [+]
ofishiate — officiate [2]
ofishus — officious [+]
ofprint — offprint
ofset — offset [+]
ofshoot — offshoot
ofside — offside
oft /en
ofthalmia — ophthalmia [+]
ofthalmologist — ophthalmologist [+]
oger — ogre [+]
ogle [2] /r
ogre /ss (fem.)
ogul — ogle [2+]
oh ★ (exclaim)
oh — O ★
ohm /ic/meter
oil [1] /y

ointment		
oister	oyster	
oiyay	oyez	
ok	oak +	
oks	ox +	
oksalic	oxalic	
oksbridge	Oxbridge	
oksbrige	Oxbridge	
oksen	oxen	
oksiasetilene	oxy-acetylene	
oksidashun	oxidation	
oksidation	oxidation	
okside	oxide +	
oksident	occident +	
oksidise	oxidise 2+	
oksigen	oxygen	
oksigenate	oxygenate 2+	
oksigenise	oxygenise 2	
oksihemoglobin	oxyhaemoglobin	
oksonian	Oxonian	
okstail	oxtail	
okstale	oxtail	
okstung	ox-tongue	
okum	oakum	
old /en/er		
olfacshun	olfaction +	
olfact ion /ory		
olfactrey	olfactory	
oligarch y /ies		
oligarkey	oligarchy +	
olimpic	Olympic +	
oliv	olive	
olive		
Olympi c /an		
om	ohm +	
ombudsman		
omega		
omelet	omelette	
omelette		
omen 1		
ominous /ly		
ominus	ominous +	
omishun	omission	
omission		
omit 3		

omlet		omelette
omnibus /es		
omnipoten ce /t		
omnipotens		omnipotence +
omnipresent		
omniscien ce /t		
omnisiens		omniscience +
omnisient		omniscient
omnivorous /ly		
omnivorus		omnivorous +
on		own 1
once		
oncoming		
oncore		encore 2
one * (single) /self		
oner		honour 1+
oner		owner +
onerable		honourable
onerabul		honourable
onerous		
onership		ownership
onerus		onerous
oniks		onyx
onion		
onist		honest +
onistey		honesty
onley		only
onlook er /ing		
only		
onomatipea		onomatopoeia +
onomatopoei a /c		
onorarey		honorary
onorarium		honorarium +
onrable		honourable
onrabul		honourable
onrush		
onset		
onslaught		
onslawt		onslaught
onslort		onslaught
onto		
ontray		entrée
ontreprener		entrepreneur +
onus		
onward /s		

199

onyx
oolit *e* /ic
ooze ² /y
opacity
opake   opaque ⁺
opal /ine
opalescen *ce* /t
opalesens   opalescence ⁺
opaque /ly
opasitey   opacity
open ¹ /er
open sesame
opera /tic/tically
operab *le* /ility
operabul   operable ⁺
operashun   operation ⁺
operat *e* ² /ive/or
operater   operator
operation /al
operetta
ophthalmi *a* /c
ophthalmolog *ist* /y
opiate
opine ²
opinion /ated
opinyun   opinion ⁺
opium
oponent   opponent
oportune   opportune ⁺
oportunism   opportunism ⁺
oportunist   opportunist
oportunitey   opportunity ⁺
opose   oppose ²⁺
oposishun   opposition
oposit   opposite ⁺
oposition   opposition
opossum
oposum   opossum

opponent
opportune /ly/ness
opportunis *m* /t
opportunit *y* /ies
oppose ² /r
opposishun   opposition
opposit *e* /ion

oppress ¹ /ion/ive
oprable   operable ⁺
oprabul   operable ⁺
opreshun   oppression
opresiv   oppressive
opress   oppress ¹⁺
opshun   option ⁺
opshunal   optional
opt ¹ /ative
opthalmia   ophthalmia ⁺
opthalmic   ophthalmic
opthalmologist ophthalmologist ⁺
opthalmology ophthalmology
optic /al/ally
optician
optimise ²
optimism
optimistic /ally
optimum
option /al/ally
optishun   optician
opulen *ce* /t
opulens   opulence ⁺
opus
or ★ (alternative)
or   awe ²★⁺
or   oar ★
or   ore ★
ora   aura
orac *le* /ular
oracul   oracle ⁺
oral ★ /ly (verbal)
oral   aural ★⁺
orangatang orang-outang
orange /ade
orang-outang
orashun   oration ⁺
orater   orator
orat *ion* /or
oratorio /s
orator *y* /ies
oratrey   oratory ⁺
orb ¹
orbit ¹ /al
orcestra   orchestra

orcestrate	orchestrate 2+	original /ity/ly	
orchard		originat e² /ion/or	
orchestra		oringe	orange +
orchestrat e² /ion/or		oriole	
orchid		orkestrate	orchestrate 2+
ordain¹		orkid	orchid
ordane	ordain¹	orlder	alder
ordeal		ornament¹ /al/ation	
ordenrey	ordinary +	ornate /ly	
order¹ /liness/ly		orning	awning
ordinal		ornitholog y /ist	
ordinance ★ (rule)		orphan¹ /age	
ordinance	ordnance ★	orspishus	auspicious
ordinar y /ily		orstralian	Australian
ordinat e² /ion		orstruck	awestruck
ordinrey	ordinary +	orsum	awesome
orditer	auditor	ort	aught ★
orditorey	auditory	ort	ought ★
orditrey	auditory	orthedoks	orthodox
ordnance ★ (survey, guns)		orthodox	
ordure		orthografey	orthography +
ore ★ (mineral)		orthograph y /ic/ical	
ore	awe 2★+	orthopaedic	
ore	oar ★	orthopeadic	orthopaedic
orfan	orphan 1+	orthoritarian	authoritarian +
orfanage	orphanage	ortolan	
orfanige	orphanage	oscilashun	oscillation +
orful	awful +	oscilation	oscillation +
organ /ist		oscillate 2★ (swing)	
organic		oscillat ion /or/ory	
organis e² /ation/er		oscillogra m /ph	
organism		oscilloscope	
orgasm		osculate 2★ (contact)	
orger	auger ★	oselot	ocelot
orger	augur 1★	oshun	ocean
orgey	orgy +	osicul	ossicle
org y /iastic/ies		osier	
orical	auricle +	osifi	ossify 4+
oriel		osius	osseous
orient /al/ally		osler	ostler
orientashun	orientation	osmium	
orientat e² /ion		osmosis	
orifice		ospray	osprey +
orifis	orifice	osprey /s	
origin		osseous	

osseus	osseous	outbid /ding	
ossicle		outbilding	outbuilding
ossifi	ossify [4+]	outboard	
ossif *y* [4] /ication		outbound	
ossilate	oscillate [2★]	outbownd	outbound
ossilation	oscillation [+]	outbrake	outbreak
ossilograf	oscillograph	outbreak	
ossilogram	oscillogram [+]	outbuilding	
ossiloscope	oscilloscope	outburst	
ost	oast	outcase	
ostensibl *e* /y		outclass [1]	
ostensibul	ostensible [+]	outcome	
ostentashun	ostentation [+]	outcri	outcry [+]
ostentashus	ostentatious	outcrop	
ostentat *ion* /ious		outcr *y* /ies	
osteo-arthritis		outdate [2]	
osteology		outdistance [2]	
osteopath /y		outdo /ing/ne	
ostintashun	ostentation [+]	outdoor /s	
ostioarthritis	osteo-arthritis	outer /most	
ostiologey	osteology	outface	
ostler		outfall	
ostracis *e* [2] /m		outfit /ter	
ostrasism	ostracism	outflank [1]	
ostrasize	ostracise [2+]	outflow	
ostrich /es		outgoing /s	
ote	oat [+]	outgrow /n/th	
oter	otter	outhouse	
oth	oath	outhowse	outhouse
other /wise		outlandish /ness	
otoman	ottoman	outlast [1]	
otter		outlaw [1] /ry	
ottoman		outlay	
ought ★ (should)		outlet	
ought	aught ★	outliing	outlying
ouija		outline [2]	
ounce		outlive [2]	
ouns	ounce	outlook	
our ★ (belonging to us)		outlying	
our	hour ★[+]	outmanoeuvre [2]	
ourly	hourly	outmanoover	outmanoeuvre
ourselves		outmatch [1]	
oust [1]		outmoded	
out [1]		outnumber [1]	
outback		outpace [2]	

outpashent	out-patient	overawe [2]	
out-patient		overawl	overall [+]
outpoor	outpour [1]	overbalance [2]	
outpost		overbalans	overbalance [2]
outpour [1]		overbaring	overbearing
output		overbearing	
outrage [2] /ous/ously		overberden	overburden [1]
outragus	outrageous	overblown	
outran		overboard	
outreach [1]		overbord	overboard
outrid e /den/ing/er		overburden [1]	
outright		overcame	
outrite	outright	overcast	
outrun /ning		overcharge [2]	
outset		overcoat	
outshin e /ing		overcom e /ing	
outshone		overcrowd [1]	
outside /r		overdew	overdue
outsize		overdo /ing/ne	
outskirts		overdose [2]	
outspoken /ness		overdraft	
outstanding /ly		overdraw /n	
outstare [2]		overdrive	
outstay [1]		overdu	overdue
outstretch [1]		overdue	
outstrip [3]		overdun	overdone
outvote [2]		overeach	overreach [1]
outward /ly/s		overeat /en/ing	
outwit [3]		overeet	overeat [+]
outworn		overestimate [2]	
ov	of ★	overflow [1]	
oval		overground	
ovarey	ovary [+]	overgrow /n/th	
ovarian		overgrownd	overground
ovar y /ies		overhand	
ovashun	ovation	overhang /ing	
ovation		overhaul [1]	
oven		overhawl	overhaul [1]
over		overhead /s	
overact [1]		overhear /ing	
overall /s		overheard	
overan	overran	overheat [1]	
overarm		overhed	overhead [+]
overate ★ (overeat)		overheet	overheat [1]
overate	overrate [2]★	overherd	overheard

overhere	overhear +	overstate ² /ment	
overhung		overstep ³	
overide	override +	overstock ¹	
overjoi	overjoy +	overstrung	
overjoy /ed		overt /ly	
overladen		overtak e /en/ing	
overland		overtaks	overtax ¹
overlap ³		overtax ¹	
overla y /id		overtern	overturn ¹
overleaf		overthrow /n	
overleef	overleaf	overtime	
overload ¹		overtire ²	
overlode	overload ¹	overtone	
overlook ¹		overtook	
overmuch		overture	
overnight		overturn ¹	
overnite	overnight	overwate	overweight
overore	overawe ²	overweight	
overought	overwrought	overwelm	overwhelm ¹+
overpass		overwerk	overwork ¹
overpower ¹		overwhelm ¹ /ingly	
overproduc e ² /tion		overw ind /ound	
overproducshun	overproduction	overwork ¹	
overran		overwownd	overwound
overrate ²★ (overvalue)		overwrought	
overrate	overate ★	oviduct	
overrawt	overwrought	ovine	
overreach ¹		oviparous	
overreech	overreach ¹	oviparus	oviparous
overrid e /den/ing		ovipositor	
overrool	overrule ²	ovoid	
overrule ²		ovoyd	ovoid
overrun /ning		ovulashun	ovulation
oversaw		ovulat e ² /ion	
oversea ★ (abroad) /s ★		ovule	
oversee ★† /ing/n/r/s ★†		ov um /a (pl.)	
†(supervise)		owe ²★ (in debt)	
overshadow ¹		ower	hour ★+
overshoot		ower	our ★
overshot		owerselves	ourselves
oversight		owl /ish	
oversite	oversight	own ¹	
oversle ep /pt		ownce	ounce
oversore	oversaw	owner /less/ship	
overspill ¹		owns	ounce

204

owst	oust[1]
owt	out[1]
owtbilding	outbuilding
owtbord	outboard
owtbound	outbound
owtbownd	outbound
owtbreak	outbreak
owtlaw	outlaw[1]+
ox /en (pl.)	
oxalic	
Oxbridge	
oxbrige	Oxbridge
oxidashun	oxidation
oxid e /ation	
oxidis e[2] /ation	
oxigenate	oxygenate[2]+
oxigenise	oxygenise[2]
oxihemoglobin	oxyhaemoglobin
Oxonian	
oxtail	
oxtale	oxtail
ox-tongue	
oxy-acetylene	
oxygen	
oxygenat e[2] /ion	
oxygenise[2]	
oxyhaemoglobin	
oyez	
oyster	
ozier	osier
ozone layer	

P

pace[2] /-maker	
pach	patch[1]+
pachwerk	patchwork
pachwork	patchwork
pachyderm /atous	
pacific /ally	
pacifis m /t	
pacif y[4] /ication/ier	
pack[1] /-horse/-ice	
package[2]	

packet	
packiderm	pachyderm+
packidge	package[2]
packing-case	
pact	
pad[3]	
paddle[2] /r/-wheel	
paddock	
paddy /-field	
pade	paid+
padie	paddy+
padlock[1]	
padock	paddock
padray	padre
padre	
padul	paddle[2]+
pady	paddy+
pagan /ism	
pag e[2] /ination	
pageant /ry	
pagentrey	pageantry
paginashun	pagination
pagoda	
paid /-up	
pail ★ (bucket)	
pail	pale[2]★
pain[1]★ (suffering) /less	
pain	pane ★
painful /ly	
pain-killer	
painstaking	
paint[1] /er	
pair[1]★ (two)	
pair	pare[2]★
pair	pear ★+
pakiderm	pachyderm+
pakidurm	pachyderm+
pal /ly	
pala ce /tial	
paladium	palladium
palankwin	palanquin
palanquin	
palas	palace+
palashul	palatial
palatabl e /y	

palatabul	palatable +
palat e /al	
palatinate	
palaver	
pale ²★ (whitish)	
pale	pail ★
paleografey	paleography
paleography	
paleolithic	
paleontolog y /ist	
paleozoic	
pale r /ly/ness/st	
palet	palette ★+
palet	pallet ★
palette ★† /-knife †(artist's board)	
palfrey	
paliass	palliasse
paliate	palliate ²+
palid	pallid +
palindrome	
palis	palace +
palisade	
pall ¹ /-bearer	
palladium	
pallet ★ (bed)	
pallet	palette ★+
palliasse	
palliat e² /ive	
pall id /or	
palm ¹ /ist/istry	
palmie	palmy
palmy	
palor	pallor
palpabl e /y	
palpabul	palpable +
palpitashun	palpitation
palpitat e² /ion	
palsie	palsy +
pals y /ied	
paltrie	paltry +
paltr y /iness	
pamflet	pamphlet +
pampas	
pamper ¹ /er	
pamphlet /eer	
pan ³ /cake	
panacea	
panache	
pan-African	
Panama	
pan-American	
panasea	panacea
panash	panache
panchromatic	
pancrea s /tic	
pancromatic	panchromatic
panda ★ (animal)	
pandemonium	
pander ¹★ (indulge)	
pane ★ (of glass)	
pane	pain ¹★+
paneful	painful +
panegyric	
panekiller	pain-killer
panel ³ /list	
panestaking	painstaking
pang	
panic /-stricken/-struck	
panick ed /ing/y	
panickt	panicked +
panier	pannier
panigiric	panegyric
panikey	panicky
panikstriken	panic-stricken
pannier	
panopl y /ied	
panorama /s	
panoramic /ally	
pansie	pansy +
pansnay	pince-nez
pans y /ies	
pant ¹	
pantaloon	
pantechnicon	
panteknicon	pantechnicon
pantheis m /t/tic	
pantheon	
panther	
panthiism	pantheism +

panthion	pantheon	paraly *se* [2] /sis/tic	
pantile		parameter	
pantograf	pantograph +	paramilitary	
pantograph /y		paramilitrey	paramilitary
pantomime		paramiter	parameter
pantrey	pantry +	paramoor	paramour
pantr *y* /ies		paramount	
papa *cy* /l		paramour	
papasey	papacy +	paramownt	paramount
paper [1] /back/-chase		paranoi *a* /c/d	
paperwait	paperweight	parapet	
paperweight		paraphernalia	
papier-mâché		paraphrase [2]	
papirus	papyrus +	paraplegi *a* /c	
papist /ical		parapleja	paraplegia +
papoose		paraselene	
paprika		parashoot	parachute [2]+
papyamashay	papier-mâché	parashootist	parachutist
papyr *us* /i (pl.)		parasilene	paraselene
parable		parasit *e* /ic/ical	
parabol *a* /ic		parasol	
parabul	parable	paratifoid	paratyphoid
parachut *e* [2] /ist		paratroop /er	
parade [2]		paratyphoid	
paradigm		parboil [1]	
paradim	paradigm	parcel [3]	
paradise		parch [1] /ment	
paradoks	paradox +	pardon [1] /able/er	
paradox /ical/ically		pardonabul	pardonable
parafernalia	paraphernalia	pare [2]★ (trim)	
paraffin		pare	pair [1]★
parafrase	paraphrase [2]	pare	pear ★+
paragon		parent /age/al/ally	
paragraf	paragraph	parenthes *is* /es (pl.)	
paragraph		parenthesise [2]	
parakeet		parenthetic /ally	
paralaks	parallax	parentige	parentage
paralax	parallax	pariah	
paralel	parallel [1]+	parie	parry [4]
paralelogram	parallelogram	parish /es/ioner	
paralise	paralyse [2]+	parishoner	parishioner
paralisis	paralysis	Parisi *an* /enne (fem.)	
paralitic	paralytic	pariside	parricide +
parallax		parisidul	parricidal
parallel [1] /ogram/ism		parit *y* /ies	

park [1] /er		part [1] /ly/-time	
parket	parquet	partak e /en/er/ing	
parking-meter		partial /ly	
parlament	parliament [+]	partialit y /ies	
parlance		participant	
parlans	parlance	participat e [2] /ion/or	
parlay [1]★ (bet)		particip le /ial	
parlay	parley [1]★	participul	participle [+]
parlementarey	parliamentary	particle	
parlementarian	parliamentarian	particul	particle
parler	parlour [+]	particular /ity/ly	
parlermade	parlour-maid	particularis e [2] /ation	
parley [1]★ (discuss)		partie	party [+]
parley	parlay [1]★	partisan /ship	
parliament /arian/ary		partishun	partition [1+]
parlour /-maid		partisipant	participant
parlous		partisipashun	participation
parlus	parlous	partisipate	participate [2+]
parm	palm [1+]	partisipation	participation
Parmesan		partisipul	participle [+]
parmist	palmist	partit ion [1] /ive	
parochial /ism/ly		partly	
parod y [4] /ies		partner [1] /ship	
parokial	parochial [+]	partook	
paroksism	paroxysm	partridge	
parole [2]		partrige	partridge
parot	parrot [1+]	part y /ies	
paroxysm		parvenew	parvenu
parquet		parvenu	
parricid e /al		pary	parry [4]
parrot [1] /-fish		pas	pass [+]
parry [4]		pasable	passable [+]
parse [2]		pasabul	passable [+]
parsec		pascher	pasture [+]
parsel	parcel [3]	pase	pace [2+]
parshal	partial [+]	pasemaker	pace-maker
parshialitey	partiality [+]	pasenger	passenger
parsimon ious /y		paserbie	passer-by
parsimonius	parsimonious [+]	paserby	passer-by
parsley		pasha	
parslie	parsley	pashence	patience ★
parsly	parsley	pashens	patience ★
parsnip		pashent	patient [+]
parson /age/ic		pashonat	passionate
parsonige	parsonage	pashun	passion [+]

pasidge	passage
pasific	pacific +
pasifier	pacifier
pasifism	pacifism +
pasifist	pacifist
pasify	pacify 4+
pasige	passage
pasiv	passive +
pasivitey	passivity
pasover	passover
paspartoo	passe-partout
pasport	passport
pass /book/es/ing/key	
passabl e /y	
passage	
passed * (did pass)	
passed	past *
passenger	
passe-partout	
passer /-by	
passige	passage
passion /ate/ately	
passive /ly	
passivity	
passover	
passport	
password	
past * (just over)	
past	passed *
pasta	
paste 2 /board	
pastel	
paster	pastor +
pasterise	pasteurise 2+
pastern	
pasteuris e 2 /ation	
pastie	pasty +
pastil	pastille
pastille	
pastime	
pastmaster	
pastor /al/ate	
pastrey	pastry +
pastr y /ies	
pastur e /age	

pasturn	pastern
past y /ies	
paswerd	password
pasword	password
pat 3 /ly/ness	
patay	pâté
patch 1 /es/work/y	
pâté	
patella	
paten	pattern 1
patency	
patensey	patency
patent 1 /able/ee/ly	
pater	patter 1+
patern	pattern 1
paternal /ism/ly	
paternalist /ic	
paternity	
path /way	
pathetic /ally	
pathological /ly	
patholog y /ist	
pathos	
patie	patty +
patience *†	
†(forbearance)	
patient /s * (under	
doctor's care)	
patina	
patio /s	
patiserey	pâtisserie
pâtisserie	
patois	
patriarch /al/y	
patriark	patriarch +
patrician	
patricide	
patrimon y /ies	
patriot /ism	
patriotic /ally	
patrishun	patrician
patriside	patricide
patrol 3	
patron /ess (fem.)	
patron age /al	

patronige	patronage +
patronise ² /r	
patten	
patter ¹ /er	
pattern ¹	
patt y /ies	
paturnal	paternal +
paturnitey	paternity
patwa	patois
paucity	
paunch /y	
pauper /ism	
pauperis e ² /ation	
pause ²★ (stop)	
pause	paws★
pave ² /ment	
pavier	paviour
pavilion	
pavilyun	pavilion
paviour	
paw ¹★ (foot, feet) /s ★	
paw	pore ²★
pawcelain	porcelain
pawch	porch +
pawferey	porphyry
pawk	pork +
pawkupine	porcupine
pawl	pall ¹+
pawlbarer	pall-bearer
pawlfrey	palfrey
pawltrey	paltry +
pawlzid	palsied
pawlzy	palsy +
pawn ¹ /broker/shop	
pawnch	paunch +
pawnografey	pornography +
pawnography	pornography +
pawper	pauper +
pawperise	pauperise ²+
pawpus	porpoise
paws	pause ²★
pawselin	porcelain
pawshun	portion ¹
pawsitey	paucity
pay /able/ee/ing/ment	

payabul	payable
paynt	paint ¹+
pe	pea+
pea /nut	
peace ★ (calm)	
peace	piece ²★+
peaceabl e /y	
peaceabul	peaceable +
peaceful /ly/ness	
peace-offering	
peach /es	
pea cock /fowl/hen	
peak ¹★ (top)	
peak	peek ¹★
peak	pique ★
peal ¹★ (of bells)	
peal	peel ¹★
peap	peep ¹
pear ★ (fruit) /-shaped	
pear	pare ²★
pear	peer ¹★+
pear	pier ★
pearage	peerage +
pearce	pierce ²
pearl ★ (gem) /y	
pearl	purl ¹★+
peasant /ry	
peat	
pebbl e /y	
pebul	pebble +
pecadillo	peccadillo
pecan	
peccadillo	
peck ¹ /er/ish	
pecock	peacock +
pectin	
pectoral	
peculat e ² /ion/or	
peculiar /ly	
peculiarit y /ies	
pecuniary	
pedagog	pedagogue +
pedagogic /al	
pedagog ue /y	
pedal ³★ (of bicycle)	

pedant /ic/ry	
peddle ²★ (sell)	
pedestal	
pedestrian crossing	
pediatric s /ian	
pediatrishun	pediatrician
pedi cure /gree/ment	
pedlar	
pedler	pedlar
pedometer	
pedul	pedal ³★
pedul	peddle ²★
peech	peach +
peek ¹★ (peep)	
peek	peak ¹★
peek	pique ★
peel ¹★ (remove skin)	
peel	peal ¹★
peep ¹	
peer ¹★† /ess (fem.)	
†(look, noble)	
peer	pier ★
peer age /less/lessly	
peet	peat
peev ed /ish/ishness	
peg ³	
pehen	peahen
peice	piece ²★+
peiceofring	peace-offering
pejorative	
pekanese	pekinese
pekansey	piquancy +
pekant	piquant
pekinese	
pekish	peckish
pektin	pectin
pektoral	pectoral
pelican	
pelit	pellet
pellet	
pell-mell	
pellucid	
pelmel	pell-mell
pelmet	
pelota	

pelt ¹	
pelusid	pellucid
pelvi s /c	
pemmican	
pen ³ /-friend/-name	
penal	
penalis e ² /ation	
penalt y /ies	
penance ★ (repentance)	
penance	pennants ★
penans	penance ★
penant	pennant +
pence	
pencil ³	
pendant ★ (ornament)	
pendent ★ (hanging)	
pending	
pendulous	
pendulum /s	
pendulus	pendulous
penetrab le /ility	
penetrabul	penetrable +
penetrashun	penetration
penetrat e ² /ion/ive	
penguin	
pengwin	penguin
penicillin	
penie	penny +
peniless	penniless +
peninsula ★(n.) /r ★(adj.)	
penis	
penisilin	penicillin
peniten ce /t	
penitens	penitence +
penitensharey	penitentiary +
penitentiar y /ies	
penkni fe /ves (pl.)	
pennant /s ★ (flags)	
pennife	penknife +
penniless /ness	
pennives	penknives
pennon	
penn y /ies	
penon	pennon
pens	pence

211

penshun	pension [1+]	perchance	
penshunabul	pensionable	perchans	perchance
penshuner	pensioner	perchase	purchase [2+]
pensil	pencil [3]	percolat *e* [2] /ion/or	
pension [1] /able/er		percushun	percussion [+]
pensive /ly/ness		percuss *ion* /ive	
pentagon /al		perda	purdah
pentameter		perdishun	perdition
pentathlon		perdition	
Pentecost		peregrin *e* /ation	
penthouse		peremptor *y* /ily/iness	
penthows	penthouse	peremtrey	peremptory [+]
penticost	Pentecost	perenial	perennial [+]
penultimate /ly		perennial /ly	
penumbra		perfecshun	perfection [+]
penurey	penury [+]	perfect [1] /ible	
penurius	penurious	perfection /ist	
penur *y* /ious		perfidey	perfidy [+]
penut	peanut	perfidius	perfidious
peonie	peony [+]	perfid *y* /ious	
peon *y* /ies		perforashun	perforation
people [2]		perforat *e* [2] /ion/or	
peper	pepper [1+]	perforce	
pepercorn	peppercorn	perform [1] /ance/er	
peperey	peppery	performans	performance
pepper [1] /corn/mint/y		perfors	perforce
pepsin /ogen		perfume [2] /ry/ries	
pep-talk		perfunctor *y* /ily	
peptic		perfunctrey	perfunctory [+]
peptides		pergative	purgative [+]
pepul	people [2]	pergatrey	purgatory
per	purr [1]	perge	purge [2+]
per annum		perhaps	
per capita		pericarp	
peradvencher	peradventure	periferal	peripheral
peradventure		periferey	periphery [+]
perambulat *e* [2] /ion/or		periferic	peripheric
perblind	purblind	perifery	periphery [+]
perceiv *e* [2] /able		perigee	
percentage		peril /ous/ously	
percepshun	perception [+]	perilus	perilous
perceptibl *e* /y		perimeter	
perceptibul	perceptible [+]	period	
percept *ion* /ive		periodic /al/ally	
perch [1] /es		periosteum	

212

peripatetic		perpetrater	perpetrator
peripher *y* /al/ic		perpetual /ly	
periscope		perpetuat *e*² /ion	
perish¹ /able/ables		perpetuity	
peristalsis		perple	purple
periton *eum* /itis		perpleks	perplex¹⁺
periwinkle		perplex¹ /ity/ities	
periwinkul	periwinkle	perport	purport¹
perjur *e*² /y		perpose	purpose⁺
perk¹ /iness/s/y		perse	purse²⁺
perkushun	percussion⁺	persecut *e*² /ion/or	
perkusiv	percussive	persepshun	perception⁺
perl	pearl★⁺	perseptible	perceptible⁺
perl	purl¹★⁺	perseption	perception⁺
perloin	purloin¹	perseptiv	perceptive
perlu	purlieu	perseve	perceive²⁺
perm¹		persever *e*² /ance	
permanenc *e* /y		pershun	Persian
permanens	permanence⁺	Persian	
permanent /ly		persist¹ /ent/ently	
permanganate		persistenc *e* /y	
permeab *le* /ility		persistens	persistence⁺
permeabul	permeable⁺	person /able/age	
permeat *e*² /ion		persona /(non) grata	
permishun	permission⁺	personal★ (private) /ly	
permisibul	permissible	personal	personnel★
permisiv	permissive⁺	personalit *y* /ies	
permiss *ion* /ible		personat *e*² /ion/or	
permissive /ness		personel	personal★⁺
permit³		personel	personnel★
permutashun	permutation	personifi	personify⁴⁺
permut *e*² /ation		personif *y*⁴ /ication/ier	
pernicious /ly/ness		personnel★ (employees)	
pernickety		personnel	personal★⁺
pernikitey	pernickety	perspective	
pernishus	pernicious⁺	perspeks	perspex
perokside	peroxide	perspektiv	perspective
peroxide		perspex	
perpechooal	perpetual⁺	perspicaci *ous* /ty	
perpechooate	perpetuate²⁺	perspicashus	perspicacious⁺
perpechual	perpetual⁺	perspicu *ous* /ity	
perpechuate	perpetuate²⁺	perspicuus	perspicuous⁺
perpendicular /ity		perspirashun	perspiration
perpetrashun	perpetration	perspir *e*² /ation	
perpetrat *e*² /ion/or		persuad *e*² /able/er	

persuashun	persuasion	pestle	
persuasion		pesul	pestle
persuasive /ly/ness		pet ³ /-name	
perswadable	persuadable	petal ³	
perswadabul	persuadable	peteat	petite
perswade	persuade ²⁺	peter ¹ /sham	
perswasion	persuasion	peticoat	petticoat
perswasiv	persuasive ⁺	petie	petty ⁺
pert /ly/ness		petiole	
pertain ¹		petish	pettish
pertane	pertain ¹	petishun	petition ¹⁺
pertinaci ous /ty		petite	
pertinashus	pertinacious ⁺	petition ¹ /er	
pertinen ce /t		petrel ★ (sea bird)	
pertinens	pertinence ⁺	petrel	petrol ★⁺
perturb ¹ /ation		petrifacshun	petrifaction
perva de ² /sive		petrifaction	
perverse /ly/ness		petrifi	petrify ⁴⁺
pervershun	perversion ⁺	petrif y ⁴ /ication	
pervers ion /ive		petrol ★ (gasoline) /eum	
pervert ¹ /er		petrol	petrel ★
pervious		petrolog y /ist	
pervius	pervious	petrul	petrel ★
pervurs	perverse ⁺	petrul	petrol ★⁺
pervurshun	perversion ⁺	petticoat	
pervursiv	perversive	pettish	
pervurt	pervert ¹⁺	pett y /ièr/iest/ily/iness	
pesable	peaceable ⁺	petul	petal ³
pesabul	peaceable ⁺	petulan ce /t	
pesant	peasant ⁺	petulans	petulance ⁺
pesarey	pessary ⁺	petunia	
pese	peace ★	peved	peeved ⁺
pese	piece ²★⁺	pevish	peevish
peseful	peaceful ⁺	pew	
peseofring	peace-offering	pewit	
peseta		pewter	
pesimism	pessimism ⁺	phaeton	
pesimist	pessimist	phalanks	phalanx ⁺
pesimistic	pessimistic	phalan x /ges/xes (pls.)	
pessar y /ies		phall ic /us	
pessimis m /t/tic		phantasm	
pest /icide		phantasmagori a /c	
pester ¹		phantom	
pestilen ce /t/tial		Pharaoh	
pestilens	pestilence ⁺	pharingeal	pharyngeal ⁺

pharinx	pharynx	phisicist	physicist
Pharis *ee* /aic		phisics	physics
pharmaceutic /al		phisik	physique ★
pharmacist		phisiologey	physiology +
pharmacolog *y* /ist		phisionomey	physiognomy
pharmacopoeia		phisiotherapist	physiotherapist +
pharmac *y* /ies		phisiotherapy	physiotherapy
pharmasey	pharmacy +	phisique	physique ★
pharmasist	pharmacist	phlebitis	
pharmasutical	pharmaceutical	phlegm /atic	
pharo	Pharaoh	phlem	phlegm +
pharyng *eal* /itis		phloem	
pharynx		phloks	phlox ★
phase [2]		phlox ★ (flower)	
phayton	phaeton	phobia	
pheasant		Phoebus	
phebus	Phoebus	phoenix	
pheniks	phoenix	phon ★ (unit of sound)	
phenix	phoenix	phone [2]★ (telephone)	
phenobarbitone		phonetic /ally	
phenol		phonograf	phonograph +
phenomenal /ly		phonograph /ic	
phenomen *on* /a (pl.)		phonolog *y* /ical	
phesant	pheasant	phony	
phial ★ (bottle)		phosfate	phosphate
philander [1] /er		phosforesence	phosphorescence
philanthrop *y* /ic/ist		phosforesent	phosphorescent
philarmonic	philharmonic	phosforous	phosphorous ★+
philatel *y* /ist		phosforus	phosphorus ★
philharmonic		phosphate	
philip	fillip [1]	phosphoresce [2] /nce/nt	
Philistine		phosphor *ous* ★ (adj.) /ic	
philolog *y* /ical/ist		phosphorus ★ (n.)	
philosofer	philosopher +	photo /-electric/stat	
philosofey	philosophy	photocopie	photocopy +
philosofical	philosophical +	photocop *y* /ies	
philosofise	philosophise [2]	photo-finish	
philosoph *er* /y		photogenic	
philosophical /ly		photograf	photograph [1]+
philosophise [2]		photograph [1] /ic/y	
philter	philtre ★	photomet *er* /ric/ry	
philtre ★ (love potion)		photon	
phisic	physic ★	photosynthesis	
phisical	physical +	phototropism	
phisician	physician	phrase [2]★ (words) /ology	

phrenetic
phrenolog *y* /ist
phthisis
phylum
physic ★ (remedy)
physic   physique ★
physical /ly
physician
physicist
physics
physiognomy
physiolog *y* /ical/ist
physiotherap *ist* /y
physique ★ (body)
pi ★ (maths)
pi   pie ★+
pianist
piano /forte
piatsa   piazza
piazza
pibald   piebald
picador
picalilli   piccalilli
picancy   piquancy +
picaniny   piccaninny
picant   piquant
piccalilli
piccaninny
piccolo /s
pich   pitch 1+
pichfork   pitchfork 1
pick 1 /axe/pocket
pickcher   picture 2+
picket 1
pickle 2
picnic /ked/ker/king
Pict /ish
pictorial /ly
picture 2 /sque
picturesk   picturesque
pidgin ★ (jargon)
pidgin   pigeon ★
pie ★ (food) /crust
pie   pi ★
piebald

piece 2★ (part) /meal
piece   peace ★
piece-work
pier ★ (jetty)
pier   peer 1★+
pierce 2
piers   pierce 2
piety
pig 3 /-iron/let
pigeon ★ (bird)
pigeon   pidgin ★
pigeon-hole 2
pigerey   piggery +
pigger *y* /ies
piggyback
pigheaded /ness
pigheded   pigheaded +
pigiback   piggyback
pigin   pidgin ★
pigin   pigeon ★
pigment 1 /ation
pig *skin* /tail
pigsti   pigsty +
pigst *y* /ies
pigtale   pigtail
pijamas   pyjamas
pikaxe   pickaxe
pike 2 /staff
piks   pyx 1
piksy   pixie +
pil   pill +
pilage   pillage 2+
pilchard
pile 2
piler   pillar +
pilerbox   pillar-box
pilfer 1 /age/er
pilgrim /age
pilgrimige   pilgrimage
pilige   pillage 2+
pilion   pillion
pill /-box
pillage 2 /r
pillar /-box
pillion

pillor *y* [4] /ies	
pillow	
pilon	pylon
pilorey	pillory [4+]
pilot [1] /age	
pilow	pillow
pilyun	pillion
pimento	
pimpernel	
pimpl *e* /y	
pimpul	pimple +
pin [3] /-prick/-up	
pinacle	pinnacle [2]
pinacul	pinnacle [2]
pinafore	
pince-nez	
pincers	
pinch [1] /er/es	
pincushion	
pincushun	pincushion
pine [2] /-cone	
pineapple	
pineapul	pineapple
ping-pong	
pinion [1]	
pink [1]	
pinnacle [2]	
pinpoint [1]	
pinsers	pincers
pint	
pinyun	pinion [1]
pionear	pioneer [1]
pioneer [1]	
pious /ly	
pip [3] /-squeak	
pipe [2] /r	
pipe -*clay* /line	
pipet	pipette
pipette	
pippin	
piquan *cy* /t	
pique ★ (anger)	
piracy	
piramid	pyramid +
pirasey	piracy

pirat *e* [2] /ical	
pire	pyre
piric	Pyrrhic +
pirite	pyrite
pirooet	pirouette [2]
pirotecnic	pyrotechnic +
pirouette [2]	
pirric	Pyrrhic +
pistachio /s	
pistil ★ (flower)	
pistol ★ (gun)	
piston	
pit [3] /fall/man	
pitance	pittance
pitans	pittance
pit-a-pat /ter	
pitch [1] /blende/er/es	
pitchfork [1]	
pitch-pine	
piteous /ly/ness	
pith /ily/iness/y	
pithon	python
pitiabl *e* /y	
pitiabul	pitiable +
pitie	pity [4+]
pitiful /ly	
pitius	piteous +
pitsicato	pizzicato
pittance	
pittans	pittance
pituitary	
pituitrey	pituitary
pit *y* [4] /iless	
pius	pious +
pivot [1] /al	
pix	pyx [1]
pixie /s	
pixy	pixie +
pizzicato	
placab *le* /ility	
placabul	placable +
placard [1]	
placat *e* [2] /ion	
place [2]★ (position)	
place	plaice ★

placenta /l		plate	plait [1]
placid /ity/ly		plateau /x (pl.)	
placket		platelet	
plagarise	plagiarise [2]+	plater	platter
plage	plague [2]	platform	
plagiaris *e* [2] /m/t		platichood	platitude +
plague [2]		platinum	
plaice ★ (fish)		platipus	platypus +
plaid		platitud *e* /inous	
plain ★ (flat land)		platitudinus	platitudinous
plain	plane [2]★	plato	plateau +
plain *er* /ness/song		platonic /ally	
plaintiff ★ (legal)		platoon	
plaintive ★ (sad) /ly		platter	
plait [1]		platypus /es	
plait	plate [2]+	plaudit	
plajarise	plagiarise [2]+	plausib *le* /ility/ly	
plak	plaque	plausibul	plausible +
plaket	placket	plawdit	plaudit
plan [3] /ner		plawsible	plausible +
plane [2]★ (smooth, aircraft)		play [1] /er/ing/mate	
		playfellow	
plane	plain ★	playful /ly/ness	
planet /arium/ary		playground	
planetrey	planetary	playgrownd	playground
plank		playrite	playwright
plankton		playwright	
plant [1] /ain/ation/er		ple	plea +
plantashun	plantation	plea /s ★ (appeal)	
plantif	plaintiff ★	plead [1] /er	
plantin	plantain	pleasant /ly/ry	
plantiv	plaintive ★+	please [2]★ (request)	
plaque		pleasur *e* /able/ably	
plase	place [2]★	pleat [1]	
plase	plaice ★	plebean	plebeian
plasenta	placenta +	plebeian	
plasid	placid +	plebian	plebeian
plasma		plebiscite	
plasmolysis		plebisit	plebiscite
plaster [1] /cast/er		plectrum	
plastic /ally/ity		pledge [2]	
plasticine		pleed	plead [1]+
plastiseen	plasticine	pleet	pleat [1]
plastisine	plasticine	plege	pledge [2]
plate [2] /ful/glass		plenary	

plenipotensharey	plenipotentiary
plenipotentiary	
plenitude	
plentie	plenty +
plentiful /ly/ness	
plentius	plenteous
plent y /eous	
plesant	pleasant +
plese	pleas *
plese	please 2*
plesurable	pleasurable
plesurabul	pleasurable
plesure	pleasure +
plethor a /ic	
pleural * (membrane)	
pleural	plural *+
pleurisy	
pli	ply 4+
pliab le /ility	
pliabul	pliable +
plian cy /t	
pliansey	pliancy +
pliers	
plight /ed	
Plimsoll /line/mark	
plimsolls	
plinth	
plite	plight +
pliwood	plywood
plod 3 /der	
ploi	ploy
plooto	Pluto
plootocracy	plutocracy +
plootocrat	plutocrat +
plootonium	plutonium
ploovial	pluvial
plot 3 /ter	
plough 1 /man/share	
plover	
plow	plough 1+
ploy	
pluck 1 /ier/iest/ily/y	
plug 3 /ger	
plum * (fruit)	
plum	plumb 1*+

plumage	
plumb 1* (weight) /line	
plumbago	
plumber	
plume 2	
plumer	plumber
plumet	plummet 1
plumige	plumage
plumline	plumbline
plummet 1	
plump 1 /er/est/ness	
plunder 1 /er	
plunge 2 /r	
pluperfect	
plural * (a few) /ism/ity	
plural	pleural *
plurisey	pleurisy
plus	
plush /y	
Pluto	
plutocrac y /ies	
plutocrasey	plutocracy +
plutocrat /ic	
plutonium	
pluvial	
ply 4 /wood	
pnemonic	mnemonic
pneumatic	
pneumonia	
poach 1 /er	
poch	poach 1+
pock /-marked	
pocket 1 /-book/-knife	
pocket-money	
podgy	
podium	
poem	
poet /ess (fem.)	
poetic /al/ally	
poetry	
pogo-stick	
poignan cy /t/tly	
poim	poem
poinancy	poignancy +
poinansey	poignancy +

219

poinant	poignant	polip	polyp
point ¹ /edly/er/less		polisey	policy +
point -*blank* /-duty		polish ¹	
poise ²		polisilable	polysyllable +
poisenous	poisonous	polite /ly/ness	
poisenus	poisonous	politecnic	polytechnic
poison ¹ /er/ous		politey	polity
pok *e* ² /er/y		politheism	polytheism +
poker-face /d		polithene	polythene
pokey	poky	politic /ian/s	
pokmarked	pock-marked	political /ly	
poks	pox	politishun	politician
pol	poll ¹★+	polity	
polar /ity		polka /dot	
polar bear		poll ¹★ (vote) /-tax	
polard	pollard +	poll	pole ★+
Polaris		pollard /ed	
polaris *e* ² /ation/er		pollen	
pole ★ (tall staff) /cat		pollinat *e* ² /ion	
pole	poll ¹★+	pollster	
pole-jump ¹		pollut *e* ² /ion	
polemic /al		polonaise	
polen	pollen	polonase	polonaise
poler	polar +	polo-neck	
polerbare	polar bear	polonium	
polerbear	polar bear	poltax	poll-tax
polese	police ²+	poltegist	poltergeist
pole-star		polterer	poulterer
pole-vault ¹		poltergeist	
poliandrey	polyandry +	poltice	poultice
poliandrus	polyandrous	poltis	poultice
polianthus	polyanthus	poltrey	poultry
police ² /man/woman		polushun	pollution
polic *y* /ies		polute	pollute ²+
poligamey	polygamy +	polution	pollution
poligamus	polygamous	polyandrey	polyandry +
poliglot	polyglot	polyandr *y* /ous	
poligon	polygon	polyanthus	
polihedron	polyhedron +	polygam *y* /ous	
polimer	polymer	polyglot	
polinashun	pollination	polygon	
polinate	pollinate ²+	polyhedr *on* /al	
polination	pollination	polymer	
polinesian	Polynesian	polymeris *e* ² /ation	
polio /myelitis		polyneshun	Polynesian

220

Polynesian	
polyp	
polysyllab *le* /ic	
polytechnic	
polytheis *m* /t/tic	
polythene	
pomace ★ (pulp)	
pomade ²	
pomegranate	
pomegranit	pomegranate
pomel	pommel ³
Pomeranian	
pomfret /cake	
pomfrit	pomfret +
pomiculcher	pomiculture
pomiculture	
pommel ³	
pomology	
pomp /osity/ous	
pompus	pompous
ponder ¹ /able	
ponderous /ly	
ponderus	ponderous +
pondrabul	ponderable
poney	pony +
poniard	
ponie	pony +
ponitale	pony-tail
pontiff	
pontificate ²	
pontoon	
pon*y* /ies /y-tail	
ponyard	poniard
poo	pooh ¹+
poodle	
poodul	poodle
poof	pouffe
pooh ¹ /-pooh	
pool	
pooley	pulley
poolit	pullet
poop ¹	
poor ★ (needy)	
poor	pore ²★
poor	pour ¹★

poor *er* /est/ly	
pop ³ /corn/gun	
pop *e* /ery/ish	
popet	poppet
pop-eyed	
popicock	poppycock
popie	poppy +
popinjay	
poplar ★ (tree)	
poplar	popular ★+
poplin	
poppet	
popp*y* /ies	
poppycock	
populace	
popular ★† /ity/ly †(well known)	
popularis *e* ² /ation	
popularitey	popularity
populas	populace
populashun	population
populat *e* ² /ion	
populer	popular ★+
populous	
populus	populous
popy	poppy +
por	paw ¹★+
por	pore ²★
porcelain	
porch /es	
porcupine	
pore ²★ (of skin)	
pore	poor ★
pore	pour ¹★
porer	poorer +
porfrey	porphyry
poridge	porridge
porige	porridge
poringer	porringer
pork /er/y	
porkupine	porcupine
pornografey	pornography +
pornograph*y* /ic	
poro *us* /sity	
porphyry	

porpoise		posse	
porpus	porpoise	possess [1] /ion/ive/or	
porridge		possi	posse
porringer		possib *le* /ility/ly	
porselin	porcelain	possibul	possible +
porshun	portion [1]	possum	
porslin	porcelain	post [1] /-card	
port /age/-hole		post office	
portab *le* /ility		postage /-stamp	
portabul	portable +	postal	
portal		post-date [2]	
portcullis		poster	
portend [1]		posterier	posterior
portent /ous		posterior	
portentus	portentous	posterity	
porter /house		postern	
portfolio		post-graduate	
portico		post-haste	
portion [1]		posthumous /ly	
portkulis	portcullis	posthumus	posthumous +
portl *y* /iness		postige	postage +
portmanteau		postilion	
portrait /ure		postilyon	postilion
portray [1] /al		post-impressionist	
portrit	portrait +	post *man* /mark	
portul	portal	post *master* /mistress	
porus	porous +	post-meridiem	
poscher	posture [2]	post-mortem	
pose [2]		postofiss	post office
poseshun	possession	postpone [2] /ment	
posess	possess [1]+	postulant	
posession	possession	postulate [2]	
posessiv	possessive	postumus	posthumous +
posey	posy +	posture [2]	
posh		post-war	
poshun	potion	posum	possum
posibilitey	possibility	pos *y* /ies	
posible	possible +	potash	
posibul	possible +	potasium	potassium
posie	posy +	potassium	
posishun	position +	potato /es	
position /al		pot-bell *y* /ied	
positive /ly/ness		poteen	
positivism		poten *cy* /t	
positron		potene	poteen

potensey	potency +
potenshul	potential +
potentate	
potential /ity/ly	
poter	potter ¹
poterey	pottery +
pot-hol e /er/ing	
pot-hook	
potie	potty
potion	
pot-pourri	
potter ¹	
potter y /ies	
potty	
pouch ¹ /es	
pouffe	
poulterer	
poultice	
poultry	
pounce ²	
pound ¹ /age	
pour ¹★ (to flow)	
pour	poor ★
pour	pore ²★
pout ¹	
poverty /-stricken	
powch	pouch ¹+
powder ¹ /y	
power ¹ /less/-station	
powerful /ly/ness	
pownce	pounce ²
pownd	pound ¹+
powns	pounce ²
powt	pout ¹
pow-wow ¹	
pox	
practicab le /ility	
practicabul	practicable +
practical /ity/ly	
practice ★ (n.)	
practician	
practise ²★ (v.)	
practishun	practician
practishuner	practitioner
practitioner	

praer	prayer +
pragmati c /sm	
prairey	prairie
prairie	
praise ² /worthy	
prance ²	
prank	
prans	prance ²
prarey	prairie
prase	praise ²+
prasee	précis ¹
praseworthey	praiseworthy
prate ²	
prattle ²	
pratul	prattle ²
prawn ¹	
pray ¹★ (say prayers)	
pray	prey ¹★
prayer /book/ful	
preach ¹ /er	
preamble ²	
preambul	preamble ²
prearrange ²	
precarious /ly/ness	
precarius	precarious +
precaution /ary	
precawshun	precaution +
precede ²★ (go before)	
precede	proceed ¹★+
precedence ★ (priority)	
precedent ★† /s ★†	
†(previous law[s])	
precedent	president ★+
precentor	
precept /or	
preceshun	procession
prech	preach ¹+
precinct	
precious /ly	
precipice	
precipis	precipice
precipitanc e /y	
precipitans	precipitance +
precipitat e ² /ion/or	
precipitous /ly	

precipitus	precipitous +
précis [1]	
precise /ly	
preclu *de* [2] /sion/sive	
preclushun	preclusion
precocious /ness	
precocity	
preconceive [2]	
preconception	
preconsepshun	preconception
preconseve	preconceive [2]
precoshus	precocious +
precositey	precocity
precursor /y	
predater	predator +
predator /y	
predecessor	
predesesor	predecessor
predestinashun	predestination
predestin *e* [2] /ation	
predetermine [2]	
predicament	
predicate [2]	
predicshun	prediction
predict [1] /able/ion	
predictabul	predictable
predilecshun	predilection
predilection	
predispos *e* [2] /ition	
prediturmine	predetermine [2]
predominance	
predominans	predominance
predominant /ly	
predominate [2]	
preegsist	pre-exist [1+]
pre-eminen *ce* /t	
pre-empt [1] /ion	
preemshun	pre-emption
preen [1]	
pre-exist [1] /ence	
prefabricat *e* [2] /ion	
prefa *ce* [2] /tory	
prefect /orial/ure	
prefer [3] /able/ably	
preference	

preferens	preference
preferenshal	preferential +
preferential /ly	
preferment	
prefiks	prefix [1]
prefis	preface [2+]
prefix [1]	
pregnanc *y* /ies	
pregnansey	pregnancy +
pregnant	
prehensile	
prehistor *ic* /y	
pre-ignition	
prejudge [2]	
prejudice [2]	
prejudicial /ly	
prejudis	prejudice [2]
prejudishal	prejudicial +
prejuge	prejudge [2]
prelate	
prelim	
preliminar *y* /ies	
preliminrey	preliminary +
prelude [2]	
premature /ly	
premeditat *e* [2] /ion	
premier *† /ship	
†(Prime Minister)	
première *†	
†(first performance)	
premise [2★] (postulate)	
premises (house)	
premiss ★ (logic)	
premium /s	
premonishun	premonition +
premonit *ion* /ory	
prenatal	
prene	preen [1]
preoccupi	preoccupy [4+]
preoccup *y* [4] /ation	
preocupashun	preoccupation
preocupy	preoccupy [4+]
prepade	prepaid
prepaid	
preparashun	preparation

preparatrey	preparatory
prepar *e* ² /ation/atory	
prepay /ing/ment	
preponderan *ce* /t	
preponderate ²	
preposess	prepossess ¹⁺
preposishun	preposition ⁺
preposition /al	
prepossess ¹ /ion	
preposterous /ly	
preposterus	preposterous ⁺
prerekwisit	prerequisite
prerequisite	
prerogative	
pres	press ¹⁺
presage ²	
presbiterian	Presbyterian
Presbyterian	
pre-school	
prescribe ²*†	
†(give directions)	
prescribe	proscribe ²*
prescripshun	prescription ⁺
prescript *ion* /ive	
presede	precede ²*
presedence	precedence *
presedence	precedents *
presedent	precedent *⁺
presedent	president *⁺
preseed	precede ²*
presence	
presens	presence
present ¹ /ation/ly	
presentabl *e* /y	
presentashun	presentation
presentiment	
presentor	precentor
presept	precept ⁺
preservashun	preservation
preservative	
preserv *e* ² /ation	
preseshun	procession
presession	procession
presher	pressure ²⁺
presherise	pressurise ²⁺

preshus	precious ⁺
presid *e* ² /ial	
presidency	
presidensey	presidency
presidenshal	presidential
president *† /ial/s *†	
†(elected head[s])	
president	precedent *⁺
presige	presage ²
presinct	precinct
presipice	precipice
presipis	precipice
presipitance	precipitance ⁺
presipitans	precipitance ⁺
presipitate	precipitate ²⁺
presipitation	precipitation
presipitous	precipitous ⁺
presipitus	precipitous ⁺
presise	precise ⁺
press ¹ /er	
press-stud	
pressure ² /-cooker	
pressuris *e* ² /ation	
prest	priest ⁺
prestege	prestige ⁺
presthood	priesthood
prestig *e* /ious	
prestigus	prestigious
presto	
presum *e* ² /ably	
presumpt *ion* /ive/uous	
presumshun	presumption ⁺
presumshus	presumptuous
presumtuous	presumptuous
presuppos *e* ² /ition	
pretekst	pretext
pretence	
pretend ¹ /er	
pretens	pretence
pretenshun	pretension
pretenshus	pretentious ⁺
pretension	
pretentious /ly/ness	
preterite	
pretext	

pretie	pretty +
prett y /ily/iness	
prety	pretty +
prevail 1	
prevalen ce /t	
prevalens	prevalence +
prevaricat e 2 /ion/or	
prevayl	prevail 1
prevenshun	prevention
prevent 1 /able/ion/ive	
preview 1	
previous /ly	
previus	previous +
prevue	preview 1
pre-war	
prey 1★ (devour)	
prey	pray 1★
prezbiterian	Presbyterian
pri	pry 4
price 2 /less	
prick 1	
prickl e 2 /y	
pricul	prickle 2+
pride 2	
prier	prior +
prierey	priory
priest /hood/ly	
prig /gish	
prim /ly/mer/mest/ness	
prima donna	
prima facie	
prima cy /te	
primar y /ies/ily	
primasey	primacy +
prime 2 /r	
Prime Minister	
primeval	
primitiv e /ism	
primogenit al /or/ure	
primordial	
primrey	primary +
primrose	
primula	
primus	
prince /ly/ss (fem.)	

principal ★ (chief) /ly	
principal	principle ★
principalit y /ies	
principle ★†	
†(moral code)	
principle	principal ★+
prins	prince +
prinsess	princess
prinsipal	principal ★+
prinsipality	principality +
print 1 /er	
prior /ess (fem.)/y	
priorit y /ies	
prise 2★ (lever)	
prise	price 2+
prise	prize 2★
prisie	prissy
prism /atic	
prison /er	
prissy	
pristene	pristine
pristine	
prithee	
prity	pretty +
privacy	
privaricate	prevaricate 2+
privasey	privacy
privashun	privation
private /ly	
privateer	
privation	
privet	
privie	privy
privilege 2	
privilige	privilege 2
privit	private +
privy	
prize 2★ (award)	
prize	prise 2★
prizm	prism +
probab le /ility/ly	
probabul	probable +
probashun	probation +
probate	
probation /ary/er	

probe ²	
problem	
problematic /al/ally	
proboscis	
procedure	
proceed ¹★ (go on) /s	
proceed	precede ²★
proceshun	procession
process ¹ /ion/ional	
proclaim ¹	
proclamashun	proclamation
proclamation	
proclaym	proclaim ¹
procrastinat e ² /ion	
procreat e ² /ion	
proctor /ial	
procura ble /tion/tor	
procurabul	procurable +
procurater	procurator
procure ² /ment	
prod ³	
prodigal /ity	
prodigey	prodigy +
prodigious /ly/ness	
prodigus	prodigious +
prodig y /ies	
produc e ² /er/ible	
product /ion/ive	
produse	produce ²+
produser	producer
profan e ² /ation	
profanit y /ies	
profecy	prophecy ★
profecy	prophesy ⁴★
profer	proffer ¹
profeser	professor +
profesey	prophecy ★
profeshonal	professional +
profeshun	profession +
profesi	prophesy ⁴★
profesor	professor +
profess ¹ /edly	
profession /alism	
professional /ly	
professor /ial	

profet	prophet +
profetical	prophetical
proffer ¹	
proficien cy /t	
profilactic	prophylactic +
profile	
profishency	proficiency +
profishensey	proficiency +
profishent	proficient
profit ¹ /less	
profitab le /ility/ly	
profitabul	profitable +
profiteer ¹	
profliga cy /te	
profound /ly	
profownd	profound +
profundity	
profus e ² /ion	
profushun	profusion
progenitor	
progeny	
prognos is /es (pl.)/tic	
prognosticat e ² /ion	
program ³★ (computer)	
programme ★†	
†(list of events)	
progreshun	progression
progress ¹ /ion/ional	
progressive /ly	
prohibishun	prohibition
prohibit ¹ /ion/ive/ory	
proibit	prohibit ¹+
projecshun	projection
project ¹ /ile/ion/or	
projeney	progeny
projeniter	progenitor
proksey	proxy +
proksimate	proximate +
proksimitey	proximity
prolapse ²	
proletaria n /t	
proliferashun	proliferation
proliferat e ² /ion	
prolific /ally	
prolog	prologue ²

prologue [2]
prolong [1]
prolongat *e* [2] /ion
promenade [2] /r
promethium
prominen *ce* /t
prominens   prominence [+]
promiscu *ous* /ity
promiscuus   promiscuous [+]
promis *e* [2] /sory
promoshun   promotion [+]
promote [2] /r
promotion /al
prompt [1] /er/ness
promulgat *e* [2] /ion
prone /ly/ness
prong [1]
pronoun
pronounce [2] /ment
pronown   pronoun
pronowns   pronounce [2+]
pronunciation
pronunsiashun   pronunciation
prood   prude [+]
proof [1] /-reader
proon   prune [2]
proov   prove [2+]
prop [3]
propaganda
propagashun   propagation
propagat *e* [2] /ion
propane
propel [3] /ler
propell *ant* (n.) /ent (adj.)
propensit *y* /ies
proper /ly
propert *y* /ies
prophecy ★ (n.)
prophesy [4]★ (v.)
prophet /ess (fem.)/ical
prophilactic   prophylactic [+]
prophyl *actic* /axis
propishiate   propitiate [2+]
propishous   propitious [+]
propishus   propitious [+]

propitiat *e* [2] /ion/or
propitious /ly
propolis
proporshonal   proportional [+]
proporshonate   proportionate
proporshun   proportion [1+]
proportion [1] /ate
proportional /ly
proposal
propos *e* [2] /ition
proposishun   proposition
propound [1]
propownd   propound [1]
proprietary
proprieter   proprietor
proprietey   propriety [+]
proprietor
proprietrey   proprietary
propriet *y* /ies
propulshun   propulsion [+]
propuls *ion* /ive
prorog   prorogue [2+]
prorog *ue* [2] /ation
prosaic /ally
proscribe [2]★ (outlaw)
proscribe   prescribe [2]★
proscripshun   proscription [+]
proscript *ion* /ive
prose
prosecushun   prosecution
prosecut *e* [2] /ion/or
prosedure   procedure
proseed   proceed [1]★[+]
proselight   proselyte [2]
proselyte [2]
proselytise [2] /r
prosess   process [1+]
prosicushun   prosecution
prosilite   proselyte [2]
prosilitise   proselytise [2+]
prosody
prospect [1] /ive/or
prospectus /es
prosper [1] /ity/ous
prosperus   prosperous

prostate ★ (gland)
prostitushun — prostitution
prostitut *e* ² /ion
prostrat *e* ² ★ (lay flat)
protactinium
protagonist
protecshun — protection
protect ¹ /ion/ive/or
protectorate
proteen — protein
protégé /e (fem.)
protein
protejay — protégé +
protene — protein
protest ¹ /ation
Protestant /ism
protocol
proton
protoplasm
prototipe — prototype +
prototyp *e* /al/ical
protract ¹ /ion/or
protrood — protrude ²
protrooshun — protrusion +
protrude ²
protrus *ion* /ive
protuberan *ce* /t
protuberans — protuberance +
proud /ly/ness
prov *e* ² /able
provenance
provenans — provenance
provender
proverb /ial
provide ² /r
providence
providens — providence
providenshul — providential
provident /ial/ially
provijun — provision +
provijunal — provisional
provinc *e* /ial
provins — province +
provinshal — provincial
provishun — provision +

provision /al/ally
proviso /ry
provocat *ion* /ive
provoke ²
provost
prow
prowd — proud +
prowess
prowibishun — prohibition
prowibition — prohibition
prowl ¹ /er
proximate /ly
proximity
prox *y* /ies
prozaic — prosaic +
prud *e* /ery/ish
pruden *ce* /t
prudens — prudence +
prudenshal — prudential +
prudential /ly
prune ²
prurien *ce* /t
pruriens — prurience +
prushan — Prussian
Prussian
pry ⁴
psalm /ist
psalter /y
pseudo /nym
psycedelic — psychedelic
psyche
psychedelic
psychiatr *ist* /y
psychic /al
psychoanalys *e* ² /is/t
psychological /ly
psycholog *y* /ist
psychopath /ic
psycho *sis* /tic
psychosomatic
psychotherap *ist* /y
psycoanalise — psychoanalyse ²+
psycologey — psychology +
psycological — psychological +
psycopath — psychopath +

229

psycosis	psychosis +	pulie	pulley
psycosomatic	psychosomatic	pulkritude	pulchritude
psycotherapist	psychotherapist +	pull [1]	
psykey	psyche	pullet	
psykick	psychic +	pulley	
ptarmigan		Pullman	
pterodactyl		pullover	
Ptolemaic system		pulman	Pullman
ptomaine		pulmonary	
ptyalin		pulmonrey	pulmonary
pu	pew	pulover	pullover
pub		pulp [1] /y	
puberty		pulpit	
pubescen *ce* /t		pulsar	
pubesens	pubescence +	pulsashun	pulsation
pubesent	pubescent	pulsat *e* [2] /ion	
pubic		pulse [2] /less	
pubis		pulser	pulsar
public /an/ation/ly		pulveris *e* [2] /ation	
publicis *e* [2] /t		puma	
publicity		pumel	pummel [3]
publish [1] /er		pumice [2]★ (lava) /-stone	
publisitey	publicity	pumice	pomace ★
publisize	publicise [2+]	pumis	pomace ★
puce		pumis	pumice [2★+]
puck		pumkin	pumpkin
pucker [1]		pummel [3]	
pudding		pump [1] /er	
puddle [2]		pumpernickel	
puding	pudding	pumpkin	
pudul	puddle [2]	pumy	pumice [2★+]
pueril *e* /ity		pun [3] /ner/nist	
puff [1] /iness/y		punch [1] /eon/es	
puffin		punchun	puncheon
pufin	puffin	punctilious /Iy/ness	
pug		punctilius	punctilious +
pugilis *m* /t/tic		punctual /ity/ly	
pugnaci *ous* /ty		punctuat *e* [2] /ion	
pugnashus	pugnacious +	puncture [2]	
pugnasitey	pugnacity	pundit	
puka	pucker [1]	pungen *cy* /t	
puke [2]		pungensey	pungency +
puker	pucker [1]	punie	puny +
pulchritude		punish [1] /able/ment	
pulcritude	pulchritude	punitive /ly	

punjency	pungency [+]	purple	
punjensey	pungency [+]	purport [1]	
punjent	pungent	purpose /ful/fully/ly	
punt [1] /er		purpul	purple
pun y /ier/iest/ily		purr [1]	
pupa /e (pl.)		purse [2] /r	
pupat e [2] /ion		pursuan ce /t	
pupie	puppy [+]	pursue [2] /r	
pupil		pursuit	
pupit	puppet [+]	pursute	pursuit
puppet /eer/ry		purulen ce /t	
pupp y /ies		purvay	purvey [1+]
		purvey [1] /ance/or	
		puse	puce

If you cannot find your word under **pur** *look under* **per**

pur anum	per annum	push [1] /-chair/y	
puray	purée	pusillanim ity /ous	
purblind		puss /y	
purceive	perceive [2+]	pussy-willow	
purcentige	percentage	put	
purchas e [2] /able		putative	
purchis	purchase [2+]	puter	pewter
purda	purdah	putie	putty [4]
purdah		putrefi	putrefy [4+]
pure /ly/r/st		putref y [4] /action	
purée		putrid	
purgat ive /ory		putrifi	putrefy [4+]
purgatrey	purgatory	putt [1] /er	
purg e [2] /ation		putty [4]	
purifi	purify [4+]	puty	putty [4]
purif y [4] /ication		puzle	puzzle [2+]
purile	puerile [+]	puzzle [2] /ment	
purist		pyatsa	piazza
puritan /ical		pye	pie [★+]
purity		pygmy	
purje	purge [2+]	pyjamas	
purjer	perjure [2+]	pylon	
purjerey	perjury	pyramid /al	
purl [1★] (knitting) /y		pyre	
purl	pearl [★+]	pyrenoid	
purlieu		pyric	Pyrrhic [+]
purloin [1]		pyrite	
purlu	purlieu	pyrotechnic /als/s	
puroolence	purulence [+]	Pyrrhic victory	
		python	
		pyx [1]	

231

Q

quack¹
quad
quadrang *le* /ular
quadrangul → quadrangle +
quadrant
quadratic
quadrennial
quadrenyal → quadrennial
quadril → quadrille
quadrilateral
quadrille
quadruped
quadruple² /t/x
quadruplicat *e* ² /ion
quadrupul → quadruple ²+
quaff¹
quagmire
quail¹
quaint /er/est/ly/ness
quake²
Quaker /ism
qualifactory
qualifi → qualify ⁴+
qualif *y* ⁴ /ication
qualitative
qualit *y* /ies
qualm
quandar *y* /ies
quandrey → quandary +
quantifi → quantify ⁴+
quantif *y* ⁴ /ication
quantitative
quantit *y* /ies
quant *um* /a (pl.)
quarantine²
quarel → quarrel ³+
quarey → quarry +
quarrel³ /some
quarr *y* /ies
quart
quarter¹ /ly/master
quartern
quartet

quarto /s
quarts ★ (fluid measure)
quartz ★ (mineral) /ite
quasar
quash¹
quaternary
quatrain
quaver¹
quay ★ (by sea)
que → cue ²★
que → queue ²★
queas *y* /iness
queen /ly
queer¹ /er/est/ly/ness
quell¹
quench¹ /able/less
querey → query ⁴+
quern
querulous /ly/ness
querulus → querulous +
quer *y* ⁴ /ies
queschun → question ¹+
quest¹
question¹ /able/ably/naire
quetzal
queue ²★ (line)
quibble² /r
quibul → quibble ²+
quich → quitch
quick /er/est/ly/ness
quicken¹
quick *sand* /silver
quid
quid pro quo
quiescen *ce* /t
quiesense → quiescence +
quiet¹ /er/est/ly
quieten¹
quietude
quiff
quill¹
quilt¹
quin
quince
quincentenary

quinine
quins   quince
quinsy
quintesence   quintessence +
quintessen *ce* /tial
quintet
quintupl *e* /et/icate
quintupul   quintuple +
quip [3]
quire ★ (of paper)
quire   choir ★
quirk
quisling
quit [3] /ter
quitch
quite
quits
quiver [1]
quixot *ic* /ry
quiz [3]
quizzical /ly
quod   quad
quodrangul   quadrangle +
quodrant   quadrant
quodratic   quadratic
quodrenial   quadrennial
quodril   quadrille
quodrilateral   quadrilateral
quodrooped   quadruped
quodruplicate   quadruplicate [2]+
quof   quaff [1]
quogmire   quagmire
quoit
quolitativ   qualitative
quolitey   quality +
quontify   quantify [4]+
quontitativ   quantitative
quontitey   quantity +
quontum   quantum +
quorantine   quarantine [2]
quorrel   quarrel [3]+
quorrey   quarry +
quorum
quoshent   quotient
quota

quot *e* [2] /able/ation
quotidian
quotient

R

rabbi /s
rabbit [1]★ (animal)
rabbit   rarebit ★
rabble
rabes   rabies
rabi   rabbi +
rabid /ly
rabies
rabit   rabbit [1]★
rabit   rarebit ★
rable   rabble
rabul   rabble
race /-course/-horse
rachit   ratchet
racial /ism/ist/ly
racis *m* /t
rack [1]★ (shelf)
rack   wrack ★
racket [1] /eer
racoon
rac *y* /ily
radar
raddle [2]
rade   raid [1]+
radial /ly
radian *ce* /t
radians   radiance +
radiashun   radiation
radiat *e* [2] /ion/or
radiater   radiator
radical ★ (political) /ly
radicle ★ (rootlet)
radio [1] /wave
radioactiv *e* /ity
radio-astronomy
radiografer   radiographer +
radiogram
radiograph *er* /y

radioisotope	
radiolog y /ist	
radiotherapy	
radish /es	
radium	
radi us /i (pl.)	
radon	
radul	raddle ²
radyal	radial ⁺
raffia	
raffish	
raffle ²	
rafia	raffia
rafish	raffish
raft ¹ /er	
raful	raffle ²
rag ³ /ger/time/wort	
ragamuffin	
ragamufin	ragamuffin
rage ²	
raglan	
raid ¹ /er	
rail ¹ /road/way	
raillery	
raiment	
rain ¹★ (water) fall/y	
rain	reign ¹★
rain	rein ¹★
raindeer	reindeer
raise ²★ (lift)	
raise	rays ★
raise	raze ²★
raisin	
raith	wraith
raja	
rak e ² /ish	
rakoon	racoon
rale	rail ¹⁺
ralerey	raillery
ralie	rally ⁴⁺
rall y ⁴ /ies	
ram ³ /mer/rod	
ramble ² /r	
rambul	ramble ²⁺
rament	raiment

ramifi	ramify ⁴⁺
ramificashun	ramification
ramif y ⁴ /ication	
ramp ¹	
rampage ² /ous	
rampagus	rampageous
rampan cy /t	
rampart	
rampige	rampage ²⁺
ramshackle	
ramshacul	ramshackle
ranch ¹ /er/es	
rancid /ity	
rancor	rancour ★⁺
ranco ur ★ (hate) /rous	
random	
randum	random
rane	rain ¹★⁺
ranee	
ranefall	rainfall
range ² /finder/r	
rangle	wrangle ²⁺
rangul	wrangle ²⁺
rank ¹ /er ★ (soldier)	
ranker	rancour ★⁺
rankle ²	
rankul	rankle ²
ransack ¹	
ransid	rancid ⁺
ransom ¹ /er	
ransum	ransom ¹⁺
rant ¹ /er	
raon	rayon
rap ³★ (knock) /per ★	
rap	wrap ★⁺
rapaci ous /ty	
rapashus	rapacious ⁺
rapasitey	rapacity
rapcher	rapture ⁺
rap e ² /er/ine/ist	
rapid /ity/ly	
rapier	
rapper	wrapper ★
rapscallion	
rapscalyon	rapscallion

rapsodey	rhapsody +	ratify⁴ /ication/ier	
rapsodise	rhapsodise²	ratio /s	
rapt ★ (absorbed)		ration¹	
rapt	wrapped ★	rational ★ (adj.) /ity/ly	
rapture /ous		rationale ★ (n.)	
rapturus	rapturous	rationalise² /ation/m	
rare /ly/r/st		rattle² /snake	
rarebit ★ (food)		ratul	rattle²+
rarefy⁴ /ication		raucous /ly	
rarifi	rarefy⁴+	raucus	raucous +
rarity /ies		ravage² /r	
rasberie	raspberry +	rave²	
rasbery	raspberry +	ravel³	
rascal /ity/ly		raven	
rase	raise²★	ravene	ravine
rase	raze²★	ravenous /ly/ness	
rasecorse	race-course	ravenus	ravenous +
rasehorse	race-horse	ravige	ravage²+
rash /er/est/ly/ness		ravine	
rashal	racial +	ravioli	
rashalism	racialism	ravish¹	
rashalist	racialist	raw /er/est/ness	
rashio	ratio +	rawcus	raucous +
rashul	racial +	rayon	
rashun	ration¹	rays ★ (light beams)	
rashunal	rational ★+	raze²★ (demolish)	
rashunalise	rationalise²+	raze	raise²★
rashunalitey	rationality	razer	razor +
rashyo	ratio +	razor /-bill/-blade	
rasie	racy +	reach¹	
rasin	raisin	reacshun	reaction +
rasism	racism +	react¹ /ive/or	
rasist	racist	reaction /ary	
raskal	rascal +	read ★† /able/er/ing	
rasp¹		†(book)	
raspberry /ies		read	red ★+
rat³ /-race/ter		read	reed¹★
ratable	rateable	readdress¹	
ratabul	rateable	readily /ness	
ratafia		readmishun	readmission
ratchet		readmission	
rate² /able/payer		readmit³ /tance	
rath	wrath +	readress	readdress¹
rather		ready /-made	
ratifi	ratify⁴+	reaf	reef¹+

reagent		rebellious /ly/ness	
reak	reek [1]★	rebelyun	rebellion
reak	wreak [1]★	rebelyus	rebellious +
real ★ (actual) /ly		reberth	rebirth
real	reel [1]★	rebild	rebuild +
realey	really	rebilt	rebuilt
realisashun	realisation	rebirth	
realis *e* [2] /able/ation		rebound [1]	
realis *m* /t		rebownd	rebound [1]
realistic /ally		rebuff [1]	
realit *y* /ies		rebuild /ing	
realm		rebuilt	
realter	realtor	rebuk *e* [2] /ingly	
realtor		rebut [3] /tal	
ream		rebutal	rebuttal
reanimat *e* [2] /ion		recalcitran *ce* /t	
reap [1] /er		recall [1]	
reapear	reappear [1]+	recalsitrance	recalcitrance +
reapearance	reappearance	recant [1] /ation	
reappear [1] /ance		recap [3]	
rear [1] /guard		recapcher	recapture [2]
rear-admiral		recapitulat *e* [2] /ion	
rearange	rearrange [2]+	recapture [2]	
reargard	rearguard	recast	
rearm [1] /ament		recede [2]	
rearrange [2] /ment		receipt [1]★ (document)	
reasemble	reassemble [2]	receit	receipt [1]★
reasembul	reassemble [2]	receiv *e* [2] /able/er	
reasershun	reassertion	recent ★ (of late) /ly	
reasert	reassert [1]+	recepshun	reception +
reasertion	reassertion	recepshunist	receptionist
reasess	reassess [1]+	receptacle	
reashorance	reassurance	receptacul	receptacle
reashorans	reassurance	reception /ist/-room	
reashore	reassure [2]+	receptive /ly/ness	
reason [1] /able/ably		receptivity	
reassemble [2]		receptor	
reassembul	reassemble [2]	receshun	recession +
reassert [1] /ion		recess [1] /ive	
reassess [1] /ment		recession /al	
reassur *e* [2] /ance		rech	retch [1]★
reath	wreath ★	rech	wretch ★
reath	wreathe [2]★	recharge [2] /able	
rebate [2]		recicle	recycle [2]
rebel [3] /lion		recidivis *m* /t	

recieve — receive [2]+
recipe
recipi — recipe
recipient
reciproc *al* /ally/ity
reciprocat *e* [2] /ion
recita *l* /tion/tive
recitashun — recitation
recite [2]
reck — wreck [1]+
reckage — wreckage
reckidge — wreckage
reckless /ly/ness
reckon [1]
reclaim [1]
reclamashun — reclamation
reclamation
reclaym — reclaim [1]
recline [2]
recluse
recognis *e* [2] /able/ably
recognishun — recognition
recognition
recoil [1]
recolect — recollect [1]+
recollect [1] /ion
recomence — recommence [2]+
recomend — recommend [1]+
recomens — recommence [2]+
recommence [2] /ment
recommend [1] /ation
recommendabl *e* /y
recompense [2]
reconcil *e* [2] /able/iation
reconcilement
recondishun — recondition [1]
recondite
recondition [1]
reconker — reconquer [1]
reconnoitre [2]
reconoiter — reconnoitre [2]
reconquer [1]
reconsider [1] /ation
reconsile — reconcile [2]+
reconstitut *e* [2] /ion

reconstruct [1] /ion/ive
recoop — recoup [1]+
record [1] /er/-player
recorse — recourse
recount [1]* (tell)
re-count [1]*†
 †(count again)
recoup [1] /ment
recouperate — recuperate [2]+
recourse
recover [1] /y
recownt — recount [1]*
recownt — re-count [1]*
recreant /ly
recreat *e* [2]* (entertain) /ion *
re-creat *e* [2]* (form anew) /ion *
recriminat *e* [2] /ion
recriminat *ive* /ory
recruit [1]
rectang *le* /ular
rectangul — rectangle +
recter — rector +
rectifi — rectify [4]+
rectifi *able* /er
rectifiabul — rectifiable +
rectif *y* [4] /ication
rectilinea *r* /l
rectilinier — rectilinear +
rectitude
recto
rector /y/ies
rect *um* /al
recumben *cy* /t
recuperat *e* [2] /ion/ive
recur [3] /rence/rent
recurens — recurrence
recycle [2]
recycul — recycle [2]
red *† /-handed
 †(colour)
red — read *+
redbreast
redbrest — redbreast
redbrick
redden [1]

redd *er* /est/ish
redeem [1] /able/er
redempt *ion* /ive
redemshun   redemption +
reden   redden [1]
redeploi   redeploy [1]+
redeploy [1] /ment
reder   redder +
redevelop [1] /ment
redie   ready +
rediffusion
redifushun   rediffusion
redifusion   rediffusion
rediley   readily +
redimade   ready-made
rediploi   redeploy [1]+
rediploy   redeploy [1]+
redirecshun   redirection
redirect [1] /ion
redistribut *e* /ion
redivelop   redevelop [1]+
redolen *ce* /t
redouble [2]
redoubt /able
redound [1]
redress [1] /ment
redskin
reduble   redouble [2]
reduc *e* [2] /ible/tion
reducshun   reduction
redundanc *y* /ies
redundansey   redundancy +
redundant
reduplicat *e* [2] /ion
redwood
re-echo [1]
reed [1]* (water-plant)
reed   read *+
reef [1] /er/-knot
reegsamin   re-examine [2]+
reek [1]* (smell)
reek   wreak [1]*
reeko   re-echo [1]
reeksport   re-export [1]+
reel [1]* (wind in)

reel
re-elect [1] /ion
reem   ream
re-enter [1]
re-entr *y* /ies
reep   reap [1]+
reer   rear [1]+
reer admiral   rear-admiral
reergard   rearguard
re-establish [1] /ment
reeve [2]
re-examin *e* [2] /ation
re-export [1] /ation
refashion [1]
refashun   refashion [1]
refector *y* /ies
refer [3] /able/ence
referee /d/ing
referend *um* /a/ums (pls.)
referens   reference
refewel   refuel [3]
refill [1] /able
refine [2] /ment
refiner *y* /ies
refit [3]
reflashun   reflation +
reflate [2]
reflation /ary
reflect [1] /ion/ive/or
refleks   reflex +
refleksiv   reflexive
reflex /ive
refloat [1]
reflote   refloat [1]
reform [1] /ation/er
reformashun   reformation
reformator *y* /ies
reformatrey   reformatory +
refracshun   refraction
refract [1] /able/ion/ive
refractor *y* /iness
refrain [1]
refresh [1] /er/ment
refrigerat *e* [2] /ion/or
refuel [3]

reel   real *+

refuge * (shelter) /e *†
  †(fugitive)
refulgen ce /t
refulgens   refulgence +
refund [1]
refurbish [1]
refus e [2] /al
refutashun   refutation
refut e [2] /able/al/ation
regain [1]
regal *† /ia/ly
  †(of a king)
regale [2]* (to feast)
regane   regain [1]
regard [1] /less
regatta /s
regen cy /t
regenerat e [2] /ion/ive/or
regicid e /al
regime /n
regiment [1] /al/ation
region /al/alism/ally
regiside   regicide +
regist er [1] /ration
registrar
registrashun   registration
registr y /ies
regreshun   regression
regress [1] /ion/ive
regret [3] /ful/fully
regretabul   regrettable +
regrettabl e /y
regular /ity/ly
regularis e [2] /ation
regularitey   regularity
regulashun   regulation
regulat e [2] /ion/or
reguler   regular +
regurgitat e /ion
rehabilitat e [2] /ion
rehash [1]
rehears e [2] /al
rehersal   rehearsal
reherse   rehearse [2]+
Reich

reign [1]* (rule)
reimburse [2] /ment
rein [1]* (of horse)
rein   reign [1]*
reincarnashun   reincarnation
reincarnat e [2] /ion
reindeer
reinforce [2] /able/ment
reinfors   reinforce [2]+
reinshore   re-insure [2]+
reinstate [2] /ment
re-insur e [2] /ance
reinvest [1] /ment
reiterashun   reiteration
reiterat e [2] /ion
rejecshun   rejection
reject [1] /ion
rejeme   regime +
rejoic e [2] /ingly
rejoin [1] /der
rejoise   rejoice [2]+
rejoovenate   rejuvenate [2]+
rejuvenat e [2] /ion
rekindle [2]
rekindul   rekindle [2]
rekwest   request [1]
rekwiem   requiem
rekwisishun   requisition
rekwisit   requisite +
rekwisition   requisition
rekwite   requite [2]+
relaks   relax [1]+
relaksashun   relaxation
relaksation   relaxation
relapse [2]
relashun   relation
relat e [2] /ion
relative /ly
relativity
relax [1] /ation
relay [1]
releaf   relief
release [2]
relegashun   relegation
relegat e [2] /ion

releif	relief
relent [1] /less/lessly	
relese	release [2]
relevan *ce* /t	
relevans	relevance +
releve	relieve [2]+
reli	rely [4]
reliabilitey	reliability
reliab *le* /ility/ly	
reliabul	reliable +
relian *ce* /t	
relians	reliance +
relic	
relief	
reliev *e* [2] /able	
religion	
religious /ly/ness	
religun	religion
religus	religious +
relinkwish	relinquish [1]+
relinquish [1] /ment	
relish [1] /able	
relm	realm
reluctan *ce* /t/tly	
reluctans	reluctance +
rely [4]	
remain [1] /der/s	
remand [1]	
remaridge	remarriage
remarie	remarry [4]+
remarige	remarriage
remark [1] /able/ably	
remarr *y* [4] /iage	
remed *y* [4] /ies	
rememb *er* [1] /rance	
remembrans	remembrance
remind [1] /er	
reminisce [2] /nce/nt	
reminisence	reminiscence
reminisens	reminiscence
reminisent	reminiscent
reminiss	reminisce [2]+
remishun	remission
remiss /ion/ly	
remit [3] /tal/tance	

remitans	remittance
remnant	
remonstran *ce* /t	
remonstrans	remonstrance +
remonstrat *e* [2] /ion/ive	
remoov	remove [2]+
remooval	removal
remorse /ful/fully	
remorseless /ly/ness	
remote /ly/r/st	
remount [1]	
removal	
remov *e* [2] /able/ability	
remownt	remount [1]
remunerat *e* [2] /ion/ive	
ren	wren
Renaissance *†	
†(historic period)	
renal	
renascen *ce* *† /t	
†(rebirth)	
rench	wrench [1]
rend [1]	
render [1]	
rendezvous [1]	
renegade [2]	
renew [1] /able/al	
renit	rennet
renium	rhenium
rennet	
renounce [2] /ment	
renouns	renounce [2]+
renovashun	renovation
renovat *e* [2] /ion/or	
renown /ed	
renowns	renounce [2]+
rent [1] /al/er	
rentul	rental
renue	renew [1]+
renunciat *e* [2] /ion	
reorganis *e* [2] /ation	
re-orientat *e* [2] /ion	
repade	repaid
repaid	
repair [1] /er	

repara *ble* /tion
reparashun   reparation
repartee /s
repast
repatriashun   repatriation
repatriat *e* [2] /ion
repay /able/ing/ment
repeal [1]
repeat [1] /able/edly
repel [3] /lent
repent [1] /ance/ant
repentans   repentance
repercushun   repercussion
repercussion
repertoire
repertory
repetishun   repetition +
repetishus   repetitious
repetiti *on* /ous/ve
repetitiv   repetitive
repetrey   repertory
repine [2]
replace [2] /able/ment
replase   replace [2]+
replay [1]
replenish [1] /ment
replet *e* /ion
repli   reply [4]+
replica
repl *y* [4] /ies
report [1] /able/er
repose [2] /ful
reposito *ry* /ies
repositrey   repository +
reprable   reparable +
reprabul   reparable +
reprehend
reprehenshun   reprehension +
reprehensibul   reprehensible
reprehensi *on* /ble
represent [1] /ation
representashun   representation
representative
represhun   repression
repress [1] /ible/ion/ive

reprieve [2]
reprimand [1]
reprint [1]
reprisal
reproach [1] /ful/fully
reprobate [2]
reproduc *e* [2] /ible
reproducshun   reproduction
reproduction
reproof /s
reprov *e* [2] /al/ingly
reptil *e* /ian
republic /an
repudiat *e* [2] /ion/or
repugnan *ce* /t
repugnans   repugnance +
repuls *e* [2] /ion
repulshun   repulsion
repulsive /ly/ness
reputashun   reputation
reput *e* [2] /able/ation
reputedly
request [1]
requiem
require [2] /ment
requisishun   requisition
requisit *e* /ion
requit *e* [2] /al
rerite   rewrite +
reritten   rewritten
rerote   rewrote
rescind [1]
rescue [2] /r
research [1] /er
reseat * (seat again)
reseat   receipt [1]*
resede   recede [2]
reseed   recede [2]
reseipt   receipt [1]*
resembl *e* [2] /ance
resembul   resemble [2]+
resent [1]* (grudge) /ment
resent   recent *+
resentful /ly
resepshonist   receptionist

resepshun	reception +	resistans	resistance +
reseptacul	receptacle	resit /ting	
reseption	reception +	resitashun	recitation
reseptionist	receptionist	resitation	recitation
reseptiv	receptive +	resite	recite 2
reseptor	receptor	resle	wrestle 2+
reserch	research 1+	resler	wrestler
reservashun	reservation	resole 2	
reserv e 2 /ation/ist		resoloot	resolute +
reservoir		resolushun	resolution
reseshun	recession +	resolute /ly/ness	
resess	recess 1+	resolution	
resession	recession +	resolve 2	
resessiv	recessive	reson	reason 1+
reset /ting		resonable	reasonable
reseve	receive 2+	resonabul	reasonable
reshuffle 2	reshuffle 2	resonan ce /t/tly	
reshuful	reshuffle 2	resonans	resonance +
resicle	recycle 2	resonat e 2 /or	
reside 2 /nce		resorce	resource +
residenc y /ies		resort 1	
residens	residence	resound 1	
residensey	residency +	resource /ful/fully	
residenshal	residential	respect 1 /ful/fully	
resident /ial		respectab le /ility/ly	
residivism	recidivism +	respectabul	respectable +
residivist	recidivist	respective /ly	
residu e /al/ary/um		respirashun	respiration
resign 1 /ation		respirater	respirator
resignashun	resignation	respir e 2 /ation/ator	
resilien ce /t/tly		respite	
resiliens	resilience +	resplenden ce /t	
resin /ous		respond 1 /ence/ent	
resind	rescind 1	respons e /ive/iveness	
resinus	resinous	responsib le /ility/ly	
resipe	recipe	responsibul	responsible +
resipie	recipe	rest 1* (repose)	
resipient	recipient	rest	wrest 1*
resiprocal	reciprocal +	restaurant	
resiprocate	reciprocate 2+	resterant	restaurant
resiprositey	reciprocity	restful /ly/ness	
resist 1 /er/ive		restitushun	restitution
resistab le /ility/ly		restitution	
resistabul	resistable +	restive /ness	
resistan ce /t		restle	wrestle 2+

242

restler	wrestler
restless	
restorashun	restoration
restor *e* ² /ation/ative	
restrain ¹ /t	
restrict ¹ /ion/ive	
restruccher	restructure ²
restructure ²	
resul	wrestle ²⁺
result ¹ /ant	
resumay	résumé ★
resume ²★ (restart)	
résumé ★ (summary)	
resumption	
resurecshun	resurrection
resurection	resurrection
resurgen *ce* /t	
resurgens	resurgence ⁺
resurrect ¹ /ion	
resus	rhesus
resuscitat *e* ² /ion	
resusitashun	resuscitation
resusitate	resuscitate ²⁺
resusitation	resuscitation
retail ¹ /er	
retain ¹ /er	
retale	retail ¹⁺
retaliat *e* ² /ion/ory	
retard ¹ /ation/er	
retayn	retain ¹⁺
retch ¹★ (vomit)	
retch	wretch ★
retenshun	retention ⁺
retent *ion* /ive	
reticen *ce* /t	
retina	
retinew	retinue
retinue	
retire ² /ment	
retisens	reticence ⁺
retisent	reticent
retoric	rhetoric ⁺
retorical	rhetorical
retort ¹	
retrace ²	

retract ¹ /able/ile/ion	
retrase	retrace ²
retread ★ (walk again)	
re-tread ¹★ (tyre)	
retreat ¹	
retred	retread ★
retred	re-tread ¹★
retreive	retrieve ²⁺
retrench ¹ /ment	
retribushun	retribution
retribut *e* ² /ion	
retriev *e* ² /able/al/er	
retroactive	
retrograde	
retrogress ¹ /ion/ive	
retrospect ¹ /ion/ive	
return ¹ /able	
reunion	
reunite ²	
reunyun	reunion
rev ³	
revali	reveille
revaluashun	revaluation
revalu *e* ² /ation	
reve	reeve ²
reveal ¹	
reveille	
revel ³ /ler/ry	
revelashun	revelation
revelation	
revelrey	revelry
revenew	revenue
revenge ² /ful/fully	
revenue	
reverberat *e* ² /ion/or	
revere ² /nce	
reverend ★ (priest)	
reverens	reverence
reverent ★† /ly	
†(respectful)	
reverey	reverie
reverie	
revers *e* ² /al/ible/ion	
revershun	reversion
revert ¹ /ible	

243

review ¹★ (survey) /er	
review	revue ★
revijun	revision
revile ²	
revis e ² /ion	
revishun	revision
reviv e ² /al	
revocabl e /y	
revokashun	revocation
revo ke ² /cation	
revolt ¹	
revolushun	revolution
revolushunise	revolutionise ²
revolushunrey	revolutionary ⁺
revolution	
revolutionar y /ies	
revolutionise ²	
revolve ² /r	
revue ★ (entertainment)	
revue	review ¹★⁺
revulshun	revulsion
revulsion	
reward ¹	
rewrit e /ten/ing	
rewrote	
rhapsodise ²	
rhapsod y /ies	
rhenium	
rhesus	
rhetoric /al	
rheumat ic /ism	
rhinoceros /es	
rhizome	
rhizomorph	
rhodium	
rhododendron	
rhomb us /i (pl.) /oid	
rhubarb	
rhyme ²★ (poetry)	
rhythm	
rhythmic /al/ally	
rib ³	
ribald /ry	
ribbon	
ricalsitrant	recalcitrant

rice ★ (food)	
rich /er/es/est/ly/ness	
ricital	recital ⁺
ricite	recite ²
rick ¹ /ety	
rickets	
rickshaw	
ricline	recline ²
ricluse	recluse
ricochet ¹	
ricooperate	recuperate ²⁺
ricroot	recruit ¹
ricshore	rickshaw
ricumbent	recumbent
ricur	recur ³⁺
ricuver	recover ¹⁺
rid /dance	
ridance	riddance
ridans	riddance
riddle ²	
rid e /den/er/ing	
rideem	redeem ¹⁺
rideemable	redeemable
rideemabul	redeemable
rideemer	redeemer
ridemshun	redemption⁺
ridge ²	
ridicule ²	
ridiculous /ly/ness	
ridiculus	ridiculous ⁺
ridownd	redound ¹
ridowt	redoubt ⁺
ridress	redress ¹⁺
riduce	reduce ²⁺
riducshun	reduction
ridul	riddle ²
ridundansey	redundancy ⁺
ridundant	redundant
riduse	reduce ²⁺
ridusible	reducible
ridusibul	reducible
rie	rye ★
rie	wry ★⁺
rife	
riff-raff	

rifinerey	refinery +	rikwest	request [1]
rifle [2] /-range		rikwire	require [2+]
riflecshun	reflection	rikwite	requite [2+]
riflect	reflect [1+]	rile [2]	
riflecter	reflector	riluctance	reluctance +
riflectiv	reflective	riluctans	reluctance +
riform	reform [1+]	riluctant	reluctant
rifract	refract [1+]	rim [3]	
rifrane	refrain [1]	rimainder	remainder
rifresh	refresh [1+]	rimand	remand [1]
rifrigerate	refrigerate [2+]	rimane	remain [1+]
rifrigerater	refrigerator	rimark	remark [1+]
rift /-valley		rimarkable	remarkable
rifulgens	refulgence +	rime [2★] (frost)	
rifulgent	refulgent	rime	rhyme [2★]
rifusal	refusal	rimember	remember [1+]
rifuse	refuse [2+]	rimembrance	remembrance
rifutal	refutal	rimembrans	remembrance
rifute	refute [2+]	rimind	remind [1+]
rig [3] /ger		riminder	reminder
rigard	regard [1+]	rimishun	remission
rigardless	regardless	rimiss	remiss +
rigata	regatta +	rimit	remit [3+]
rige	ridge [2]	rimitance	remittance
riger	rigor ★	rimitans	remittance
riger	rigour ★	rimonstrativ	remonstrative
riggle	wriggle [2]	rimoov	remove [2+]
right [1★] (correct)		rimorse	remorse +
right	rite ★	rimorsless	remorseless +
right	write ★+	rimote	remote +
righteous /ly/ness		rimunerate	remunerate [2+]
rightful /ly		rimuneration	remuneration
rigid /ity/ly		rinasance	Renaissance ★
rigmarole		rinasance	renascence ★+
rigor ★ (stiffness)		rinasant	renascent
rigour ★ (severity)		rind	
rigreshun	regression	rinew	renew [1+]
rigresiv	regressive	rinewable	renewable
rigress	regress [1+]	rinewabul	renewable
rigret	regret [3+]	rinewal	renewal
rigretable	regrettable +	ring [1★] (circle, bell)	
rigretabul	regrettable +	ring	wring ★
rigretful	regretful	ring er ★† /leader/let †(horse)	
rigul	wriggle [2]		
rike	Reich	ringer	wringer ★

245

rink	
rinkle	wrinkle [2]
rinkul	wrinkle [2]
rinoceros	rhinoceros [+]
rinoserus	rhinoceros [+]
rinounce	renounce [2+]
rinownse	renounce [2+]
rinse [2]	
rinuable	renewable
rinuabul	renewable
rinual	renewal
rinue	renew [1+]
rinunsiashun	renunciation
rinunsiate	renunciate [2+]
rinunsiation	renunciation
riot [1] /ous/ously	
riotus	riotous
rip [3] /per	
ripair	repair [1+]
ripare	repair [1+]
ripe /r/st/ly/ness	
ripeel	repeal [1]
ripeet	repeat [1+]
ripel	repel [3+]
ripen [1]	
ripent	repent [1+]
ripentance	repentance
ripentans	repentance
ripentant	repentant
ripine	repine [2]
riple	ripple [2]
riplete	replete [+]
ripli	reply [4+]
riport	report [1+]
ripose	repose [2+]
ripositrey	repository [+]
ripple [2]	
ripreshun	repression
ripress	repress [1+]
ripreve	reprieve [2]
riprisal	reprisal
riproch	reproach [1+]
riprochful	reproachful
riproof	reproof [+]
riproov	reprove [2+]

ripublic	republic [+]
ripublican	republican
ripudiate	repudiate [2+]
ripugnance	repugnance [+]
ripugnans	repugnance [+]
ripugnant	repugnant
ripul	ripple [2]
ripulse	repulse [2+]
ripulshun	repulsion
ripulsiv	repulsive [+]
ripute	repute [2+]
riquest	request [1]
riquire	require [2+]
riquite	requite [2+]
ris e *(get up)/en/er/ing	rice *
rise	
risemblans	resemblance
risemble	resemble [2+]
risembul	resemble [2+]
risent	resent [1*+]
risentful	resentful [+]
riserch	research [1+]
riserve	reserve [2+]
riservist	reservist
riside	reside [2+]
risign	resign [1+]
risilience	resilience [+]
risilient	resilient
risilyant	resilient
risilyens	resilience [+]
risist	resist [1+]
risistable	resistable [+]
risistabul	resistable [+]
risistance	resistance [+]
risistans	resistance [+]
risistant	resistant
risital	recital [+]
risite	recite [2]
risk [1] /ier/iest/y	
riski ly /ness	
risolve	resolve [2]
risorce	resource [+]
risorceful	resourceful
risort	resort [1]
risotto	

246

risound	resound [1]	riter	writer
risource	resource +	rithe	writhe [2]
risourceful	resourceful	rithm	rhythm
risownd	resound [1]	rithmic	rhythmic +
rispect	respect [1]+	riting	writing
rispectable	respectable +	ritire	retire [2]+
rispectful	respectful	ritort	retort [1]
rispectiv	respective +	ritracshun	retraction
rispire	respire [2]+	ritract	retract [1]+
rispite	respite	ritraction	retraction
risplendence	resplendence +	ritreet	retreat [1]
risplendens	resplendence +	ritrevable	retrievable
risplendent	resplendent	ritreval	retrieval
rispond	respond [1]+	ritreve	retrieve [2]+
rispondence	respondence	ritten	written
rispondens	respondence	ritual /ism/ist	
risponsible	responsible +	riturn	return [1]+
risponsibul	responsible +	rityoual	ritual +
risponsiv	responsive	rival [3] /ry	
rissole		riveal	reveal [1]
rist	wrist +	rivenge	revenge [2]+
ristband	wristband	rivengeful	revengeful
ristlet	wristlet	river	
ristore	restore [2]+	rivere	revere [2]+
ristrain	restrain [1]+	**rivet** [1]	
ristraint	restraint	rivijun	revision
ristrict	restrict [1]+	rivile	revile [2]
ristwatch	wrist-watch	rivise	revise [2]+
risult	result [1]+	rivishun	revision
risultant	resultant	rivision	revision
risume	resume [2]★	rivival	revival
risurgence	resurgence +	rivive	revive [2]+
risurgens	resurgence +	rivocable	revocable +
risurgent	resurgent	rivocabul	revocable +
rit	writ	rivoke	revoke [2]+
ritaliate	retaliate [2]+	rivolt	revolt [1]
ritard	retard [1]+	rivolv	revolve [2]+
ritchus	righteous +	rivolver	revolver
rite ★ (ceremony)		rivue	review [1]★+
rite	right [1]★	rivue	revue ★
rite	write ★+	**rivulet**	
riteful	rightful +	rivulshun	revulsion
ritenshun	retention +	rivulsion	revulsion
ritention	retention +	rivursal	reversal
ritentiv	retentive	rivurse	reverse [2]+

rivurt	revert [1+]
riward	reward [1]
ro	roe ★+
ro	row [1]★+
roach [1] /es	
road ★ (highway)	
road	rode ★
roadworth y /iness	
roam [1]	
roan	
roar [1] /er	
roast [1]	
rob [3] /ber	
robber y /ies	
robe [2]	
roberey	robbery +
robin redbreast	
robot	
robust /ly/ness	
roch	roach [1+]
rock [1] /er/y	
rock -cake /garden	
rocker y /ies	
rocket [1] /eer/ry	
rocking -chair /-horse	
rococo	
rode ★(did ride)	
rode	road ★
rodedendron	rhododendron
rodent	
rodeo /s	
rodeworthey	roadworthy +
rodio	rodeo +
rodium	rhodium
roe ★ (deer) /buck	
roe	row [1]★+
rog	rogue +
rogish	roguish
rogu e /ery/ish	
roial	royal +
roialtey	royalty
rol	role ★
rol	roll [1]★+
rolcall	roll-call
role ★ (of an actor)	

roli poli	roly-poly
rolick	rollick [1+]
roll [1]★ (move) /-call/er	
roller-skate [2]	
rollick [1] /er	
rolling-pin	
roly-poly	
Roman Catholic	
romance [2]	
romans	romance [2]
romantic /ally/ism	
Romany	
romboid	rhomboid
rombus	rhombus +
rome	roam [1]
romp [1] /er	
rondayvoo	rendezvous [1]
rondo /s	
rone	roan
rong	wrong [1+]
rongful	wrongful +
roo	rue [2+]
roobarb	rhubarb
rooble	rouble
roobul	rouble
rood ★ (church)	
rood	rude ★+
roodiment	rudiment +
roodimentrey	rudimentary
roof [1] /less	
rooful	rueful
rooge	rouge [2]
rooin	ruin [1+]
rooinashun	ruination
rooination	ruination
rooinous	ruinous +
rooinus	ruinous +
rook [1] /ery/eries	
rool	rule [2+]
roolet	roulette
room /ful/iness/y	
roomatic	rheumatic +
roomatism	rheumatism
roomer	rumour [1]
roomey	roomy

roon	rune
roopee	rupee
rooral	rural +
roose	ruse
roost [1] /er	
root [1]★ /-crop/less	
root	route ★
roothless	ruthless +
rootine	routine
rootstock	
rop e [2] /iness/y	
rope-ladder	
ropey	ropy
ror	roar [1]+
rort	wrought +
rosarey	rosary +
rosar y /ies	
rose ★ /-bud/-tree	
rose	rows ★
roset	rosette
rosette	
rosewood	
rosie	rosy +
rost	roast [1]
roster	
rostrum /s	
ros y /ily/iness	
rot [3] /ter	
rota /s	
rotarey	rotary +
rotar y /ies	
rotashun	rotation
rotat e [2] /able/ion	
rote ★ (repetition)	
rote	wrote ★
roten	rotten +
roter	rotor
roth	wrath +
rotor	
rotten /ly/ness	
rotund /a/ity	
rouble	
rouge [2]	
rough ★ (coarse) /age	
rough-and-ready	

rough-and-tumble	
roughen [1]	
rough er /est/ly/ness	
rough-shod	
rought	wrought +
roulette	
round [1] /er/est/ly/ness	
roundabout	
Roundhead	
round -table /-up	
rous e [2] /ingly	
rout [1]★ (defeat)	
route ★ (way)	
routeen	routine
routine	
rove [2] /r	
row [1]★ (boat) /er	
rowdie	rowdy +
rowd y /ies/ily/iness	
rownd	round [1]+
rowndabout	roundabout
rowndhed	Roundhead
rowndup	round-up
rows ★ (lines)	
rowse	rouse [2]+
rowt	rout [1]★
rowze	rouse [2]+
royal /ly/ty	
royaltey	royalty
rub [3] /ber	
rubarb	rhubarb
rubbish /y	
rubble	
rubicund	
rubie	ruby +
rubish	rubbish +
rubric	
rubul	rubble
rub y /ies	
rucksack	
rudder	
rudd y /iness	
rude ★(offensive)/ly/r/st	
rude	rood ★
ruder	rudder

249

rudie	ruddy +	run /ner/ning/way	
rudiment /ary		runaway	
rue² /ful/fully		rune	
ruf	rough ★+	runerup	runner-up
ruf	ruff ★	rung ★†	
ruf and redy	rough-and-ready	†(step, did ring)	
ruf and tumbul	rough-and-tumble	rung	wrung ★
ruff ★ (collar, bird)		runner-up	
ruff	rough ★+	runt	
ruffage	roughage	rupcher	rupture²
ruffen	roughen¹	rupea	rupee
ruffian /ism/ly		rupee	
ruffle²		rupture²	
ruffley	roughly	rural /ly	
rufidge	roughage	ruse	
rufige	roughage	rush¹	
rufle	ruffle²	rushun	Russian
rufshod	rough-shod	rusit	russet
ruful	rueful	rusk	
rufyan	ruffian +	rusler	rustler
rugbe	Rugby	russet	
Rugby		Russian	
rugged /ly/ness		rust¹ /less/y	
rugid	rugged +	rustic /ity	
ruin¹ /ation		rusticat e² /ion	
ruinashun	ruination	rusti er /est/ly/ness	
ruinous /ly		rustle² /r	
ruinus	ruinous +	rust-proof	
ruksac	rucksack	rusul	rustle ²+
rule² /r		rut³	
rum /ba/my		ruthenium	
rumatic	rheumatic +	ruthless /ly/ness	
rumatism	rheumatism	rye ★ (grain)	
rumble²		rye	wry ★+
rumbul	rumble²	ryly	wryly
rumer	rumour¹	rythm	rhythm
rumidge	rummage²	rythmic	rhythmic +
rumige	rummage²		
ruminat e² /ion/ive			
rummage²			
rumour¹			
rump /steak			
rumple²		saans	seance
rumpul	rumple²	sabath	sabbath +
rumpus /es		sabatical	sabbatical
		sabbat h /ical	

S

saber	sabre +
sable	
sabotage ²	
sabre /-toothed	
sabul	sable
sacarin	saccharin
saccharin	
sacerdotal	
sachel	satchel
sachet	
sack ¹ /ful	
sackarin	saccharin
sacrament	
sacred /ly/ness	
sacrement	sacrament
sacrific e ² /ial	
sacrifise	sacrifice ²+
sacrifishal	sacrificial
sacrileg e /ious	
sacrilige	sacrilege +
sacriligus	sacrilegious
sacrosanct	
sacsophone	saxophone +
sad /der/dest/ly/ness	
sadden ¹	
saddle ² /r/ry	
saden	sadden ¹
sadis m /t	
sadul	saddle ²+
safari /s	
safe /ly/r/st/ty	
safegard	safeguard ¹
safeguard ¹	
saffron	
safire	sapphire
saftie	safety
sag ³	
saga /s	
sagaci ous /ty	
sagashus	sagacious +
sagasitey	sagacity
sage /ly/ness	
sago	
said	
sail ¹★ (of boat) /or	

sail	sale ★+
sailsman	salesman
saint /hood/ly	
sake	
sakshorn	saxhorn
saksofone	saxophone +
sakson	Saxon +
saksophone	saxophone +
salar y ⁴ /ies	
sale ★† /ability/able	
†(of goods)	
sale	sail ¹★+
salesman	
salie	sally ⁴+
salien ce /t	
saliens	salience +
salin e /ity	
saliva /ry/tion	
sallow /ness	
sall y ⁴ /ies	
salm	psalm +
salmon	
salon	
saloon	
saloot	salute ²+
salow	sallow +
salsify	
salt ¹ /iness/y	
salt -cellar /-lick	
salter	psalter +
saltpeter	saltpetre
saltpetre	
salubri ous /ty	
salubrius	salubrious +
salutar y /iness	
salutashun	salutation
salut e ² /ation	
salvage ²	
salvashun	salvation
salvation	
salv e ² /able	
salver	
salvidge	salvage ²
salvige	salvage ²
salvo /s	

251

samaritan		sap³	
samarium		saper	sapper
same /ness		sapien *ce* /t	
samon	salmon	sapiens	sapience⁺
samovar		sapling	
sample² /r		sapper	
sampul	sample²⁺	sapphire	
sanatorium /s		sarcasm	
sancshun	sanction¹	sarcastic /ally	
sanctifi	sanctify⁴⁺	sarcofagus	sarcophagus⁺
sanctif *y*⁴ /ication		sarcophag *us* /i (pl.)	
sanctimonious /ly		sardine	
sanctimonius	sanctimonious⁺	sardonic /ally	
sanction¹		sargant	sergeant⁺
sanctity		sari	
sanctuar *y* /ies		sarjent	sergeant⁺
sanctum /s		sarm	psalm⁺
sand¹ /y		sartorial	
sandal /-wood		sary	sari
sandle	sandal⁺	saserdotle	sacerdotal
sandpaper¹		sash /es	
sandwhich	sandwich¹⁺	sashable	satiable
sandwich¹ /es		sashabul	satiable
sane ★ (not mad) /ly/ness		sashay	sachet
sane	seine²★	sashiate	satiate²
sang-froid		Satan /ic	
sanguin *e* /ary		satchel	
sangwin	sanguine⁺	sate²	
sanitary		sateen	
sanitashun	sanitation	satelight	satellite
sanitation		satellite	
sanitey	sanity	saten	sateen
sanitrey	sanitary	saterday	Saturday
sanity		satiable	
sankshun	sanction¹	satiabul	satiable
sanktify	sanctify⁴⁺	satiate²	
sanktimonius	sanctimonious⁺	satin	
sanktitey	sanctity	satir *e* /ist	
sanktuarey	sanctuary⁺	satirical /ly	
sanktum	sanctum⁺	satirise²	
Sanskrit		satisfacshun	satisfaction
sant	saint⁺	satisfactor *y* /ily	
Santa Claus		satisfactrey	satisfactory⁺
Santa klaws	Santa Claus	satisfiabul	satisfiable
santeem	centime	satisf *y*⁴ /iable/action	

saturashun	saturation
saturat *e*² /ion	
Saturday	
Saturn	
sauce ★ (liquid) /boat/pan	
sauce	source ★
saucer	
saucerer	sorcerer +
saucerey	sorcery
sauci *er* /est/ly/ness	
saucy	
sauna	
saunter ¹	
sausage	
sausie	saucy
savage ² /ly/ry	
savana	savannah
savannah	
save ²★ (hoard)	
saver	savour ¹★+
savier	saviour
savige	savage ²+
savigrey	savagery
saviour	
savorey	savoury
savour ¹★ (flavour) /y	
savyer	saviour
saw ★ (cut) /n	
saw	soar ¹★
saw	sore ★+
sawcer	saucer
sawcy	saucy
sawdid	sordid +
sawdust	
sawna	sauna
sawnter	saunter ¹
saws	sauce ★+
saws	source ★
sawser	saucer
sawsey	saucy
sawsier	saucier +
saxhorn	
saxofone	saxophone +
Saxon /y	
saxophon *e* /ist	

say /ing	
sayance	seance
scab ³ /by	
scabbard	
scabees	scabies
scabies	
scaffold	
scald ¹	
scal *e* ² /y	
scaliwag	scallywag
scallop	
scallywag	
scalp ¹ /er	
scalpel	
scamp ¹	
scamper ¹	
scampi	
scan ³ /ner	
scandal /ous/ously	
scandalise ²	
scandium	
scanshun	scansion
scansion	
scant /ily/iness/y	
scapegoat	
scapula /r	
scar ³	
scarab	
scarce /ly/ness/r	
scarcit *y* /ies	
scare ² /crow/monger/y	
scaretso	scherzo
scar *f* /fs/ves (pls.)	
scarf-pin	
scarif *y* ⁴ /ication	
scarlatina	
scarlet	
scarsitey	scarcity +
scate	skate ²+
scathe ² /less	
scatter ¹ /-brain	
scavenge ² /r	
sceme	scheme ²+
scenario /s	
scene ★ (of a play) /ry	

253

scenic /ally
scent [1]★ (smell)
scepter   sceptre
sceptic /al/ally/ism
sceptre
scerge   scourge [2]
scermish   skirmish [1+]
schedule [2]
schematic /ally
scheme [2] /r
scherzo /s
schism /atic
schist
schizofrenia   schizophrenia [+]
schizoid
schizophreni *a* /c
schnaps
scholar /ly/ship
scholastic /ism
school [1] /boy/girl
schooner
sciatic /a
scien *ce* /tist
scientific /ally
scintillat *e* [2] /ion
scion
scission
scissors
scitsofrenia   schizophrenia [+]
sclerosis
sclerotic
scoff [1] /er
scolar   scholar [+]
scolarship   scholarship
scolastic   scholastic [+]
scold [1] /er
scone
scool   school [1+]
scoop [1]
scoot [1] /er
scorch [1] /er/ingly
score [2] /r
scorn [1] /ful/fully
scorpion
scorpyun   scorpion

Scot /ch/tish
scot-free
Scots *man* /woman
scoundrel /ism/ly
scour [1] /er
scourge [2]
scout [1]
scower   scour [1+]
scowl [1]
scowndrel   scoundrel [+]
scowt   scout [1]
scrabble [2]
scrabul   scrabble [2]
scrag [3] /gy
scram [3]
scramble [2]
scrambul   scramble [2]
scrap [3] /-book/-heap
scrape [2] /r
scrapp *y* /ily/iness
scrapy   scrappy [+]
scratch [1] /es
scrawl [1]
scrawny
scream [1] /er
scree
screech [1] /es/-owl
screed [1]
screen [1]
screw [1] /driver/y
screwtinise   scrutinise [2]
scribble [2] /r
scribe [2]
scribul   scribble [2+]
scrimige   scrimmage
scrimmage
scrimp [1] /y
scripcher   scripture [+]
script /-writer
scriptur *e* /al
scroful *a* /ous
scroll
scroo   screw [1+]
scrotum
scrounge [2] /r

254

scrownge — scrounge [2+]
scrub [3] /ber/by
scruff /ier/iest/y
scrum half
scrummage
scrumptious /ly/ness
scrumshus — scrumptious [+]
scrunch [1] /es
scruple [2]
scrupul — scruple [2]
scrupulous /ly/ness
scrutinise [2]
scrutiny /ies/eer
scud [3]
scuffle [2]
scuful — scuffle [2]
scul — scull [1★+]
scul — skull [★+]
sculerey — scullery [+]
scull [1★] (boat) /er
sculler y /ies
sculpcher — sculpture [2]
sculpt or /ress (fem.)
sculpture [2]
scum [3] /my
scupper [1]
scurf /iness/y
scurge — scourge [2]
scurie — scurry [4]
scurilus — scurrilous [+]
scurrilous /ly
scurry [4]
scurv y /ily
scury — scurry [4]
scuttle [2]
scutul — scuttle [2]
scythe [2]
sea ★ (water) /-gull
sea — see [★+]
seafar er /ing
seal /ed/er/ing ★ (fasten)
sea -level /-lion
sealing — ceiling ★
sealskin
seam ★ (join in cloth)

seam — seem [1★]
seaman /ship
seamstress
seam y /ier/iest
sean — scene [★+]
sean — seen ★
seance
seans — seance
sear [1★] (scorch)
sear — seer ★
search [1] /es/er
sea shore /side/weed
seasick /ness
season [1] /able/ably
seasonal /ly
seasor — seesaw [1]
seat [1]
seaworth y /iness
sebaceous
sebashus — sebaceous
secaters — secateurs
secateurs
secede [2]
seceshun — secession
secession
seclu de [2] /sion
second [1] /ly/-rate
secondar y /ily
secondrey — secondary [+]
secrecy
secresey — secrecy
secret /ive/ly
secretaria l /t
secretar y /ies
secret e [2] /ion
sect /arian
section /al/ally
sector
secular /ism
secularis e [2] /ation
secur e [2] /able/ely
securitey — security [+]
securit y /ies
sed — said
sedashun — sedation [+]

255

sedate /ly/ness	
sedat *ion* /ive	
sedentary	
sedentrey	sedentary
seder	cedar
sedge	
sedila	cedilla
sediment /ation	
sedishun	sedition +
sedishus	seditious
sedit *ion* /ious	
seduce ² /r	
seducshun	seduction
seduction	
seductive /ly	
sedulous /ly	
sedulus	sedulous +
seduse	seduce ²+
see *† /ing/n *†	
†(with eyes)	
see	sea *+
seed ¹* (of plants)	
seed	cede ²*
seed *iness* /ling/y	
seefarer	seafarer +
seege	siege
seek /er/ing	
seel	seal +
seeling	ceiling *
seeling	sealing *
seem ¹* (appear)	
seem	seam *
seeman	seaman +
seemey	seamy +
seeml *y* /ier/iest/iness	
seemstress	seamstress
seen	scene *+
seenerey	scenery
seenic	scenic +
seep ¹ /age	
seepige	seepage
seer * (prophet)	
seer	sear ¹*
seesaw ¹	
seese	cease ²+

seesfire	cease-fire
seesher	seizure
seeshore	seashore +
seesick	seasick +
seeside	seaside
seet	seat ¹
seeth	seethe ²
seethe ²	
seeworthey	seaworthy +
seeze	seize ²
sefalic	cephalic +
sefalitis	cephalitis
sege	sedge
segment /ation	
segregashun	segregation
segregat *e* ² /ion/ive	
seige	siege
seine ²* (fishing net)	
seism *ic* /ometer	
seismograph /ic	
seismolog *y* /ist	
seize ²	
seizure	
sekaters	secateurs
sekstant	sextant
sekstet	sextet
sekston	sexton
seksual	sexual +
sekt	sect +
sekwel	sequel
sekwence	sequence +
sekwens	sequence +
sekwester	sequester ¹
sekwestrate	sequestrate ²+
sekwin	sequin
selandine	celandine
selcius	Celsius
seldom /ly	
selebritey	celebrity +
select ¹ /ion/or	
selective /ly	
selenium	
seler	cellar *
seler	seller *
selerey	celery

seleritey	celerity		semi-final	
self /ish/ishness			semikwaver	semiquaver
self-assured			semilunar	
self-centred			seminal	
self-confiden ce /t			seminar /y	
selfconfidens	self-confidence +		semi-precious	
self-conscious /ly/ness			semipreshus	semi-precious
selfconshus	self-conscious +		semiquaver	
self-contained			Semit e /ic	
self-control			semitone	
self-respect /ing			semitrey	cemetery +
self-righteous /ly/ness			semolena	semolina
self-service			semolina	
selibacy	celibacy +		sena	senna
selibasey	celibacy +		senario	scenario +
selibat	celibate		senat	senate +
selibrant	celebrant		senat e /or	
selibrate	celebrate ²+		senater	senator
sell ★ (goods) /er ★			send /er	
sell	cell ★		senil e /ity	
seller	cellar ★		senilitey	senility
Sellotape			senior /ity	
selofane	cellophane		senna	
selsius	Celsius		senotaf	cenotaph
selt	Celt +		sensashun	sensation
seltic	Celtic		sensashunal	sensational +
selular	cellular		sensation	
selule	cellule		sensational /ism/ly	
seluloid	celluloid		sense ² /less	
selulose	cellulose		senser	censer ★
selvage			senser	censor ¹★+
selvige	selvage		sensher	censure ²+
semafor	semaphore		senshience	sentience +
semantic /s			senshooal	sensual +
semaphore			sensib le /ility/ly	
semblance			sensibul	sensible +
semblans	semblance		sensitise ²	
semen			sensitiv e /ely/ity	
semester			sensitivitey	sensitivity
semibreve			sensorey	sensory
semicercul	semicircle +		sensorious	censorious
semicirc le /ular			sensorius	censorious
semicolon			sensory	
semi-conductor			sensual /ist/ity/ly	
semi-detached			sensus	census +

sent * (did send)
sent | cent *
sent | scent [1]*
sentenarey | centenary [+]
sentenarian | centenarian
sentence [2]
sentenial | centennial [+]
sentens | sentence [2]
sentenshus | sententious [+]
sententious /ly
sentenyal | centennial [+]
senter | centre [2+]
senter forwud | centre-forward
sentien ce /t
sentigrade | centigrade
sentigram | centigram
sentileter | centilitre
sentiment
sentimental /ist/ity/ly
sentimentalise [2]
sentimeter | centimetre
sentinel
sentipede | centipede
sentor | centaur
sentral | central [+]
sentralise | centralise [2+]
sentralitey | centrality
sentrey | sentry [+]
sentrifugal | centrifugal [+]
sentrifuge | centrifuge
sentripetal | centripetal
sentr y /ies
sentuple | centuple
senturey | century [+]
senturion | centurion
senyor | senior [+]
senyoritey | seniority
separat e [2] /ion/ist/or
seperate | separate [2+]
sephalic | cephalic [+]
sephalitis | cephalitis
sepia
sepoi | sepoy
sepoy
September

septer | sceptre
septic
septicaemia
septisemia | septicaemia
sepulchr e /al
sepulker | sepulchre [+]
sequel
sequen ce /tial
sequester [1]
sequestrat e [2] /ion/or
sequin
ser | sir
seraf | seraph [+]
serafic | seraphic
seramic | ceramic [+]
seraph /s/ic
serch | search [1+]
serebral | cerebral [+]
serees | series
serenade [2]
serendipity
seren e /ely/ity
serenitey | serenity
seres | series
sereze | cerise
serf * (slave) /dom
serf | surf [1]*[+]
sergeant /-major
serial *† /ly
  †(part of a story)
serial | cereal *
serialis e [2] /ation
seribelum | cerebellum
seribrum | cerebrum
serid | serried
series
serimonial | ceremonial [+]
serimonius | ceremonious [+]
serimuney | ceremony [+]
serious /ly/ness
serius | serious [+]
serlier | surlier [+]
serloin | sirloin
serly | surly *
sermise | surmise [2]

sermon	
sermonise [2]	
sermownt	surmount [1]
sername	surname
serpass	surpass [1]
serpent /ine	
serplis	surplice ★
serplus	surplus ★
serprise	surprise [2]
serrated	
serried	
sertaks	surtax [+]
sertax	surtax [+]
sertifi	certify [4+]
sertifiable	certifiable [+]
sertificat	certificate [2+]
sertify	certify [4+]
sertintey	certainty [+]
sertitude	certitude
serum	
servant	
servay	survey [1+]
servaylans	surveillance
serve [2] /r	
servical	cervical
service [2] /ability/able	
serviet	serviette
serviette	
serviks	cervix [+]
servil e /ity	
servitude	
servival	survival
servive	survive [2+]
serviver	survivor
servix	cervix [+]
sesashun	cessation
sese	cease [2+]
seseed	secede [2]
seseshun	secession
seshun	cession ★
seshun	session ★
sesion	cession ★
sesion	session ★
sesium	caesium
sesless	ceaseless

sesmic	seismic [+]
seson	season [1+]
sesonable	seasonable
sesonabul	seasonable
sesonal	seasonal [+]
sespit	cesspit
sespool	cesspool
sessashun	cessation
sessesion	secession
session ★ (period)	
session	cession ★
set /ting/-square	
setea	settee
seter	setter
setle	settle [2+]
settee	
setter	
settle [2] /ment/r	
setul	settle [2+]
setulment	settlement
seudo	pseudo [+]
seudonim	pseudonym
sevear	severe [+]
seven /teen/teenth/th	
sevent y /ies/ieth	
sever [1] /ance˙	
several /ly	
severans	severance
sever e /ely/ity	
severitey	severity
sew [1★†] /er ★† /ing/n ★†	
†(with a needle)	
sew er [1★†] /age/erage	
†(public drain)	
sewn	sown ★
sex /ed/iness/less	
sextant	
sextet	
sexton	
sexual /ity/ly	
sezarian	Caesarean
Sezer	Caesar
sfere	sphere [2+]
sferical	spherical
sferoid	spheroid

259

sfincter	sphincter	shan't (shall not)	
sfinks	sphinx +	shant	shan't
sfinx	sphinx +	shant y /ies	
sha	shah	shape ² /liness/ly	
shabbi ly /ness		shaperon	chaperon ¹+
shabb y /ier/iest		sharad	charade
shaby	shabby +	share ² /holder/r	
shack		shark	
shackle ²		sharlot	charlotte
shad e ² /y		sharp /er/est/ly/ness	
shadervre	chef-d'oeuvre	sharpen ¹ /er	
shadow ¹ /y		sharpshooter	
shaft		shasee	chassis
shagay da fare	chargé-d'affaires	shater	shatter ¹
shagg y /iness		shatow	chateau +
shagie	shaggy +	shatter ¹	
shagrin	chagrin +	shave ² /n/r	
shah		shawl	
shak	shack	shea f ¹ /ves (pl.)	
shake *† /down/n/r		shear * (clip) /s	
†(agitate)		shear	sheer ¹*
shake	sheik *	sheath * (n.)	
shakey	shaky +	sheathe ²* (v.)	
shak y /ily/iness/ing		shed /ding	
shal	shall	shedule	schedule ²
shalaton	charlatan	sheef	sheaf ¹+
shalay	chalet	sheek	chic *
shale		sheek	sheik *
shalet	chalet	sheen	
shall		sheep /-dog/skin	
shallot		sheepish /ly/ness	
shallow /er/est/ness		sheer ¹* (thin, steep)	
sham ³ /mer		sheer	shear *+
shamble ²		sheet ¹	
shambul	shamble ²	shef	chef
shame ² /-faced/less		sheik * (Arab chief)	
shameful /ly		sheik	chic *
shampane	champagne	sheild	shield ¹
shampoo ¹		shel	shell ¹+
shamrock		shelac	shellac +
shamwa	chamois	sheld	shield ¹
shandeleer	chandelier	shel f /ves (pl.)	
shandie	shandy +	shelfish	shellfish
shand y /ies		shell ¹ /fish	
shank		shellac /ked/king	

260

shelter [1] /er
shelve [2]
shemeez · chemise
sheperd · shepherd [1+]
sheperds pie · shepherd's pie
shepherd [1] /ess (fem.)
shepherd's pie
sherbet
sherie · sherry [+]
sherif · sheriff [+]
sheriff /s
sheroot · cheroot
sheropodey · chiropody [+]
sherry /ies
shery · sherry [+]
sheth · sheath [*]
sheth · sheathe [2*]
shevaler · chevalier
sheves · sheaves
shevron · chevron
shi · shy [4+]
shic · chic [*]
shic · sheik [*]
shicanerey · chicanery
shield [1]
shifon · chiffon
shift [1] /ily/iness/less/y
shiling · shilling
shilling
shilly-shally [4] /ier
shily shaly · shilly-shally [4+]
shimeric · chimeric [+]
shimmer [1] /y
shin [3]
shin e [2] /er/y
shingle [2]
shingles
shingul · shingle [2]
shinguls · shingles
ship [3] /ment/per
shipreck · shipwreck [1]
ship shape /wright
shipwreck [1]
shire
shirk [1] /er

shirt /ing/y
shivalrey · chivalry [+]
shivalrous · chivalrous
shivalrus · chivalrous
shiver [1] /y
shnaps · schnaps
shoal [1]
shock [1] /-absorber/er
shoddi ly /ness
shodd y /ier/iest
shodie · shoddy [+]
shody · shoddy [+]
shoe /lace/string
shofer · chauffeur
sholder · shoulder [1]
shole · shoal [1]
shoo · shoe [+]
shood · should [+]
shook
shoolace · shoelace
shoostring · shoestring
shoot [*] (gun) /er
shoot · chute [*]
shooting /-brake
shop [3] /keeper/per
shoplift [1] /er
shop-soiled
shop-steward
shore [2*] (prop up)
shore · sure [*+]
shoretey · surety [+]
shorley · surely [*]
shorn
short /age/ly
short bread /cake
short-circuit [1]
shorten [1]
shorthand
short-sighted /ness
short sited · short-sighted [+]
shot
should /n't
shoulder [1]
shout [1] /er
shove [2]

261

shovel³ /ler	
shovinism	chauvinism⁺
shovinist	chauvinist
show /down/ily/ing/n/y	
shower¹ /-bath/y	
showt	shout¹⁺
shrank	
shrapnel	
shred³ /der	
shreek	shriek¹
shrew /ish/ishly	
shrewd /er/est/ly/ness	
shriek¹	
shrift	
shrike	
shrill¹ /er/est/ness/y	
shrimp	
shrine²	
shrink /age/ing	
shrivel³	
shroo	shrew⁺
shrood	shrewd⁺
shroud¹	
Shrovetide	
shrowd	shroud¹
shrub /bery	
shrug³	
shrunk /en	
shudder¹	
shuffle² /r	
shuful	shuffle²⁺
shugar	sugar¹⁺
shun³	
shunt¹	
shurbet	sherbet
shurk	shirk¹⁺
shurt	shirt⁺
shut /ter/ting	
shuttle² /cock	
shutul	shuttle²⁺
shuv	shove²
shuvel	shovel³⁺
shy⁴ /er/est/ly/ness	
si	sigh¹
sianide	cyanide

siatic	sciatic⁺
sibernetics	cybernetics
sibilant	
sibling	
sicamore	sycamore
sicedelic	psychedelic
siciatrey	psychiatry
sicick	psychic⁺
sick /ly/ness	
sicken¹	
sickle	
siclamate	cyclamate
siclamen	cyclamen
siclic	cyclic⁺
siclist	cyclist⁺
siclometer	cyclometer
siclone	cyclone⁺
siclops	Cyclops
siclostile	cyclostyle
siclotron	cyclotron
sicoanalise	psychoanalyse²⁺
sicofant	sycophant⁺
sicologey	psychology⁺
sicological	psychological⁺
sicopath	psychopath⁺
sicosis	psychosis⁺
sicosomatic	psychosomatic
sicotherapey	psychotherapy
sicotherapist	psychotherapist⁺
sicotic	psychotic
sicul	cycle²
side² /board/line/ways	
sider	cider
sidle²	
sie	sigh¹
siege	
sienna	
siense	science⁺
sientific	scientific⁺
sientist	scientist
siesta	
sieve²	
sieze	seize²
sifer	cipher¹
sifilis	syphilis⁺

sifon	siphon [1]+	silidge	silage
sift [1]		silie	silly +
sigar	cigar +	silige	silage
sigaret	cigarette	silinder	cylinder
sigh [1]		silindrical	cylindrical +
sight [1]★ (see) /less		silk /ily/iness/y	
sight	cite [2]★+	sill	
sight	site [2]★	sillable	syllable +
sightsee r /ing		sillabub	
sign [1]★ /er/-writer		sill y /ier/iest/ily/iness	
sign	sine ★	silo	
signacher	signature	silogise	syllogise [2]+
signal [3] /ler		silogism	syllogism
signalise [2]		silooet	silhouette [2]
signator y /ies		siluet	silhouette [2]
signature		silvan	
signet ★ (ring)		silver [1] /y	
signet	cygnet ★	sily	silly +
signifi	signify [4]	simbiosis	symbiosis +
significan ce /t/tly		simbiotic	symbiotic
significans	significance +	simbol	cymbal ★+
signify [4]		simbol	symbol ★+
signpost [1]		simbolical	symbolical +
signul	signal [3]+	simbolise	symbolise [2]+
sikedelic	psychedelic	simbolism	symbolism
sikey	psyche	siment	cement [1]+
sikiatrist	psychiatrist +	simer	simmer [1]
sikiatry	psychiatry	simfoney	symphony +
sikick	psychic +	simian	
siks	six +	similar /ly	
sikstey	sixty +	similarit y /ies	
silable	syllable +	similer	similar +
silabus	syllabus +	similitude	
silage		simmer [1]	
silence [2] /r		simmetrey	symmetry +
silens	silence [2]+	simpathetic	sympathetic +
silent /ly		simpathise	sympathise [2]+
silestial	celestial +	simpathy	sympathy +
silf	sylph +	simper [1]	
silhouette [2]		simple /r/st/ton	
siliam	cilium	simplifi	simplify [4]+
silic a /osis		simplif y [4] /ication	
silicon ★ (hard mineral)		simplisitey	simplicity
silicone ★ (compound in polish)		simpl y /icity	
		simposium	symposium +

simptom	symptom +	sinopsis	synopsis +
simptomatic	symptomatic	sinoptic	synoptic
simpul	simple +	sinoshoor	cynosure
simpulton	simpleton	sinovial	synovial
simulashun	simulation	sinse	since
simulat e ² /ion/or		sinsere	sincere +
simultaneous /ly		sinseritey	sincerity
simultanius	simultaneous +	sintactic	syntactic
sin ¹ /ner		sintaks	syntax +
sinagog	synagogue	sintax	syntax +
sinamon	cinnamon	sinthesis	synthesis +
since		sinthesise	synthesise ²+
sincer e /ity		sinthetic	synthetic
sinch	cinch +	sinue	sinew +
sincopate	syncopate ²+	sinuous	
sindicalism	syndicalism +	sinus /es/itis	
sindicate	syndicate ²+	sinuus	sinuous
sindrome	syndrome	sion	scion
sine ★ (maths)		sip ³	
sine	sign ¹★+	sipher	cipher ¹
sinecamera	cine camera	siphon ¹ /age	
sinecure		sipress	cypress
sinepost	signpost ¹	sir	
sinew /y		sirca	circa
sinful /ly/ness		sircharge	surcharge ²
sing /er/ing		siren	
singe ²		siringe	syringe ²
single ² /-minded		sirloin	
singul	single ²+	siro stratus	cirro-stratus
singular /ity		sirocco	
singuler	singular +	sirocumulus	cirro-cumulus
sinic	cynic +	sirosis	cirrhosis
sinical	cynical +	sirup	syrup +
sinima	cinema +	sise	size +
sinimatograf	cinematograph +	sishun	scission
sinimatograph	cinematograph +	sismic	seismic +
sinisism	cynicism	sismograf	seismograph +
sinister		sismologey	seismology +
sink /er/ing		sissers	scissors
sinkromesh	syncromesh	sist	cyst +
sinkronise	synchronise ²+	sistem	system +
sinod	synod +	sistematic	systematic
sinonim	synonym +	sistematise	systematise ²+
sinonimus	synonymous	sister(s)/-in-law	
sinonym	synonym +	sistern	cistern

sistitis	cystitis	skeptic	sceptic +
sistole	systole	skepticul	sceptical
sit /-in/ter/ting		skeptisism	scepticism
sitadel	citadel	skermish	skirmish 1+
sitashun	citation	skert	skirt 1+
site 2★ (place)		skerting bord	skirting-board
site	cite 2★+	skertso	scherzo +
site	sight 1★+	sketch 1 /ier/ily/iness/y	
siteseeing	sightseeing	skew 1 /-whiff	
siteseer	sightseer +	skewer 1	
sitey	city +	ski 1★ (sport) /er	
sithe	scythe 2	ski	sky 4★+
sitie	city +	skid 3	
sitizen	citizen +	skiff 1	
sitologey	cytology	skil	skill +
sitric acid	citric acid	skilful /ly/ness	
sitron	citron +	skilite	skylight
sitrus	citrus	skill /ed	
situashun	situation	skim 3 /-milk	
situat e 3 /ion		skimp 1 /ily/iness/y	
siv	sieve 2	skin 3 /ner/ny	
sivere	severe +	skin-deep	
sivic	civic +	skin-div er /ing	
sivil	civil +	skiney	skinny.
sivilian	civilian	skinflint	
sivilisashun	civilisation	skintilate	scintillate 2+
sivilise	civilise 2+	skip 3	
sivilitey	civility +	skipper	
sivit	civet	skirl 1	
six /th/thly		skirmish 1 /es	
sixteen /th		skirt 1 /ing-board	
sixt y /ies/ieth		skiscraper	skyscraper
siythe	scythe 2	skism	schism +
size /able/ably		skist	schist
sizemic	seismic +	skit /tish	
sizers	scissors	skitsofrenia	schizophrenia +
sizul	sizzle 2	skittle 2	
sizzle 2		skitul	skittle 2
skate 2 /board/r		skitzoid	schizoid
skedule	schedule 2	sku	skew 1+
skee	ski 1★+	skulk 1	
skein		skull ★ (head) /-cap	
skelet on /al		skull	scull 1★+
skematic	schematic +	skunk	
skeme	scheme 2+	skurl	skirl 1

265

If you cannot find your word under **skw** look under **squ**

skwable   squabble [2]
skwod   squad
skwodron   squadron
skwolid   squalid [+]
sky [4][*][†] /-blue/-high
  [†](atmosphere)
sky   ski [1][*][+]
skyatic   sciatic [+]
skylark
skylight
skylite   skylight
skyscraper
slack [1] /er/est/ly/ness
slacken [1]
slain
slake [2]
slaken   slacken [1]
slam [3]
slander [1] /er/ous
slane   slain
slang /y
slant [1]
slap [3] /dash/stick
slash [1] /er
slat *e*[2] /y
slattern /ly
slaughter [1] /-house
Slav /onic
slav *e*[2] /ish/ishness/ery
slawter   slaughter [1][+]
slay [*] (kill) /ing
slay   sleigh [*]
sleazy
sled
sledge /-hammer
sleek /ness
sleep /ing/y
sleepi *er* /est/ly/ness
sleepless /ness
sleet [1] /y
sleeve /d/less

slege   sledge [+]
sleigh [*] (for snow)
slender /ness
sleuth
slew
sli   sly [+]
slice [2]
slick [1]
slid *e* /ing
slight [1] /er/est/ly/ness
slim [3] /mer/mest/ness
slim *e* /ier/iest/y
sling /er
slip [3] /way
slipper /iness/y
slipshod
slise   slice [2]
slit /ting
slite   slight [1][+]
slither [1]
sliver
slo   sloe [*]
slo   slow [1][*][+]
slobber [1] /er
sloe [*] (plum)
sloe   slow [1][*][+]
slog [3] /ger
slogan
sloop
sloose   sluice [2]
slooth   sleuth
slop [3] /py
slope [2]
sloppi *er* /est/ly/ness
slosh [1]
slot [3] /machine
sloth /ful
slouch [1]
slough [1][*] (dead skin)
slough [*] (swamp)
sloven /liness/ly
slow [1][*][†] /er/ly/-worm
  [†](not quick)
slow   slough [*]
slowch   slouch [1]

slowerm	slow-worm	smug /ger/gest/ly/ness	
sludg e /y		smuge	smudge [2+]
slue	slew	smuggle [2] /r	
sluff	slough [1*]	smugul	smuggle [2+]
slug /gard/gish		smurch	smirch [1+]
sluge	sludge +	smurk	smirk [1]
sluice [2]		smut /tiness/ty	
slum [3] /mer/my		snack	
slumber [1] /ous		snag [3]	
slump [1]		snail [1]	
slung		snake [2] /-bite	
slunk		snale	snail [1]
slur [3]		snap [3] /dragon/shot	
slush /y		snapp er /ily/ish/y	
slut /tish		snare [2]	
sly /er/est/ly/ness		snarl [1] /er	
smack [1]		snatch [1] /es	
small /er/est/pox		sneak [1] /ingly/ily	
smarmy		sneek	sneak [1+]
smart [1] /er/est/ly/ness		sneer [1]	
smarten [1]		sneeze [2]	
smash [1] /er		snicker [1]	
smatter [1]		snide	
smear [1] /y		sniff [1] /er/y	
smeer	smear [1+]	sniffle [2]	
smell [1] /ier/iest/ing/y		sniful	sniffle [2]
smelling-salts		snigger [1]	
smelt [1] /er		snip [3] /pet	
smirch [1] /es		snipe [2] /r	
smirk [1]		snivel [3] /ler	
smit e /ing		sno	snow [1+]
smith /y/ies		snobb ery /ish/ishness	
smithereens		snoberie	snobbery +
smithey	smithy	snobish	snobbish
smitten		snooker [1]	
smock [1]		snoop [1] /er	
smog		snooze [2]	
smoke [2] /r/-stack		snore [2] /r	
smok ier /iest/y		snorkel	
smolder	smoulder [1]	snorkle	snorkel
smooth [1] /er/est/ly/ness		snort [1] /er	
smote		snot /ty	
smother [1]		snout	
smoulder [1]		snow [1] /drift/drop/fall	
smudg e [2] /y		snowball [1]	

snow-plough		soften [1]	
snowt	snout	software	
snub [3]		softwear	software
snuff [1]		sogg *y* /iness	
snuffle [2]		sogie	soggy [+]
snuful	snuffle [2]	Soho	
snuggle [2]		soia	soya
snugul	snuggle [2]	soil [1]	
so ★ (in this way)		soiray	soirée
so	sew ★[+]	soirée	
so	sow [1]★	soiya	soya
soak [1]		sojern	sojourn [1+]
soap [1] /y		sojourn [1] /er	
soar [1]★ (to fly)		soke	soak [1]
soar	sore ★[+]	solace [2]	
sob [3]		solar /ium	
sober [1]		solar plexus	
sobriety		solar system	
sobrikay	sobriquet [+]	solas	solace [2]
sobriquet /s		solder [1]	
soccer		soldering iron	
sociab *le* /ility/ly		soldier [1] /ly/y	
sociabul	sociable [+]	sole ★ (shoe) /ly	
social /ite/ly		sole	soul ★[+]
socialis *e* [2] /ation		solecism	
socialis *m* /t/tic		soleful	soulful [+]
societ *y* /ies		solem	solemn [+]
sociolog *y* /ical/ist		solemn /ity/ly	
sock [1]		solemnis *e* [2] /ation	
socker	soccer	solemnitey	solemnity
socket		solenoid	
soda /-water		solesism	solecism
sodden		sol-fa	
soden	sodden	solger	soldier [1+]
sodium		solicit [1] /ation/ude	
sodom *y* /ite		solicit *or* /ous	
sofen	soften [1]	solid /er/est/ity/ly	
sofism	sophism [+]	solidarity	
sofist	sophist	solidifi	solidify [4+]
sofisticashun	sophistication	solidif *y* [4] /ication	
sofisticate	sophisticate [2+]	solilokwise	soliloquise [2]
sofistication	sophistication	solilokwy	soliloquy [+]
sofistrey	sophistry	soliloquise [2]	
sofmore	sophomore	soliloqu *y* /ies	
soft /er/est/ly/ness		solisit	solicit [1+]

solisiter	solicitor +	soop	soup
solisitous	solicitous	soot * (black powder) /y	
solisitus	solicitous	soot	suit ¹*+
solitar y /ily/iness		sooth /sayer	
solitrey	solitary +	soothe ²	
solitude		soovenir	souvenir
soljer	soldier ¹+	sop ³ /py	
solo /ist		sope	soap ¹+
solstice		sophis m /t/try	
solstis	solstice	sophisticat e ² /ion	
solub le /ility		sophomore	
solubul	soluble +	soporific	
solushun	solution	soprano /s	
solution		sorcer er /ess (fem.)/y	
solv e ² /able		sord	sword
solven cy /t		sordid /ly/ness	
solvensey	solvency +	sordust	sawdust
somber	sombre +	sore * (hurt) /ly/r/st	
sombraro	sombrero +	sore	saw *+
sombre /ly/ness		sore	soar ¹*
sombrero /s		sorey	sorry +
some *† /body/how		sorie	sorry +
†(a few)		sorna	sauna
some	sum ³*	sornter	saunter ¹
some one /what/where		sorow	sorrow ¹+
somersalt	somersault ¹	sorrel	
somersault ¹		sorrow ¹ /ful/fully	
somnolen ce /t		sorr y /ier/iest	
somnolens	somnolence +	sors	sauce *+
son * (male child)		sors	source *
sonar		sort ¹* (kind) /er	
sonata		sort	sought *
sonde		sortee	sortie
soner	sonar	sortie	
song /-bird/ster		sorul	sorrel
sonic		soshable	sociable +
son(s)-in-law		soshabul	sociable +
sonnet		soshal	social +
sonor ous /ity		soshalise	socialise ²+
sonorus	sonorous +	soshalism	socialism +
soo	sue ²	soshalist	socialist
soocher	suture	soshalistic	socialistic
sooflay	soufflé	soshiologey	sociology +
sooit	suet	soshiologist	sociologist
oon /er		sosidge	sausage

sosietey	society +	spanner	
sosige	sausage	Spanyard	Spaniard
sot /tish		spanyel	spaniel
sotto voce		spar ³	
soufflé		spare ²	
sought * (did seek)		spark ¹ /ing-plug	
soul * (spirit) /less		sparkle ² /r	
soul	sole *+	sparkul	sparkle ²+
soulful /ly		sparo	sparrow +
sound ¹ /er/est/less/ness		sparrow /-hawk	
soundproof ¹		spars	sparse +
soup		sparse /ly/ness	
sour ¹ /er/est/ish/ness		sparsity	
source * (origin)		Spartan	
source	sauce *+	spase	space ²+
souse ²		spashal	spatial
south /erly/ern		spashus	spacious
souvenir		spasm	
sou'-wester		spasmodic /ally	
sovereign /ty		spastic /ism	
soverin	sovereign +	spate	
soviet		spatial	
sovrentey	sovereignty	spatter ¹	
sow ¹* (cast seed, pig)		spatula /te	
sow	sew ¹*+	spawn ¹	
sown * (seed)		speak /er/ing	
sown	sewn *	spear ¹ /head	
sownd	sound ¹+	special /ist/ly	
sowndproof	soundproof ¹	specialis e ² /ation	
sowr	sour ¹+	specialt y /ies	
sowse	souse ²	species	
sowth	south +	specifi	specify ⁴+
sow-wester	sou'-wester	specific /ally	
soya		specif y ⁴ /ication	
spac e ² /ious		specimen	
spade /-work		specious /ness	
spagetti	spaghetti	speck ¹	
spaghetti		speckle ²	
span ³		spectacle	
spaner	spanner	spectacular /ly	
spangle ²		spectator	
spangul	spangle ²	specter	spectre +
Spaniard		spectr e /al	
spaniel		spectrograf	spectrograph
spank ¹		spectrograph	

spectroscop *e* /ic
spectr *um* /a (pl.)
speculashun   speculation
speculat *e* [2] /ion/or
speculative /ly
speech /less
speed [1] /y
speedi *er* /est/ly/ness
speedometer
speek   speak +
speeker   speaker
speeking   speaking
speer   spear [1]+
speerhed   spearhead
spekul   speckle [2]
spel   spell +
spelbownd   spellbound
spel *l* /ling/t
spellbound
spend /er/thrift
sperm /-whale
spermatozo *on* /a (pl.)
spern   spurn [1]
spert   spurt [1]
speshal   special +
speshalise   specialise [2]+
speshalist   specialist
speshaltey   specialty +
speshes   species
speshialtey   specialty +
speshus   specious +
spesifi   specify [4]+
spesific   specific +
spesificashun   specification
spesify   specify [4]+
spesimen   specimen
spew [1]
spher *e* [2] /ical/ically
spheroid
sphincter
sphinx /es
spi   spy [4]+
spic *e* [2] /y
spici *er* /est/ly/ness
spick and span

spider /y
spik *e* [2] /y
spil *l* /ling/t
spin [3] /ner/neret
spinach
spinaker   spinnaker
spindl *e* /y
spindul   spindle +
spin *e* /al/eless
spiney   spinney +
spinidge   spinach
spinige   spinach
spinnaker
spinney /s
spinster /hood
spiracle
spiral [3] /ly
spire
spirichooal   spiritual +
spirichooalise   spiritualise [2]+
spirichooalist   spiritualist +
spirit [1] /less
spiritual /ly
spiritualis *e* [2] /ation
spiritualist /ic
spise   spice [2]+
spisey   spicy
spisier   spicier +
spit /ting/toon
spite [2] /ful/fulness
spitfire
spittle
spitul   spittle
splash [1] /-down
splay [1]
spleen
splender   splendour
splendid
splendour
splice [2]
splint [1]
splinter [1]
splise   splice [2]
split /ting
splutter [1]

spoil [1] /sport/t	
spoke /n	
spokes *man* /woman	
spoliashun	spoliation +
spoliat *ion* /or	
spong *e* [2] /er/y	
sponser	sponsor [1]
sponsor [1]	
spontaneity	
spontaneous /ly/ness	
spontanius	spontaneous +
spontenaitey	spontaneity
spoof [1] /er	
spool	
spoon [1] /-fed/ful	
spoonerism	
spoor [1]★ (track)	
spoor	spore ★
sporadic /ally	
sporan	sporran
spore ★ (seed, germ)	
spore	spoor [1]★
sporn	spawn [1]
sporran	
sport [1] /ive/ively	
sportsman	
spot [3] /-check/ty	
spotlight [1]	
spotlite	spotlight [1]
spouse	
spout [1]	
spowse	spouse
spowt	spout [1]
sprain [1]	
sprane	sprain [1]
sprang	
sprawl [1]	
spray [1] /er	
spread /ing	
spread-eagle [2]	
spred	spread +
spree	
spri	spry +
sprightl *y* /ier/iest	
spring /-board/bok	

springtime	
spring *y* /iness/ing	
sprinkle [2] /r	
sprinkul	sprinkle [2]+
sprint [1]	
sprite /ly	
sprocket	
sproose	spruce +
sprout [1]	
sprowt	sprout [1]
spruce /ly	
sprung	
spry /er/est	
spu	spew [1]
spume [2]	
spunge	sponge [2]+
spunk	
spur [3]	
spurious /ly/ness	
spurius	spurious +
spurm	sperm +
spurn [1]	
spurt [1]	
sputter [1]	
sputum	
sp *y* [4] /ies	
squabble [2]	
squabul	squabble [2]
squad	
squadron	
squalid /ly	
squall [1]	
squalor	
squander [1]	
square [2] /ly	
squash [1]	
squat [3] /ter	
squaw	
squawk [1] /er	
squeak [1] /er/y	
squeal [1] /er	
squeamish /ly/ness	
squeeze [2]	
squelch [1]	
squerm	squirm [1]

squert	squirt [1]	stale /ness	
squib		stalemate [2]	
squid		stalion	stallion
squiggle [2]		stalk [1] /er	
squigul	squiggle [2] .	stall [1]	
squint [1]		stallion	
squir e [2] /archy		stalwart	
squirm [1]		stalwert	stalwart
squirrel		stalyun	stallion
squirt [1]		stamen	
squod	squad	stamer	stammer [1]+
squodron	squadron	stamina	
squoler	squalor	stammer [1] /er	
squolid	squalid +	stamp [1] /er	
squonder	squander [1]	stampede [2]	
squosh	squash [1]	stance	
squot	squat [3]+	stanch [1]* (stop flow)	
stab [3]		stanch	staunch *
stabilis e [2] /ation/er		stand /-by/point/still	
stability		standard	
stable [2]		standardis e [2] /ation	
stabul	stable [2]	standerd	standard
staccato		standerdise	standardise [2]+
stacher	stature	stane	stain [1]+
stachooery	statuary	stank	
stack [1]		stans	stance
stadi um /a/ums (pls.)		stanza	
staf	staff [1]+	stapes	
staff [1] /s		staple [2] /r	
stag		stapul	staple [2]+
stage [2] /-coach		star [3] /less/light/ry	
stager	stagger [1]	starboard	
stagger [1]		starbord	starboard
stagnant		starch [1]	
stagnashun	stagnation	stare [2]* (gaze)	
stagnat e [2] /ion		stare	stair *+
staid * (steady)		starecase	staircase
staid	stayed *	starie	starry
stain [1] /less		stark	
stair * (step) /case		starling	
stair	stare [2]*	start [1] /er	
stake [2]* (post)		startle [2]	
stake	steak *	startul	startle [2]
stalactite * (down)		starvashun	starvation
stalagmite * (up)		starv e [2] /ation/eling	

stashun	station [1+]
stashunrey	stationary ★
stashunrey	stationery ★
state [2] /less/ment	
stately /ier/iest/iness	
static /ally/s	
station [1] /ary ★ (at rest)	
stationer /y ★ (paper)	
statistic /ian/s	
statistical /ly	
statistishun	statistician
statuary	
statue /sque/tte	
statuesk	statuesque
statuet	statuette
stature	
status	
statut e /ory	
staunch ★ (true)	
staunch	stanch [1]★
stave [2]	
stawk	stalk [1+]
stay /ed ★† /ing	
†(remained)	
stayed	staid ★
steadfast /ly/ness	
steadie	steady [4+]
stead y [4] /ier/iest/ily	
steak ★ (beef)	
steak	stake [2]★
steal ★ (take) /ing	
steal	steel [1]★+
stealth /ily/iness/y	
steam [1] /er	
stedfast	steadfast +
stedy	steady [4+]
steed	
steel [1]★ (metal) /y	
steel	steal ★+
steem	steam [1+]
steep [1] /er/est/ly/ness	
steeple /chase/jack	
steepul	steeple +
steer [1] /able/age	
stelar	stellar

stellar	
stelth	stealth +
stem [3]	
stench /es	
stencil [3] /ler	
stenografey	stenography +
stenograph y /er/ic	
stenotipe	stenotype [2]
stenotype [2]	
stensil	stencil [3+]
step [3]★ (pace) /-ladder	
step	steppe ★
step brother /sister	
step daughter /son	
step father /mother	
steppe ★ (plain)	
ster	stir [3]
sterdey	sturdy +
stereo /phonic	
stereoscop e /ic	
stereotype [2]	
steril e /ity	
sterilis e [2] /ation	
sterilitey	sterility
sterio	stereo +
steriofonic	stereophonic
sterioscope	stereoscope +
steriotipe	stereotype [2]
sterjun	sturgeon
sterling	
stern /er/est/ly/ness	
sternum	
stethoscope	
stevedore	
stew [1]	
steward /ess (fem.)	
sti	sty [4+]
stich	stitch [1+]
stick /er/ing/s ★ (wood)	
sticking-plaster	
stickleback	
stickler	
Sticks	Styx ★
stick y /ily/iness	
stif	stiff +

274

stifen   stiffen ¹+
stiff /er/est/ly
stiffen ¹ /er
stifle ²
stiful   stifle ²
stigma /s/ta (pls.)
stigmatise ²
stil   still ¹+
stilberth   still-birth +
stile * (steps)
stile   style ²*+
stiletto /s
stilise   stylise ²+
stilish   stylish
stilist   stylist
still ¹ /ness
still -*birth* /-bȯrn
stilt ¹
stilus   stylus +
stimie   stymie +
stimulashun   stimulation
stimulat e² /ion/ive/or
stimul us /i (pl.)/ant
sting /er/ing
sting y /ier/iest/ily/iness
stink /er/ing
stint ¹
stipel   stipple ²
stipend
stipendiar y /ies
stipple ²
stiptic   styptic
stipul   stipple ²
stipulashun   stipulation
stipulat e² /ion/or
stir ³
stirrup
stirup   stirrup
stitch ¹ /es
stoat
stock ¹ /broker/taking
stockade
stockie   stocky +
stocking
stockman

stockpile ²
stock-still
stock y /ier/iest/iness
stodg e² /y
stoge   stodge ²+
stoic /al/ally
stoicism
stoisism   stoicism
stoke ² /r
stole /n
stolid /ity
stoma /s/ta (pls.)
stomach ¹ /-ache
stone ² /mason
stonewall ¹ /er
ston y /ier/iest/ily
stood
stooge ²
stook ¹
stool ¹
stoop ¹
stop ³ /cock/page/per
stoper   stopper
storage
store ² /house
storekeeper
storey * (floor level) /s
storey   story *+
storidge   storage
storie   storey *+
storie   story *+
storige   storage
stork
storm ¹ /ier/iest/y
stormi ly /ness
stor y * (narrative) /ies
story   storey *+
stote   stoat
stout /er/est/ly/ness
stove ²
stow ¹ /age/away
stowige   stowage
stowt   stout +
straddle ²
stradul   straddle ²

straf	strafe [2]	streemline	streamline [2]
strafe [2]		street	
straggle [2] /r		strength	
stragul	straggle [2+]	strengthen [1]	
straight ★ (line)		strenth	strength
straight	strait ★	strenthen	strengthen [1]
straightaway		strenuous /ly/ness	
straighten [1]		strenuus	strenuous [+]
straightforward		streptococc us /i (pl.)/al	
strain [1] /er		stress [1]	
strait ★ (sea passage)		stretch [1] /er	
strait	straight ★	strew /ing	
straitaway	straightaway	strewn	
straiten	straighten [1]	striccher	stricture
straitforwerd	straightforward	stricken	
strait-jacket		stricneen	strychnine
strait-laced		strict /er/est/ly/ness	
strand [1]		stricture	
strane	strain [1+]	strid e /ing	
strange /ly/ness/r/st		striden cy /t	
strangle [2]		stridensey	stridency [+]
strangul	strangle [2]	strife	
strangulat e [2] /ion		strik e /er/ing	
strap [3] /hanger		strike-break er /ing	
stratagem		string /ing/y	
strate	straight ★	stringen cy /t	
strate	strait ★	stringensey	stringency [+]
strategey	strategy [+]	strip [3] /per	
strategic /ally		stripe [2]	
strateg y /ies/ist		stripling	
stratifi	stratify [4+]	striv e /en/ing	
stratif y [4] /ication		stroboscop e /ic	
stratoscope		strode	
stratosfere	stratosphere [+]	stroke [2]	
stratospher e /ic		stroll [1] /er	
strat um /a (pl.)		strong /er/est/ly/ness	
straw		strontium	
strawberie	strawberry [+]	stroo	strew [+]
strawberr y /ies		strooen	strewn
stray [1]		strove	
streak [1] /y		struck	
stream [1]		struckcher	structure [+]
streamline [2]		structur e /al/ally	
streek	streak [1+]	struggle [2]	
streem	stream [1]	strugul	struggle [2]

276

strum³ /mer	
strung	
strut³	
strychnine	
stu	stew¹
stuard	steward⁺
stub³	
stubbl e /y	
stubborn /ly/ness	
stubern	stubborn⁺
stubul	stubble⁺
stucco¹	
stuck	
stud³	
student	
studey	study⁴⁺
studio /s	
studious /ly/ness	
studius	studious⁺
stud y⁴ /ies	
stuf	stuff¹⁺
stuff¹ /y	
stuffi er /est/ly/ness	
stuko	stucco¹
stultifi	stultify⁴⁺
stultif y⁴ /ication	
stumac	stomach¹⁺
stumble²	
stumbul	stumble²
stump¹	
stun³	
stung	
stunk	
stunt¹	
stupefi	stupefy⁴⁺
stupef y⁴ /action	
stupendous /ly/ness	
stupendus	stupendous⁺
stuper	stupor
stupid /er/est/ity/ly	
stupify	stupefy⁴⁺
stupor	
sturdie	sturdy⁺
sturd y /ier/iest/ily/iness	
sturgeon	

sturgon	sturgeon
sturgun	sturgeon
sturling	sterling
sturn	stern⁺
sturnum	sternum
stuter	stutter¹⁺
stutter¹ /er	
stuward	steward⁺
st y⁴ /ies	
styl e²*† /ish/ist	
†(manner)	
style	stile ★
stylis e² /ation	
stylus /es	
stymie /d	
styptic	
Styx ★ (river)	
suage	sewage
suav e /ely/ity	
subaltern	
subcomitee	subcommittee
subcommittee	
subconscious /ly	
subconshus	subconscious⁺
subcontinent	
subcontract¹ /or	
subdivide²	
subdivishun	subdivision⁺
subdivisi on /ble	
subdue²	
subedit¹ /or	
suberb	suburb⁺
suberban	suburban
sub-human	
subjecshun	subjection
subject¹ /ion/ive/ivity	
subjoogate	subjugate²⁺
subjugat e² /ion	
subjunctive	
sublet /ting	
sublimat e² /ion	
sublim e /inal	
submachine-gun	
submarine	
submerg e² /ence/ible	

submershun	submersion +	subtenant	
submersi *on* /ble		subtend [1]	
submishun	submission +	subterfuge	
submisiv	submissive	subterranean	
submiss *ion* /ive		sub-title [2]	
submit [3]		subtitul	sub-title [2]
submurge	submerge [2+]	subtle /ness/r/st	
subnormal		subtlet *y* /ies	
subordinat *e* [2] /ion		subtly	
suborn [1] /ation/er		subtracshun	subtraction
subpena	subpoena [1]	subtract [1] /ion	
sub-plot		subtropical	
subpoena [1]		suburb /an/ia	
subscribe [2] /r		subvershun	subversion +
subscription		subvers *ion* /ive	
subsekwent	subsequent +	subversiv	subversive
subsequent /ly		subvert [1] /er	
subservien *ce* /t		subvurt	subvert [1+]
subserviens	subservience +	subway	
subsidarey	subsidiary +	succeed [1]	
subside [2] /nce		success /ful/fully	
subsidens	subsidence	success *ion* /ive/or	
subsidey	subsidy +	succinct	
subsidiar *y* /ies		succour [1]★ (help)	
subsidis *e* [2] /ation		succulen *ce* /t	
subsid *y* /ies		succumb [1]	
subsist [1] /ence		such	
subsistens	subsistence	sucher	suture
subsoil		suck [1]	
subsonic		sucker ★ (victim, one who sucks)	
subsoyl	subsoil	sucker	succour [1]★
substance		suckle [2]	
substandard		suckshun	suction
substans	substance	suckulens	succulence +
substanshal	substantial +	suckulent	succulent
substanshiate	substantiate [2+]	suckumb	succumb [1]
substantial /ly/ity		sucrose	
substantiat *e* [2] /ion		sucseed	succeed [1]
substantive		sucseshun	succession +
substashun	substation	sucsess	success +
substation		sucsesser	successor
substitushun	substitution	sucsessful	successful
substitut *e* [2] /ion		sucsessiv	successive
substrat *um* /a (pl.)		sucsint	succinct
subtefuge	subterfuge		

suction		sulferus	sulphurous
sudden /ly/ness		sulfide	sulphide
sudo	pseudo +	sulfuric asid	sulphuric acid
sudonim	pseudonym	sulie	sully [4]
suds		sulk [1] /ily/iness/y	
sue [2]		sullen	
suède		sully [4]	
suer	sewer [1]★+	sulphate	
suet		sulphide	
sufer	suffer [1]+	sulphur /ous	
suffer [1] /ance/er		sulphuric acid	
suffice [2]		sultan /a (fem.)/ate	
sufficien cy /t		sultrey	sultry +
suffiks	suffix [1]+	sultr y /ily/iness	
suffise	suffice [2]	suly	sully [4]
suffishency	sufficiency +	sum [3]★ (total)	
suffishent	sufficient	sum	some ★+
suffix [1] /es		sumbody	somebody
suffocat e [2] /ion		sumhow	somehow
suffrage /tte		summari ly /ness	
suffus e [2] /ion		summarise [2]	
sufocashun	suffocation	summar y ★ (account)/ies	
sufocate	suffocate [2]+	summer /time/y ★†	
sufocation	suffocation	†(of summer)	
sufrajet	suffragette	summerise	summarise [2]
sufrance	sufferance	summit	
sufrige	suffrage +	summon [1]★ (call forth)	
sufuse	suffuse [2]+	summons [1]★ (before court)	
sugar [1] /y		sump	
sugeschun	suggestion	sumptuous /ly/ness	
sugest	suggest [1]+	sumshus	sumptuous +
sugestion	suggestion	sumun	summon [1]★
sugestiv	suggestive	sumuns	summons [1]★
suggest [1] /ion/ive		sumwere	somewhere
suicid e /al		sumwun	someone +
suige	sewage	sun [3]★† /beam/dial/ny	
suiside	suicide +	†(planet)	
suit [1]★† /ability		sun	son ★
†(clothes)		sun inlaw	son(s)-in-law
suit	suet	sunbathe [2]	
suitab le /ility/ly		sunbern	sunburn +
suite ★ (rooms)		sunburn /t	
suitor		sundae ★ (ice cream)	
sulfate	sulphate	Sunday ★ (day of week)	
sulfer	sulphur +	sundrey	sundry +

sundr *y* /ies		supervis *e* [2] /ion/or/ory	
sung		supervishun	supervision
sunk /en		supine	
sunlight		suplant	supplant [1+]
sunlite	sunlight	suple	supple [+]
sunni *er* /est/ly/ness		suplement	supplement [1+]
sun *rise* /stroke		suplicate	supplicate [2+]
sun-tan [3]		suport	support [1+]
sup [3] /per ★ (meal)		suposishun	supposition
super ★ (fantastic)		suposition	supposition
super	supper ★	supositrey	suppository [+]
superabundan *ce* /t		supplant [1] /er	
superannuat *e* [2] /ion		supple /ness	
superb /ly		supplement [1] /ation	
supercargo /es		supplementary	
supercharge [2]		suppli	supply [4+]
supercilious /ly/ness		suppliant	
superconductor		supplicat *e* [2] /ion/ory	
superficial /ity/ly		suppl *y* [4] /ier/ies	
superfine·		support [1] /er	
superfishal	superficial [+]	suppos *e* [2] /ition	
superflooous	superfluous [+]	supposior *y* /ies	
superflu *ous* /ity		suppress [1] /ible/ion/or	
superhuman		suppurat *e* [2] /ion	
superier	superior [+]	supremasey	supremacy
superimpos *e* [2] /ition		suprem *e* /acy/ely	
superintend [1] /ent		supreshun	suppression
superior /ity		supress	suppress [1+]
superlative		supression	suppression
super *man* /men (pl.)		suprintend	superintend [1+]
supermarket		supul	supple [+]
supernacheral	supernatural [+]	sur	sir
supernatural /ly		surayalism	surrealism [+]
supernova		surayalist	surrealist
supernumerar *y* /ies		surca	circa
superpos *e* [2] /ition		surcharge [2]	
supersede [2]		surcit	circuit [1+]
supersilious	supercilious [+]	surcitrey	circuitry
supersilius	supercilious [+]	surcitus	circuitous
supersonic		surcul	circle [2]
superstishun	superstition [+]	surcularise	circularise [2+]
superstishus	superstitious	surculashun	circulation
superstitio *n* /us		surculate	circulate [2+]
superstructure		surculer	circular
superven *e* [2] /tion		surcumfleks	circumflex

surcumflex	circumflex	surogat	surrogate
surcumfrance	circumference	suround	surround [1]
surcumfrans	circumference	surownd	surround [1]
surcumnavigate	circumnavigate [2+]	surpass [1]	
surcumscribe	circumscribe [2]	surplice ★ (robe)	
surcumscripshun	circumscription	surplis	surplice ★
surcumscription	circumscription	surplus ★ (excess)	
surcumsise	circumcise [2+]	surprise [2]	
surcumsision	circumcision	surrealis *m* /t	
surcumspecshun	circumspection	surrender [1]	
surcumspect	circumspect [+]	surreptitious /ly/ness	
surcumstans	circumstance	surrogate	
surcumstanshul	circumstantial [+]	surround [1]	
surcumstantial	circumstantial [+]	surt	cert
surcumvent	circumvent [1+]	surtaks	surtax [+]
surcus	circus [+]	surtax /es	
sure ★† /ly ★†/r/st †(certain[ly])		surtin	certain [+]
		surtn	certain [+]
sure	shore [2★]	survant	servant
sureptishus	surreptitious [+]	survay	survey [1+]
sureptitious	surreptitious [+]	survaylans	surveillance
suret *y* /ies		surve	serve [2+]
surf [1★] (sea) /er		surveillance	
surf	serf ★[+]	survey [1] /or	
surface [2]		survice	service [2+]
surfdom	serfdom	surviet	serviette
surfeet	surfeit [1]	survile	servile [+]
surfeit [1]		survilitey	servility
surfis	surface [2]	survis	service [2+]
surfit	surfeit [1]	surviv *e* [2] /al/or	
surge [2]		susceptib *le* /ility	
surgeon		suseptible	susceptible [+]
surger *y* /ies		suseptibul	susceptible [+]
surgun	surgeon	suspect [1]	
surley	surely ★	suspend [1] /er	
surli *er* /est/ly/ness		suspense	
surloin	sirloin	suspenshun	suspension [+]
surly ★ (uncivil)		suspens *ion* /ory	
surly	surely ★	suspicion	
surmise [2]		suspicious /ly/ness	
surmon	sermon	suspishun	suspicion
surmonise	sermonise [2]	suspishus	suspicious [+]
surmount [1]		sustain [1]	
surmownt	surmount [1]	sustayn	sustain [1]
surname		sustenance	

281

sustenans	sustenance	swerve [2]	
sut	soot *+	swet	sweat [1]+
sutable	suitable +	sweter	sweater
sutabul	suitable +	swich	switch [1]+
suter	suitor	swift /er/est/ly/ness	
suthen	southern	swig [3]	
sutherley	southerly	swill [1] /er	
sutle	subtle +	swim /mer/-suit	
sutletey	subtlety +	swimming /-pool	
sutul	subtle +	swindle [2] /r	
suture		swindul	swindle [2]+
swab [3]		swin e /ish	
swaddle [2]		swing * (move) /ing	
swade	suède	swinge * (beat) /ing	
swadul	swaddle [2]	swipe [2]	
swagger [1] /er		swirl [1]	
swain		swish [1]	
swallow [1] /er		Swiss /roll	
swam		switch [1] /back	
swamp [1] /y		swivel [3]	
swan [3] /sdown		swizul	swizzle [2]
swane	swain	swizzle [2]	
swank [1] /y		swob	swab [3]
sware	swear +	swollen	
swarm [1]		swollow	swallow [1]+
swarthy		swomp	swamp [1]+
swash [1]		swon	swan [3]+
swastika		swoon [1]	
swat [3] /ter		swoop [1]	
swath * (line of cut grass)		swop [3]	
swathe [2]* (bandage)		sword	
sway [1]		swor e /n	
swear /-word		swostika	swastika
sweat [1] /er/y		swot [3] /ter	
Swed e /ish		swum	
sweep /er/ing/stake		swung	
sweet * (sugary)		swurl	swirl [1]
sweet	suite *	swurv	swerve [2]
sweetchestnut		sybarit e /ic	
sweeten [1]		sycamore	
sweet *heart* /ly/meat		sycedelic	psychedelic
sweetpea		syciatrey	psychiatry
swell [1]		syciatrist	psychiatrist +
swelter [1]		sycick	psychic +
swept		sycoanalise	psychoanalyse [2]

sycoanalisis	psychoanalysis
sycofant	sycophant +
sycologey	psychology +
sycological	psychological +
sycologist	psychologist
sycopath	psychopath +
sycophant /ic	
sycosis	psychosis +
sycosomatic	psychosomatic
sycotherapey	psychotherapy
sycotherapist	psychotherapist +
sycotic	psychotic
syfilis	syphilis +
sygnet	cygnet ★
sylf	sylph +
syllab *le* /ic	
syllabus /es	
syllogis *e* ² /m	
sylph /like	
symbio *sis* /tic	
symbol ★ (sign) /ic	
symbol	cymbal ★+
symbolical /ly	
symbolis *e* ² /m	
symmetr *y* /ical/ically	
sympathetic /ally	
sympathey	sympathy +
sympathise ² /r	
sympath *y* /ies	
symphon *y* /ies/ic	
symplify	simplify ⁴+
symposi *um* /a (pl.)	
symptom /atic	
synagog	synagogue
synagogue	
synchronis *e* ² /ation/m	
syncopat *e* ² /ion	
syncope	
syncromesh	
syndicalis *m* /t	
syndicat *e* ² /ion	
syndrome	
synic	cynic +
synod /al/ical	
synonym /ous/ously	

synops *is* /es (pl.)	
synoptic	
synovial	
syntaks	syntax +
synta *x* /ctic	
synthes *is* /es (pl.)	
synthe *sise* ² /tic/tically	
sypher	cipher ¹
syphili *s* /tic	
syphon	siphon ¹+
syringe ²	
syrup /y	
system /atic/atically	
systematis *e* ² /ation	
systole	

T

tab ³	
tabard	
tabb *y* /ies	
tabernacle	
tabernacul	tabernacle
tabie	tabby +
table ²	
tableau /x (pl.)	
tablespoon /ful	
tabl *et* /oid	
tablit	tablet +
tablo	tableau +
tabloyd	tabloid
taboo ¹ /s	
tabor	
tabul	table ²
tabular	
tabulashun	tabulation
tabulat *e* ² /ion/or	
tabuler	tabular
tabulspoon	tablespoon +
taby	tabby +
tacit /ly	
taciturn /ity	
tack ¹	
tackey	tacky +

283

tackle ² /r		tam *e* ² /able	
tackul	tackle ²⁺	tam-o'-shanter	
tack *y* /iness		tamper ¹	
tact /less/lessly		tampon	
tactful /ly/ness		tan ³ /ner/nery/neries	
tactic /al/ian/s		tandem	
tactile		taner	tanner
tactishun	tactician	tang	
tacul	tackle ²⁺	tangent /ial	
tadpole		tangerine	
taffeta		tangib *le* /ility/ly	
tafita	taffeta	tangibul	tangible ⁺
tag ³		tangle ²	
tail ¹*† /less		tango ¹ /s	
†(follow, of animals)		tangul	tangle ²
tail	tale *	tanic	tannic ⁺
tailor ¹ /-made		tanjent	tangent ⁺
taint ¹		tanjerene	tangerine
tak *e* /en/ing		tank /age/ard/er/ful	
takey	tacky ⁺	tanni *c* /n	
taks	tax ¹⁺	tant	taint ¹
taksashun	taxation	tantalis *e* ² /ingly	
taksi	taxi ⁺	tantalum	
taksidermey	taxidermy ⁺	tantamount	
talc /um		tantamownt	tantamount
tale * (story)		tantrum	
tale	tail ¹*⁺	tap ³ /-dancing/-root	
talent /ed		tape ² /worm	
talie	tally ⁴⁺	tape measure	
talie ho	tally-ho	tape recorder	
talisman /s		taper ¹* (candle, narrow)	
talk ¹ /ative/er		taper	tapir *
talk	talc ⁺	tapestr *y* /ies	
talkum	talcum	tapioca	
tall /est/ness		tapir * (animal)	
tallow		tapistrey	tapestry ⁺
tall *y* ⁴ /ies		tar ³	
tally-ho		taragon	tarragon
talon		tarantella * (dance)	
talor	tailor ¹⁺	tarantula * (spider)	
talow	tallow	tardie	tardy ⁺
tamarisk		tard *y* /ily/iness	
tamber	tambour ⁺	tare * (weed)	
tamboreen	tambourine	tare	tear *⁺
tambour /ine		target	

argit	target	tawny	
arie	tarry [4]	tax [1] /able/ation	
arif	tariff	taxashun	taxation
ariff		taxi /cab/meter/s	
armac		taxiderm y /ist	
armigan	ptarmigan	Te Deum	
arn		tea ★ (drink) /cup/pot	
arnish [1]		tea	tee ★+
arpaulin		teach /able/er/ing	
arporlin	tarpaulin	teajuncshun	T-junction
arragon		teak	
arry [4]		teal	
arsals		team [1] ★ (group) /ster	
arsus		team	teem [1]★
art /let		team-work	
artan		tear ★ (crying) /ful	
artar		tear ★ (rip) /ing	
arter	tartar	tear	tier ★
artrate		tease [2] /r	
asit	tacit +	teaspoon /ful	
asiturn	taciturn +	teat	
ask /master		teath	teeth ★
assel [3]		teathe	teethe [2]★
assul	tassel [3]	teatime	
aste [2] /less/r		teatotler	teetotaller
asteful /ly/ness		teatotul	teetotal +
ast ier /iest/y		tech	teach +
atle	tattle [2]	techer	teacher
atoo	tattoo [1]+	technical /ly	
atter [1]		technicalit y /ies	
attle [2]		techni cian /que	
attoo [1] /er		technocrac y /ies	
atul	tattle [2]	technocrat /ic	
aught ★ (did teach)		technolog y /ical/ically	
aught	tort ★	tecneek	technique
aunt [1] /er		tecnical	technical +
aurus		tecnicalitey	technicality +
aut ★ (tight) /ly/ness		tecnician	technician +
aut	taught ★	tecnishun	technician +
aut	tort ★	tecnocracy	technocracy +
auten [1]		tecnologey	technology +
autolog y /ical		teddy-bear	
aven	tavern	tedibare	teddy-bear
vern		tedi um /ous/ously	
wdr y /ily/iness		tedius	tedious

tee * (golf) /d/ing	
tee	tea *+
teech	teach +
teek	teak
teel	teal
teem 1* (swarm)	
teem	team 1*+
teenage /r	
teese	tease 2+
teet	teat
teeter 1	
teeth * (pl. of tooth)	
teethe 2* (develop teeth)	
teetotal /ism/ler	
tegument	
tekneek	technique
teknical	technical +
teknicalitey	technicality +
teknician	technician +
teknishun	technician +
teknocracy	technocracy +
teknocrasey	technocracy +
teknologey	technology +
teknological	technological
tekscher	texture
tekst	text +
tekstile	textile
telecommunications	
telefone	telephone 2+
telefonist	telephonist
telegraf	telegraph 1+
telegram	
telegraph 1 /ic/ist/y	
teleks	telex 1
telemeter	
telepath y /ic	
telephon e 2 /ic/ist	
telephoto /graph	
teleprinter	
telescop e 2 /ic/y	
teletipe	teletype
teletype	
televise 2	
televishun	television
television	

telex 1	
telicomunications	telecommunicatic
telie	telly
telifone	telephone 2+
telifoto	telephoto +
teligraf	telegraph 1+
teligram	telegram
telimeter	telemeter
teliprinter	teleprinter
teliscope	telescope 2+
teliscopic	telescopic
telitipe	teletype
telivise	televise 2
telivishun	television
telivision	television
tell /er/ing/-tale	
tellurium	
telly	
telurium	tellurium
temerity	
temper 1	
temperacher	temperature
temperament /al	
temperance	
temperans	temperance
temperat e /ure	
temperit	temperate +
tempest /uous	
tempestuus	tempestuous
temple	
tempo /s	
temporal /ly	
temporar y /ily	
temporis e 2 /r	
temprament	temperament +
temprecher	temperature
tempremental	temperamental
tempt 1 /ation/er	
temptashun	temptation
tempul	temple
temtashun	temptation
ten /fold/th/thly	
tenab le /ility	
tenabul	tenable +
tenacious /ly	

tenacity		
tenanc*y* /ies		
tenansey	tenancy +	
tenant /ry		
tenashus	tenacious +	
tenasitey	tenacity	
tend [1]		
tendenc*y* /ies		
tendensey	tendency +	
tendenshus	tendentious	
tendentious		
tender [1] /er/est/ly/ness		
tenderhooks	tenterhooks	
tendon		
tendril		
tenement /-house		
tener	tenor ★	
tenet		
teniment	tenement +	
tenis	tennis	
tennis		
tenon /-saw		
tenor ★ (voice)		
tenor	tenure ★	
tense /ly/ness/r/st		
tenshun	tension	
tensile		
tension		
tent		
tentacle		
tentacul	tentacle	
tentative /ly		
tenterhooks		
tenuous /ly/ness		
tenure ★ (possession)		
tenuus	tenuous +	
tenyer	tenure ★	
tepid /ity/ly		
teracota	terracotta	
terafurma	terra firma	
terain	terrain	
terapin	terrapin	
terass	terrace [2]	
terban	turban +	
terbid	turbid +	

terbine	turbine
terbium	
terbo	turbo +
terbot	turbot
terbulence	turbulence +
terbulens	turbulence +
terbulent	turbulent
tergid	turgid +
terible	terrible +
teribul	terrible +
terific	terrific +
terify	terrify [4]
teritorey	territory +
teritorial	territorial +
terjid	turgid +
terkey	turkey +
terkish	Turkish
terkwoise	turquoise
term [1]	
termagant	
terminable	
terminabul	terminable
terminal /ly	
terminat*e* [2] /ion	
terminological /ly	
terminolog*y* /ies	
termin*us* /i (pl.)	
termite	
termoil	turmoil
tern ★ (bird)	
tern	turn [1]★+
ternip	turnip
terodactil	pterodactyl
teror	terror +
terorism	terrorism
terorist	terrorist
terpentine	turpentine
terpitude	turpitude
terra firma	
terrace [2]	
terracotta	
terrain	
terrapin	
terrestrial	
terribl*e* /y	

terribul	terrible +	thach	thatch [1]+
terrier		thalidomide	
terrifi	terrify [4]	thallium	
terrific /ally		than	
terrify [4]		thank [1] /less	
territorial /ly		thankful /ly	
territor y /ies		thanksgiving	
terror /ism/ist		that /'s (that is)	
terroris e [2] /ation		thatch [1] /er	
terse /ly/ness		thaw [1]	
tershan	tertian +	thay	they +
tertia n /ry		the	
tertle	turtle	theater	theatre
teselashun	tessellation	theatre	
teselate	tessellate [2]+	theatrical /ly	
teselation	tessellation	theft	
tespoon	teaspoon +	theif	thief +
tessellat e [2] /ion		their ★ (possession) /s ★	
test [1] /-tube		their	there ★
testament		theirs	there's ★
testat e /or/rix (fem.)		theis m /t/tical	
testes	testis +	theives	thieves
testicle		theivish	thievish
testicul	testicle	them /selves	
testie	testy +	them e /atic	
testifi	testify [4]+	thence /forth/forward	
testif y [4] /ier		thens	thence +
testimon y /ial		theocra cy /tic	
testimonyal	testimonial	theocrasey	theocracy +
test is /es (pl.)		theodolite	
test y /ily/iness		theolog y /ian/ical/ist	
tetanic	titanic	theolojun	theologian
tetanus		theorem	
tetatet	tête-à-tête	theoretic /al/ally	
tête-à-tête		theorey	theory +
tether [1]		theorise [2]	
tetragon /al		theor y /ies/ist	
tetrahedr on /al		theosofey	theosophy +
tetrarch /y		theosoph y /ical/ist	
tetrark	tetrarch +	therapeuti c /st	
Teutonic		therapey	therapy +
texcher	texture	theraputic	therapeutic +
text /ual/ually		therap y /ist	
textile		therd	third +
texture		there ★ (that place)	

288

there	their *+
there	they're *
therefore	
therem	theorem
there's * (there is)	
theres	theirs *
theretic	theoretic +
theretical	theoretical
therey	theory +
therise	theorise 2
therist	theorist
therm /al/ally	
thermion /ic	
thermite	
thermocouple	
thermocuple	thermocouple
thermodynamic /s	
thermo-electric /ity	
thermomet er /ric/ry	
thermonuclear	
thermos	
thermostat /ic/ically	
thersday	Thursday
therst	thirst 1+
therstey	thirsty
therteen	thirteen +
therty	thirty +
thesaur us /i (pl.)	
these	
thes is /es (pl.)	
they /'re * (they are)	
thi	thigh
thick /er/est/ly/ness/set	
thicken 1 /er	
thie f /ves (pl.)/vish	
thigh	
thimble /ful	
thimbul	thimble +
thime	thyme *
thin 3 /ly/ner/nest	
thine	
thing	
think /er/ing	
third /ly	
thirm	therm +

thiroyd	thyroid
thirst 1 /ily/y	
thirteen /th	
thirtie	thirty +
thirt y /ies/ieth	
thisis	phthisis
thisle	thistle +
thisorus	thesaurus +
thistl e /y	
thisul	thistle +
thither	
tho	though
thole	
thong	
thor	thaw 1
thoraks	thorax +
thora x /cic	
thorium	
thorn /y	
thorough /ly	
thorough bred /fare	
thort	thought
thortful	thoughtful +
thortless	thoughtless +
those	
though	
thought	
thoughtful /ly/ness	
thoughtless /ly/ness	
thousand /th	
thowsand	thousand +
thrall 1	
thrash 1	
thread 1 /bare	
threat	
threaten 1	
thred	thread 1+
thredbare	threadbare
three-dimensional	
three fold /pence	
three-quarters	
thresh 1 /er	
threshold	
thret	threat
threten	threaten 1

threw * (did throw)
threw   through *
threwout   throughout
thrice
thrift /less/y
thrifti er /est/ly/ness
thrill [1] /er
thrise   thrice
thriv e /en/ing
throat /y
throb [3]
throe * (pain) /s *
throe   throw *[+]
thrombosis
throne * (chair of state)
throne   thrown *
throng [1]
throo   threw *
throo   through *
throt   throat [+]
throttle [2]
throtul   throttle [2]
through * (penetrated)
through   threw *
throughout
throve
throw *† /ing/n *†/s *†
    †(hurl[ed, s])
throw   throe *[+]
thrum [3]
thrush /es
thrust /er/ing
thud [3]
thug /gery
thulium
thum   thumb [1]
thumb [1]
thump [1]
thunder [1] /bolt/ous
thunderstorm
thunderstruck
thunderus   thunderous
thurer   thorough [+]
thurerbred   thoroughbred [+]
thurerfare   thoroughfare

thurm   therm [+]
thurmal   thermal
thurmion   thermion [+]
thurmite   thermite
thurmocuple   thermocouple
thurmodinamic   thermodynamic [+]
thurmoelectric   thermo-electric [+]
thurmometer   thermometer [+]
thurmonucliar   thermonuclear
thurmos   thermos
thurmostat   thermostat [+]
thurmyon   thermion [+]
Thursday
thurst   thirst [1+]
thurteen   thirteen [+]
thurty   thirty [+]
thus
thwack [1]
thwart [1]
thwort   thwart [1]
thyme * (herb)
thyroid
tialin   ptyalin
tiara /s
tibia
tic * (twitch)
tick [1] * (sound) /er
ticket
tickl e [2] /er/ish
tickul   tickle [2+]
ticoon   tycoon
tidal
tiddler
tiddlywinks
tide /less
tidie   tidy [4+]
tidi ly /ness
tidings
tidliwinks   tiddlywinks
tidul   tidal
tid y [4] /ier/iest/ily/iness
tie /d
tier * (layer)
tier   tire [2*+]
tier   tyre *

tiff[1]	
tiffin	
tifoid	typhoid
tifoon	typhoon⁺
tifus	typhus⁺
tig *er* /ress (fem.)	
tight /-laced/rope	
tighten[1]	
tight *er* /est/ly/ness	
tights	
tike	tyke
tile[2]	
tilige	tillage
till[1] /able/age/er	
tilt[1]	
timber[1]	
time[2]*† /keeper/less †(duration)	
time	thyme★
timepeace	timepiece
timepiece	
timid /er/est/ity	
timorous /ly/ness	
timorus	timorous⁺
timpan *o* /i (pl.)/ist	
timpanum	tympanum⁺
tin[3] /foil/ny	
tincture	
tinder /y	
tinge[2]	
tingle[2]	
tingul	tingle[2]
tinie	tiny⁺
tinkcher	tincture
tinker[1]	
tinkle[2]	
tinkul	tinkle[2]
tinsel[3] /ly	
tint[1]	
tin *y* /ier/iest/ily/iness	
tip[3] /ster	
tipe	type[2]⁺
tiperiter	typewriter⁺
tipical	typical⁺
tipify	typify[4]

tipist	typist
tipit	tippet
tiple	tipple[2]⁺
tipografey	typography⁺
tippet	
tipple[2] /r	
tipsey	tipsy⁺
tips *y* /ily/iness	
tiptoe[2]	
tipul	tipple[2]⁺
tirade	
tiraney	tyranny⁺
tiranical	tyrannical⁺
tiranise	tyrannise[2]⁺
tirannical	tyrannical⁺
tirant	tyrant
tiranus	tyrannous
tire[2]*† /less/lessly †(grow weary)	
tire	tyre★
tiresome /ly/ness	
tiresum	tiresome⁺
tiro	
tishoo	tissue⁺
tishue	tissue⁺
tissue /-paper	
Titan	
titanic	
titanium	
titbit	
tite	tight⁺
titen	tighten[1]
titer	tighter⁺
titerope	tightrope
tites	tights
tithe /-barn	
titillat *e*[2] /ion	
titivat *e*[2] /ion	
title /d	
titm *ouse* /ice (pl.)	
titmowse	titmouse⁺
titrat *e*[2] /ion	
titter[1]	
tittle-tattle	
titul	title⁺

titul tatul	tittle-tattle
titular	
tituler	titular
T-junction	
to ★ (towards) /day	
to	too ★
to	two ★+
to and fro	
toad /stool/y	
toast¹ /er	
tobacco /nist	
tobaco	tobacco +
toboggan¹ /er	
tocsic	toxic +
tocsicologey	toxicology +
tocsin ★ (bell)	
tocsin	toxin ★
toddle² /r	
toddy	
tode	toad +
todle	toddle ²+
todstool	toadstool
todul	toddle ²+
tody	toddy
toe ★ (on foot)	
toe	tow ¹★+
tofee	toffee
toffee	
together	
toggle	
togul	toggle
toi	toy ¹+
toil¹ /er	
toilet /ry	
token	
toksic	toxic +
toksicologey	toxicology +
tole	toll ¹+
tolemaic sistem	Ptolemaic system
tolerabl e /y	
tolerabul	tolerable +
toleran ce /t	
tolerans	tolerance +
tolerashun	toleration
tolerat e ² /ion	

toll¹ /-bar/-gate	
tolrable	tolerable +
tolrabul	tolerable +
tomahawk	
tomahork	tomahawk
tomane	ptomaine
tomato /es	
tomb /stone	
tomboi	tomboy
tomboy	
tome	
tomfoolery	
tomorrow	
tomtit	
ton ★ (weight) /nage	
ton	tun ★
tonal /ity	
tone /less	
tongs	
tongue² /-tied/-twister	
tonic	
tonight	
tonite	tonight
tonsher	tonsure +
tonsil /litis	
tons ure /orial	
too ★ (also)	
too	to ★+
too	two ★+
took	
tool¹	
toom	tomb +
toomstone	tombstone
toor	tour ¹+
toot¹	
tooth /ache/less	
toothake	toothache
tootle²	
tootul	tootle ²
top³ /-heavy/sail	
topas	topaz
topath	towpath
topaz	
topic /al/ally	
tople	topple ²

topografer	topographer
topografey	topography +
topografic	topographic
topograph y /er/ic/ical	
topple ²	
topsy-turvy	
topul	topple ²
torch /light	
torcher	torture ²+
torchlite	torchlight
tordrey	tawdry +
toreador	
torenshal	torrential
torent	torrent +
torential	torrential
torero	
torey	Tory +
torid	torrid
torie	Tory +
torism	tourism
torist	tourist
torment ¹ /or	
tornado /es	
tornament	tournament
torney	tawny
tornt	taunt ¹+
torpedo ¹ /-boat/es	
torper	torpor
torpid /ity	
torpor	
torrenshal	torrential
torrent /ial	
torrid	
torshun	torsion +
torsion /al	
torso /s	
tort * (law)	
tort	taught *
tort	taut *+
torten	tauten ¹
tortoise /-shell	
tortologey	tautology +
tortuous /ly/ness	
torture ² /r	
tortus	tortoise +

tortuus	tortuous +
torus	Taurus
Tor y /ies	
toss ¹ /-up	
tost	toast ¹+
total ³ /ity/ly	
totalis e ² /ator	
totalitey	totality
totem pole	
totter ¹	
totul	total ³+
touch ¹ /ier/iness/y	
touchstone	
touchwood	
tough /er/est/ly/ness	
toughen ¹	
tour ¹ /ism/ist	
tournament	
tourniket	tourniquet
tourniquet	
tousle ²	
tout ¹	
tow ¹* (pull) /age	
tow	toe *
toward /s	
towel ³	
tower ¹	
town /hall	
towpath	
towsl	tousle ²
towt	tout ¹
toxic /ity	
toxicolog y /ist	
toxin * (poison)	
toxin	tocsin *
toy ¹ /s/shop	
toylet	toilet +
toyul	toil ¹+
trace ² /able/r/ry	
trache a /otomy	
tracing-paper	
track ¹ /er	
tracshun	traction
tract	
tract able /ion/or	

tracter	tractor
trade² /r/sman	
tradishun	tradition +
tradishunal	traditional
tradition /al/ally	
traduce²	
traduse	traduce²
traffic /ked/king	
trafic	traffic +
traged y /ies	
tragic /al/ally	
trail¹ /er	
train¹ /ee/er	
traipse²	
trait	
traitor /ous	
trajector y /ies	
trajectrey	trajectory +
trajedey	tragedy +
trakia	trachea +
trakiotomey	tracheotomy
trakshun	traction
tram /car/-line	
trammel³	
tramp¹	
trample²	
trampoline	
trampul	trample²
tramul	trammel³
trance	
trane	train¹+
trankwil	tranquil +
trankwilise	tranquillise²+
trankwilitey	tranquillity
tranquil /lity/ly	
tranquillis e² /er	
trans	trance
transact¹ /ion	
transatlantic	
transceiver	
transcend¹ /ence/ental	
transcribe²	
transcript /ion	
transend	transcend¹+
transendence	transcendence

transendental	transcendental
transept	
transfer³ /able/ence	
transferens	transference
transfiger	transfigure²+
transfigur e² /ation	
transfiks	transfix¹
transfix¹	
transform¹ /ation/er	
transformashun	transformation
transfus e² /ion	
transfushun	transfusion
transgreshun	transgression
transgress¹ /ion/or	
transien ce /t/tly	
transiens	transience +
transishun	transition +
transister	transistor
transistor	
transistoris e²	
transit /ive/ory	
transition /al	
translashun	translation
translat e² /able/ion/or	
translater	translator
translucen ce /t	
translusens	translucence +
translusent	translucent
transmigrat e² /ion	
transmishun	transmission
transmission	
transmit³ /ter	
transmut e /ation	
transparen ce /cy/t	
transparens	transparence +
transparensey	transparency
transpir e² /ation	
transplant¹ /ation	
transport¹ /ation/er	
transportashun	transportation
transpos e² /ition	
transsever	transceiver
trans-ship³ /ment	
transverse /ly	
transvershun	transversion

transversion	
transvesti *sm* /te	
trap ³ /per	
trapez *e* /ium/oid	
trapse	traipse ²
trase	trace ²⁺
trash /y	
trasing paper	tracing-paper
trate	trait
trater	traitor ⁺
traterous	traitorous
traterus	traitorous
trauma /tic	
travail ¹	
travale	travail ¹
travel ³ /ler/ogue	
travelog	travelogue
traverse ²	
travest *y* /ies	
trawl ¹ /er	
trawma	trauma ⁺
tray /s	
treacherey	treachery ⁺
treacher *y* /ous	
treacl *e* /y	
treacul	treacle ⁺
tread /ing/le	
treason /able/ous	
treasonus	treasonous
treasure ² /r	
treasur *y* /ies	
treat ¹ /able/ment	
treatise	
treatiss	treatise
treat *y* /ies	
trebl *e* ² /y	
trebul	treble ² ⁺
trecherey	treachery ⁺
trecherus	treacherous
tred	tread ⁺
tree	
treecul	treacle ⁺
treet	treat ¹⁺
treetie	treaty ⁺
treetis	treatise

treetment	treatment
trefoil	
trefoyul	trefoil
trek ³ /ker	
trellis-work	
tremble ²	
trembul	tremble ²
tremendous /ly	
tremendus	tremendous ⁺
tremer	tremor
tremor	
tremulous	
tremulus	tremulous
trench ¹ /es	
trenchan *cy* /t	
trenchansey	trenchancy ⁺
trend ¹ /y	
treo	trio ⁺
trepidashun	trepidation
trepidation	
treshur	treasure ²⁺
treshurey	treasury ⁺
treson	treason ⁺
trespass ¹ /er/es	
tressul	trestle
trestle	
tri	try ⁴⁺
trial	
triang *le* /ular	
triangul	triangle ⁺
triangulat *e* ² /ion	
trianguler	triangular
trib *e* /al/alism	
tribul	tribal
tribulashun	tribulation
tribulation	
tribun *e* /al	
tributar *y* /ies	
tribute	
tributrey	tributary ⁺
trice	
triceps	
tricicul	tricycle
trick ¹ /ery/ster/y	
tricki *er* /est/ly/ness	

trickle [2]		trooant	truant
tricuspid		troobadoor	troubadour
tricycle		trooism	truism
trident		trooley	truly
trifle [2] /r		troop [1]★ (military)	
triful	trifle [2]+	troop	troupe ★
trigger [1]		troos	truce
trigonometr y /ic		trooth	truth
trill [1]		troothful	truthful +
trilogy		troph y /ies	
trim [3] /mer		tropic /al/ally	
trimaran		tropism	
trinity		troposfere	troposphere
trinket		troposphere	
trio /s		trorma	trauma +
triode		trormatic	traumatic
trip [3]★ (fall)		trot [3] /ter	
tripartite		troubadour	
tripe ★ (food)		trouble [2] /-maker	
triple [2] /t		troubleshooter	
triplicat e [2] /ion		troublesome	
tripod		trough	
tripos		trounce [2]	
triptick	triptych	trouns	trounce [2]
triptych		troup	troop [1]★
tripul	triple [2]+	troupe ★ (actors)	
trise	trice	trousers	
trisicul	tricycle	trousseau /x (pl.)	
trite /ly		trout	
triumf	triumph [1]+	trowel	
triumph [1] /al/ant		trownce	trounce [2]
trivia /l/ly		trowns	trounce [2]
trivialise [2]		trowsers	trousers
trivialit y /ies		trowt	trout
trod /den		truan cy /t	
trofey	trophy +	truansey	truancy +
troley	trolley +	truble	trouble [2]+
trolie	trolley +	trubul	trouble [2]+
troll [1]		truce	
trolley /s		truck	
trollop		truculen ce /t	
trolop	trollop	trudge [2]	
trombon e /ist		tru e /er/est/ism/ly/th	
troo	true +	truf	trough
trooancy	truancy +	truffle	

truful	truffle
truge	trudge [2]
trulie	truly
trump [1]	
trumpet [1] /er	
truncat e [2] /ion	
truncheon	
trunchon	truncheon
trundle [2]	
trundul	trundle [2]
trunk /-line	
trusow	trousseau +
truss [1] /es	
trust [1] /ee/ful/fully	
trustwerthey	trustworthy +
trustworth y /iness	
truthful /ly/ness	
tr y [4] /ier/ies	
trycicle	tricycle
tsar	
tub [3] /biness/by	
tuba /s	
tub e [2] /ular	
tuber /cle/cular	
tubercul osis /ous	
tuch	touch [1]+
tuchstone	touchstone
tuchwood	touchwood
tuchy	touchy
tuck [1] /er	
Tuesday	
tuf	tough +
tuffen	toughen [1]
tuft [1]	
tug [3] /-of-war	
tuishun	tuition
tuition	
tuk	tuck [1]+
tuksedo	tuxedo
tulip	
tumble [2] /r	
tumbul	tumble [2]+
tumer	tumour
tumour	
tumult /uous	
tumultuus	tumultuous
tumulus	
tun * (large cask)	
tun	ton *+
tuna	
tundra	
tun e [2] /able/er	
tuneful /ly/ness	
tuney	tunny +
tung	tongue [2]+
tungsten	
tungtied	tongue-tied
tunic	
tunie	tunny +
tunige	tonnage
tunnel [3] /ler	
tunn y /ies	
tunul	tunnel [3]+
turban /ed	
turbid /ity	
turbine	
turbo /-alternator	
turbo-generator	
turbo-jet	
turbo-prop	
turbot	
turbulen ce /t	
turbulens	turbulence +
tureen	
turet	turret +
turf [1] /s/ves (pls.)	
turgid /ity	
turjid	turgid +
turkey /s	
Turkish	
turkwoise	turquoise
turm	term [1]
turminable	terminable
turminabul	terminable
turminal	terminal +
turminate	terminate [2]+
turmination	termination
turminologey	terminology +
turminological	terminological +
turminus	terminus +

turmite	termite	twilight	
turmoil		twilite	twilight
turn [1]★ (rotate) /er		twill [1]	
turn	tern ★	twin [3]	
turn *coat* /key/pike		twine [2]	
turnikay	tourniquet	twinge [2]	
turniket	tourniquet	twinkle [2]	
turnip		twinkul	twinkle [2]
turn *stile* /table		twirl [1]	
turpentine		twise	twice
turpitude		twist [1] /er	
turquoise		twit [3]	
turret /ed		twitch [1] /es	
turse	terse +	twitter [1]	
turshan	tertian +	two ★ (number) /-way	
tursharey	tertiary	two	to ★+
turtian	tertian +	two	too ★
turtle		twodle	twaddle [2]
turtul	turtle	two *fold* /pence	
tusday	Tuesday	twurl	twirl [1]
tusk [1] /er		tyalin	ptyalin
tussle [2]		tycoon	
tusul	tussle [2]	tyfoid	typhoid
tutel *age* /ary		tyfoon	typhoon +
tutelige	tutelage +	tyfus	typhus +
tuter	tutor [1]+	tyke	
tutonic	Teutonic	tympano	timpano +
tutor [1] /ial		tympan *um* /a (pl.)	
tuxedo		type [2] /script	
twaddle [2]		typeriter	typewriter +
twain		typewrit *er* /ing/ten	
twang [1]		typho *on* /nic	
twayn	twain	typh *us* /oid	
tweak [1]		typical /ly	
tweed		typifi	typify [4]
tweek	tweak [1]	typify [4]	
tweezers		typist	
twel *fth* /ve		typografey	typography +
twelth	twelfth +	typograph *y* /er/ic	
twent *y* /ies/ieth		tyranical	tyrannical +
twice		tyrannical /ly	
twich	twitch [1]+	tyrann *ise* [2] /ous	
twiddle [2]		tyran *ny* /t	
twidul	twiddle [2]	tyre ★ (of a car)	
twig [1]		tyre	tire [2]★+

298

U

u
ubikwitey   ewe *
ubikwitus   ubiquity +
ubiquit y /ous   ubiquitous
U-boat
ucalyptus   eucalyptus +
Ucarist   Eucharist
uclid   Euclid
udder
ufemism   euphemism
ufemistic   euphemistic +
ufoney   euphony +
uforia   euphoria +
uforic   euphoric
ug   ugh
ugenic   eugenic +
ugh
uglie   ugly +
ugl y /ier/iest/iness
ukaliptus   eucalyptus +
ukarist   Eucharist
ukelalee   ukulele
uksorius   uxorious
ukulele
ulcer /ous
ulcerat e ² /ion
ulna
ulogey   eulogy +
ulogise   eulogise ²+
ulogism   eulogism
ulser   ulcer +
ulserate   ulcerate ²+
ulserous   ulcerous
ulserus   ulcerous
ulterier   ulterior
ulterior
ultimate /ly
ultimatum /s (pl.)
ultramarine
ultramicroscopic
ultrasonic
ultra-violet
umbilical

umbrage
umbrella
umbridge   umbrage
umpire ²* (referee)
umpire   empire *
umpteen
unable
unabridged
unabriged   unabridged
unabul   unable
unacceptable
unaccompanied
unaccompnid   unaccompanied
unaccountable
unaccustomed
unacowntable   unaccountable
unacquainted
unacseptable   unacceptable
unacseptabul   unacceptable
unacumpanid   unaccompanied
unacustomd   unaccustomed
unaded   unaided
unadulterated
unaffected
unafrade   unafraid
unafraid
unaided
unalloyed
unaloid   unalloyed
unanimity
unanimous /ly
unanimus   unanimous +
unanserable   unanswerable +
unanswer able /ed
unapproachable
unaprochable   unapproachable
unaprochabul   unapproachable
unarmed
unashamed
unasked
unaskt   unasked
unassisted
unassuming
unatacht   unattached
unatainable   unattainable

299

unattached		uncanny /ily/iness	
unattainable		uncared-for	
unattended		unceremonious /ly	
unauthorised		unceremonius	unceremonious [+]
unavail *able* /ing		uncertain /ty/ties	
unavalabul	unavailable [+]	unchangable	unchangeable
unavaling	unavailing	unchangeable	
unavoidabl *e* /y		uncharitable	
unavoydable	unavoidable [+]	uncharitabul	uncharitable
unaware /s		uncharted	
unawthorised	unauthorised	unchristian	
unbalanced		uncivil /ised	
unbalanst	unbalanced	unclaimed	
unbarable	unbearable [+]	unclamed	unclaimed
unbarabul	unbearable [+]	uncle	
unbearabl *e* /y		unclean	
unbeat *able* /en		uncomfortabl *e* /y	
unbecoming		uncomfortabul	uncomfortable [+]
unbeknown		uncomftable	uncomfortable [+]
unbeleif	unbelief	uncomited	uncommitted
unbelevable	unbelievable [+]	uncommitted	
unbelevabul	unbelievable [+]	uncommon	
unbelief		uncommunicative	
unbeliev *able* /ing		uncompromising	
unbelievabul	unbelievable [+]	unconcern /ed	
unbend /ing		uncondishnal	unconditional [+]
unbenown	unbeknown	unconditional /ly	
unberden	unburden [1]	unconected	unconnected
unbeten	unbeaten	unconfirmed	
unbiased		unconfurmd	unconfirmed
unbiast	unbiased	uncongenial	
unbidden		unconnected	
unblemished		unconquerable	
unblemisht	unblemished	unconscionable	
unborn		unconscious /ly/ness	
unbounded		unconshonable	unconscionable
unbowed		unconshonabul	unconscionable
unbownded	unbounded	unconshus	unconscious [+]
unbridled		unconstitutional	
unbriduld	unbridled	uncontrolabul	uncontrollable
unbroken		uncontrollable	
unburden [1]		unconvenshunal	unconventional
unbutton [1]		unconventional	
uncalled-for		unco-operative	
uncanie	uncanny [+]	unco-ordinated	

uncooth   uncouth
uncorroborated
uncouple [2]
uncoupul   uncouple [2]
uncouth
uncover [1]
uncristian   unchristian
uncritical
uncshun   unction [+]
unct *ion* /uous
uncul   uncle
uncultivated
uncumftable   uncomfortable [+]
uncuple   uncouple [2]
uncuver   uncover [1]
undated
undaunted
undawnted   undaunted
undeceive [2]
undecided
undecieve   undeceive [2]
undefended
undeniable
undeniabul   undeniable
under /arm/bid
undercarige   undercarriage
undercarriage
undercloth *es* /ing
undercover
undercurrent
undercut /ting
undercuver   undercover
underdog
underdone
underdun   underdone
underfed
undergo /ing/ne
undergraduate
undergroth   undergrowth
underground
undergrownd   underground
undergrowth
underhand
underl *ie* /ying
underline [2]

underling
undermand   undermanned
undermanned
undermine [2]
underneath
undernourish [1] /ment
undernurish   undernourish [1+]
underpass [1]
underprivileged
underrate [2]
underrite   underwrite [+]
underrote   underwrote
undersell /ing
undersigned
undersined   undersigned
undersised   undersized
undersized
understand /able
understatement
understood
understud *y* [4] /ies
undertak *e* /er/ing
underto   undertow
undertone
undertook
undertow
underwait   underweight
underware   underwear
underwater
underwear
underweight
underwerld   underworld
underworld
underwrit *e* /ing/ten
underwrote
undeservd   undeserved
undeserved
undeseve   undeceive [2]
undesirable
undesirabul   undesirable
undeterd   undeterred
undetermind   undetermined
undetermined
undeterred
undieing   undying

301

undifended	undefended	unfaned	unfeigned
undignifide	undignified	unfare	unfair +
undignified		unfasen	unfasten [1]
undisciplined		unfashionable	
undisided	undecided	unfashnable	unfashionable
undisiplind	undisciplined	unfasten [1]	
undo /ing/ne		unfathful	unfaithful +
undornted	undaunted	unfavourabl *e* /y	
undoubted /ly		unfavrable	unfavourable +
undowted	undoubted +	unfeigned	
undress [1]		unfit [3] /ness	
undu *e* /ly		unfold [1]	
undulat *e* [2] /ion/ory		unforeseen	
undying		unforgetabul	unforgettable
unearned		unforgettable	
unearth [1] /ly		unfortunate /ly	
uneas *y* /ily		unfounded	
uneatable		unfownded	unfounded
uneatabul	uneatable	unfriendl *y* /iness	
unecessary	unnecessary +	unfurl [1]	
uneconomic /al/ally		unfurnished	
uneducated		unfurnisht	unfurnished
uneek	unique +	ungainly	
unekspected	unexpected	unganley	ungainly
unekwal	unequal +	ungarded	unguarded
unemploiabul	unemployable +	ungodly	
unemploy *able* /ed/ment		ungovernable	
unenterprising		ungracious /ly	
unequal /led/ly		ungrammatical /ly	
unequivocal		ungrashus	ungracious +
unering	unerring	ungrateful	
unerned	unearned	ungreatful	ungrateful
unerring		unguarded	
unerth	unearth [1]+	unguent	
unesessary	unnecessary +	unguvernabul	ungovernable
unesey	uneasy +	unguvnable	ungovernable
unetable	uneatable	unguvnabul	ungovernable
uneven /ness		unhallowed	
uneventful		unhalowd	unhallowed
unexpected		unhapie	unhappy +
unfailing /ly		unhappi *ly* /ness	
unfaind	unfeigned	unhapp *y* /ier/iest	
unfair /ly/ness		unhealthy	
unfaithful /ly/ness		unheard-of	
unfaling	unfailing +	unhelthy	unhealthy

302

unherdov	unheard-of
unhinge [2]	
unholesum	unwholesome
unholy	
unhurdov	unheard-of
unicellular	
unicicle	unicycle
unicorn	
unicycle	
unidentified	
unifi	unify [4+]
uniform /ity	
unif*y* [4] /ication	
unikwivocal	unequivocal
unilateral /ly	
unimpeachable	
uninhabit *able* /ed	
uninteligibul	unintelligible +
unintelligib *le* /ility	
union /ism/ist	
unique /ly/ness	
uniquivocal	unequivocal
uniselular	unicellular
unisicul	unicycle
unison	
unit /ary	
unitarian /ism	
unite [2]	
unit*y* /ies	
uniun	onion
universal /ity/ly	
universe	
universit*y* /ies	
univursal	universal +
univurse	universe
univursitey	university +
unjust	
unjustifi *able* /ed	
unjustifiabul	unjustifiable +
unkempt	
unkemt	unkempt
unkind /ness	
unknow *ing* /n	
unkristian	unchristian
unkshun	unction +

unkshus	unctuous
unkwalified	unqualified
unkweschunable	unquestionable +
unlawful /ly	
unleash [1]	
unleavened	
unlesh	unleash [1]
unless	
unlevend	unleavened
unlicensed	
unlike /ly	
unlimited	
unlisensd	unlicensed
unload [1]	
unlock [1]	
unlode	unload [1]
unluck*y* /ier/iest/ily	
unlukey	unlucky +
unmanageable	
unmanigable	unmanageable
unmannerly	
unmarid	unmarried
unmarried	
unmask [1]	
unmenshunable	unmentionable
unmentionable	
unmistakabl *e* /y	
unmistakabul	unmistakable +
unmitigated	
unmoovd	unmoved
unmoved	
unnacheral	unnatural +
unnamd	unnamed
unnamed	
unnatural /ly	
unnecessar*y* /ily	
unnerv *ed* /ing	
unnesessarey	unnecessary +
unnowing	unknowing +
unnown	unknown
unnumberd	unnumbered
unnumbered	
unnurvd	unnerved +
unobserv *ant* /ed	
unobtrusive	

303

unoccupied		unready /iness	
unocupied	unoccupied	unreal /istic	
unoffending		unreasnable	unreasonable +
unofficial /ly		unreasonabl e /y	
unoficial	unofficial +	unrecognis able /ed	
unofishul	unofficial +	unrecognisabul	unrecognisable +
unopend	unopened	unredabul	unreadable
unopened		unredey	unready +
unorthorised	unauthorised	unreel	unreal +
unpack [1]		unrekwited	unrequited
unpaid		unreleved	unrelieved
unparaleld	unparalleled	unreliab le /ility	
unparalleled		unreliabul	unreliable +
unparlamentrey	unparliamentary	unrelieved	
unparliamentary		unremitting	
unpayd	unpaid	unrequited	
unpick [1]		unreservedly	
unpleasant /ness		unresnable	unreasonable +
unplesant	unpleasant +	unresponsive	
unpopular /ity		unrest	
unpopuler	unpopular +	unrestraind	unrestrained
unpractical		unrestrained	
unprecedented		unrighteous	
unprejudiced		unrimitting	unremitting
unprejudist	unprejudiced	unripe	
unpremeditated		unritchus	unrighteous
unprepard	unprepared	unritten	unwritten
unprepared		unrivald	unrivalled
unprepossessing		unrivalled	
unpresedented	unprecedented	unroll [1]	
unpretenshus	unpretentious	unruffled	
unpretentious		unrufld	unruffled
unprincipled		unrufuld	unruffled
unprinsipld	unprincipled	unruly	
unprintable		unsafe	
unprintabul	unprintable	unsaid	
unprofeshnal	unprofessional +	unsatisfactor y /ily	
unprofessional /ly		unsatisfactrey	unsatisfactory +
unqualified		unsatisfied	
unquestionabl e /y		unsavorey	unsavoury +
unquestionabul	unquestionable +	unsavour y /iness	
unrap	unwrap [3]	unscathed	
unravel [3]		unscientific	
unreadable		unscrupulous /ly	
unreadabul	unreadable	unscrupulus	unscrupulous +

304

unseasnabul	unseasonable
unseasonable	
unseat [1]	
unsed	unsaid
unseeing	
unseeml y /iness	
unseen	
unseet	unseat [1]
unselfish /ly/ness	
unseremonius	unceremonious +
unsermowntable	insurmountable
unsertan	uncertain +
unsettle [2]	
unsetul	unsettle [2]
unsientific	unscientific
unsightl y /iness	
unsitely	unsightly +
unsivil	uncivil +
unsivilised	uncivilised
unskathd	unscathed
unskild	unskilled
unskilful	
unskilled	
unsociabl e /y	
unsofisticated	unsophisticated
unsolicited	
unsolisited	unsolicited
unsootable	unsuitable
unsootabul	unsuitable
unsophisticated	
unsoshable	unsociable +
unsoshabul	unsociable +
unsound	
unsownd	unsound
unspeakabl e /y	
unspekabul	unspeakable +
unspoiled	
unspoyld	unspoiled
unstable	
unstabul	unstable
unstead y /ily/iness	
unstedey	unsteady +
unsubstanshiated	unsubstantiated
unsubstantiated	
unsuccessful /ly	

unsucsesful	unsuccessful +
unsuitable	
unsuitabul	unsuitable
unsullied	
unsupported	
unsurmountable	insurmountable
unsurtan	uncertain +
unsuspected	
unsutable	unsuitable
unsutabul	unsuitable
untactful /ly	
untenable	
untenabul	untenable
unthinkable	
unthinkabul	unthinkable
unti	untie +
untide	untied
untid y /ier/iest/ily/iness	
unt ie /ied/ying	
untieing	untying
until	
untimely	
untimley	untimely
unto	
untold	
untouchable	
untouchabul	untouchable
untoward	
untraceable	
untrasable	untraceable
untrasabul	untraceable
untroo	untrue
untrooth	untruth
untroothful	untruthful +
untrue	
untruth	
untruthful /ly/ness	
untuchable	untouchable
untuchabul	untouchable
untuterd	untutored
untutored	
unuch	eunuch
unuk	eunuch
unushual	unusual +
unusual /ly	

unvail	unveil [1]	upon	
unvareying	unvarying	upper /most	
unvarnished		uppish /ness	
unvarnisht	unvarnished	upright	
unvarying		upris e /ing	
unveil [1]		uprite	upright
unwanted		uproar /ious/iously	
unwarey	unwary [+]	uprore	uproar [+]
unwarrant able /ed		uprorius	uproarious
unwarrantabul	unwarrantable [+]	upset /ting	
unwar y /ily		upshot	
unweldey	unwieldy	upside-down	
unwell		upstairs	
unwerkable	unworkable	upstares	upstairs
unwerkabul	unworkable	upstart	
unwerthey	unworthy [+]	upstream	
unwholesome		upstreem	upstream
unwieldy		upward	
unwilling		upwerd	upward
unwind /ing		ur	err [1]
unwise /ly		uranium	
unwitting /ly		Uranus	
unworantable	unwarrantable [+]	Urazian	Eurasian
unworantabul	unwarrantable [+]	urban	
unworkable		urban e /ely/ity	
unworkabul	unworkable	urbanis e [2] /ation	
unworldl y /iness		urbun	urban
unworth y /iness		urchin	
unwound		urea	
unwownd	unwound	ureter	
unwrap [3]		urethra	
unwritten		urge [2] /ncy/nt	
unyun	onion	urinate [2]	
upbrade	upbraid [1]	urin e /al/ary	
upbraid [1]		urithmics	eurhythmics
upbringing		urjensey	urgency
update [2]		urjent	urgent
upheaval		url	earl [+]
upheld		urley	early [+]
upheval	upheaval	urlier	earlier [+]
uphill		urmin	ermine
uphold /ing		urn ★ (vase)	
upholster [1] /er/y		urn	earn [1]★[+]
uphoney	euphony [+]	urnest	earnest [+]
upkeep		urolog y /ist	

Uropian	European
urstwile	erstwhile
urth	earth [1+]
urthen	earthen +
urthkwake	earthquake
urthquake	earthquake
us e^2 /able/age/er	
useful /ly/ness	
useless	
userp	usurp [1+]
usher [1] /ette (fem.)	
usheret	usherette
usless	useless
usorius	usurious
usual /ly	
usurp [1] /ation/er	
usur y /ious	
utensil	
uter	utter [1+]
uter us /ine	
uthanasia	euthanasia
uther	other +
utherwise	otherwise
utilis e^2 /able/ation	
utilitarian /ism	
utilit y /ies	
utmost	
Utopia /n	
utríc le /ular/ulus	
utter [1] /ance/ly	
uvula /r	
uxorious	
uxorius	uxorious

V

vacanc y /ies	
vacansey	vacancy +
vacant /ly	
vacashun	vacation
vacat e^2 /ion	
vaccinat e^2 /ion/or	
vaccine	
vacillat e^2 /ion	

vacseen	vaccine
vacsinashun	vaccination
vacsination	vaccination
vacsine	vaccine
vacu ous /ity	
vacuum	
vacuus	vacuous +
vagabond /age	
vagar y /ies	
vage	vague +
vagina	
vagran cy /t	
vagransey	vagrancy +
vague /ly/r/st	
vail	vale *
vail	veil [1]*
vain *(proud)/er/est/ly	
vain	vane *
vain	vein [1]*
vainglor $ious$ /y	
vainglorius	vainglorious +
vajina	vagina
valance	
valans	valance
valay	valet [1]
vale * (valley)	
vale	veil [1]*
valedicshun	valediction +
valedict ion /ory	
valentine	
valer	valour +
valerus	valorous
valese	valise
valet [1]	
valiant	
valid /ity	
validashun	validation
validat e^2 /ion	
valise	
valley /s	
valor	valour +
valo ur /rous	
valt	vault [1]
valuashun	valuation
valu e^2 /able/ation/er	

307

valueless	
valv *e* /ular	
valy	valley +
valyu	value 2+
valyuble	valuable
valyubul	valuable
valyuer	valuer
valyuless	valueless
vamp 1	
vampire	
Van de Graaff generator	
vanadium	
vandal /ism	
vane ★ (weather)	
vane	vain ★+
vane	vein 1★
vangard	vanguard
vanglorey	vainglory
vanglorious	vainglorious +
vanglorius	vainglorious +
vanguard	
vanilla	
vanish 1	
vanity /-bag	
vankwish	vanquish 1
vanquish 1	
vantage	
vantidge	vantage
vantige	vantage
vaper	vapour +
vapid	
vaporis *e* 2 /ation/er	
vaporus	vaporous
vapo *ur* /rous	
varia *ble* /bility/tion	
variabul	variable +
varian *ce* /t	
varians	variance +
variashun	variation
varicose	
varie	vary 4+
variegated	
variet *y* /ies	
varikose	varicose
varius	various

varnish 1 /er	
var *y* 4 /iation/ious	
vascular	
vase	
Vaseline	
vasillate	vacillate 2+
vasleen	Vaseline
vast /er/est/ly/ness	
Vatican	
vault 1	
vaunt 1	
veal	
vech	vetch +
vector	
veel	veal
veemence	vehemence +
veemens	vehemence +
veement	vehement
veer 1	
vegetable	
vegetarian /ism	
vegetashun	vegetation
vegetat *e* 2 /ion/ive	
vegtable	vegetable
vegtabul	vegetable
vehemen *ce* /t	
vehic *le* /ular	
veiculer	vehicular
veil 1★ (disguise)	
veil	vale★
vein 1★ (blood)	
vein	vain ★+
vein	vane ★
veks	vex 1+
veksashun	vexation
veksashus	vexatious
veksation	vexation
veksatious	vexatious
vekter	vector
veld	
vellum	
velocit *y* /ies	
veloors	velours
velositey	velocity +
velours	

velt	veld
velum	vellum
velvet /een	
vena cava	
venal /ity/ly	
vencher	venture [2]+
vend [1] /or	
vendetta	
veneer [1]	
venerab le /ility	
venerabul	venerable +
venerashun	veneration
venerat e [2] /ion	
venereal	
venerial	venereal
veneshun	Venetian
Venetian	
venge ance /ful	
vengence	vengeance +
vengens	vengeance +
venial	
venison	
venom /ous	
venomus	venomous
venous * (of veins)	
venous	Venus *
vent [1]	
ventilashun	ventilation
ventilat e [2] /ion/or	
ventral /ly	
ventrical	ventricle
ventricle	
ventrilokwism	ventriloquism +
ventriloquis m /t	
venture [2] /some	
venturous	
venturus	venturous
Venus * (planet)	
venus	venous *
venyet	vignette
eraci ous /ty	
eranda	
erashus	veracious +
erasitey	veracity
erb /al/ally/atim	

verbiage	
verbos e /ity	
verdant	
verdict	
verdur e /ous	
verge [2]	
verger	
verie	very
verifi	verify [4]+
verif y [4] /iable/ication	
verily	
verisimilitude	
verit y /ies/able/ably	
vermicelli	
vermilion	
vermin /ous	
vermouth	
vernacular	
vernal	
versatil e /ity	
verse /s * (poetry)	
verses	versus *
versif y [4] /ication	
version	
versus * (against)	
vertebra /e (pl.)/l/te	
verteks	vertex +
vert ex /ices (pl.)	
vertical /ly	
vertig o /inous	
verve	
very	
vesa	visa
vescher	vesture [2]
vespers	
vessel	
vest [1] /ment	
vestal	
vestibule	
vestig e /ial	
vestrie	vestry +
vestr y /ies	
vestul	vestal
vesture [2]	
vesul	vessel

vet [3]		victor y /ies	
vetch /es		victual [3] /ler	
vetenarey	veterinary +	video /-frequency	
vetenrey	veterinary +	vidio	video +
veteran		vie /d	
veterinar y /ies		vieing	vying
veto [1] /es		view [1] /er	
vex [1] /ation/atious		view-point	
vexashun	vexation	viger	vigour +
vexashus	vexatious	vigil /ance/ant/ante	
veza	visa	vigilans	vigilance
vezave	vis-à-vis	vignette	
vi	vie +	vigorus	vigorous
via		vigo ur /rous/rously	
viab le /ility		vijun	vision +
viabul	viable +	Viking	
viaduct		viksen	vixen
vial ★ (glass)		vilan	villain +
vial	vile ★+	vile ★† /ly/ness/r/st	
vial	viol ★+	†(loathsome)	
viands (pl.)		vile	vial ★
vibrant		vile	viol ★+
vibrashun	vibration	vilidge	village +
vibrat e [2] /ion/or		vilifi	vilify [4]+
vicar /age		vilif y [4] /ication/ier	
vicarious /ly		vilige	village +
vicarius	vicarious +	villa	
vice		village /r	
vice versa		villain /ous/y	
vice-chancellor		villaney	villainy
vice-president		villanus	villainous
vicer	vicar +	vill us /i (pl.)	
viceregal		vindicashun	vindication
viceroi	viceroy +	vindicat e [2] /ion/or	
viceroy /alty/alties		vindictive	
vicinity		vine /ry	
vicious /ly/ness		vinegar /y	
vicissitude		viniger	vinegar +
vicount	viscount +	vintage	
vicownt	viscount +	vintidge	vintage
victim		vintige	vintage
victimis e [2] /ation		vinul	vinyl
victor /ious/iously		vinyet	vignette
victorey	victory +	vinyl	
victorius	victorious	viol ★ (music) /a/in/inist	

viol	vial ★	visiditey	viscidity
viol	vile ★+	visinitey	vicinity
violashun	violation	vision /ary	
violat e² /ion/or		visionrey	visionary
violen ce /t		visissitude	vicissitude
violens	violence +	visit¹ /ant/ation/or	
violet		visitashun	visitation
violoncello /s		visiter	visitor
violonchelo	violoncello +	viskositey	viscosity
viper /ish/ous		vista	
virgin /al/ity		visual /ly	
Virgo		visualis e² /ation	
viril e /ity		visul	visual +
virilitey	virility	visulise	visualise ²+
virolog y /ist		vital /ity/ly/s	
virtual /ly		vital	victual ³+
virtu e /osity/ous		vitalis e² /ation	
virtuoso		vitalitey	vitality
virulen ce /t		vitamin	
virulens	virulence +	vitaminis e² /ation	
virus		vitiat e² /ion	
visa		vitreous	
visage		vitrifi	vitrify ⁴+
vis-à-vis		vitrif y⁴ /ication	
viscera /l		vitriol /ic	
viscid /ity		vitrius	vitreous
viscos e /ity		vitul	vital +
viscositey	viscosity	vituperat e² /ion/ive/or	
viscount /ess (fem.)		viul	vial ★
viscous		viul	vile ★+
viscuus	viscous	viva voce	
vise	vice	vivac ious /ity	
vise chanseler	vice-chancellor	vivashus	vivacious +
vise president	vice-president	vivasitee	vivacity
visera	viscera +	vivavosi	viva voce
viseregal	viceregal	vivid /ly/ness	
viseroi	viceroy +	vivifi	vivify ⁴+
visevursa	vice versa	vivif y⁴ /ication	
vishiate	vitiate ²+	viviparous	
vishun	vision +	viviparus	viviparous
vishunrey	visionary	vivisecshun	vivisection
vishus	vicious +	vivisect¹ /ion/or	
visib le /ility/ly		vixen	
visibul	visible +	vocabular y /ies	
visid	viscid +	vocal /ist/ly	

311

vocalis *e* ² /ation
vocashun   vocation ⁺
vocation /al
vocative
vocifer *ate* ² /ous
vociferus   vociferous
vodka
voge   vogue
vogue
voice ²
void ¹
voiige   voyage ²⁺
voiiger   voyager
voile
vois   voice ²
volatil *e* /ity
volatilis *e* ² /ation
volcanic
volcano /es
voley   volley ¹⁺
volishun   volition ⁺
volition /al
volkano   volcano ⁺
volley ¹ /s
volt /age/meter
volub *le* /ility/ly
volubul   voluble ⁺
volum *e* /etric/inous
voluminus   voluminous
voluntar *y* /ily
volunteer ¹
voluntrey   voluntary ⁺
voluptu *ous* /ary
voluptuus   voluptuous ⁺
vomit ¹
voraci *ous* /ty
vorashus   voracious ⁺
vorasitey   voracity
vornt   vaunt ¹
vorteks   vortex ⁺
vort *ex* /exes/ices (pls.)
vorticella
vosiferate   vociferate ²⁺
vosiferus   vociferous
votar *y* /ies

vote ² /r
votive
vouch ¹ /er
vouchsafe ²
vow ¹
vowch   vouch ¹⁺
vowchsafe   vouchsafe ²
vowel
vowul   vowel
voyage ² /r
voyd   void ¹
voys   voice ²
vue   view ¹⁺
vulcanis *e* ² /ation
vulcher   vulture
vulgar /ity
vulgaris *e* ² /ation/m
vulnerab *le* /ility
vulnerabul   vulnerable ⁺
vulnrable   vulnerable ⁺
vulture
vulva
vurb   verb ⁺
vurchoo   virtue ⁺
vurchual   virtual ⁺
vurchuous   virtuous
vurchuus   virtuous
vurgin   virgin ⁺
vurginitey   virginity
vurgo   Virgo
vurtue   virtue ⁺
vurtuoso   virtuoso
vurtuous   virtuous
vwal   voile
vye   vie ⁺
vying

W

wack   whack ¹
wad /ding
waddle ²
wade ² /r
wadle   waddle ²

wadul	waddle ²	walow	wallow ¹
wafe	waif	walrus /es	
wafer		walts	waltz ¹⁺
waffle ² /-iron		waltz ¹ /er	
wafle	waffle ²⁺	wan ★ (pale) /ness	
waft ¹		wan	won ★
waful	waffle ²⁺	wander ¹★ (roam) /er/lust	
wag ³ /gish/tail		wander	wonder ¹★⁺
wage ²		wane ²	
wager ¹		wangle ² /r	
waggle ²		wangul	wangle ²⁺
wagon /er/ette		wanskot	wainscot ¹⁺
wagul	waggle ²	want ¹	
waif		wanton /ness	
wail ¹★ (cry)		war ³ /-paint/-path	
wail	whale ★⁺	warant	warrant ¹⁺
wainscot ¹ /ing		warantee	warranty ⁺
waist ★ (body) /coat		warble ² /r	
waist	waste ²★⁺	warbul	warble ²⁺
wait ¹★† /er/ress (fem.)		ward ¹ /er/room	
†(stay for)		warden	
wait	weight ★⁺	wardrobe	
waitey	weighty	ware ★ (avoid) /s ★†	
waive ²★ (give up)		†(goods for sale)	
waive	wave ²★⁺	ware	wear ★⁺
waiver ¹★ (law)		ware	where ★
waiver	waver ¹★⁺	warehouse	
wake ² /ful/fulness		warehowse	warehouse
waken ¹		waren	warren
waks	wax ¹⁺	wares	wears ★
wakswork	waxwork	warey	wary ⁺
walabey	wallaby ⁺	warf	wharf ⁺
wale	wail ¹★	war *fare* /like	
wale	whale ★⁺	warior	warrior
walk ¹ /-over		warm ¹ /er/est/ly/ness/th	
walkie-talkie		warmonger ¹	
walking-stick		warn ¹	
wall ¹ /flower/paper		warp ¹	
wallab *y* /ies		warrant ¹ /able	
wallah		warrant *y* /ies	
wallet		warren	
wallop ¹		warrior	
wallow ¹		wart /y	
walnut		warves	wharves
walop	wallop ¹	war *y* /ily/iness	

313

was		weakly	weekly *+
wash [1] /able/er		weal * (state)	
washed-up		weal	wheel [1]*+
wasl	wassail [1]	weald * (district)	
wasn't (was not)		weald	wield [1]*
wasnt	wasn't	wealth /ier/iest/iness/y	
wasp /ish		wean [1]	
wassail [1]		weapon	
wast *e* [2]*† /age/er/rel		wear *† /able/er/ing/s *†	
†(squander)		†(have on the body)	
waste	waist *+	wear	ware *+
wasteful /ly/ness		wear	where *
wat	watt *+	wearey	weary [4]+
wat	what *+	wearisome	
watch [1] /ful/fulness		wears	wares *
wate	wait [1]*+	wear *y* [4] /ier/iest/ily/iness	
wate	weight *+	weasel	
water [1] /cress/fall		weat	wheat +
waterlogged		weather [1]*† /cock	
water *mark* /tight		†(atmosphere)	
waterproof [1]		weather	whether *
watt * (power) /age		weathervane	
wave [2]*† /form/length		weatmeal	wheatmeal
†(water, gesture)		weave [2]* (make fabric) /r	
wave	waive [2]*	weave	we've *
waver [1]* (falter) /er		web [3] /-footed/-toed	
waver	waiver [1]*	wed [3] /ding/lock	
wawlts	waltz [1]+	Wedensday	Wednesday
wax [1] /en/work		wedge [2]	
way * (direction) /side		Wednesday	
way	weigh [1]*+	wee * (small)	
way	whey *	weed [1] /s/y	
waybridge	weighbridge	weedul	wheedle [2]
wayfare [2] /r		week *† /day/end	
way *lay* /laid/laying		†(seven days)	
wayward		week	weak *+
waywerd	wayward	weeken	weaken [1]
we * (us)		weekling	weakling
we	wee *	weekl *y* * (every week) /ies	
weak *† /ling/ness		weel	weal *
†(feeble)		weel	wheel [1]*+
weak	week *+	weelbarrow	wheelbarrow
weaken [1]		weeld	weald *
weak *er* /est/ly *† /ness		weeld	wield [1]*
†(sickly)		weelrite	wheelwright

ween	wean [1]	were ★ (to be)	
weep /er/ing/y		were	where ★
weevil		were	whirr [1]★
weeze	wheeze [2]+	we're ★ (we are)	
wege	wedge [2]	wereabouts	whereabouts
weigh [1]★† /bridge		wereas	whereas +
†(how heavy)		wereby	whereby
weight ★† /less/lessness/y		werefor	wherefore
†(heaviness)		weren't (were not)	
weild	weald ★	werever	wherever
weild	wield [1]★	werewol f /ves (pl.)	
weir ★ (dam)		werey	weary [4]+
weird /er/est		werisum	wearisome
weja	ouija	werk	work [1]+
welch [1]★ (cheat)		werkbox	workbox +
welch	Welsh ★	werker	worker
welcome [2]		werkshop	workshop
weld [1] /er		werl	whirl [1]★+
welfare		werl	whorl [1]★
welk	whelk	werld	world +
welkin		werldwide	worldwide
we'll ★ (we will)		werligig	whirligig
well [1]★ (spring) /-advised		werm	worm [1]+
well-appointed		werse	worse +
well-balanced		wersen	worsen [1]
well-behaved		wership	worship [3]+
well-being /-bred		werst	worst
wellingtons		wersted	worsted
well-meaning		werth	worth +
well-nigh /-to-do		werthey	worthy +
welp	whelp [1]	werthwiul	worthwhile
Welsh ★ (from Wales)		werwoolf	werewolf +
welter [1]		wesel	weasel
welth	wealth +	Wesleyan	
wen	when +	weslian	Wesleyan
wence	whence	west /erly/ern/ward	
wench [1] /es		westernis e [2] /ation	
wend [1]		westwerd	westward
wenever	whenever	wet [3]★† /ness/ter/test	
went		†(soaked)	
wepon	weapon	wet	whet [3]★
wept		wether	weather [1]★+
wer	weir ★	wether	whether ★
werd	weird +	wethercock	weathercock
werd	word +	wethervane	weathervane

315

we've ★ (we have)

weve   weave [2]★+

wevil   weevil

whack [1]

whal e ★† /er/ing
  †(mammal)

whar f /ves (pl.)

what ★† /ever/soever
  †(question)

what   watt ★+

wheat /en/meal

whedul   wheedle [2]

wheedle [2]

wheel [1]★ /barrow

wheelwright

wheez e [2] /ily/y

whelk

whelp [1]

when /ever/soever

whence

whens   whence

where ★ (which place)

where   ware ★+

where   wear ★+

where   were ★

whereabouts

where as /by/ever

wherefore

where upon /withal

wherl   whirl [1]★+

wherl   whorl [1]★

whet [3]★ (sharpen)

whether ★ (if)

whether   weather [1]★+

whey ★ (milk)

which ★ (which one)

which   witch ★+

whiff [1]

Whig ★ (political)

whil e ★ (during) /st

while   wile [2]★+

whim /sical

whimper [1]

whimsie   whimsy +

whims y /ies

whine [2]★ (complain)

whinn y [4] /ies

whip [3] /cord

whipper-snapper

whippet

whirl [1]★† /igig
  †(swing round)

whirl   whorl [1]★

whirr [1]★ (whirl)

whisk [1]

whisker /ed

whiskey ★†
  †(alcohol—Irish)

whisky ★†
  †(alcohol—Scotch)

whisper [1] /er

whist

whistle [2] /r

whisul   whistle [2]+

whit ★ (particle, jot)

white /bait/r/st

whiten [1]

whitewash [1]

whither ★ (where)

whiting

Whitsun

whittle [2]

whitul   whittle [2]

whiz [3]

who /ever

whoa ★ (stop)

whole ★ (complete)

whole   hole [2]★+

whole-hearted

wholesale /r

wholesome /ly

wholly ★ (fully)

wholly   holey ★

wholly   holy ★

whom

whoop [1]★ (shout)

whoop   hoop [1]★

whooping cough

whop [3]

whore [2] /monger

whorl ¹*†
  †(ring of leaves)
whorl   whirl ¹*+
who's * (who is or has)
whose * (possessive)
whur   whirr ¹*
whurl   whirl ¹*+
whurl   whorl ¹*
why
wick /er
wicked /er/est/ly
wide /ly/r/st
wide awake /spread
widen ¹
widow ¹ /er
width
wield ¹* (hold and use)
wield   weald *
wi fe /ves (pl.)
wiff   whiff ¹
wig ³* (hair)
wig   Whig *
wiggl e² /y
wigul   wiggle ²+
wigwam
wild /er/est/ly/ness
wilderness
wil e²* (trick) /iness/y
wile   while *+
wilful /ly/ness
will ¹ 'power'-o'-the-wisp
willow /y
willy-nilly
wilst   whilst
wilt ¹
wim   whim +
wimin   women +
wimper   whimper ¹
wimsey   whimsy +
wimsical   whimsical
win /ner/ning
vince ²
winch ¹ /es
wind ¹*† /bag/ward
  †(make short of breath)

wind * (turn)/er/ing
window /-pane/-sill
wind y /ier/iest/iness
wine * (drink) /-cellar
wine   whine ²*
wineglass /es
wing ¹
wink ¹
winkle ²
winkul   winkle ²
winnow ¹
winsome /ness
winter ¹
wintrie   wintry
wintry
wip   whip ³+
wipcord   whipcord
wipe ² /r
wipper snapper whipper-snapper
wippet   whippet
wire ² /less
wir iness /y
wirl   whirl ¹*+
wirl   whorl ¹*
wirr   whirr ¹*
wisdom
wise /acre/ly/r/st
wish ¹ /ful
wishy-washy
wisk   whisk ¹
wisker   whisker +
wiskey   whiskey *
wiskey   whisky *
wisp
wisper   whisper ¹+
wist   whist
wistful /ly/ness
wistle   whistle ²+
wisul   whistle ²+
wit * (flair, humour)
wit   whit *
witch * (hag) /es
witch   which *
witcher y /ies
wite   white +

317

witen	whiten [1]	wolop	wallop [1]
witer	whiter	wolow	wallow [1]
witewash	whitewash [1]	woman /kind/ly	
with /al		womb	
withdraw /al/ing/n		women (pl.) /folk	
withdrew		won * (did win)	
withdroo	withdrew	won	wan *+
wither [1]* (decay)		wonder [1]*† /ful/fully	
wither	whither *	†(remarkable thing)	
withers		wonder	wander [1]*+
withheld		wondrous	
withhold /ing		wondrus	wondrous
within		wont * (accustomed)	
without		wont	want [1]
withstand /ing		wont	won't *
witing	whiting	won't * (will not)	
witness [1] /es		wonton	wanton +
witsun	Whitsun	woo [1] /er	
witti *cism* /ness		wood * (lumber) /cut	
wittle	whittle [2]	wood	would *
witt *y* /ier/iest/ily		wooden /ly/ness	
witul	whittle [2]	woof	
wiz	whiz [3]	wool /len/liness	
wizard		woolf	wolf [1]+
wizened		wooll *y* /ies	
wo	whoa *	wooman	woman +
wo	woe *+	woomb	womb
wobbl *e* [2] /y		woond	wound [1]*
woble	wobble [2]+	wop	whop [3]
wobul	wobble [2]+	wor	war [3]+
woch	watch [1]+	worant	warrant [1]+
wod	wad +	worantie	warranty +
wodle	waddle [2]	worble	warble [2]+
wodul	waddle [2]	worbul	warble [2]+
woe * (grief) /begone		word /ily/ing/y	
woe	whoa *	word	ward [1]+
woeful /ly		worden	warden
wofle	waffle [2]+	wordrobe	wardrobe
woft	waft [1]	wore	
woful	waffle [2]+	woren	warren
woful	woeful +	worf	wharf +
wolabey	wallaby +	worfare	warfare +
wolet	wallet	work [1] /able/aday/er	
wol *f* [1] /ves (pl.)		work *box* /shop	
wolla	wallah	worl	whirl [1]*+

worl	whorl 1★	wren	
world /liness/ly/wide		wrench 1	
worm 1 /wood		wrest 1★ (pull away)	
worm	warm 1+	wrestle 2 /r	
wormunger	warmonger 1	wresul	wrestle 2+
worn /-out		wretch ★†	
worn	warn 1	†(unhappy person)	
worp	warp 1	wri	wry ★+
worrier	warrior	wriggle 2	
worr y 4 /ies/ier		wrigul	wriggle 2
vors e /t		wring ★ (squeeze)	
worsen 1		wringer ★ (machine)	
worship 3 /per		wrinkle 2	
worsted		wrinkul	wrinkle 2
wort	wart +	wrist /band/let/-watch	
worth /less/while		writ	
worth y /ier/iest/ily		writ e ★† /er/ing/ten	
wos	was	†(put words on paper)	
wosh	wash 1+	writhe 2	
wosht up	washed-up	wrong 1 /doer	
wosl	wassail 1	wrongful /ly	
wosnt	wasn't		
wosp	wasp +	wrort	wrought +
wot	watt ★+	wrote ★ (did write)	
wot	what ★+	wrought /-up	
wotch	watch 1+	wrung ★ (squeezed)	
wotchful	watchful	wry ★ (distorted) /ly	
wotever	whatever	wun	one ★+
wotsoever	whatsoever	wun	won ★
would ★ (conditional)		wunce	once
would	wood ★+	wunder	wonder 1★+
wound 1★ (injure)		wundrus	wondrous
wound ★ (did turn)		wuns	once
wove /n		wunself	oneself
wrack ★ (seaweed)		wur	whirr 1★
wraith		wurey	worry 4+
wrangle 2 /r		wurl	whirl 1★+
wrangul	wrangle 2+	wurl	whorl 1★
wrap ★ (pack) /per ★ /ping		wurligig	whirligig
wrapped ★ (packed)			
wrath /ful			
wreak 1★ (inflict)			
wreath ★ (flowers)			
wreathe 2★ (twist)			
wreck 1 /age			

X

xenofobia		xenophobia +	
xenophob ia /e/ic			
xeroks		Xerox 1	

319

Xerox [1]
X-ray [1]
xylofone — xylophone
xylophone

Y

y — why
yacht [1] /sman
yak
yam
yank [1]
Yankee
yap [3]
yard /age
yarn [1]
yashmak
yaw [1]★ (of ship)
yaw — yore ★
yaw — your ★+
yawl [1]
yawn [1]
yay — yea
yea
yeald — yield [1]
year /ling
yearn [1]
yeast
yeer — year +
yeest — yeast
yeld — yield [1]
yell [1]
yellow /ish
yelow — yellow +
yelp [1]
yeoman /ry
yerling — yearling
yern — yearn [1]
yes
yest — yeast
yesterday
yet
yeti
yety — yeti

yew ★ (tree)
yew — ewe ★
yew — you ★
yewse — use [2]+
yewsery — usury +
yewshual — usual +
yewsual — usual +
yiddish
yield [1]
yodel [3] /ler
yodle — yodel [3]+
yoga
yogert — yogurt
yogurt
yoke ★ (round neck)
yoke — yolk ★
yokel
yokle — yokel
yolk ★ (of egg)
yolk — yoke ★
yoman — yeoman +
yonder
yore ★ (years ago)
yore — yaw [1]★
yore — your ★+
yorself — yourself +
yorselves — yourselves
yot — yacht [1]+
yotsman — yachtsman
you ★ (person)
you — ewe ★
you — yew ★
youboat — U-boat
you'll ★ (you will)
young /er/est/ster
your ★† /s
  †(belonging to you)
your — yaw [1]★
your — yore ★
your — you're ★
you're ★ (you are)
yoursel f /ves (pl.)
youth /ful
ytterbium
yttrium

yule *† /tide
  †(Christmas)

yule	you'll ★
yung	young +
yungster	youngster
yurn	yearn 1
yuse	use 2+
yuseful	useful +
yuserey	usury +
yusual	usual +
yutensil	utensil
yuterine	uterine
yuterus	uterus +
yuth	youth +
yutilise	utilise 2+
yutilitarian	utilitarian +
yutilitee	utility +
yutopia	Utopia +

Z

zan y /ies	
zar	tsar
zeal /ous	
zealot	
zebra	
zeel	zeal +
zefer	zephyr
zelot	zealot
zelus	zealous
zenith	

zenofobia	xenophobia +
zenophobia	xenophobia +
zepher	zephyr
zephyr	
zeplin	Zeppelin
Zeppelin	
zerconium	zirconium
zero /s	
zeroks	Xerox 1
zerox	Xerox 1
zest /ful	
Zeus	
zigospore	zygospore
zigote	zygote
zigzag 3	
zilofone	xylophone
zilophone	xylophone
zinc	
zink	zinc
Zion /ism/ist	
zip 3 /per/-fastener	
zirconium	
zither	
zodiac	
zon e 2 /al	
zoo /logical/logy	
zoologey	zoology
zoom 1	
Zulu	
zus	Zeus
zygospore	
zygote	

APPENDIX I
Some Spelling Rules

A. y always stays when adding -ing but changes to i before adding -ed, e.g.:

    carry, carrying, carried   terrify, terrifying, terrified

B. i before e except after c, e.g.:

    field, mischievous, relief   deceive, perceive, receipt

Note that there are exceptions to the above rules.

C. q is always followed by u, e.g.: conquer, frequent, queen

D. all at the beginning of a word loses one l, e.g.: already, altogether, always
The double l is retained in hyphenated words such as all-fours and all-round, but the words all right should always be written as two separate words.

E. A word accented on its last syllable and ending with a single consonant preceded by a vowel doubles that consonant on adding **-ed** and **-ing** e.g.:

    prefer   preferred   preferring

Words of this type, not accented on the last syllable, do **not** double the last consonant, e.g.:

    benefit   benefited   benefiting

With words ending in -l, the final consonant is generally doubled whether the last syllable is accented or not, e.g.:

    travel   travelled   travelling

THE FORMATION OF PLURALS

1. Most words, including those ending in silent -e, add -s, e.g.:
   airport, airports
   sausage, sausages

2. Words ending in -ay, -ey, -oy, or -uy add -s, e.g.:
   day, days   toy, toys
   abbey, abbeys   guy, guys

3. Words ending in -fe change f to v and add -s, e.g.:
   knife, knives

4. Some words ending in -f change f to v and add -es, e.g.:
   half, halves   loaf, loaves

5. Some words ending in -f add -s, e.g.:
   chief, chiefs
   handkerchief, handkerchiefs
   But note that some words ending in -f can either add -s or change f to v and add -es, e.g.:
   hoof, hoofs *or* hooves
   scarf, scarfs *or* scarves

6. Words ending in -ff usually add -s, e.g.:
   cliff, cliffs
   sheriff, sheriffs

7. Words ending in -o add -s or -es, e.g.:
   concerto, concertos
   dynamo, dynamos
   buffalo, buffaloes
   domino, dominoes

8. Words ending in -ch, -s, -sh, -x, or -z add -es, e.g.:
   church, churches   thrush, thrushes
   gas, gases   box, boxes
   dress, dresses   buzz, buzzes

9. Words ending in -y (but not -ay, -ey, -oy, or -uy: see Note 2) change the y to an i and add -es, e.g.:
   baby, babies
   family, families

10. Some words form their plurals mainly by changing their vowels (or some of their vowels), e.g.:

foot, feet	mouse, mice
goose, geese	tooth, teeth
man, men	woman, women

11. One word adds -**en**:
    ox, oxen
    One word adds -**ren**:
    child, children

12. Words ending in -u̲s̲ change u̲s̲ to **i**, e.g.:
    bacillus, bacilli
    fungus, fungi
    radius, radii
    rhombus, rhombi
    terminus, termini

13. Words ending in -i̲s̲ change i̲s̲ to -**es**, e.g.:
    analysis, analyses
    basis, bases
    metamorphosis, metamorphoses

14. Words ending in -e̲x̲ add -**es** or change e̲x̲ to -**ices**, e.g.:
    apex, apexes *or* apices
    index, indexes *or* indices
    vortex, vortexes *or* vortices

15. Words ending in -i̲x̲ add -**es** or change i̲x̲ to -**ices**, e.g.:
    appendix, appendixes *or* appendices
    helix, helices
    matrix, matrixes *or* matrices

16. Some words ending in -a̲ simply add -**s**, e.g.:
    aroma, aromas
    drama, dramas
    idea, ideas
    but note:
    alga, algae
    antenna, antennae
    formula, formulas *or* formulae
    stoma, stomas *or* stomata

17. Some words ending in -u̲m̲ simply add -**s**, e.g.:
    museum, museums
    premium, premiums
    but note:
    aquarium, aquariums *or* aquaria

bacterium, bacteria
curriculum, curricula
memorandum, memorandums
        or memoranda
stadium, stadiums *or* stadia

18. Words ending in -o̲n̲ usually add -**s**, e.g.:
    electron, electrons
    neutron, neutrons
    but note:
    phenomenon, phenomena

19. Words ending in -e̲a̲u̲ add -**x**, e.g.:
    bureau, bureaux
    chateau, chateaux
    plateau, plateaux
    Note that some dictionaries allow a plural in -**s** for some of these words.

20. Some words have the same spelling for both the singular and the plural forms, e.g.:

bison	grouse	sheep
deer	salmon	trout

21. Compound words.
    Logically, the most important word should be changed into the plural, as, for example:
    brother-in-law, brothers-in-law
    man-of-war, men-of-war
    but note:
    court-martial, court-martials
    lord justice, lords justices

22. Some words are used only in the singular form, e.g.:

arithmetic	goodness	magic
courage	logic	music

23. Some words are used only in the plural form, e.g.:
    mathematics
    Among words frequently used in their plural form are:

acoustics	physics	tactics
athletics	politics	

24. Pairs.
    The following nouns do not have a singular form:

entrails	pliers	trousers
pincers	scissors	tweezers

324

APPENDIX II
Abbreviations in General Use

A. Advanced (level of G.C.E.)
A.A. Automobile Association
A.B.M. anti-ballistic missile
acc., a/c account
A.D. in the year of our Lord
A.D.C. aide-de-camp
A.F.C. Air Force Cross
A.F.M. Air Force Medal
a.m. before noon
Ave. avenue
A.W.O.L. absent without leave

B.A. Bachelor of Arts
Bart. Baronet
B.B.C. British Broadcasting Corporation
B.C. before Christ
B.D. Bachelor of Divinity
B.Ed. Bachelor of Education
B.E.M. British Empire Medal
Benelux Belgium–Netherlands–Luxembourg Union
B.M. Bachelor of Medicine
B.M.A. British Medical Association
B.Mus. Bachelor of Music
B.R. British Rail
B.R.C.S. British Red Cross Society
B.Sc. Bachelor of Science
B.S.T. British standard time, British summer time

C. Centigrade
c., ca. about
C.A.B. Citizens' Advice Bureau
C.A.C.M. Central American Common Market
CARICOM Caribbean Community
C.B.E. Commander of the British Empire
C.B.I. Confederation of British Industry
C.C. County Council
C.E.N.T.O. Central Treaty Organisation
C.G.M. Conspicuous Gallantry Medal
C.G.S. Chief of General Staff
C.H. Companion of Honour
Ch.B. Bachelor of Surgery

C.I.D. Criminal Investigation Department
C.-in-C. Commander-in-Chief
C.M.E.A. (COMECON) Council for Mutual Economic Assistance
C.N.D. Campaign for Nuclear Disarmament
C.O. Commanding Officer
c/o care of
C.O.D. cash on delivery
Con. Conservative
C.S.E. Certificate of Secondary Education

D.B.E. Dame Commander of the British Empire
D.C.L. Doctor of Civil Law
D.C.M. Distinguished Conduct Medal
D.D. Doctor of Divinity
D.D.T. dichlor-diphenyl-trichlorethane (insecticide)
D.F.C. Distinguished Flying Cross
D.F.M. Distinguished Flying Medal
D.M. Doctor of Medicine
D.Mus. Doctor of Music
DNA deoxyribonucleic acid
D.O.E. Department of the Environment
D.Phil. Doctor of Philosophy
Dr. Doctor
D.Sc. Doctor of Science
D.S.C. Distinguished Service Cross
D.S.M. Distinguished Service Medal
D.S.O. Distinguished Service Order

E.E.C. European Economic Community
E.F.T.A. European Free Trade Association
e.g. for example
E.S.N. educationally subnormal
E.S.P. extrasensory perception
Esq. Esquire

F. Fahrenheit
F.A. Football Association

325

F.A.O. Food and Agriculture Organisation

F.B.A. Fellow of the British Academy

f.o.c. free of charge

F.R.S. Fellow of the Royal Society

G.A.T.T. General Agreement on Tariffs and Trade

G.B. Great Britain

G.B.E. Dame or Knight Grand Cross of the British Empire

G.C. George Cross

G.C.E. General Certificate of Education

G.D.P. gross domestic product

G.D.R. German Democratic Republic

G.H.Q. General Headquarters

G.L.C. Greater London Council

G.M. George Medal

G.M.T. Greenwich mean time

G.N.P. gross national product

G.P. general practitioner

G.P.O. General Post Office

H.E. His Excellency; His Eminence

H.M. Her Majesty

H.M.I. Her Majesty's Inspector

H.M.S. Her Majesty's Ship

H.M.S.O. Her Majesty's Stationery Office

H.N.C. Higher National Certificate

H.N.D. Higher National Diploma

Hon. honorary; Honourable

h.p. hire purchase; horsepower

H.Q. Headquarters

H.R.H. Her (His) Royal Highness

I.B.R.D. International Bank for Reconstruction and Development (World Bank)

I.C.C. International Chamber of Commerce

I.C.F.T.U. International Confederation of Free Trade Unions

I.C.I. Imperial Chemical Industries

i.e. that is

I.L.O. International Labour Organisation

I.M.F. International Monetary Fund

I.O.U. I owe you

I.Q. intelligence quotient

I.R.A. Irish Republican Army

I.T.V. Independent Television

J.E.T. Joint European Torus

J.P. Justice of the Peace

K.B.E. Knight Commander of the British Empire

K.C.B. Knight Commander of the Bath

Kt. Knight

Lab. Labour

L.A.F.T.A. Latin American Free Trade Association

lat. latitude

lbw leg before wicket

L.E.A. Local Education Authority

Lib. Liberal

LL.B., LL.D. Bachelor, Doctor of Laws

long. longitude

L.P. long-playing (of gramophone records, etc.)

L.S.D. lysergic acid diethylamide (hallucinogenic drug)

L.T.A. Lawn Tennis Association

Ltd. Limited

L.V. luncheon voucher

M.A. Master of Arts

M.B. Bachelor of Medicine

M.B.E. Member of the British Empire

M.C. Military Cross; Master of Ceremonies

M.C.C. Marylebone Cricket Club

M.D. Doctor of Medicine

M.F.H. Master of Foxhounds

M.O.H. Medical Officer of Health

M.P. Member of Parliament

m.p.g. miles per gallon

m.p.h. miles per hour

MS., MSS. manuscript(s)

M.Sc. Master of Science

N.A.S.A. National Aeronautics and Space Administration

N.A.T.O. North Atlantic Treaty Organisation

N.B. note well

N.C.O. non-commissioned officer

N.H.S. National Health Service

N.I. National Insurance

No. number

nr. near

N.S.P.C.C. National Society for the Prevention of Cruelty to Children

O. Ordinary (level of G.C.E.)
O.A.P. old aged pensioner
O.A.S. Organisation of American States
O.A.U. Organisation of African Unity
O.B.E. Officer of the British Empire
O.D.E.C.A. Organisation of Central American States
O.E.C.D. Organisation for Economic Co-operation and Development
O.H.M.S. On Her Majesty's Service
O.M. Order of Merit
O.N.C. Ordinary National Certificate
O.N.D. Ordinary National Diploma
op. cit. in the work named
O.P.E.C. Organisation of the Petroleum Exporting Countries

P.A.Y.E. pay as you earn
P.E. physical education
Ph.D. Doctor of Philosophy
P.M. Prime Minister
P.O. post office; postal order
P.O.W. prisoner of war
P.S. postscript
P.T.O. please turn over

Q.C. Queen's Counsel

R. Regina; Rex
R.A. Royal Academy; Royal Artillery
R.A.C. Royal Automobile Club
R.A.D.A. Royal Academy of Dramatic Art
R.A.F. Royal Air Force
R.A.M. Royal Academy of Music
R.C. Roman Catholic
R.C.A. Royal College of Arts
R.C.M. Royal College of Music
Rev., Revd. Reverend
R.G.S. Royal Geographical Society
R.H.S. Royal Horticultural Society
R.I.P. may he (she, they) rest in peace
R.M. Royal Marines; Royal Mail
R.N. Royal Navy
r.p.m. revolutions per minute
R.S.P.C.A. Royal Society for the Prevention of Cruelty to Animals
R.S.V.P. please reply
Rt. Hon. Right Honourable

s.a.e. self-addressed envelope
S.A.L.T. Strategic Arms Limitation Treaty

S.A.Y.E. save as you earn
S.C.M. State Certified Midwife
S.E.A.T.O. South-East Asia Treaty Organisation
S.O.S. distress signal
S.R.N. State Registered Nurse
St. Saint; street
S.T.D. subscriber trunk dialling

T.A.S.S. Soviet Telegraph Agency
T.B. tuberculosis
T.N.T. trinitrotoluene (high explosive)
T.U.C. Trades Union Congress

U.A.R. United Arab Republic
U.D.C. Urban District Council
U.D.I. Unilateral Declaration of Independence
U.F.O. unidentified flying object
U.N. United Nations
U.N.D.P. United Nations Development Programme
U.N.E.S.C.O. United Nations Educational, Scientific and Cultural Organisation
U.N.I.C.E.F. United Nations International Children's Emergency Fund
U.S. United States
U.S.A. United States of America
U.S.S.R. Union of Soviet Socialist Republics

V.A.T. value added tax
V.C. Victoria Cross
V.D. venereal disease
V.H.F. very high frequency
V.I.P. very important person

W.C.C. World Council of Churches
W.H.O. World Health Organisation
W.I. West Indies; Women's Institute
W.R.A.C. Women's Royal Army Corps
W.R.A.F. Women's Royal Air Force
W.R.N.S. Women's Royal Naval Service
W.R.V.S. Women's Royal Volunteer Service

Y.H.A. Youth Hostels Association
Y.M.C.A. Young Men's Christian Association
Y.W.C.A. Young Women's Christian Association

APPENDIX III
Common Forenames

MEN
Adrian
Alan, Allan
Andrew
Anthony, Antony
Barry
Brian, Bryan
Bruce
Charles
Christopher
Claude
Clive
Cyril
Derek
Desmond
Douglas
Edmund
Edward, Ted
Eugene
Ewen, Ewin
Francis
Frederick, Fred
Gareth
Gary
Geoffrey
George
Gerald, Gerry
Giles
Gordon
Graham
Guy
Harold, Harry
Howard, Howerd
Hugh
Humphrey
Ian
Jack
James, Jim
Jeremy, Jerry
John
Jonathan
Julian
Keith
Kenneth
Leonard

Lewis
Malcolm
Mathew, Matt
Michael, Mike
Neil
Nicholas, Nick
Nigel
Oliver
Patrick, Paddy
Peter
Philip
Richard, Dick
Robert, Bob
Roger
Ronald
Roy
Sean
Sidney
Simon
Stephen, Steven
Terence, Terry
Thomas
Timothy
Tony
Trevor
Wayne
William

WOMEN
Alice
Alison
Angela, Angie
Ann, Anne
Anthea
Barbara
Belinda
Bridget
Carol, Carole
Caroline
Carolyn
Catherine, Cathy
Charlotte
Christine
Clare
Daphne

Dawn
Deborah, Debby
Denise
Diana
Doreen
Eileen
Elaine
Elizabeth, Betty
Ellen
Emily
Emma
Evelyn
Felicity
Fiona
Frances
Gillian, Jill
Hazel
Heather
Helen
Hilary
Irene
Isabel, Isobel
Jacqueline
Jane
Janet
Janice
Jean
Jennifer, Jenny
Jill
Joan
Joanna
Joy
Joyce
Judith, Judy
Julia
Julie
Karen
Laura
Lesley
Lilian
Linda, Lynda
Lisa, Liza
Lorna
Louise
Lynn

Margaret, Maggie
Marian
Marie
Marilyn
Marion
Marjorie
Mary
Miranda
Miriam
Monica
Natalie
Olivia
Pamela
Patricia
Paula
Pauline
Penelope, Penny
Phillipa
Phillis, Phyllis
Rachel
Rebecca
Rosemary
Ruth
Sally
Sandra, Sandy
Sarah
Sharon
Sheila
Shirley
Sonia
Stephanie
Susan, Sue
Suzanne
Sylvia
Theresa, Tessa
Tina
Tracy
Vera
Veronica
Victoria, Vicky
Virginia
Vivian
Wendy
Yvonne
Zoe

APPENDIX IV

The British Isles

APPENDIX V

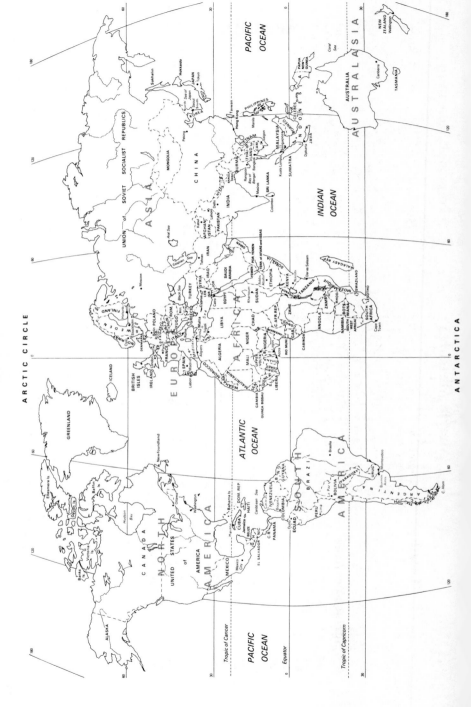

Metric Measures

Length

1 millimetre (mm)		= 0.039 in
1 centimetre (cm)	= 10 mm	= 0.394 in
1 metre (m)	= 100 cm	= 1.094 yd
1 kilometre (km)	= 1000 m	= 0.621 mile

Surface or Area

1 sq cm (cm²)	= 100 mm²	= 0.155 in²
1 sq m (m²)	= 10000 cm²	= 1.196 yd²
1 sq km (km²)	= 100 ha	= 0.386 mile²
1 hectare (ha)	= 10000 m²	= 11960 yd²

Volume and Capacity

1 cu cm (cm³)		= 0.061 in³
1 cu dm (dm³)	= 1000 cm³	= 61.02 in³
1 cu m (m³)	= 1000 dm³	= 1.308 yd³
1 litre (l)	= 1 dm³	= 1.760 pints
1 hectolitre (hl)	= 100 l	= 2.750 bushels

Weight

1 milligram (mg)		= 0.015 grain
1 gram (gm)	= 1000 mg	= 0.035 oz
1 kilogram (kg)	= 1000 g	= 2.205 lb
1 tonne (t)	= 1000 kg	= 0.984 ton

Temperature Conversion

$C = \frac{5}{9} (F - 32)$ $F = (\frac{9}{5} C) + 32$

98.4° Fahrenheit = 36.9° Centigrade
32° Fahrenheit = 0° Centigrade
50° Fahrenheit = 10° Centigrade
68° Fahrenheit = 20° Centigrade
212° Fahrenheit = 100° Centigrade

Imperial Measures

Length

1 inch (in)		= 2.540 cm
1 foot (ft)	= 12 in	= 30.48 cm
1 yard (yd)	= 3 ft	= 0.914 m
1 mile	= 1760 yd	= 1.609 km
1 nautical mile	= 6080 ft	= 1.852 km

Surface or Area

1 sq in (in²)		= 6.452 cm²
1 sq ft (ft²)	= 144 in²	= 9.290 dm²
1 sq yd (yd²)	= 9 ft²	= 0.836 m²
1 rood	= 1210 yd²	= 1012 m²
1 acre	= 4840 yd²	= 0.405 ha
1 sq mile	= 640 acres	= 259.0 ha

Volume and Capacity

1 cu in (in³)		= 16.39 cm³
1 cu ft (ft³)	= 1728 in³	= 0.028 m³
1 cu yd (yd³)	= 27 ft³	= 0.765 m³
1 pint	= 4 gills	= 0.568 l
1 gallon (gal)	= 8 pints	= 4.546 l
1 bushel	= 8 gal	= 36.37 l
1 fluid ounce	= 8 fl drachms	= 28.41 cm³
1 pint	= 20 fl oz	= 568.2 cm³

Weight

1 ounce (oz)	= 437.4 grains	= 28.35 g
1 pound (lb)	= 16 oz	= 0.454 kg
1 stone	= 14 lb	= 6.350 kg
1 cwt	= 8 st	= 50.80 kg
1 ton	= 20 cwt	= 1.016 tonnes

Time

1 min	= 60 sec	
1 hr	= 60 min	= 3600 sec
1 day	= 24 hr	
1 year	= 365 days (366 in leap year)	

APPENDIX VII

Common Chemical Compounds

Common name	Chemical name	Formula
Alcohol, grain	Ethanol	CH_3CH_2OH
Alcohol, wood	Methanol	CH_3OH
Baking soda	Sodium hydrogen carbonate	$NaHCO_3$
Borax	Disodium tetraborate	$Na_2B_4O_7$
Brimstone	Sulphur	S
Calomel	Mercury(I) chloride	Hg_2Cl_2
Carbolic acid	Phenol	C_6H_5OH
Carbon tetrachloride	Tetrachloromethane	CCl_4
Carborundum	Silicon carbide	SiC
Chalk	Calcium carbonate	$CaCO_3$
Chloroform	Trichloromethane	$CHCl_3$
Cooking salt	Sodium chloride	$NaCl$
Corn syrup	Glucose, dextrose	$C_6H_{12}O_6$
Diamond	Carbon	C
Dry ice	Carbon dioxide (solid)	CO_2
Ethyl	Lead tetraethyl	$Pb(C_2H_5)_4$
Fire damp	Methane	CH_4
Glycerine	Glycerol	$C_3H_5(OH)_3$
Graphite	Carbon	C
Iron pyrites	Iron disulphide	FeS_2
Laughing gas	Dinitrogen oxide	N_2O
Lime water	Calcium hydroxide solution	$Ca(OH)_2$
Lye (or caustic soda)	Sodium hydroxide	$NaOH$
Magnesia	Magnesium oxide	MgO
Marble	Calcium carbonate	$CaCO_3$
Marsh gas	Methane	CH_4
Milk of magnesia	Magnesium hydroxide (with water)	$Mg(OH)_2$
Moth balls	Naphthalene	$C_{10}H_8$
Muriatic acid	Hydrochloric acid	HCl
Oil of vitriol	Sulphuric acid	H_2SO_4
Peroxide	Hydrogen peroxide	H_2O_2
Potash	Potassium carbonate	K_3CO_3
Quartz	Silicon dioxide	SiO_2
Quicklime	Calcium oxide	CaO
Quicksilver	Mercury	Hg
Sal ammoniac	Ammonium chloride	NH_4Cl
Saltpetre	Potassium nitrate	KNO_3
Sand	Silicon dioxide (impure)	SiO_2
Soap	Sodium stearate	$C_{17}H_{35}COONa$
Sugar (cane or beet)	Sucrose	$C_{12}H_{22}O_{11}$
Vinegar	Ethanoic acid (with water)	CH_3COOH
Water glass	Sodium silicate	Na_2SiO_3
Zinc white	Zinc oxide	ZnO

APPENDIX VIII
Physical Constants, Conversion Factors and Units

There are nine basic units in the SI system (Système international d'unités)

Quantity	Name of unit	Symbol
length	metre	m
mass	kilogram	kg
time	second	s
electric current	ampere *	A
thermodynamic temperature	kelvin *	K
amount of substance	mole	mol
luminous intensity	candela	cd
plane angle	radian	rad
solid angle	steradian	sr

In addition there are a number of derived units

Quantity	Name of unit	Symbol
force	newton *	N
energy	joule *	J
power	watt *	W
electric charge	coulomb *	C
potential difference	volt *	V
electric resistance	ohm *	Ω
frequency	hertz *	Hz
customary temperature	degree Celsius	°C

The asterisk (*) indicates that the names of the relevant units begin with a small letter when they are written out in full, but are symbolised by a capital letter.

Special prefixes and symbols are used to indicate multiples and sub-multiples of the basic units in powers of ten

Multiple	Prefix	Symbol
10^{18}	exa	E
10^{15}	peta	P
10^{12}	tera	T
10^{9}	giga	G
10^{6}	mega	M
10^{3}	kilo	k
10^{-1}	deci	d
10^{-2}	centi	c
10^{-3}	milli	m
10^{-6}	micro	μ
10^{-9}	nano	n
10^{-12}	pico	p
10^{-15}	femto	f
10^{-18}	atto	a

APPENDIX IX

PERIODIC TABLE OF THE ELEMENTS

H 1 Hydrogen																	He 2 Helium
Li 3 Lithium	Be 4 Beryllium											B 5 Boron	C 6 Carbon	N 7 Nitrogen	O 8 Oxygen	F 9 Fluorine	Ne 10 Neon
Na 11 Sodium	Mg 12 Magnesium											Al 13 Aluminium	Si 14 Silicon	P 15 Phosphorus	S 16 Sulphur	Cl 17 Chlorine	Ar 18 Argon
K 19 Potassium	Ca 20 Calcium	Sc 21 Scandium	Ti 22 Titanium	V 23 Vanadium	Cr 24 Chromium	Mn 25 Manganese	Fe 26 Iron	Co 27 Cobalt	Ni 28 Nickel	Cu 29 Copper	Zn 30 Zinc	Ga 31 Gallium	Ge 32 Germanium	As 33 Arsenic	Se 34 Selenium	Br 35 Bromine	Kr 36 Krypton
Rb 37 Rubidium	Sr 38 Strontium	Y 39 Yttrium	Zr 40 Zirconium	Nb 41 Niobium	Mo 42 Molybdenum	Tc 43 Technetium	Ru 44 Ruthenium	Rh 45 Rhodium	Pd 46 Palladium	Ag 47 Silver	Cd 48 Cadmium	In 49 Indium	Sn 50 Tin	Sb 51 Antimony	Te 52 Tellurium	I 53 Iodine	Xe 54 Xenon
Cs 55 Caesium	Ba 56 Barium	La 57 Lanthanum	Hf 72 Hafnium	Ta 73 Tantalum	W 74 Tungsten	Re 75 Rhenium	Os 76 Osmium	Ir 77 Iridium	Pt 78 Platinum	Au 79 Gold	Hg 80 Mercury	Tl 81 Thallium	Pb 82 Lead	Bi 83 Bismuth	Po 84 Polonium	At 85 Astatine	Rn 86 Radon
Fr 87 Francium	Ra 88 Radium	Ac 89 Actinium	104	105													

Ce 58 Cerium	Pr 59 Praseodymium	Nd 60 Neodymium	Pm 61 Promethium	Sm 62 Samarium	Eu 63 Europium	Gd 64 Gadolinium	Tb 65 Terbium	Dy 66 Dysprosium	Ho 67 Holmium	Er 68 Erbium	Tm 69 Thulium	Yb 70 Ytterbium	Lu 71 Lutetium
Th 90 Thorium	Pa 91 Protactinium	U 92 Uranium	Np 93 Neptunium	Pu 94 Plutonium	Am 95 Americium	Cm 96 Curium	Bk 97 Berkelium	Cf 98 Californium	Es 99 Einsteinium	Fm 100 Fermium	Md 101 Mendelevium	No 102 Nobelium	Lr 103 Lawrencium

Acknowledgements

In preparing this dictionary the following books have been particularly useful to me as resource material:

Cassell's New Spelling Dictionary
L. B. and D. Firnberg, Cassell, 1976

Authors' and Printers' Dictionary
F. Howard Collins, Oxford University Press, 11th rev. ed., 1973

The Concise Oxford Dictionary
Ed. J. B. Sykes, Oxford University Press, 6th ed., 1976

Maxwell's Illustrated Colour Dictionary
Ed. J. P. Brasier-Creach, M.A. and
B. A. Workman, M.A. ILSC, London, 1969

The Oxford School Dictionary
Joan Pusey, Oxford University Press, 3rd rev. ed., 1974

The Perfect Speller
Harriet Wittels and Joan Griesman, Grosset & Dunlap, New York, 1973

I have benefited greatly from the help and advice of many people and schools. I would like to acknowledge the help of: Miss Judy Black, Miss Georgina Cox, Mr Gordon Files, Mrs Edna Goldman, Mr Oliver Gregory, Mrs Gretchen Ingram, Mr C. R. Jacobs, Mrs Jean Price, Mrs Olive Robinson, Miss Avital Talmor and the teachers of Shepherds' Hill Middle School, Oxford. However, any mistakes contained in the dictionary are entirely my responsibility.

Special thanks are also due to Mr Vince Edmonds, Mr Ben Bolt, and in particular to Mr John Hine of the Editorial Production Department at Pergamon Press, Oxford.

The final acknowledgement goes to my family who helped me out in so many ways and particularly to my father, without whose invaluable advice, constant encouragement and support this project would never have got off the ground.